THE ESSENCE
OF CAPITALISM

D0807517

for Peter Curtis

THE ESSENCE
OF CAPITALISM

The Origins
of Our Future

Humphrey McQueen

BLACK
ROSE
BOOKS

Montréal/New York/London

2-21-2004
WW
$28.99

Copyright © 2003 BLACK ROSE BOOKS

No part of this book may be reproduced or transmitted in any form, by any means electronic or mechanical including photocopying and recording, or by any information storage or retrieval system—without written permission from the publisher, or, in the case of photocopying or other reprographic copying, a license from the Canadian Reprography Collective, with the exception of brief passages quoted by a reviewer in a newspaper or magazine.

Black Rose Books No. GG318

National Library of Canada Cataloguing in Publication Data

McQueen, Humphrey, 1942-
The essence of capitalism : the origin of our future / Humphrey McQueen

Includes bibliographical references and index.
ISBN: 1-55164-221-2 (bound) ISBN: 1-55164-220-4 (pbk.)

1. Coca-Cola Company--History. 2. International business enterprises--Case studies. I. Title.

HD9349.S634C63 2003   338.8'876362   C2002-904815-X

Cover design: Associés libres

BLACK ROSE BOOKS

C.P. 1258	2250 Military Road	99 Wallis Road
Succ. Place du Parc	Tonawanda, NY	London, E9 5LN
Montréal, H2X 4A7	14150	England
Canada	USA	UK

To order books:

In Canada: (phone) 1-800-565-9523 (fax) 1-800-221-9985
email: utpbooks@utpress.utoronto.ca

In United States: (phone) 1-800-283-3572 (fax) 1-651-917-6406

In the UK & Europe: (phone) London 44 (0)20 8986-4854
(fax) 44 (0)20 8533-5821 email: order@centralbooks.com

Our Web Site address: http://www.web.net/blackrosebooks

A publication of the Institute of Policy Alternatives of Montréal (IPAM)

Printed in Canada

Contents

INTRODUCTION **The Origins of Our Future**

At an owner-operated drug store in Atlanta in 1886, a soda-fountain proprietor sold the world's first Coca-Cola by pouring syrup from a bottle before topping the glass up with carbonated water. Today, Coca-Cola concentrate is distributed worldwide to be consumed from billions of cans, bottles and cups made with materials unknown in the 1880s. When that first Coca-Cola was drunk, bread was often baked at home with ingredients purchased from a store-keeper who weighed flour into the newly invented paper bag. Our daily loaf is now sliced, packaged in plastic, and branded by one transnational corporation to be sold through supermarkets owned by another. Soap was cut from unmarked slabs. Now both sides of the shopping aisles are stacked with brand-name cleaning products, marketed by global giants such as Proctor & Gamble.

This sprawl of household commodities was supported by so many white goods and electrical gadgets that by the 1950s 'the average American home' was pictured 'as a small factory'.[1] At the time,

English novelist and social critic J. B. Priestley coined 'Admass' as his short-hand for

> the whole system of an increasing productivity, plus inflation, plus a rising standard of material living, plus high-pressure advertising and salesmanship, plus mass communications, plus cultural democracy and the creation of the mass mind, the mass man.[2]

The Essence of Capitalism sorts through Priestley's tumble of causes and effects to connect the transformation of everyday life with the concentration of control and the expansion of capital.

The stories told throughout *The Essence of Capitalism* are also the origins of our future which we must make in circumstances not entirely of our choosing. Monopolisers and marketeers limit our options. We cannot wish ourselves back to the era of corner stores. Many processes of capital accumulation are irreversible. Moreover, capital must go on expanding in order to survive, which is why its sustainable development is antipathetic to every ecological equilibrium.

The captains of industry have more choices than their employees but even the most powerful executives retain their power only when their decisions coincide with the logic of capital growth. That condition overrides any good intent. A Coca-Cola lawyer, who was also a Papal Knight, wrote to The Company's chairman about a mutual acquaintance whose death bed he had visited:

> He is a believing Christian, knows that his soul will live on forever but there seems to stop. In his conversations it is apparent that he is much more interested in The Coca-Cola Company and the Trust Company of Georgia than in preparation for a future life.[3]

That dying friend knew what kept a man a capitalist. So did the international currency speculator George Soros when he observed early in 1999 that

> If I allowed moral considerations to influence my investment decisions, it would render me an unsuccessful competitor. And it would

not in any way influence the outcome because there would be someone else to take my place at only a marginally different price.[4]

Had Soros behaved otherwise, his fortunes would have been taken
from him by capitalists who had not tired of 'the restless never-
ending process of profit-making'.[5] Nestlé chief Helmut Maucher
underscored the point: 'I am not against culture and ethics but we
cannot live on that'.[6] Instead, every firm feeds on three kinds of
expropriation: of natural resources; of the values added by physical and mental effort to those raw materials and to the products
made from them; and by besting rival corporations engaged in the
other two.

The Essence of Capitalism offers a short history of the long twentieth century, from the 1870s to the present, as a precondition for
understanding the world we face. By setting out the structures of
monopolising capitals, the book's thematic analysis provides a means
to comprehend the dynamics concealed by the blizzard of scraps
called 'the news'. The economic anthropologist Karl Polanyi
described the victory of the market over society in the middle of
the nineteenth century as the great transformation, the title of his
1944 masterwork. The processes set in motion by that upheaval
provided the foundations for a second great transformation beginning in the 1870s. The contrasts are clear: war moved from
occasional eruption to perpetual dynamic; a few corporations mar-
ginalised the multitude of family businesses; the state and
corporations brought an end to the first episode of free trade; the
visible hand of marketeers sidelined price competition as the sales
effort burgeoned; and consumer sovereignty was redefined to match
the needs of capital. Surpluses replaced scarcity for many in the
First World while starvation supplanted sufficiency through swathes
of the Third.

More of the world's population and resources became subject to the corporatised market: 'the control of the economic system
by the market', Polanyi stressed, 'means no less than the running
of society as an adjunct to the market. Instead of economy being
embedded in social relations, social relations are embedded in the
economic system'.[7] Whereas the Emperor's writ once stopped at

the village gate, most of what goes on in society today is related to the expansion of capital. Businesses have taken over the replenishment of our capacity to labour through their provision of food, drink and leisure, offering KFC in place of pot-roast chicken, Sprite not home-made lemonade, videos instead of parlour games.

Polanyi's great transformation had been led by English experiences of science-based farming and the factory system, powered by water, horses and steam, and financed through the joint-stock company. The second wave since the 1870s has been carried forward by the American System of mass manufacturing, organised through oligopolies and excited by the merger of advertising with entertainment.

The essence of capitalism is capital's need to expand. That drive exists because of the relationships between competing capitals and between capital and labour. To survive against those two pressures, each firm must reduce the unit cost of production, which leads to producing ever more. Because the extra must be sold if a profit is to be earned, mass marketing is the companion of mass manufacture. The essence of capitalism is not internal to capital but operates through its links to human and natural resources.

My treatment of global developments since the 1870s can be introduced by sketching developments in my own understanding. In writing *Australia's Media Monopolies*, I proposed two reasons for taking advertising as the key link between capitalism and the mass media. First, advertising stimulates the demand for commodities. Secondly, advertisers package audiences to sell to retailers. In attempting to revise *Australia's Media Monopolies*, I recognised that the mass media were only a delivery system for one element within the sales effort. Far from advertising's being the key link, it is only 'a tiny, tiny part of marketing'.[8] I came to see mass marketing as a matrix connecting production with consumption through retail credit (hire purchase and cards), merchandising (department and chain stores), and the movement of goods (air freight) or of consumers (drive-ins).

To chart these circuits, I attached my analysis to one of the products being promoted: Coca-Cola. The Company and its beverages offer gilded threads through the labyrinth of marketing, monopolising and management. The Coca-Cola Company is not a template for every corporation. No such ideal type can exist. Coca-Cola becomes typical whenever its opportunities and obstacles overlap with those of all other businesses. That is why to know only Coca-Cola is not to know even Coca-Cola; and why my investigations tracked across a variety of firms. Many of the comparisons are with other mass marketeers, including Gillette, McDonald's, Proctor & Gamble, Rowntrees and Sears. Reference is also made to heavier manufacturers, General Electric, General Motors and Standard Oil; to financiers such as the House of Morgan; and to knowledge managers, IBM and Microsoft. The context helps us to distinguish the forces that impinge on all firms from the practices peculiar to Coca-Cola.

Although each chapter will traverse one feature of capitalism, the world of getting and spending is never as neat as a contents page. Some topics must reappear—franchising, for instance, is the subject of chapter five but returns in the chapter on monopoly competition.

Part One deals with the organisation of capital, connecting the nation-*market*-state and the invention of the corporation with the geographical extension of trade. It reviews the training of managers and their relationship to owners.

The second part sets out the workings of capital by taking up the management of investment by financiers and accountants. Franchising is examined as a device to fund expansion through garnering other people's money.

Part Three looks at the means by which oligopolisation has become the norm, beginning with the swell of monopolisers in the late nineteenth century and moving to the recent tidal wave of mergers and acquisitions. We see why anti-trust actions have done little more than streamline this concentration. Because competition has been intensified, not eliminated, the phrase 'monopolising capitals' is preferred when describing this dominance of oligopolies. (Should the book be called 'The essence of monopolising capitals'?) The nature of competition within a system of oligopolised industries is explored through price discrimination, price fixing and price cutting.

The fourth part surveys mass marketing and asks what is a market? and when did it become dominant? The ability of firms to manage demand as well as supply explains why capital can use marketing to absorb overproduction. To that end, advertisements debase information, thereby undermining consumer sovereignty. Advertising is the best known yet least effective element in the sales effort. Its achievement is not selling one brand over another but in stimulating total demand by encouraging debt. Attention is drawn to how brands contribute to oligopoly power. Monopolising is monitored around the planet by weaving overseas sales and investments by US firms into the rise of the USA as a global power. By responding to changes in both production and selling through the pursuit of worldwide niches, globalisation is adding enzymes to a process until recently called imperialism.

Part Five is the crux of the book because the reproduction and control of the workforce is the pre-requisite for capital's expansion. An experience of the steel-master Andrew Carnegie has lasting and universal significance. In 1856, the 21-year old Carnegie was amazed by his earliest dividend cheque which, as he reminisced, was 'the first penny of revenue ... that I had not worked for with the sweat of my brow'.[9] Not for the last time, other workers had done that for him, as they still do for all shareholders. For that to happen, the workforce must be organised for production and disorganised for struggle. The relatively low labour costs at Coca-Cola have not exempted The Company from union-busting, whether in Georgia or Guatemala. The obsession with time derives from the purchase of labour power for a given period during which managers must maximise returns on the price paid in wages and conditions. Because capital must go faster or falter, every aspect of life is accelerating.

The final part joins the debate over what constitutes human nature. An investigation into human needs sidelines explanations in terms of physiological or social drives in favour of capital-induced ones. The ways in which capital alters needs are explored through how corporations shape our taste in fluids, and by showing how sweeteners have come to occupy their place in Western diets. The book closes with reflections on the prospects for nature under the rule of capital. The genetic manipulation by corporations such as Monsanto is pondered to see whether what Polanyi called 'the juggernaut, improvement' can be turned.

Asked why the great transformation has turned everyday life inside out, common sense voices two clichés. The first reaches back to original sin to lament greed and laziness as no more than one can expect from human nature with its selfish gene. The second conventional wisdom puts the responsibility onto technology as a perpetual motion machine, largely beyond human control. The answers offered below treat human nature and technologies as supports for the prime mover of capital accumulation. That explanation leads into economics, from which experts have scared the public away by jargon and algebra. Descriptive economics lets us understand how we got where we are now, where the capitalist system is headed, and what we can do to redress its social inequalities and environmental plunder. Without an understanding of capitalism's dynamic, reform projects must misfire. This book is not a manifesto of what should be done. Rather, it is a reminder of what we are up against. Thus equipped, our effort to avert catastrophe will become even more productive.

PART ONE

Visible Hands

CHAPTER 1 # The Nation-Market-State

> To found a great empire for the sole purpose of raising up a people
> of customers, may at first sight appear a project fit only for a nation
> of shopkeepers. It is, however, a project altogether unfit for a nation
> of shopkeepers; but extremely fit for a nation whose government
> is influenced by shopkeepers.
>
> Adam Smith, *The Wealth of Nations*, 1776[1]

Nations are recent developments, pillars for the nineteenth-century transformation of societies into market-directed economies. The rise of the nation-state was in reality the rise of a nation-*market*-state, with the government extending its territories and functions in keeping with the expansion of capital.

The term 'market' came to denote both a system of exchange and its geographical extent. In her 1933 study of monopolising, Joan Robinson concluded that 'a large nation, with a large internal market within the orbit of its political control, has important economic advantages over a small one'. The integration of Europe is drawing the earliest nation-market-states towards a continent-market-state because a 'group of nations that can succeed in agreeing to behave as if, for certain purposes, they were one, thus scores a benefit for all of them in competition with the outside world'.[2]

Globalisation is weakening some nation-market-states, but by no means all. That the budgets for several US corporations are bigger than those of many countries does not by itself make those transnationals more powerful than the nation-market-states with which they deal. In 1998, revenues at General Motors reached $161 billion, but this was only 60 per cent of the Pentagon's $267 billion expenditure. The socialist government of Chile in the early 1970s was stronger than IT&T and Anaconda Copper until the CIA and other Washington agencies came to the aid of those firms. That intervention followed decades of manoeuvring with Chilean capitalists, including the local Pepsi bottler, who also ran a daily newspaper as a CIA conduit.[3] It was the force of the US state behind the US corporations that tipped the scales.

The state attempts for capital what managers cannot achieve through corporations. For example, the establishment of the US Federal Reserve in 1913–14 did what no pool of bankers had been able to achieve. J. P. Morgan had herded fellow financiers together for self-protection during a financial crisis in 1907, but a central bank would always be at the ready, able to assist producers as well as their lenders. When cotton prices fell by 75 per cent during 1920, the Federal Reserve in Atlanta more than doubled its advances to prevent growers from panicking and 'dumping' their products on the market.[4] Confronted by the 1998 hedge funds crisis, Federal Reserve chairman Alan Greenspan dared not leave Wall Street to the force of the market, but captained a rescue mission in a realm where he had no legislative authority.

The state takes the lead beyond the financial sector. In 1945, US President Harry Truman agreed that the federal government should finance fundamental research in science because it had 'been basic United States policy that Government should foster the opening of new frontiers'. In 1999, Al Gore spelt out the state's role in technological change when he promised to 'make the long-term investment...that most companies cannot afford'. A principal researcher at the US Department of Agriculture identified its 'mission' as being to help US producers succeed 'in the face of foreign competition'.[5]

After free marketeers spent the 1970s and 1980s calling for the dismantling of interventionist states, the World Bank strengthened Third World regimes so that they could contain the unrest sparked by the exchange-rate crisis in 1997. Faced by this underwriting of what experts euphemise as an 'effective' state, one must ask: effective for whom? and against whom?

The inspirer of free-market economics, Adam Smith, was not embarrassed to tell his students that 'Laws and government may be considered in...every case as a combination of the rich to oppress the poor, and preserve to themselves the inequality of the goods'.[6] A century later, the Supreme Court of West Virginia agreed that 'unless the government intervene to protect property...property would cease to exist'.[7] Then, as now, property meant the productive resources that capitalists had at their disposal. The threat came from those who had only their own labour to sell. That is why capitalists praised the militia who cut down strikers, thanked judges who jailed union leaders, and honoured civil servants who supervised the trade in indentured labourers.

Another task for the state is to hold the ring among competing corporations. In 1887, after railroad entrepreneurs had failed to abide by voluntary agreements on traffic and rates, the US Congress established an Interstate Commerce Commission to act as referee for such pooling arrangements. The Commission helped railroad managers to restrict competition, disappointing the merchants and farmers. It also reassured British investors, who had become reluctant to lend after being swindled by railroad speculators. Later, in the pit of the 1930s depression, regulators benefited the established soft-drink manufacturers by outlawing 'destructive competitive practices' in the industry.[8] Those measures protected oligopolies such as Coca-Cola against price-cutting by wildcat firms. Similarly, the chief concern behind amendments to the anti-trust laws in the 1950s was always 'to protect some business firms against others, chiefly larger ones, and to prevent business from being shut out of any particular market'.[9]

Corporations prefer not to go it alone. Capitalists rarely stand for election, despite Henry Ford's fantasy of running for the US presidency in 1924, when he invited Coca-Cola president Robert Woodruff to be his running mate.[10] Rather, US businessmen join cabinets by invitation. In the 1940s, one of the world's largest cotton traders, William Clayton, became Assistant Secretary of State for Economic Affairs; he approached the economic revival of Europe on the principle that firms such as his own would 'need markets— big markets—in which to buy and sell'.[11] The president of General Motors, Charles E. Wilson, defended his nomination as Secretary of Defense in 1953 by observing that what was 'good for our country was good for General Motors and vice versa'.[12]

Company executives were also asked for advice on appointments. In 1931, Woodruff of Coca-Cola was being consulted as a matter of course over the selection of federal judges.[13] He later served on the Business Advisory Council that represented the views of capital to the president. Woodruff's associates recognised that by the 1960s he had built the Trust Company of Georgia into 'probably the greatest political power in the State'.[14] Yet, when one of Coca-Cola's attorneys called Woodruff a member of the 'governing classes', he affected not to understand what the phrase meant. 'I am working for a great many more people than are working for me,' he replied.[15] The gap between how a magnate is viewed and how he sees himself indicates how intricate are the paths between corporations and the nation-market-state. The 'governing classes' can exist because the state supports the corporations in a multitude of ways.

Tariffs

Even the most obliging government cannot sweeten everyone's pot at the same time. Tariffs are one means by which capitalists redistribute wealth among themselves. The US sugar tariff, for instance, remains a battleground among a hierarchy of interest groups. On top are beet and cane farmers, who are protected against all comers. The benefits flood to the larger producers, with half the money going to one per cent of the growers:

The industry wrote the bills which were presented to Congress. It is not surprising, therefore, that the program protected its authors rather than the small farmer... Most small operators [in 1970] did not even know of the Sugar Act and only about half of them received any technical aid from the Agriculture Department. Unlike his well-organised larger competitor, the small farmer did not have a powerful lobby.[16]

Even less protected were the field labourers, whose low wages and bad conditions kept down the costs of raw sugar to industrial users such as Coca-Cola. By the late 1980s, to preserve one job in the sugar industry cost taxpayers and consumers $76 000, five times the average national wage. US householders paid more than twice the world price for their sugar. Second prize went to the refiners, for whom the tariff provided indirect protection against competitors off shore.

Free trade and protectionism are not opposites. Both promote competing interests within capital: 'the free-trade doctrine... is believed only by those who will gain an advantage from it.'[17] The US administration supports free trade when it serves US corporations as the most powerful traders. Until the 1950s, US administrations promoted the interests of United Fruit around Central America by sending in the Marines. In 1999, Washington backed United Fruit bananas by taking the European Union to the World Trade Organisation.

The nation-market-state remains a key player in globalisation, as the US government demonstrates when it imposes its version of free trade on other countries. After Gillette sought to close down production in France in the late 1980s, the French government applied pressure and offered inducements. When Paris threatened a boycott, Gillette 'turned to Washington higher-ups, who ordered the American ambassador to France, William Rogers, to instruct [the French minister of industry] to withdraw the threats or face retaliation against French products sold in the United States'.[18]

Washington now deploys Special Trade Negotiators to open up Japan; in 1853, Commodore Perry fired cannon. To get Kodak into Japan, the US Department of Commerce intervened to make up for the US firm's incompetence. The USA still uses its military capacity as a backstop in negotiations. The wisdom of former US Secretary of State George Shultz that 'negotiations are a euphemism for capitulation if the shadow of power is not cast across the bargaining table' applies to trade as much as other conflicts.[19] Flag follows trade when the US Fleet patrols the Middle East to secure oil. If war is the violent method of erecting and demolishing economic borders, protectionism is an alternative path to comparable ends.

A warfare state

Wars are not interruptions to economic life but rather its continuation by other means. They reallocate markets and shift dominance. Borders have been determined by a clash of arms. The English subordinated Wales, Scotland and Ireland. Prussia dominated a unified Germany through a series of wars in the 1860s; the Sardinians tried to do much the same with the Italian peninsula.

Militarising the mechanisms of production and exchange had begun long before the rise of the market-directed economy:

> For instance, it was in the army that the ancients first fully developed a wage system... Here too the first use of machinery on a large scale... The division of labour *within* one branch was also first carried out in the armies. The whole history of the forms of bourgeois society is very strikingly epitomised here.[20]

Notwithstanding Tolstoy's depiction of the battlefield as chaos, the synchronised loading and close-order firing of muskets around 1600, like parade-ground drill from the 1770s, presaged the regularities of mass production in factories. During the second half of the eighteenth century, Frederick the Great of Prussia extended his fascination with mechanical toys to fashioning fighting units that would act as automata. 'Among these reforms were the introduction of ranks and uniforms, the extension and standardisation of regulations...the creation of a command language, and systematic training'.[21] Each foot soldier was to be an exchangeable part. The tasks of keeping an army in the field became as specialised as the economic division of labour beloved by Kaiser Frederick's contemporary, Adam Smith. The vision shared by philosopher and king would conquer workshops and continents. Eli Whitney demonstrated the mass production of rifles out of standardised parts from 1801. A century later, F. W. Taylor installed chains of command and regularised the pattern of work at the Watertown arsenal. Military training and battlefield experience did more than Taylor's time-and-motion studies to inculcate the discipline of the production line.

According to capitalism's most venerable management consultant, Peter Drucker, the 'first conscious and systematic application of management principles was not in a business' but for the reorganisation of the US Army in 1901 by Secretary of War Elihu Root, who had been attorney to steel-maker Andrew Carnegie.

> World War I made clear the need for a formal organisational structure. Managing tens of millions of soldiers and refocusing whole economies on war production made formal organisation indispensable. They showed, however, that...Carnegie's functional structure was not the right one for massive undertakings. Their highly centralised management just couldn't work on that scale. Decision-making had to be pushed down into the organisation.[22]

These experiences prepared the ground for the multi-divisional enterprise, which business historian Alfred D. Chandler Jr championed as the model for corporate management, though he was less than forthcoming on its debt to war-making. Yet the concept of middle management derived from the military mode. Between 1923 and 1954, General Woods, who had supervised building the Panama Canal, ran Sears Roebuck as if it were an army.

Because engineers and architects were experienced in the direction of men and materials, they officered millions of conscripts during World War One, honing command skills to be carried back to supervisory professions in civilian life. For instance, W. D. Scott developed a rating scale to allocate recruits to tasks appropriate to their skills and personalities, classifying three million GIs according to aptitude tests that he would apply to salesmen in the 1920s.

In the early 1920s, the US Navy, fearful that the British would hold a monopoly over radiotelegraphy, sponsored the Radio Corporation of America through General Electric, with the federal government represented on the RCA board. Rearmament, not the New Deal, brought the USA back from the 'steepest economic descent in its history' during 1937.[23]

The adaptation of war-time systems to corporate planning continued in 1945 when the Ford Motor Company hired a squad of whiz kids from the military's Office of Statistical Control. On that team was Robert McNamara, who had taught at Harvard's Business School and would become US Secretary of Defense in the 1960s. Their strategy at Ford was to 'divide the company into divisions and to separate staff and line, a main organisational principle in the military'.[24] Meanwhile, at General Electric, the management structure ascended from 190 departments (battalions) through 46 divisions (regiments) and 10 groups (divisions) to a CEO (Commander-in-Chief). 'Accustomed to military hierarchies from service in World War Two, most GE-ers adapted easily to the strict new lines of authority'.[25] In general, 'autarchic military bureaucracies, not civilian agencies, have provided the closest approximation to industrial planning'.[26]

Having learnt from the rapid increase in consumer demand after World War Two, General Motors responded to the Korean conflict in 1950 with 'new plant facilities for defense production that ultimately could be used for commercial operations'.[27] President Eisenhower warned in 1960 that the US 'military-industrial complex' had 'the potential for the disastrous rise of misplaced power'. His draft had noted the congressional pressure to spend on armaments to maintain local employment, a process known as warfare Keynesianism. In 1962, the chairman of the Senate Armed Services Committee, Georgia's Richard B. Russell, reflected that 'there is something about buying arms...which causes men not to reckon the dollar cost'.[28]

In 1970, outlays on the armed services supported one civilian job in twelve. The rise of the national security state represented more than political influence by defence contractors. Since the 1940s, the arms sector has accounted for 80 per cent of US research and development expenditures. The Internet is only the Pentagon's latest gift to commerce.[29] Throughout the 1980s, the Reagan and Thatcher administrations both lifted military spending while proclaiming the virtue of small government. The end of the Cold War in 1991 gave the Pentagon the task of finding new enemies against which to sign more business contracts, as in the proposed anti-missile system.

The militarised mind

A militarisation of business ideologies accompanied the regimenting of work. Joseph Wharton told students in 1890 that the business school named in his honour would 'instil a sense of the coming strife' in which each manager would be a 'soldier'.[30] The Harvard case study took over training methods used for Prussian officers. The ex-editor of the *Harvard Business Review* compared the business school with West Point, contending that its MBA courses made 'managers good "fighters" on economic battlefields'.[31] Another insider account of the Harvard School previewed a third World War 'fought on the shelves of your neighbourhood shopping centre'.[32] In tune with this mentality, in 1997 Sears hired the three-star general who had been in charge of logistics during the Gulf War 'to shorten supply lines'.[33] PepsiCo designated its sales force in Germany the Panzer Unit. At a 1995 training session, Monsanto executives 'created four different "worlds" and began "war-gaming" with external forces such as US farm policy and global views on technology'.[34]

Master of the marketing universe Marion Harper quoted Clausewitz's *On War*: 'If you decide you can't win the battle, change the battlefield'.[35] Because that text is too long for most managers to read, the 2400-year-old *The Art of War* by Sun Tzu became a best-seller with a 1995 edition packaged as *The Art of War for Executives*. PepsiCo chief Roger Enrico valued it 'as a constant reminder that good ideas, properly utilised, are worth as much as heavy weapons'. Connecting his relaxation to his work, Enrico read mostly military strategy, just as in Vietnam he had learnt 'principles that would have important applications in my business career'. [36] When John Sculley joined PepsiCo in 1967 he found that his fellow executives 'were the kind of people who would rather be in the Marines than in the Army'.[37] Enrico's successor as CEO was another ex-marine. The language of Vietnam infected the vocabulary of US business until the managerial fat in one takeover target 'had to be napalmed', while the raiders saw themselves 'charging right through the rice paddies . . . taking no prisoners'.[38] Later, the consolidation of Coca-Cola bottlers became known as 'the engulf war'.[39]

A refreshing war

In 1941, Coca-Cola's 'reputation for managerial ability' and 'operating high speed production lines' convinced Washington to put The Company's managers in charge of an ammunitions factory in Alabama. Coca-Cola offered its Times Square neon space to promote war loans. After a Coca-Cola executive moved in as a bureau head at the Office of War Information, junior staff created a mock poster of a Coca-Cola bottle wrapped in an American flag, with the caption 'Step right up and get your four delicious freedoms. It's a refreshing war.'[40]

Coca-Cola was only one of many firms to depict itself as a 'symbol of a way of life for which a war is being waged'.[41] From 1943, the corporate-controlled War Advertising Council paraded its image of business as more patriotic than the government or unions. Executives needed to regain ideological dominance after a decade of depression and fascism during which, as a vice-president with the *New York Herald-Tribune* complained, the public had been persuaded 'that the criminal class of America was made up of the owners and executives of American corporations'.[42]

Coca-Cola's rise to globalism came during World War Two when The Company promised to supply all US troops with Coke at the standard price of five cents a bottle. In 1943 the Allied Commander in Europe, General Dwight Eisenhower, cabled Washington: 'On early convoy, request shipment three million bottled Coca-Cola, and complete equipment for bottling, washing, capping same quantity twice monthly'.[43] He hoped to boost morale. With thirty-six bottling plants built by the army around the world, Coca-Cola had become so commonplace by July 1945 that an officer in Germany requested a case every week as his right.

In Australia, Coca-Cola colonels requisitioned the four existing plants to supply the half-million US troops who followed General MacArthur after his PT boat, stocked with Coke, had fled the Philippines. 'So little market penetration had been made before the war that many an Australian tasted Coca-Cola for the first time when it was taken into their homes by soldiers, sailors, or airmen to whom they extended their hospitality.'[44] Coca-Cola also placed its coolers in civilian offices. The story of a Yank in Fremantle giving his week's salary for a single bottle determined one Australian serviceman to secure a franchise for his home town of Adelaide. No marketeer, however, would ever have been so crazy as were the gods in August 1944, when a Liberator bomber shed a carton of 'coco cola' onto an Adelaide wash-house.[45]

Taxes

Wars cost money, which means more taxes, and taxes at any level annoyed the hell out of the owner of Coca-Cola, Asa Candler. In 1902, he won a suit for the return of $29 500 in taxes imposed on Coca-Cola to finance the 1898 invasion of Cuba, from which he had benefited directly. Candler wanted the spoils, but declined to pay his share. World War One required even more taxes. Because Washington regarded soft drinks as non-essentials, they were subjected to a volley of charges.[46] Federal taxes soared again in 1939, with Coca-Cola paying one dollar in every 200 collected from corporations. The senior senator from Georgia, who chaired the Finance Committee, was able to block the reintroduction of a luxury tax.

In 1930, Georgia's Governor, Eugene Talmadge, had seen a tax on intangibles as a way to raise revenues without offending the rural-dominated Assembly. To escape this penalty, Coca-Cola re-incorporated in Delaware and began a long campaign to install a tax regime in Georgia more favourable to its long-term interests.

Coca-Cola's lawyer summarised the steps he had taken to defeat the Talmadge impost:

> The first was to secure a Constitutional amendment and enabling acts putting into effect a reasonable intangible tax law in Georgia whereby intangible property, such as money, foreign stocks, etc, would be taxed at a reasonable rate in accordance with the practice in other States. This took ten years and led into all other kinds of collateral legislation.[47]

The attorney did not confine his endeavours to the law or to the State Assembly, but employed a journalist to dispatch two items every week to eighty-seven newspapers, vetting every column himself. This 'reader salesmanship' aimed to create a climate of opinion in favour of a 2 per cent general sales tax instead of a luxury tax on soft drinks. One column was full of populist rhetoric aimed at farmers, while the other was directed to the better-educated.[48] Woodruff appreciated that it 'would be impossible for us to find a better friend' than the editor of the *Atlanta Constitution*.[49] Public opinion was both a marketing tool and a political weapon.

After Georgia went dry in 1907, liquor interests in the State Senate had used discriminatory legislation to attack Coca-Cola, but Asa Candler refused to buy off his chief tormentor.[50] Once the ban on alcohol became nationwide, State governments compensated for the resulting loss of revenue by imposing a 'nuisance tax' on soft drinks.[51] Coca-Cola aimed to prevent the States from introducing sales taxes that discriminated against The Company's product, because an impost that fell on soda pop but not on sweets or ice creams could redirect juvenile spending. So successful was its lobbying that by 1925 South Carolina was the only State with a tax specifically on bottled drinks. In reporting the 1938 California election results, Coca-Cola's Los Angeles office put the 'Tax Assessor for Los Angeles County', who was 'a personal friend', on a par with the Governor and the US Senator.[52] To defeat a 1950 discriminatory tax in West Virginia, 'everything was done and everybody consulted and used that might have been helpful'.[53]

Consultants

Consultation is an amiable word. Just how cosy it is depends on how the talks are conducted. Because the state must balance competing and changing interests, the first task for any corporation is to make its voice heard above the throng, whether through lawsuits, social contacts, corruption or political donations. These approaches are never mutually exclusive. Woodruff called upon them as appropriate until, in the words of an ex-Governor, the 'General Assembly always realised that what's good for Coke is good for Georgia'.[54]

The rules of the consultancy game were spelt out in a 1969 judgement awarding damages of $175 000 to a partner in Coca-Cola's legal firm, Robert B. Troutman, who had claimed the sum as his fee for representations to President Kennedy on behalf of a railroad company in 1963. The corporation contended that it had never hired Troutman but rather had asked him to influence the president. The judge instructed the jury that while 'it is illegal to agree, for hire, to bring personal or political influence to bear on a public official', it was permissible for lawyers to use their personal contacts to secure a hearing. Without that distinction, 'many perfectly innocent citizens would be deprived of an opportunity to have the merits of their case considered'. In adding that 'not every citizen knows a President', the judge failed to recognise that a corporation with links to a lawyer on speaking terms with the nation's chief executive was less likely to go unheard than most voters. The jury decided that Troutman's interventions were professional services deserving a fee, not the trading of favours that would attract a prison sentence.[55]

The fine line is also fuzzy. Corporate lawyers simultaneously maintain social contacts by promoting a charity, fulfil their duties as citizens by supporting candidates for public office, and seek access to their community and political associates on behalf of their clients. Few lawyers embodied this round of activities more completely, and certainly none with more grace, than Ralph Hayes, Coca-Cola's bachelor about Washington, New York and Wilmington. Born Alfonso Lamont in Ohio, Hayes had entered public life as an assistant to the Secretary of War in 1917. As an attorney, Hayes held few illusions: 'What I am trying to do, of course, is to reconstruct...a basis for asserting that the words of the definition Congress wrote into the Export-Import Act really mean, or should be read as meaning, the opposite of what they appear to state'. In the next sentence, Hayes joked that the research for this interpretation was being conducted by the director of the New York Community Trust, that is, by himself, in a role that smoothed his contact with the rich and influential. In 1938, Robert Woodruff joked that Walter Lippmann, author of *Public Opinion*, should write Hayes's biography.[56] As Hayes's career underscored, success is a matter of who you know. A press secretary for Ronald Reagan summed up: 'Facts determine about half a decision... The other half is whose ear you can get.'[57]

Some interactions between capital and the state happen just because their representatives move in the same circles, where friendships develop and good turns deserve each other. Such was the case when Woodruff told FBI Director J. Edgar Hoover that 'to me, you are the personification of "the American Ideal"—and that is why I am proud to be one of your "fans"'. A few years later, Woodruff again offered to assist Hoover, but did not specify areas for their co-operation. At the time, their common concerns included Negro activists, Reds and unionists, in particular the Teamsters.[58]

The national chairman of the Democratic Party, James Farley, was another social lubricator. He quit President Roosevelt's inner circle in 1940 to become president of Coca-Cola Export. In 1946, Farley accepted an invitation from New York's Archbishop Francis Spellman to travel to Rome to witness His Grace's installation as a cardinal. Four years later, Spellman interested himself in the Rome franchise for Coca-Cola, hoping to secure it for

> his very personal friend, Count Enrico [sic] Galleazzi, who is the closest friend of the Pope. He is the financial and political adviser to the Pope and Governor of the Vatican State... He is the number one man for social and political contacts in Italy and picked DeGaspieri as Premier of Italy. He is also the man who

consummated the plan for releasing $4 000 000 in blocked lire for Hollywood companies.

In a follow-up audience, His Eminence affected to have 'no particular concern in this matter' but said he was merely trying to grant Coca-Cola 'a favour in putting us in touch with people...we might want to work with'. [59]

Not every arrangement can be left to the serendipities of clubland. Early in 1945, the head of Monsanto sought Robert Woodruff's advice on selecting 'Our Man in Washington': 'As we are moving into a managed economy, I believed the person in charge of the proper kind of liaison with the tops of government agencies will occupy one of the important positions in a company, just as it did in Nazi Germany'.[60] Five months later, a Monsanto official phoned Atlanta to suggest that, because Monsanto's president in Canada was 'well acquainted with the Controller of Chemicals' there, he 'might be helpful' in arranging the import of a scarce ingredient for the Coca-Cola syrup.[61]

The personal style of a Hayes or a Farley always needed institutional supports. From the 1920s, Coca-Cola employed a public-relations firm. Its owner became president of The Company in 1955, and remained a senior official until his death in 1969. Coca-Cola's subsequent Washington lobbyists—Williams and Jensen—also served J. P. Morgan, Texaco and Genetech.

Plutocracy

The Standard Oil Company, one wit observed, had done 'everything with the Pennsylvania legislature except refine it'.[62] The same could be alleged of sugar refiners and the US Congress. After leading the 1946 campaign to end sugar rationing months earlier than advised by the Agriculture Department, the junior Senator from Wisconsin, Joe McCarthy, earned the label of 'the Pepsi Cola kid' and a loan of $20 000 from one of its bottlers. 'I'd do that for any friend', the open-handed franchise-holder declared.[63]

Between 1979 and 1994, with 100 lobbyists in Washington, sugar growers donated $12 million to support the election of legislators favourable to their cause. One-fifth of that sum came from the Fanjul family, who had fled Cuba at the same time as Coke's Goizueta. In the 1986 and 1988 congressional elections, Political Action Committees funded by sugar and corn-syrup producers donated $2 million to members of the House of Representatives to re-enact the quota system.[64] By 1995, 'Senators who voted the way the sugar industry wanted had received an average of $13 473 over the previous six years from sugar-industry PACs. Those who voted to eliminate the subsidy received an average of just $1, 461'.[65]

Corporations seek to soften attitudes more often than they buy a one-off vote. The liberal Republican Walter Mack boasted that no sooner had he taken charge of Pepsi in the 1930s than he told 'all our bottlers to get involved in local politics and to make size-able contributions to their state senators and members of congress', irrespective of affiliation.[66] A Coke executive in Los Angeles in the late 1930s was a golfing buddy of the Democrat governor and friendly with a Republican candidate for the Senate. The Fanjul family proved equally non-partisan: 'One brother, José, was the vice chairman of [Republican] Bob Dole's finance committee during the 1996 GOP primaries, while the other, Alfonso, served on President Clinton's finance committee'.[67] As a Southern concern, Coca-Cola began as pro-Democrat, leaving Pepsi little option but to be pro-Republican. Few corporations, however, can afford to indulge the political preferences of their executives; most must contribute to both major parties. Politicians similarly remain flexible in their treat-ment of competing interests. As a congressman from a sugar-growing State advertised: 'I can't be bought. But I can be rented'.[68]

Hail to the Chief

Woodruff did not meet Eisenhower until four years after the gen-eral had ordered the biggest Coke in history. Thereafter, they went huntin', shootin' and fishin' at Woodruff's estates. The channels of influence were reversed in 1951 when Georgia Senator Walter George proposed cutting military and economic aid for Europe. Eisenhower, then NATO commander in Paris, believed that such a reduction 'would most certainly make it impossible' for him to fulfil his mission. He had an aide write to Woodruff pointing out that 'Ike cannot communicate with Senator George, [but] there is no reason why you shouldn't'. Woodruff had daily access to the Senator whenever Congress debated matters of interest to Coca-Cola. Their friendship had been confirmed in 1935 when Woodruff made the Senator a personal loan of $2500.[69] After Eisenhower agreed to run as Republican candidate for the presidency in 1952, Woodruff marshalled a group of Augusta Golf Club members, all anti-New Deal Democrats, 'to go all-out' for Eisenhower, but he failed to get many white Georgians to switch to the party that had freed the slaves, few of whose descendants dared to register to vote.

Eisenhower's vice-president, Richard Nixon, asked for a job with Coca-Cola in 1962 before becoming a senior partner with Pepsi's legal firm; some of the contacts he made there turned up in the Watergate affair. Wayne Andreas of Archer-Daniels-Midland, a grain oligopoly and supplier of corn syrup to Coca-Cola, gave $100 000 to Nixon's 1971 re-election fund. Another cheque from Andreas became the first item in the paper trail from the Watergate burglars to Nixon's campaign committee.[70] Andreas also stayed close to Democrat Senator and 1968 presidential candidate Hubert Humphrey. In 1978, Andreas placed $72 000 in a stock trust for an ex-aide of Humphrey's when he became a Commissioner with the Commodity Futures Exchange, the body that oversaw Andreas's grain trade. Andreas had lent an aircraft to a Senator Robert Dole before he became the Republican candidate in 1996.[71] Capital can afford no loyalties greater than its own expansion.

Woodruff did not know Jimmy Carter before the latter made his move for the governorship of Georgia, but they got together in time for the 1970 poll. Afterwards, Carter appointed Woodruff an admiral in the Georgia Navy. Coca-Cola president Paul Austin took an interest in Carter and arranged for him to be made a member of the Trilateral Commission, a body set up in July 1973 by David Rockefeller of the Chase Manhattan Bank, with the twin tasks of making democracy safe for oil and giving Japan a role in managing the world. Carter attended every meeting of the commission alongside US, European and Japanese power-brokers; it was his graduate seminar in international affairs. When he became US president, associates from the commission would run his administration's foreign policy. The commission's report on US democracy had tipped Carter off to the ruse of pretending to be no more than a peanut grower: 'the candidate who could make himself or herself appear to be an outsider, had the inside road to political office'.[72]

Carter was in the White House when the price for raw sugar dropped back to around 8 cents a pound in 1977, spurring US growers to request increased protection. Coca-Cola responded through its Sugar Users Group with a call to replace the tariff with a bounty, which would lower their costs. Because the new system did not start until 1 January 1978, Coca-Cola could stockpile and thereby save a further $24 million under a law that became known as the Coca-Cola Bill.

*

In the assessment made by Alfred Du Pont Chandler Jr, the leading historian of US business, the corporation, during the twentieth century, became 'the most powerful institution in the American economy and its managers the most influential group of economic decision makers'.[73] This judgement undermines the liberal position that the USA has neither a power elite nor a ruling class. Chandler's thesis also challenges the constitutional order by setting business above government of, by and for the people. The controls concentrated in corporations overwhelm the choices left to small businesses and individual consumers. Nonetheless, corporations can never rule the world. That task requires the nation-market-states that legitimised the existence of corporations in the late nineteenth century.

CHAPTER 2 **A Law Unto Themselves**

The industrial corporation...has proved the most effective device
for extending technology which man has ever known...The greatest
invention of them all.

Henry B. du Pont, vice-president,
E.I. du Pont de Nemours & Co., 1959.[1]

Corporations are now as ubiquitous as Cola-Cola signs, yet in the
1880s their legal status remained in doubt. Once this threat was
averted, the 'modern business enterprise took the place of market
mechanisms in co-ordinating the activities of the economy and allocating its resources'.[2] Corporations produced 75 per cent of all US
manufactures by 1900, leading the president of Columbia University
to proclaim them the greatest single discovery of modern times,
greater than steam or electricity. The creation of corporations confirmed that 'social not technical invention was the intellectual
mainspring of the Industrial Revolution'.[3]

The origins of the corporation provide our second vantage point
for perceiving the great transformation wrought by monopolising
capitals since the 1870s. It was the expansion of capital that gave

rise to the corporation, not the other way around. To identify the corporation as 'an underlying dynamic in the development of modern industrial capitalism' is to assign it too large a role.[4] Had incorporation been blocked by legislatures or in the courts, the juggernaut of growth would have forced some other path. Each phase in the development of capitals has created new business structures. The corporation has flourished for 130 years only by undergoing relentless changes. Even if capitalism proves to be 'the end of history', its corporate form remains open to renewal and subject to decay.[5]

From the 1840s, the consolidation of individual capitals into joint-stock companies helped entrepreneurs through their next round of expansion. That achievement intensified pressures to accept change as the only constant, whether in the law or in economics. Yet to acknowledge the permanence of impermanence was not to reconcile oneself to being wrecked in capital's 'perennial gale of creative destruction'.[6] Against such tempests, incorporation promised continuity beyond the career of an inventor or entrepreneur. When Alfred Marshall, a founder of modern economics in England, published his *Principles* in 1890, he could not conceive of any firm as having a life much beyond the career of its founder, extending at most to his heir. New Jersey legislators saw further in 1896 when they removed the cap on the legal life of corporations.

Capitalists could wait for neither courts nor legislatures, still less for scholars. In the USA, railroads tunnelled through the assumptions that had bounded businesses within political territories. From the 1870s, the rules were being stretched to allow entrepreneurs the legal room to match the geographical spaces across which they operated. Acceptance of the non-government corporation spread after the United Kingdom granted a general right to incorporate in 1862. In Japan, the Meiji oligarchs borrowed the most advanced techniques in their determination not to be colonised, hoping to leapfrog their economy into the era of concentration that they saw overtaking their rival empires. Hence, five years after the 1868 Restoration, Tokyo made erstwhile samurai invest their government bonds in joint-stock companies in order to approach the scale required for survival against foreign traders. Japan's leading banker 'attributed his country's industrial success largely to the effective introduction of the joint stock company'. Of course, forms were adapted to tradition: by the 1890s, the old trading houses— *Zaibatsu*—had reorganised themselves as 'holding companies in the centre' to control 'a string of joint-stock companies'.[7]

This chapter connects the reinvention of the corporation in the late nineteenth century with the breakdown of restrictions on inter-state trade in the USA. It then traces the renovation of the trust into a higher form of business organisation. The next section shows how these patterns of management were strengthened to cope with monopolising before the invention of the multi-divisional corporation of the 1920s, which then supplied a matrix for the transnational enterprise in the 1960s.

Creation myths

Throughout the eighteenth century, corporations had been creatures of the British Crown, which awarded immunity from competition in exchange for public work. After the American War of Independence, State administrations in the US continued to grant monopolies over canals and railroads. These mercantilist privileges were both prescriptive and proscriptive: a company chartered to construct railroads could not build a hotel for its passengers. Because the States rather than the federal government were the authorising powers, corporations' capacities ended at State borders. The common law was averse to corporations doing business in what were called 'foreign' States. 'Foreign' here referred not to Germany but to other members of the Union, making New York foreign to New Jersey.

New Jersey's incorporation laws set the pace in clearing the path. In 1846, the State legislature excused stockholders from responsibility for all of the company's debts, a refuge known as limited liability. Amendments in 1849 removed the requirement for stockholders to subscribe the whole of the company's capital. This change permitted companies to expand beyond the resources of their promoters. New Jersey lawmakers came to regard 'the corporation as a means of bringing the savings of many into efficient use as capital for the development of resources and the promotion of industries'.[8] The corporation as a vehicle to promote a public interest had given way to the engorgement of private capitals.

Legislators also welcomed the fees to be earned from attracting firms to incorporate within their jurisdiction. From 1865, New Jersey permitted its corporations to conduct some operations interstate. Nonetheless, each charter of incorporation still had to be passed as a piece of special legislation, an arrangement which encouraged corruption. After 1875, New Jersey abolished this stipulation and enlarged the sphere in which businesses could operate. Debts could exceed capital and the purchase of additional properties could be financed by the issue of further stock. New Jersey law had caught up with business practices, but only for the moment.

Competition among States for revenues eventually 'eliminated almost every restriction on mergers'.[9] In 1888, New York outlawed the use of the trust instrument as a device for takeovers. Neighbouring New Jersey at once relaxed its law to permit certain corporations to hold stock in each other. When New York followed suit in 1892, New Jersey went further by removing trade from the provisions of its conspiracy law, thereby inscribing space for combinations and cartels. New Jersey next authorised its corporations to behave as if they were individuals allowed to deal in each other's stocks. Thereafter, every New Jersey corporation could be used as a holding company. At the start of the second round of mergers in 1899, sixty-one incorporations, each with capital of more than $10 million, were registered in New Jersey, against sixty in the other forty-five States combined.

The Fourteenth Amendment

In 1868, radical Abolitionists thought they had guaranteed the citizenship of the recently freed slaves by the Fourteenth Amendment to the Constitution:

> All persons born or naturalised in the United States, and subject
> to the jurisdiction thereof, are citizens of the United States and of
> the State wherein they reside. No State shall make or enforce any
> law which shall abridge the privileges or immunities of citizens of

the United States; nor shall any State deprive any person of life, liberty, or property, without due process of law; nor deny to any person within its jurisdiction the equal protection of the laws.

Corporations at once wanted that due process provision to apply to them. Because their charters could be revoked by the legislatures, every election could produce a majority anxious to punish a business by revoking its right to exist. Railroad companies in particular sought to protect themselves from populist resentment against extortionate freight charges.

One attempt to stretch the due process of the Fourteenth Amendment to corporations reached the Supreme Court in 1873, when butchers in New Orleans opposed a public health measure granting a monopoly over slaughtering. In deciding against the butchers, the court also weakened the Amendment's intended defence of human dignity by finding that, because the second sentence specified 'citizens of the United States', it did not protect 'privileges or immunities' within particular States.

As a defence of the Negro, the Fourteenth Amendment fell into disuse until the 1920s. Instead, lawyers spied in the words 'nor shall any State deprive any person of life, liberty, or property, without due process of law' a fortress for modern corporations. This section referred to 'persons', and did not contain the qualification 'of the United States'. If corporations were persons, they would be entitled to the protection of due process under the Fourteenth Amendment.

Before the late 1880s, persons could be corporations, but not the other way around. *Laissez-faire* conservatives identified corporations with individual entrepreneurs, not with giants such as Standard Oil. The Supreme Court dismissed the first attempt to present corporations as persons on the grounds that the Constitution referred to 'persons born or naturalised' in the United States and endowed with 'life, liberty, and property'.[10]

Then, in 1882, a California railroad company paid ex-Senator Roscoe Conkling $5000 to inform the Ninth Circuit Court that when he had drafted the Fourteenth Amendment in 1867, he had written 'person' not 'citizen' because he intended the term to include corporations. It was indeed the case that, when the amendment was being drafted at the end of the Civil War, corporations with inter-state businesses had been petitioning Congress for relief from State penalties and prohibitions. Muckrakers would cite Conkling's claim as proof of a conspiracy in 1867. The truth was that in 1882 Conkling made a 'daring misuse' of the evidence. He had not conspired in 1867, but he did perjure himself fifteen years later.[11]

A no less inspired railroad counsel guided the Supreme Court away from its assumption that a person had to be either born or naturalised. Adam and Eve, the lawyer reminded the bench, were neither born nor naturalised but, like corporations, had been cre-ated. If due process were reserved for citizens born or naturalised, humankind's progenitors must remain in the limbo where the rail-roads were being shunted. Although the attorney acknowledged that corporations were not citizens, they were as much natural per-sons as Eve or any freed slave, and hence entitled to due process.

With the bench weary of philosophising its way out of prece-dents, the chief justice announced at the start of yet another California railroad appeal in 1886 that his court would hear no more submissions on whether equal protection could apply to cer-tain corporations, because 'We are all of the opinion that it does'.[12] For several decades thereafter, corporations could challenge any leg-islation that limited their operations, anticipating that such shenanigans would find favour in the Supreme Court.

In 1892, the *American Law Review* voiced outrage that 'consti-tutional ordinances earned on the field of battle and intended as charters of human liberty, have been turned into the shield of incor-porated monopoly'.[13] This denunciation over-simplified a process which continued to be convoluted and uneven. Although protec-tion for ex-slaves had been abandoned almost before it began, the Supreme Court nonetheless had hoped to quibble its way out of States' Rights. Due process for businesses was complete only when the 1895 railroad strike scared the bench into converting the Sherman Anti-Trust Act into a defence of corporations against wage-earners, just as it had read the Fourteenth Amendment as liberating bondholders, not bondsmen. Thus, by 1900, State and federal courts, along with their legislatures, had reconstructed 'due process' to protect most contracts and corporations against governmental restrictions.

The Coca-Cola Company

In Coca-Cola's home State of Georgia, the power to incorporate had followed English common law until the 1840s, when a series of Acts and rulings established 'the free right to incorporate for profit'.[14] The law 'allowed individuals to pool their capital to create manufacturing' as part of the Industrial Gospel preached by sectional interests against the dominant New England cotton millers.[15] After defeat in battle, Georgia's politicians suspected the corporation of being 'yet another attempt to subjugate...the South's own small companies to Northern rule'.[16] 'Only after the fumblings and uncertainties of 100 years did Georgia judges swear by the new book of Genesis in which it was written that, while 'man is one person created by the Almighty', a corporation is 'an artificial person created by law for specific purposes'.[17]

The building of Coca-Cola benefited from the judiciary's acceptance of these doctrines. Its principal owner, Asa Candler, incorporated one collection of Coca-Cola partners in 1888 for $12 000. He did so again in 1892, this time with a nominal capital of $100 000. He 'had in mind the sale of a considerable amount of stock...to get the capital which seemed necessary to establish the business on a sound basis'.[18] He contacted brokers in the northeast, but these Yankees had dodges of their own on which to splurge, so he retained 90 per cent of the stock himself.

In deciding to incorporate his still tiny firm, Candler was keeping up with the transformation of the US economy. The meat packer Swift incorporated in 1882, Duke Tobacco in 1885, Proctor & Gamble in 1890 to raise funds to export, A&P Stores and Quaker Oats in 1901, Pepsi in 1902, and Henry Ford in 1903. H. J. Heinz waited until 1905, when its sales were a million times greater than Coca-Cola's had been at incorporation.

Incorporation could also be a snare for investors. Extrapolating from a putative annual profit of $100 000, the promoter would set the value of his concern at $1 million. He would then sell 499 999 shares at one dollar, retain control, and have almost half a million in cash. The originator of Coca-Cola, Dr Pemberton, had conceived some such scheme in 1885–86 when he incorporated his Chemical Company with a nominal capital of $160 000.

Interstate trade

In 1787, the confusions and conflicts caused by the colonies 'imposing their own tariffs on overseas and interstate produce' had led the Philadelphia Convention to give the Federal Congress constitutional power over 'Commerce with foreign nations, and among the States'. Although the States could no longer levy tariffs against each others' goods, they retained policing powers to incorporate businesses, charter tradesmen, inspect merchandise and license pedlars—opportunities enough to impede trade.

Local traders pressured State administrations to enforce anti-foreign regulations. By the mid-nineteenth century, most States had protected their own manufacturers and merchants by penalising those from across the border. Georgia, for example, made life harder for non-resident salesmen by demanding a separate licence to sell in each of its counties. Not until the late 1880s did the courts invalidate special taxes on 'foreigners'. When Washington failed to legislate against these impediments, a door opened for judicial activism on behalf of producers who needed to profit from a continental market but were boxed in by State laws. 'The rise of big business was a prerequisite for the emergence of a national market', more than the other way around.[19] As disputes reached the Supreme Court, distinctions between commerce and manufacture taxed the resourcefulness of the justices, although the hair-splitting made less and less sense against the sprawl of trade.

The Singer Sewing Machine Company had led the fight against restrictions on mass marketing by establishing its own sales outlets. By 1879, Singer had 530 retail stores, from which radiated thousands of door-to-door salesmen. During the 1870s, 'Singer's counsel prompted the Court to deduce from the commerce clause a new, fundamentally important constitutional right: the right of American businessmen, even without congressional license, to engage in interstate transactions on terms of equality with local merchants and manufacturers'.[20] In 1880, Singer defeated a Virginia law which would have forced it to abandon its own sales network and rely on local shopkeepers.

By the mid-1880s, mass producers had shattered the regime under which thousands of manufacturers had held local monopolies. The area that a factory could expect to supply trebled between 1880 and 1900. In Coca-Cola's first decade, its salesmen were travelling beyond Georgia. Without reinterpretation of the US Constitution, the sale in Virginia of a syrup made in Georgia would not have been secure. Health inspections by any of the States could still trip out-of-town pedlars, but when Minnesota used its pure food laws to exclude beef slaughtered in Illinois, the Supreme Court found in favour of the Chicago meat trust. Hence, just when Coca-Cola began to move beyond Georgia, the court lessened the likelihood that the policing powers of the States could be deployed against the sale of Candler's 'foreign' beverage.

The altered legal environment allowed Candler to expand more readily. It also pitted his family business against a handful of corporations. Had Coca-Cola appeared twenty years sooner, it might well have withered inside Georgia, forbidden to trade outside its State of manufacture. Had it appeared twenty years later, some triumphant predecessor might have offered the Candlers a bottling franchise. Candler took over Coca-Cola just as the law assured capitalists of their right to spread geographically as well as financially.

The trusts

The corporations that emerged in the last half of the nineteenth century proved more successful than their precursors. Initial growth, however, could never guarantee longevity. Firms therefore sought to block entrants, to manage production and to stabilise prices through a spread of devices, none more inventive than the trust.

Throughout the 1870s, John D. Rockefeller had taken over companies as if those transactions were between individual persons. By holding property in several States and owning stock in other corporations, his Standard Oil Company (SOC) left its legal standing precarious. A demand for $3 million in back taxes to Pennsylvania on properties held outside that State spurred SOC to restructure its ownership through a creative application of the common-law trust, under which activities could be conducted in secret and without governmental approval. A trust company hitherto had been used when a trustee had several clients who did not know each other. SOC adapted this procedure so that 'the controlling voting stock in a number of rival corporations was transferred to one corporation in exchange for the latter's trust certificates. Market policies were thus centralised in the hands of a small group'.[21]

The late nineteenth century is called petroleum's age of 'illumination and lubrication', a motto applicable to Henry Flagler, SOC's secretary-treasurer. Flagler had learnt much from his dealings with railway companies when he had negotiated reductions of freight charges for Rockefeller. In 1875, he initiated a Central Refiners Association, the members of which then leased their plant to the association in return for stock. This venture pointed towards the holding company as a vehicle for limiting competition. As long as States forbade corporations to own each other, members of a railroad pool had to trust each other, which they knew better than to do. Flagler glimpsed a way forward by turning a gentlemen's agreement into a legal bond. His first step down this path came with SOC's takeover of the Long Island Oil Company, which he transferred to himself as trustee. For that advance, the legal and common usage of the word 'trust' coincided: one person held property on behalf of another. The beneficiary of Flagler's trusteeship remained unstated, because in law it could not be Standard Oil. If cross-examined, Flagler would say that he held the trust for a few friends who happened to own Standard Oil.

In 1879, Flagler replaced individual trustees with a joint trust of three friends in Ohio who happened to be on the staff of SOC. This arrangement still allowed Rockefeller to tell the truth, if not the whole truth, when he swore that SOC did not own a catalogue of 1003 companies. They were owned by his office boys, those amicable Ohio trustees who distributed profits for the benefit of individual stockholders in Standard Oil. When those stockholders signed a trust agreement on 2 January 1882 to set up Standard Oil

Companies in several States of the Union, their new contract united these corporations into one company. For the first time, all SOC properties and stocks came under a single trust. Profits went into the trust to be distributed as dividends to its certificate-holders, as the stockholders had become. The modern corporation had been made paper.

Shareholders were reluctant to trade their real property for trust certificates until the legality of the new system was clear. Investors liable for losses, however, were anxious to swap, a feature not mentioned nowadays when trust is posited as the virtue of a market-directed economy. Indeed, the trust became an instrument for deceit. When Ernest Woodruff organised a syndicate of bankers to take over The Coca-Cola Company in 1919, he did so through a voting trust, the standard bankers' device for keeping power out of the hands of the shareholders. Three years later, he set up Coca-Cola International Corporation solely as a holding company of common stock in The Coca-Cola Company to wrest control away from his erstwhile banking partners. The Woodruffs in turn arranged their shares in Coca-Cola International through a holding company.

Because SOC already owned 90 per cent of the petroleum industry before John D. Rockefeller and Flagler formed the trust in 1882, their motives were unlike those of most capitalists who followed their lead. In manipulating the time-honoured purposes of the trust, SOC sought legal security and managerial efficiencies to sustain its dominance over the market. Its emulators, by contrast, used the trust to pursue their monopolising. This aim was most widespread among railroad companies, where trust was 'usually a euphemism for Pierpont [Morgan] and three or four of his cronies'.[22]

The uses of the trust as a legal instrument for the growth of capital had not been apparent until Rockefeller's men clawed their way through them. Rockefeller acknowledged that 'all we saw at the moment was the need to save ourselves from wasteful conditions'.[23] His tasks between 1870 and 1890 had 'constantly assumed larger proportions'.[24] He and Flagler were not blind, but they could not see around corners. When one plan to dominate refining encountered obstructions, they found another way to open up additional realms to consolidate and restructure.

Games theorists have tried to calibrate the 'degree of foresight possessed by competitors' during the 1890s merger movement.[25] Such calculations are inappropriate because businessmen were in the same fog as the lawyers, politicians and judges who had to scramble after rapid changes in the structure of industries and the management of firms: 'most of the legal problems that corporations confronted had to be negotiated case-by-case within each State'.[26] Decades of experimentation were needed to build up sufficient examples for any of the participants to comprehend the copiousness being raised on their mundanities. Each obstacle offered opportunities to enter 'into new geographical and related product markets'.[27]

*

In gathering together autonomous operations, the trust as holding company foreshadowed the multi-divisional corporation, which was perfected by the du Ponts around 1920, when they added a central office to allocate resources and monitor performance. That geometry of controls coupled with the complexities of business organisation required the turning of management into a profession.

CHAPTER 3 **Hands-On**

> Once upon a time, the organisation of...the firm was a black box.
> Into this box went labour and capital, and out came products...
> Some venturesome economists have wondered what the black box
> contained.
>
> Armen A. Alchian and Susan Woodward, 1988[1]

Economists have hypnotised themselves with invisible hands. Just
as theologues believed that angels carried the planets on their orbits
around the earth, so have neo-classical economists placed their faith
in the force of the market. Markets, however, can make nothing.
Owners and managers, merchandisers and bureaucrats, consumers
and labourers carry forward the expansion of capital. That growth
calls for more than the guiding hand of the state. Corporations need
specialists in research, manufacture, finance and marketing.

Today it appears normal that all these activities take place inside
the one firm. Before the 1870s, few businesses reached beyond their
localities or ran to more than one product line. Family-sized concerns held no hierarchies beyond parent and child, craftsman and
apprentice. Alfred D. Chandler Jr documented how in 'many sectors

of the economy the visible hand of management replaced what Adam Smith referred to as the invisible hand of market forces'.[2] Executives and their gurus welcome his hypothesis, which elevates their own activities, while economists look down on a conclusion drawn from the archives rather than from algebra.

This chapter examines the rise of the manager from two angles. The first segment explores the relationship between managers and owners. The second part introduces management failure, then outlines the attempts to overcome that impediment to capital's expansion through specialist education, scientific management and corporate planning. The next chapter will take up some financial aspects of management.

Managerialism

Capitalists must reinvest if they are to survive as capitalists. Deciding how much to plough back and how much to consume is part of every economic process. That choice confronted Asa Candler in 1891, when he was sole owner and manager of Coca-Cola, as much as it does a suburban retiree today watching her portfolio of Coca-Cola shares. Disagreements between owners and managers over investment did not appear with the drawing of functional distinctions between families and managers, or between personal managers and professional ones. Even where 'the basic goal of large companies—either managerial or owner-dominated—is profits *and* growth', these 'inseparable objectives' require the allocation of funds between dividends and reserves.[3] At issue is whether to return capital to shareholders for some alternative expenditure or to retain those monies to improve the earnings of the firm.

Attempts by executives to recapitalise their establishments have brought them into conflict with investors clamouring for dividends. Minority shareholders once sued Henry Ford for ploughing back profits. Nonetheless, it is misleading to suggest that owners indulge their whims, while managers make rational investments.

The split between owners and managers has never been absolute. Interactions are invariably more layered because owners remain active, managers become owner–directors, and new investors are appointed directors. The president and chairman of General Motors from 1923 to 1946, Alfred P. Sloan Jr, was also one of its largest individual shareholders. As he put it in his memoirs, 'The shareholder's point of view is natural to me. I have always taken a strong stand for the shareholders, especially in such matters as...the payment of dividends'.[4] Similarly, in 1998, McDonald's new CEO spent his first day phoning the firm's twenty largest investors: 'That's who I work for. At the end of the day, this is all about shareholder value'.[5] In the 1990s, departments of investor relations were added to corporate structures in an effort to slow the churn of share trading, which grew from 12 per cent of shares per annum in 1960 to 75 per cent in 1998. The power of owners over their manager asserted itself on 1 December 1999, when the largest stock-holder in Coca-Cola, Warren Buffett, told Coca-Cola's chairman and CEO, Doug Ivester, that he 'was no longer the man who should be running Coke'. Four days later, Ivester resigned.[6] Harvard's business school has no case study of an editor sacking Rupert Murdoch, a pleasure still reserved for his bankers.

Owners also remained managers. Many corporations 'grew to maturity while dominated by an entrepreneur who remained thoroughly in command of policy despite relinquishing day-to-day control of operations to a staff of professional managers'.[7]

At Coca-Cola, the Candler family stayed in control for thirty years until 1919, when they were bought out by a syndicate headed by Ernest Woodruff, who 'refused to invest in companies whose management had little or no ownership'.[8] His son Robert would not have become known as The Boss at Coca-Cola had his father not captained its acquisition. Thereafter, the childless Robert Woodruff nurtured every senior executive, a rite of succession which mimicked the Irish custom of Tanistry, whereby the inheritance passes to the most capable near relative, a practice 'prevalent also in numerous American industries'.[9]

Executives have turned themselves into owners. At General Motors the Bonus Plan created 'an owner-management group' in the early 1920s.[10] From the late 1980s, Coca-Cola executives became part-owners through exercising stock options in their remuneration packages. By 1989, Coke's chairman, Roberto Goizueta, held $600 million worth of shares; his reward for 1991 included a million shares in the company, then valued at $83.40 each. His successor had Coca-Cola stock with a market value of $206 million and un-exercised vested options worth $139 million.

Whereas managers once were praised for guarding the long-term prospects of their firms against shareholders grasping after dividend cheques, executives are now accused of 'mortgaging the present',[11] diluting the worth of their companies by not charging their stock options against current income. Senior managers have made even more spectacular gains from leveraged buy-outs, in which they put up 10–15 per cent of the bidding price to take over corporations they had been employed to run on the shareholders' behalf.

Management failure

The achievements of the visible hands of executives, whether owners or employees, have been incontrovertible. Yet management failure is as significant as market or regulatory failure and cannot always be prevented by a suite of Harvard MBAs. Alongside the hand-books that provide executives with a security blanket, such as *The Art of War and the Art of Management*, a place should be reserved for Norman Dixon's *On the Psychology of Military Incompetence* (1976).

Business Week in 1993 listed New Coke as one of its top ten 'world-class flops'.[12] Most of the other nine failed so completely that they are not remembered at all, though the corporations that promoted them were the most successful in their fields, including Ford, Du Pont, Time and IBM. If these companies were so rich, why were they not smarter? One answer is that practices that once brought success had become obstacles to change. Procedures that strike analysts as daft today are the detritus of bright ideas adopted to dispel some previous difficulty. Hence, Diet Coke and New Coke cannot be counterpoised as triumph against disaster. The distance between The Company's high flyer and its prize failure narrows once we recognise that both were launched in response to weak-ness in the line leaders, TAB and Classic Coke.

Before Goizueta took over in 1980–81, some senior executives recognised that there was 'no-one really running the company', which had fallen victim to 'paralysis through analysis'.[13] Goizueta established a 'Spanish Inquisition' of financial controls, which cleared up some problems but could not prevent new ones. The $250 million research budget for the 1983 launch of Diet Coke failed to predict its almost total displacement of TAB, Coca-Cola's original diet line. Goizueta, in turn, did not learn from that mistake to question the positive figures from the trial release of New Coke. Nor did outside experts ensure quality advice. The consultants he brought in to crunch numbers on the acquisition of Columbia Pictures overlooked the earnings from its film library, which proved a goldmine. Small wonder then that his successor worried about 'the arrogance of success', while the head of marketing talked of 'the Coca-Cola rash', which erupts when 'you lose your humility'.[14]

Historians are always in danger of treating categories such as History, Capital or Technology as if they were persons. To treat human beings 'as personifications instead of as individuals' is to bow down before abstractions. Similarly, business historians fail when they treat the enterprise as if it had 'a life of its own'.[15] The corporation does not make history. It is 'in the person of the capitalist' that capital is endowed with 'intelligence and will'.[16] Yet the scholars' worship of the market or the multi-divisional corporation is a perverse acknowledgement of the constraints set on our wishes by the accumulation of capital.

'Individualism has gone, never to return', John D. Rockefeller observed in retirement. The reason for its demise was Rockefeller's success with the trust movement, which 'was the origin of the whole system of modern economic administration'.[17] Sixty years later, the CEO at Sears, Ed Brennan, said he would like to have the time to re-read Ayn Rand. His choice of author suggests nostalgia for a form of capitalism which has been vanquished by corporations such as his. The Sears Tower was nearer to Kafka's *Castle* than to the visions of the architect-as-hero in Rand's *Fountainhead*. Alexander Calder's modernist mobile in the tower's mezzanine was 'singularly unappreciated' by the firm's organisation men.[18] Brennan was just one more chief executive falling for the impossible dream that individual enterprise is compatible with oligopoly.

To tame the rugged individualist, however, is not to erase characters, their foibles or temperaments. Equally, to acknowledge the idiosyncrasies of owners and managers need not reduce the history of capitalism to goodies and baddies, inspired inventors and robber barons, Edison and Rockefeller, geniuses and entrepreneurs. Corporate cultures do not eliminate the influence that personality has on profit rates. By 1980, Coca-Cola's marketing supremo, Sergio Zyman, had become known as the 'Aya Cola', whereas executives at Sears nominated a colleague as the man they would choose for a father. Coke bottlers perceived its backslapping president Donald Keough and patrician chairman Roberto Goizueta as good cop and bad cop, a contrast which benefited The Company.

The advice that a Coca-Cola lawyer gave Robert Woodruff on how to present himself for his official photograph comes closer than any flow-chart to capturing the disorganisation generated by senior executives:

> Have the studio come to your office—and don't pose there, either.
> I don't want to see a neat pile of papers in front of you as if you
> were some Colonel of Industry. I want to see the documentary
> chaos that surrounds you; those stacks of home-work behind you
> that make the place look like a hoo-rah's nest in a hurricane...I
> want a photograph that shows you as your friends and hired-hands
> have to put up with you.[19]

Management has to keep this disorder within bounds so that profits emerge despite incapacities and irrationalities at every level. Institutions always need human beings to operate them, no matter how thoroughly those individuals are buttoned down beneath grey flannel suits—the Proctoids at Proctor & Gamble, or the foot soldiers at General Electric. In compiling his histories of business management, Alfred D. Chandler Jr ignores the impetus derived from emotions such as envy, lust and avarice—'revenge first, then money and sex', as one advertising executive listed the qualities needed for success.[20]

At Sears in the late 1970s, whenever the vice-presidents in charge of buying and selling 'sat down together...the effort to unify the company was set back again'.[21] Others were close to fisticuffs. Its finance department behaved like Hoover's FBI, keeping files on expense accounts to use in boardroom battles. About the same time, Coca-Cola's chairman and president were not speaking to each other as a result of failure to resolve disputes with the bottlers.

Writing in the mid-1970s, Chandler claimed: 'Men came and went. The institution and its offices remained', so that 'once a managerial hierarchy had been formed and had successfully carried out its function of administrative co-ordination, the hierarchy itself became a source of permanence, power, and continued growth'.[22] These achievements could also impede growth when precepts implanted by the founders outlasted their usefulness. Coca-Cola took less than four years to break from the Asa Candler mould because an economic slump in 1920–23 required immediate action. Although Robert Woodruff retired in 1955, he maintained his authority for a further thirty years through a three-man finance committee, which one colleague described as 'visible evidence of the transmigration of souls'.[23]

Woodruff's influence was reinforced by the ages of the other board members. In 1979, he was eighty-nine years old and his fellow directors averaged seventy. Only one of the fourteen was under fifty. None was from the Pepsi Generation. The board procrastinated over price increases and resisted new products and bottle sizes. As the head of PepsiCo sneered, 'Coke didn't need to innovate': the old man's 'single perception' had proved 'so brilliant that it needed no revision'.[24] By practising Emerson's maxim that 'an institution is the lengthened shadow of a man', Woodruff stunted Coca-Cola.

Corporations have adopted various means to maintain their momentum as they grew beyond the reach or grasp of any individual. Three discussed below are specialist education, scientific management and strategic planning. In practice, these solutions overlapped. The Joseph Wharton who donated $100 000 to found a business school at the University of Pennsylvania was the same Joseph Wharton who paid the founder of scientific management, Frederick William Taylor, $35 a day to bring efficiency to the steelworks in that State.

Specialist education

J. Pierpont Morgan complained to his father in the autumn of 1875 that he was having difficulty finding partners for their bank:

> The longer I live the more apparent becomes the absence of brains—particularly soundly balanced brains. You would be surprised...to see how few business men there are unexceptionable in character, ability, experience, and association to fit such a position.[25]

Perhaps that is why Pierpont hired the most handsome applicants, who became known as 'J. P.'s Ganymedes'. Elsewhere, his criteria of brains and character had to be met.

By 1880, commercial colleges in the USA were training 50 000 students a year to become clerks, but no one was preparing executives to back up entrepreneurs. Joseph Wharton set out to remedy that lack. In the 1840s Wharton had been apprenticed to the dry-goods trade, where he learned 'the business procedures created by the medieval Italians: book credit and double-entry bookkeeping'.[26] From there he made one fortune from zinc, a second from nickel, a third from iron and, though a Quaker, a fourth from armaments. These enterprises taught him that 'systematic instruction cannot be expected from the over-worked heads of any great establishment'.[27] So he funded the University of Pennsylvania in 1881 to educate a business elite in the liberal arts and social sciences.

When Harvard's Graduate School of Business Administration opened in 1908, that discipline was still in search of both its content and an appropriate pedagogy. The Harvard curriculum was more technical than Pennsylvania's, adding economic geography to units in accounting, commercial law and railway practice. The case-study method, later complemented by student placement with corporations, countered the allegation that administration could not be taught except by doing.[28]

Although Wharton had anticipated a demand for tertiary courses in business administration, he did not expect to mass-produce managers along with workers and commodities. Yet such was the result. In 1900, two-thirds of senior executives in the USA had no formal business education. By 1950, almost all the top personnel had been to college, while 160 business schools and 400 university departments were passing out 50 000 graduates and 5000 Masters candidates a year. This swell of students did not meet Wharton's call for quality. The Business School at Columbia was a backwater by the 1950s, stamping out technicians, not strategists. Both the Carnegie and Ford Foundations published reports in 1959 calling on the universities 'to create more intellectual content in the field, to improve the quality of both students and faculty, to eliminate trivia'.[29]

Management in the USA before the 1920s was the preserve of the works engineer. Because Coca-Cola had no works to speak of, it employed few engineers and so had little experience of managerialism. Coca-Cola recruited Harvard graduates but was not committed to formal training until the 1960s, when it instituted Harvard School courses for bottlers and company managers, including overseas participants. When the Chief Financial Officer, Doug Ivester, needed to master marketing in 1990, Coca-Cola reverted to an apprenticeship model by commissioning its erstwhile marketing supremo, Sergio Zyman, to tutor Ivester on Saturday mornings for more than a year. Zyman himself had pulled out of a Harvard course in order to take charge of the 1980 launch of Diet Coke. Emory University in Atlanta, though endowed by the Candlers and Woodruffs, did not develop its school of business until the mid-1990s. PepsiCo's first Harvard MBA was John Sculley, who in 1967 introduced the marketing department to an analytic assessment of its campaigns. Previously, 'Pepsi had always operated by gut instinct'.[30]

Before 1990, Harvard's business school had 50 000 graduates and was producing 700 more each year; a third of the top officers in *Fortune*'s 500 biggest corporations could put the MBA brand label after their names. By contrast, Japanese firms trained their people in house, giving credence to the jibe that the Japanese economy thrived between 1960 and 1990 because its corporations employed no lawyers, no economists and no Harvard MBAs. In like mood, the Hong Kong tycoon Robert Kuok, whom Coca-Cola selected as its springboard into China, scoffed in 1997: 'When I hear somebody's got an MBA, I have a feeling of dread because normally they come to me with an over-pompous sense of their own importance...So they learn painful lessons at my expense'.[31]

Tertiary qualifications for executives could be delayed, even ignored as at McDonald's, without ruining the business. Those options were not open when it came to the supervision of the workforce. Indeed, the control of labour has been at the heart of management training.

Scientific management

Rather than 'searching for some unusual or extraordinary man'—that genius who kept all accounts in his head, whether to avoid taxes or to save himself the trouble of writing them down—firms sought to redress their talent deficit by imposing Frederick W. Taylor's 'systematic management'.[32] Routine would compensate for a want of flair. At Wharton's Bethlehem Steel, Taylor shifted control over the flow of production from the workmen to the office planners. 'The office was beginning, but only beginning, to dominate the shop'.[33] The time-and-motion study aspects of scientific management have been exaggerated since; by 1914, no more than 50000 workers were under Taylor's system. Scientific management provided a Utopian vision more than a checklist of practices, becoming a generic term for a host of attempts to cope with the complexities of mass production and worldwide distribution.

Railroads were among the first corporations to establish complex administrations, since, by definition, a railroad company operates at a distance from its centre. One railway superintendent explained that, while he could give fifty miles of track his personal attention, a track of five hundred miles required a different system of control, because authority had to be divided between headquarters staff and employees down the line.

For the office to run the shop, someone had to run the office. Here too, Standard Oil had built better than it knew. Under its deed of trust, the nine trustees would 'exercise general supervision over the affairs of the said several Standard Oil companies'.[34] A structure originally devised to disguise monopolisation created circumstances in which the directors took on more power to become their own working managers.

Rockefeller thus oversaw SOC's diverse undertakings through a swarm of committees. After he shifted to New York in 1883, the trustees—now better called executives—met almost daily. Instead of waiting upon decisions by a majority of the stockholders, Rockefeller would co-opt two or three directors to handle each aspect of the firm's business. Between them, Rockefeller and SOC's secretary–treasurer, Flagler, belonged to every committee, and together they formed a supervisory executive. Yet Rockefeller's managerial practices were never a complete success. The New York office 'continued to reflect the melange of companies based upon historical precedent, personal predilections, State corporation requirements, and tax laws. Even such an orderly mind as that of the company's General Counsel did not have a complete picture of it'.[35]

Resistance to the new forms of office management was wide and deep. J. Pierpont Morgan operated a 'posh sweatshop' and held no directors' meetings before the financial panic of 1907. The scarcely literate Henry Ford feared managers with a 'genius for organisation', and left piles of accounts unopened. The task for 'autocrats' such as Sloan at General Motors was to devise networks of delegation. Managers invented more rules than products, accounting for stock and labour as well as for cash.

Attaching the term 'scientific' to both socialism and management allied them with the ideologies of progress being crafted around technological innovation. Just as socialism held out a promise for workers, so 'the cult of efficiency'[36] stiffened the bosses' resolve to keep their employees hard at it. The chief engineer at General Electric, Charles Steinmetz (1865–1923), thought himself a socialist, and offered his services to the Soviet government. He believed that the age of the individual was over and that the corporation represented the highest form of collectivism. In 1928, the first Soviet five-year plan was welded together by another engineer, not an economist.

Strategic planning

George Orwell's *Nineteen Eighty-Four* (1949) popularised the idea
of convergence between Soviet ministries and US corporations. Sixty
years earlier, radicals had asked: 'What is the difference between
U.S. Steel as it might be organised by Mr Morgan, and a Department
of Steel as it might be organised by the Government?'[37] In terms
of managerial practices, the distance was not great. Nor was it vast
in 1988, when a study reported that Soviet and US managers both
tended 'to assume that there exist greater differences and fewer
commonalties than we in fact found'.[38] The corporate executives
and ministerial apparatchiks were united, however, in claiming cost
advantages from supplying their own resources and services. They
said they absorbed the costs that would have come from transact-
ing those deals with outsiders.

The closeness of the two systems is revealed by asking which of
these two descriptions of industries is about the United States and
which about the Soviet Union?

I. One study found 'chains of command' with parallel lines of
authority for counter-checking 'with extreme use of incessant pressure...to meet explicit short-run production goals'.[39]

II. Another investigation found nine layers of bureaucracy that once
had been a 'means of disciplining the organisation had started to
strangle' its productivity. When the financial controller imposed
arbitrary targets, 'managers often would refuse to invest in essential equipment [and] even close down factories'.[40]

The first statement comes from a 1959 US survey of Soviet industry, the second from an in-house critique of General Electric twenty
years later.

Those parallels cannot blot out the differences. The Soviet system
imploded, while US oligopolies bestride our world. Yet that outcome had not always been clear. Throughout the 1930s, capitalism
was mired in depressions while the Soviet Union passed through
industrial take-off. The Dneiper dam was the equal of the Tennessee

Valley Authority, and the Red Army as formidable against Hitler as the US military. After 1945, central planning restored the eight years of Soviet production lost in the war, helping the USSR to lead the exploration of space in 1957. In 1960, when Khrushchev told US businessmen that the Soviets would bury capitalism through peaceful competition, a bull market in shovels was not irrational. By 1990, the battle was over. Indeed, it had been lost before 1980. The central planners had been fair enough at lump business, but disastrous with consumer items: 'The early critics of socialist central planning...were clearly on target in their emphasis on the magnitude of the task that any putative planning authority must face in any economy that involves many goods'.[41]

Yet similar encumbrances prevailed at Sears, where buyers told the suppliers to overcharge so that the regional stores could build up a fund which would be channelled back to those suppliers through marketing outlays. Other bottlenecks were circumvented by nepotism. The head of men's apparel acknowledged: 'The only way I get things done is 'cause I know a few guys in the field from the old neighbourhood. But it's a hell of a way to run a candy store.'[42] As in the Soviet system, managers at Sears got around obstacles by inserting yet another layer of organisation. Comparable behaviour clogged Proctor & Gamble, where a brand manager in the early 1980s had to rewrite a memo '460 times in six months', and where the minutes for formal meetings were 'typed in advance'.[43]

Whether planning an economy or running a firm, managers use their positions to accrue wealth. The number of bureaucrats required to allocate resources under socialist planning enhanced 'their potential to extract bureaucratic rents'.[44] Managers in the capitalist corporation did much the same: 'The men in control of a corporation can operate in their own interests, and can divest a portion of the asset fund of income stream to their own uses, such is their privilege', concluded a 1933 survey of US business. Its author argued that these new 'autocrats' had 'powers which are absolute and not limited by any implied obligation with respect to their use'.[45]

The best was yet to come. After 1970, it was a rare CEO in the USA who was without a company jet to take him away for a weekend of golf. Share options and leveraged buy-outs have since showered US managers with rewards as vast as any the Brezhnev clan extracted from the Soviet proletariat. Executives underwrote the value of their benefits by having their corporations go into debt to buy back stock and thus keep up the share price of their options.

In the United Kingdom, the earnings of management consultants went up by 443 per cent between 1980 and 1987, while outlays on physical stocks increased by only 63 per cent. Worldwide, the consultancy game had garnered $230 billion. The 1998 merger frenzy generated close to $2 billion in fees and $72 billion in restructuring charges, or 22 cents in every dollar for the top 500 companies. The push to replace managerial privileges with shareholder value failed. Instead, the institutional investors and Wall Street brokers gorged on fees and the managers gave themselves stock options.

The 'potential to extract rents' was never confined to the dress circle. Corporations in the West were as loaded down with office staff as any state-owned plant. General Electric made every general manager in 1960 'hire a full-time strategic planner...to create a formal strategic plan each year':

> That hefty document, the product of more man-hours than anyone dared count, went up to one of the forty-six SBUs [Strategic Business Units], which would subject it to intense scrutiny. The SBUs in turn would send on the plan to a newly created staff at headquarters.[46]

Similarly, Nabisco generated volumes of projections about every crumb of its workings. Service divisions expanded while their productivity defied measurement, until middle management was downsized in the 1980s as a crude way to push up output.

Had it not been for Electronic Data Processing, the entire workforce of Sears and the Soviet Union would have been engaged on their respective plans. In the early 1970s, the Soviet Minister for Chemical Industries wanted more memory for his IBM 360–50 so that he could control 30 000 factories. He saw mainframes as the means to centralise everything, not as an aid to rationalise resources between his centre, the regions and localities. The IBM vice-president who disparaged the minister's ambition failed to notice that his own company suffered from a comparable malaise. The mainframe was like IBM itself, built for huge command systems, but slow to turn. Ten years later, RJR Nabisco emulated the Soviet minister by attempting 'to assemble a telecommunications and computer system that would tie together the whole empire. It was like we'd been bought by the federal government.'[47]

Managers claim that strategic planning is essential to their corporations. Why else are they paid? Yet in the late 1970s, when Sears sought to improve its performance by examining the methods employed by AT&T, NCR and Texas Instruments, it discovered that 'none of them seemed to be such avid planners'; even IBM had 'gotten into highly disciplined planning quite recently'.[48] Wal-Mart's founder, Sam Walton, fessed up: 'We didn't have systems. We didn't have ordering programs. We didn't have a basic merchandise assortment.'[49]

One firm which did not simply muddle through was Proctor & Gamble; its marketing department policed its campaigns. That approach was much admired by Goizueta, who put an end to five-year plans at Coca-Cola, claiming they looked too far ahead to concentrate the mind. His subordinates had to meet three-year targets. At RJR Nabisco, the new CEO, Ross Johnston, declared: 'Planning, gentlemen, is "What are you going to do next year that's different from what you did this year? All I want is five items".'[50]

Business strategists and their socialist counterparts extracted more in rewards than they contributed to efficiencies. Why were more than enough capitalist titans able to break through administrative sclerosis to carry their system forward while Soviet ministries were unable to escape bureaucratisation? The pat answer is that strategic planning inside firms 'can occur precisely because the market furnishes it with the necessary prices for the factor inputs that would be absent in a full-blown state ownership situation'.[51]

That account underplays the extent to which monopolising and the internalising of transactions get around the discipline of price. Some advocates of free trade are now calling for the force of the market to penetrate corporations. Any reversal of the past century's rule by the visible hand of management would open the way to the dislocations that the firm had been created to preclude. Managerial dilemmas for market-directed economies have not disappeared just because the Soviets failed to overcome theirs.

PART TWO

Values in Motion

All things float with equal specific gravity
in the constantly moving stream of money.
Georg Simmel, 1902[1]

CHAPTER 4 # Cash Flows

My estate would be worth—if I were dead—and it was care-
fully handled about $700, 000—debts paid. If I live five years
more and succeed as desired... it would be approximately one
million. I have not in cash $5000 today. I've kept my body
and my stuff continuously invested. Don't talk of this letter
except to <u>God</u>.

Asa Candler, 1908[2]

'I never keep money', Asa Candler wrote to his brother, Bishop
Warren Candler, in 1913. 'Money is not meant to be hoarded. Myself
and all I have I try to keep righteously active'.[3] Asa's boast that he
kept his money in play was an exaggeration; he had invested so
much in real estate that cash was not always or readily available
for new projects. Nor did his success with Coca-Cola weaken his
conviction that security resided in real estate and cotton, investments which continued the South's plantation mentality of cleaving
to land as the low-risk asset that never lost its value. Uncertainty
over the security of bank savings encouraged capitalists to buy real

properties. The federal government did not guarantee deposits until after the 1930s crash.

Access to cash would not have made Asa Candler any kind of capitalist. To become a capitalist, he had to advance his 'stuff' to make it grow. By that criterion, Candler embodied the expansion of capital. In 1890, he had been just about broke when he closed out his entire stock of 'drugs, paints, oil, glass, perfumery and fancy articles' for $50 000.[4] By 1908, his assets totalled $700 000. Five years later, he was worth $3.76 million.

Wealth alone could not make either Candler or Robert Woodruff a capitalist. Both gave away millions, which was not the essence of a capitalist, because those donations would not come back with their increment of profit. Woodruff's lawyers assured him that his largesse would not endanger the expansion of his fortune: 'Such contributions now are largely money which would otherwise be paid in taxes to the government'.[5] He could remain a capitalist while acting the benefactor.

Within the cycles of capital's expansion, money acts as intermediary between the resources to be worked on and the resultant commodities, which must be sold if a profit is to be realised. Money becomes capital only when it joins this cycle of buying resources to sell for more money with which to buy further resources. For this circuit to proceed, financial institutions had to be constructed to supply media for exchange, to speed and secure the transfer of those instruments, and to lend capitalists the extra funds for expansion. Neither cash nor credit is capital until it is launched on its augmentation. A new generation of bankers came to lend but stayed to manage. Accounting developed as a system of control when trade spread beyond the reach of an individual.

Exchange

The great transformation in the nineteenth century produced 'a completely monetarized economy', [6] but not a cashed-up one. Most people were settling their bills with money, not through barter; these pay-outs were often quarterly, or even only once a year. The cash economy remained a mess, with 7000 banks issuing notes in

1860. Counterfeiters flourished amid the disruptions of the Civil War, until most US currency was as suspect as Confederate dollars were worthless. The value of local banknotes also fluctuated according to the supply of commercial paper in each district.

In general, the economy was cash poor. Pennies were as scarce as hen's teeth, so grocers rounded prices up to the nearest nickel (five cents), as in the standard charge for a Coca-Cola. The drugstore that sold the first Coca-Cola in 1886 had ordered 1000 new pennies that year from the mint to lift sales by shaving prices. By the 1880s there were enough coins and notes for the National Cash Register Company to sell its machines to storekeepers. The chronic shortage of national banknotes became acute in 1891, with only $2.50 per head in circulation. After 600 banks failed during the 1893 crash, the public hoarded cash, making paper money so desirable that Wall Street brokers traded it on the kerb. Matters again became chaotic in 1907 when, for 'every dollar in currency, there were $6.00 in deposits', leaving the banks vulnerable to demands for cash.[7] A panic that year saw withdrawals capped at $100 per week.

Before the 1850s, small-scale manufacturers with limited sales territories had got along by issuing notes of long-term credit. Cash became more desirable during the Civil War, causing vendors to offer discounts and impose thirty-day deadlines for settlement. Established firms relied on an alternative system of unsecured notes, which were promises to pay a nominated sum by a given date, like Antonio's bond to Shylock in *The Merchant of Venice*. These notes were traded across the country. A deposit-rich bank in Philadelphia might buy one from a manufacturing chemist in Atlanta and sell it back to a wholesaler of spices in Boston, taking a percentage in fees. Corporations settled some accounts with stocks and bonds.[8]

Businesses also used cheques to transfer funds; by 1914, 90 per cent of commercial transfers were in that form. Asa Candler sent out cheques to pay for rebates on large orders, and for items obtained from out of town. He was less keen on receiving them, because the clearing of cheques was a slow and uncertain process. Candler used a cash box to hold the wherewithal to pay for local wages and materials. During the forty years to 1913, as the financial system became more sophisticated, 'the fraction of money held as currency' fell from one-third to one-eighth.

Delivery

Because capitalists do not retrieve their investments or their profits until they are paid for their produce, a safe and speedy transfer of funds is essential for capital to continue its cycle of expansion. In Coca-Cola's earliest days, its travellers carried considerable sums of cash 'since accounts were normally paid once a year and very frequently with gold'.[9] Until the 1930s, corner shops paid the Coca-Cola drivers 'in cash—no credit, no cheques, nothing but cash'.[10]

Valuables were transported by express companies such as the Adams Express, which operated all over the United States by 1861. On the outbreak of the Civil War, some Adams employees incorporated a Southern Express Company in Georgia. Using railroads, steamboats and stage lines, the breakaway boasted that it would move a slave or a packet of pins. In the 1880s, Candler used this Atlanta-based company to transport syrup and promotional materials. Express companies and banks developed the money-order business, which helped to transmit funds between druggists, travelling salesmen and company headquarters.

During the 1830s, the USA had abandoned its continent-wide banking network. Fearful of big money, authorities and electors encouraged the establishment of thousands of small banks. After the Civil War, the federal government chartered a handful of national banks. Individual States still had to grant a 'foreign' bank the right to operate across their territories. This patchwork was barely adequate when the economy was rural and parochial. The momentum from continental markets required the transfer of funds between firms hundreds of miles apart.

To speed up commercial payments, bankers set up regional clearing houses early in the twentieth century, including one in Atlanta. In reaction to the 1907 financial crisis, Congress finally legislated for a central banking system in 1913; all national banks had to belong, and State-chartered ones could join if they met solvency criteria. One of the new Federal Reserve's twelve regional offices was in Atlanta.

Financiers

In replacing the invisible hand of market forces, financiers have had as much effect on the expansion of capital as did the 'modern business enterprise' under 'the visible hand' of managers. The establishment of a continental market across the USA drew together manufacturers, railroads and bankers. Railroads were incorporated as banks and vice versa, as with the Georgia Railroad and Banking Company. Railways marshalled funds from a horde of investors. Speculators did as much as engineers to redirect corporate behaviour, taking more than 'a first step away from family capitalism'.[11] A biographer of Andrew Carnegie wrote that his switch from speculating in bonds to building a steelworks 'marked the transition of Carnegie from capitalist to entrepreneur'.[12] In fact, Carnegie had moved from being one kind of capitalist to another. Money in a bank is capital when it is on loan to another capitalist who provides its chance to fluoresce.

Smaller businesses borrowed in the hope that rising sales would cover their debts. Often as not they went bust, as happened to Henry Heinz and his partners when their purchase of the 1875 crop ran too far ahead of pickle sales. Long-term financing came with the corporation. John D. Rockefeller recalled that in his early days he 'had worn out the knees of my pants begging credit at the banks'.[13] He later made enough from Standard Oil to establish his own bank, now CitiGroup.

Industrialists invited bankers in to clear up the bankruptcies that followed the 1893 crash. These financiers stayed on as stockholders and executive directors, cementing the interpenetration of manufacturers with money minders. At Winston-Salem in North Carolina, for example, managers moved back and forth between the Wachovia Bank and R.J.Reynolds tobacco.

The financier Henry Villard backed Thomas Edison through his research and development phases before the bankers Drexel Morgan stepped in after the 1907 slump. They cut off credit to unprofitable experiments at Thomas A. Edison, Inc. (TAE) and initiated the divisional structure that Alfred Sloan would adapt for General Motors in the 1920s. The organisational methods that the younger Edison devised for TAE after 1910 drew on his 'contacts in banking and accounting'.[14]

No team of in-house managers had a greater effect on the structure of corporations than the House of Morgan, which arranged half the capitalisation during the merger rush of 1898–1902, thereby creating a new industry in 'the production of monopolies'.[15] Journalists coined the term 'Morgan-isation' for reorganisation. J. Pierpont Morgan explained that once he had rescued a concern he became 'morally responsible for its management to protect it, and I generally do protect it'. His bank floated $2 billion in securities during the decade to 1912, by which time his partners held 72 directorships in 112 corporations, 78 of which banked with his house.[16] His hand was not so much invisible as covert. Yet Morgans were not omniscient. Sneering at the idea that automobiles would ever outnumber horses, they lost the opportunity in 1907 to finance General Motors.

Confederate dollars

Capital had always been harder to obtain in the South than in the north-east. Credit became precarious after the Confederacy's defeat in 1865. The word of a gentleman no longer sufficed. Mortgages were exacted. Banks would lend for only 60 or 90 days, after which borrowers had to turn to moneylenders. Merchants were an alternative source of credit but set their annual interest rates between 50 and 140 per cent. Every business in the New South suffered from its 'chronic malady, a shortage of liquid capital'.[17]

Asa Candler went into banking because it gave him access to other people's money. During the 1907 crash, he took charge of a bank, then made its small depositors wait ten years to get back 50 cents in the dollar. He set up the Candler Investment Co. in 1903 under the motto *Ad Mortem Fidelis* (Faithful Unto Death); he was president of the Central Bank and Trust Corporation, which financed Coke's Chicago bottlers, and he held a sizeable interest in the Atlanta

National Bank, which supervised a $3 million bond offer for the State of Georgia in 1908.

A more puissant Atlanta banker was Ernest W. Woodruff, who had joined the Trust Company of Georgia shortly after its founding in 1891 and served as its president from 1904 to 1922. Under his direction, the Trust Company did for the South what Morgan achieved for the whole nation. In 1910, Woodruff supervised the merger of nine ice and coal companies, 'the largest transaction ever handled by any Southern institution exclusively on its own resources'. Other consolidations included Atlantic Steel, Empire Oil, and the cotton company Continental Gin. 'Let me tell you', he told the steel makers, 'what you need out there is a reorganisation; the Trust Company is going to do that for you; it is going to save you.'[18] In 1915, Morgan invited the Trust Company to act as 'local manager for a syndicate participating in the Anglo-French war loan'.[19] In 1917, the Trust Company became one of the first State banks to join the Federal Reserve. By 1946, Trust Company directors were linked to 200 businesses. Ernest Woodruff and his son, Robert, were more esteemed in the South for their presidencies of the Trust Company than for their stake in Coca-Cola.

For the takeover of The Coca-Cola Company in 1919, Ernest Woodruff relied on the Trust Company of Georgia, which advertised loans at 6 per cent to anyone who would buy Coca-Cola stock, approving $3.5 million at a single session. As an historian of the Trust Company observed: 'it was somewhat difficult to tell whether the Trust Company was acting as agent for its officers and directors, or whether the officers and directors were acting as agents for the bank'.[20] The Trust Company acquired Coca-Cola stock in lieu of fees. Woodruff had allied his bank with Morgans through the Georgia-born Eugene Stetson, a vice-president of the Guaranty Trust of New York. Stetson became a member of the finance committee at Coca-Cola and of the voting trust that controlled the soft-drink maker between 1919 and 1922. Stetson also represented Woodruff in the sugar trade with Cuba, and in the company's renegotiation of its contract with franchised bottlers.

Bankers could be a source of instability. Ernest Woodruff joined the speculative frenzy of the late 1920s, operating a pool in Coca-

Cola stock, and was almost caught out with promises to supply shares he did not own. He was saved when his son covered the shortfall with an issue of Class A stock, dividends on which took priority over the common stock.[21] In 1932, when the ending of Prohibition sparked fears of a collapse in soft-drink sales, rumours circulated that Southern banks would liquidate their stock in The Coca-Cola Company. Some bankers did move against Coca-Cola, making 600 short sales in thirty days.

Each year, The Coca-Cola Company had to assemble the funds to retire Class A stock, pay dividends and expand operations. For example, the only way The Company could have been free of debt by the end of 1935 would have been to buy 'absolutely no raw materials'.[22] The Trust Company of Georgia, acting as *de facto* financial division of The Coca-Cola Company, lent it $6 million that year alone. In the 1950s, the Trust Company carried its Coca-Cola stock 'as a secondary capital reserve'.[23] By 1974, that backstop was worth more than $100 million, although the Trust Company listed its book value at only $100 000. The Trust Company's successor, Sun Trust, remains one of Coca-Cola's two largest stockholders with some 7 per cent.

In the late 1970s, Coca-Cola no longer had a reserve available for takeovers, though its debts were negligible. To obtain the $80 million needed to buy into bottlers, president Paul Austin issued new stock, thereby costing The Company more than a bank loan would have done. Because Atlanta generated its funds internally, it had lost the habit of pricing its capital as it would if it had borrowed from an outside bank. The return on investment was below 10 per cent. When Roberto Goizueta took charge of the company, he would complain: 'We're liquidating our business, borrowing money at 16 per cent and investing it at 8 per cent. You can't do that forever.'

From the beginning of his reign in 1980, Goizueta decreed that every part of The Company would have to pay its way. He extended cost-accounting precepts to the funds for investment, which would be advanced at a set rate. 'When you start charging people for their capital', he reflected in 1993, 'all sorts of things happen'. He turned the pressure up a notch by demanding a 20 per cent return. Divisions that could not meet this target would be sold: projects that did not promise that rate of return were denied a hearing.[24]

Accountants

Once money comes into a firm, whether from sales or from financiers, all sides need to know how it is faring. Managers keep track of their inventories. Stockholders want to be satisfied that dividends express the true position of their investments. Alongside scientific management, professional education and strategic planning, accounting became the fourth control mechanism within the corporation:

> As the trust and holding corporations gained headway, popular writers and prominent authorities predicted that such businesses would fail. Their belief was founded upon the view that no one person or board of directors could successfully master such large organisations in a competitive environment. But accounting administrative control systems being developed during this period provided the information and means of direction to place at the disposal of management factors relevant to operations.[25]

Share trading and taxation also tightened the auditing requirements, which in turn stimulated stocktaking and other procedures beyond the confines of a cashbook.

Early in the thirteenth century, a Pisan mathematician, Leonardo Fibonacci, had adopted Arabic numbers to simplify commercial accounts. Within a century, 'reckoning schools' were teaching traders how to add up and subtract; multiplication and division remained as advanced as differential calculus is today. By 1400, Italian traders had developed double-entry bookkeeping to detect fraud by employees.

Not much changed during the next 450 years. Handwriting in the style of Coca-Cola's brand label was the nineteenth-century bookkeeper's pride. In 1896, New York became the first State to register certified accountants. When the Federal Reserve opened its office in Atlanta in 1914, its staff purchased a ledger and wrote

'the names of the banks in alphabetical order, and the amount...
to be posted opposite each name...If the cash letter was not paid
in full, we had difficulty in showing the exception due to lack of
space.'[26] Loose-leaf folders came into use in the 1920s.

Railroads proved the exception that set the new rules. Track
engineers developed systems to control operations in detail in real
time, while the chicanery of stock promoters led to controls by gov-
ernment-backed auditors. Engineers carried through the transition
from bookkeeping to accounting because of the keenness of their
mathematical skills, the multiplicity of their activities, and their need
for daily returns. Even so, during the rate-cutting wars of the 1870s,
railroads often did not know whether they were making a profit.

Andrew Carnegie learnt the principles of cost accounting on the
Pennsylvania Railroad before carrying them over to his iron and
steel works. Previously, foundries had operated as a 'lump business'
where owners evaluated their profit by deducting total costs from
total revenues. Carnegie became obsessed with finding out how
cheaply his workers had made something rather than how much
had been earned in selling it. He saw the latter as 'a temporary
result, due possibly to special conditions of trade, but the other
means a permanency that will go on with the works as long as they
last'.[27]

Not every capitalist emulated Carnegie. Many assumed that as
long as 'new plants and bank balances kept going up, expenses
were obviously well below income'.[28] Billy Durant at General Motors
skipped over the problems of co-ordinating the twenty firms he had
combined in 1909: 'There was no uniform bookkeeping procedure,
no clear control over inventories'.[29] US insurance companies—
despite their actuarial roots—had not 'developed proper accounting
and book-keeping procedures' in the early 1900s, a failure which
helped executives to misappropriate millions.[30] Similarly, Henry
Ford never employed a 'more sophisticated method of learning unit
cost than dividing the number of units produced into the year's
total expenditures', like any lump business.[31] Until his grandson,
Henry II, took charge in 1945, the whole corporation 'had financial statements like a country grocery store', enabling its top
managers to steal. Henry II hyperbolised but slightly when he

claimed that one department 'figured their costs by weighing the pile of invoices on a scale'. After he instituted detailed costings in the late 1940s, he discovered that his firm was selling passenger vehicles at a loss. Around the same time, Bloomingdale's learned that the cost of promoting certain lines was greater than their mark-ups.

The complexities of asset depreciation defeated even the railroad companies. A professional accounting journal in Britain admitted in 1881 that 'it is impossible to lay down any fixed principles' for depreciation.[32] The issue of 'historical cost' continues to divide auditors, because technological changes erode the value of equipment, while inflation increases its replacement costs. In the USA, asset accounting faded as an issue after 1878, when the Supreme Court ruled that a railroad could charge only actual expenditures against profits. Investors and the courts feared that depreciation charges were a scam for transferring profits from stockholders to promoters. The minority of firms that did allow for depreciation dropped the charge in lean years when it would have reduced dividends. Railroads recognised some of the accounting procedures required to calculate working capital and the flow of funds, but most US estimates of depreciation remained elementary well into the twentieth century. The presumption among businessmen, auditors and judges was that so long as the assets were kept in good repair they would hold their value, so the cost of maintenance should be charged against that year's earnings. One result was that businesses continued trading while insolvent because they had failed to calculate all their costs.

The five-cent Titan

Canny about costs, Asa Candler boasted: 'In Philadelphia we had an engine and a boiler but in Los Angeles we were able to rent power cheaper than we could install machinery. It costs us only 50c a day for the days we are actually running machinery.'[33] Candler could be a capitalist without owning properties so long as he had access to the money to rent them. Property becomes capital only when it is active in the social relations of adding value. Hence, he remained a capitalist whether he bought equipment in Philadelphia or hired it in Los Angeles. Candler chose between leasing and ownership on the basis of relative cost.

Despite Candler's economising, Coca-Cola's costs skyrocketed as effective demand increased from 8855 gallons in 1890 to 281 000 by 1899. At the start of the new century, Asa confided in his eldest son, Howard:

> This day closes a busy, worrisome week. After closing last year's books we discovered greatly to my surprise that our profits were very much less in proportion to business than in any year since we began. We have grown so large and so many to be paid etc that money goes out in great torrents.[34]

Coca-Cola had encountered the parameter that governs the fortunes of every firm. Indeed, it is 'the normal case of modern industry' that 'the operation of a larger quantity of means of production... [is] necessarily connected with a simultaneous drop in the rate of profit'.[35] That this tendency is ever present does not mean the rate of profit falls at all times for every firm. Capitalism has flourished through the creation of counter-forces, such as the corporation, mass marketing and labour discipline. That is the genius of managers, and an informing concept of this book.

Vigilance could contain but not prevent the rise in unit costs. After financial and stock controls had been devised, they still needed to be enforced, which was never easy. Howard Candler lamented in 1919 'how hard it is to make branch office accountants understand radical changes in detail'.[36] Disasters with Coca-Cola's sugar supplies in 1919–20 were in part an accounting failure. At the peak of that crisis, Howard Candler warned the Woodruff syndicate that Coke's bottling contracts were so vast as to require 'an immense amount of personal service, skill in manufacture and details of office and executive management, almost beyond calculation'.[37]

Robert Woodruff tightened financial controls in the 1920s to get out of debt, but his watchfulness was undermined by incompetence among distributors. Druggists and grocers often 'did not know even approximately where they stood financially'.[38] They made few inventory checks and did not provide for their own salaries, or for their families' dipping into stock or helping themselves to petty cash. For their part, the Coke bottlers were mostly self-made men who had struck it lucky by securing a franchise before 1910. By the late 1930s, franchised bottlers had to put 'more skill into planning a series of truck routes properly' than Atlanta needed for the production of syrup.[39] Not all agents possessed the necessary training or talents. These troubles multiplied as Coke's international sales grew. Shortly before Coca-Cola opened its operations in Sydney in 1937, the *Australasian Grocer* printed an article which began: 'Few traders have a correct idea as to what constitutes profit'. A companion piece explained why profit was not gross income minus outgoings.[40]

In Atlanta, information was still partial and tardy in 1946. After Woodruff received a five-page summary on bank balances, his staff at once requested 'any other report…which would enable him to keep more generally informed concerning the Company's operations'.[41] He thereafter got the comparisons of expenses that had been detailed for the auditors. Clearly, The Boss had been running on less than full knowledge. In the 1950s, Coca-Cola began using IBM punch-card machines to monitor sales.

By the 1960s, corporations employed senior executives whose functions 'were confined to finance and long-term strategy'.[42] This specialisation had unanticipated consequences at Coca-Cola. According to Roberto Goizueta, so wide was the gulf between production and finance that, by 1981, 'none of our operating executives could even read a balance sheet'.[43] The pressure to manage money carried chief financial officers to the chairmanships of Coca-Cola and McDonald's.

Elsewhere, managers misled themselves and each other. IBM persisted with a version of lump business into the 1980s, setting a 'single profit-margin goal for the entire company' and assigning the bulk of 'development costs…to the hugely profitable mainframe division…Everyone else got a free ride, making it hard to spot problems.'[44] Meanwhile at Sears, field offices were muddling their statistical returns so as to frustrate any effort by head office to direct regional finances. A future CEO got around this obfuscation by requesting data on unrelated aspects of the business, then using the answers to calculate the numbers he sought. After he identified losses, he still had to get local managers to act on them, which they would not always do because of power structures and social networks. In 1997, the company's president of retail stores lamented: 'Facts were ignored in favour of telling tales inside the Indian tribe'.[45]

Businesses also persisted with accounting procedures which had been developed for conditions which no longer prevailed. Early in the 1980s, a Harvard professor of accounting had argued that the auditing systems appropriate for the fabrication of metals were misleading when applied to their processing. He called for

> systems that truly reflect advances and declines in an operation in the light of its particular product mix, market strategy, and production technology. Contemporary cost accounting and management control systems…are no longer providing accurate signals about the efficiency and profitability of internally managed transactions… [T]he availability of the 'visible hand' to effectively manage the myriad transactions that occur in a complex hierarchy has been severely compromised.[46]

That difficulty was compounded by intangibles, especially when they were used for stock-market peculation.

Creative accounting

Accounting allows capitalists to conceal the condition of their investments as well as to reveal it. The creation of accounting principles has been matched by unprincipled creative accounting. When nineteenth-century bookkeepers stole, they pocketed receipts without entering them in the cash book. Their successors help corporations to avoid tax, bamboozle creditors and excite the stock market. In the 1929–30 crash, Gillette managers pretended that they had sold inventory that had merely been forwarded overseas. They operated a stock pool to keep up the share price before revealing that their company had not earned its 1930–31 dividend. Seventy years later, Gillette again masked its position by reporting shipments as sales.[47]

In 1974, the professor of accounting at Columbia University, Abe Briloff, laid down Briloff's Law: 'whenever ants swarm, the pot not only will contain a bit of honey, but also will be filled with accounting ploys'. McDonald's, he continued, had just overstated income and 'induce[d] the capability for future earnings exaggeration' by misrepresenting the cost of real-estate purchases.[48] Investors were entitled to ask: where's the beef? In the early 1980s, IBM bloated its earnings by abandoning 'its normally ultraconservative accounting policies so that it could treat some of its new leases as sales, counting all the revenue and profit up front rather than a bit at a time as the money actually came in'.[49]

A former editor of the *Harvard Business Review* acknowledged in 1990 that 'minimum acceptable accounting standards are the norm' in the USA because auditors feared loss of work if they probed too deeply. [50] The poachers had snared the gamekeepers with consultancy fees, which made up half of the revenue of auditing firms. Individual accountants also held shares in the firms they were checking. Auditing and accounting have become as much a part of the problem as a solution to the difficulties of knowing how well capital is expanding. The chairman of the US Securities and Exchange Commission, Arthur J. Levitt Jr, declared that the accountancy profession has become 'almost oblivious to the words "public interest".' He pushed for a rule which would prevent accountants from auditing firms for which they do consultancy work. The profession responded by donating $10 million to candidates for the 2000 elections.[51]

Champion investor Warren Buffett has complained about executives who draw the bull's-eye around the arrow. Deception had become so ubiquitous by April 1998 that the *Economist* took it for granted that 'accounts are...bottom-up affairs: firms decide what profit they want to report and then fill in the numbers accordingly'.[52] Six months later, SEC chairman Levitt characterised annual reports and quarterly earnings statements as a 'game of nods and winks', warning that 'integrity may be losing out to illusion'. In March 2000, *Fortune* magazine mocked the 'accounting gimmicks' surrounding IT stocks as Wall Street's answer to the magic acts that divert patrons at Las Vegas casinos.[53]

Rupert Murdoch's accountants arranged the affairs of Newscorp Investments so that it 'paid no net British corporation tax' in the eleven years to 1998, despite announcing group profits of £1.4 billion.[54] At other times, their 'loosey-goosey' numbers enhanced the reported profits in order to soothe financiers.[55] By operating on Australian procedures, Murdoch's accountants in 1997–98 converted what would have been a loss of $155 million under US rules into a profit of $561 million.[56]

During the 1980s, the price of a Coca-Cola share went from $100 to $1231, beating the leading stock-market average by three to one. The Company achieved this increase by 'managing earnings through periodic gains and charges, using some pretty complex accounting'. Wall Street accepted 'Coke's version of events because The Company has delivered the goods in the past and because many analysts are intimidated by The Company'.[57]

Coke's prestidigitators revalued capital in two ways. First, payment of executives with stock options was not charged against current income. Had Coca-Cola booked options to its wages bill, its 1996 profit would have been halved. The US Financial Accounting Standards Board failed to have the big six auditing firms include such costs in profit-and-loss reports. Corporate America howled against the proposal: 'If we have to record a reduction in income by 40 per cent, our stock options will be worthless, we won't be able to keep employees. It would destroy all American business and Western civilisation'.[58]

Coke's second redefinition of capital emerged after 1986, when Goizueta split most of the physical assets off to the partly owned subsidiary, Coca-Cola Enterprises, while holding the income-generating and intangible properties in The Coca-Cola Company. By 1996, the intangible assets of The Coca-Cola Company were valued at $19 billion, but the market value of its shares was nearly ten times higher. By contrast, with $21 billion in physical assets, Coca-Cola Enterprises had a market value of only $15.7 billion. The difference arose because the income was being channelled into The Company while Enterprises carried the debts.

After The Coca-Cola Company presented its 'market capitalisation as the sum of the values of its brand and its management
systems', [59] auditors had to sign off on intangibles under headings
that had been developed to depreciate machinery. PepsiCo
announced in 1998 that it was about to separate its bottling operations from its intangibles, a move its executives claimed had
'nothing to do with accounting'.[60] As one investment analyst put
it, the contrivance of putting all the profit-earners in one basket 'is
pretty fake, actually'.[61] The Financial Accounting Standards Board
in 1998 mooted consolidation of the accounts of The Coca-Cola
Company and Coca-Cola Enterprises. That recombination would
have cut short-term earnings to The Company and forced it to
reclaim billions in debt. Matters got murkier when the Asian crisis
reduced revenues for Coca-Cola Enterprises. The Company then
poured $1.2 billion into its quasi-subsidiary, but called this loan
'pre-paid expenses'. Coca-Cola Enterprises recorded the amount in
a way which made 'their operating income look higher'.[62]

Technical difficulties in accounting help managers to mislead
investors, and themselves. These problems intensified in the 1990s
when no one knew how to put a number on knowledge in an information economy. Coca-Cola, Sara Lee, Nike and Sony lifted their
share prices by pumping their assets up with newly minted intangibles such as brand strength and intellectual property. A 1999 cover
story in *Accounting & Business* admitted 'that there is a long way
to go for generally accepted and endorsed practices' to manage,
calculate and report these intangible assets. Even the definition of
an intangible remains a muddle of processes, products and prospects.
Three methods of valuing intellectual capital are on offer:

- The first is the simplest to operate, and to dismiss, because
  it determines the 'missing value' by deducting the physical
  assets from the market prices of all the company's shares. The
  difference is the worth of the intangibles. This method pre-
  supposes that the share price is a measure and not a wish.
  For its merger with Time-Warner, America Online (AOL)
  offered its shares at a 25 per cent discount, which the

> *Economist* saw as 'an extraordinary admission...that their shares were not worth what the market said'.[63]

- The second approach requires one more year of primary school arithmetic but suffers from the same circularity of relying on the share price. The task here is to establish the ratio between the total price that the market puts on a firm's shares and the replacement costs of its assets. The method does not determine the worth of the intangibles in a particular firm, only its relative position.

- The third measure involves a procession of elementary sums, which need not detain us long, since the first step is to identify 'average pre-tax earnings for three years', a figure which few Information Technology start-ups have attained.[64]

Fortune acknowledged in 1999 that the accounting profession had found no way 'to assign a specific value and useful life' to information or other intangibles: 'Throwing up its hands, accounting regards these treasures as worth zero...until someone pays for them. Then, suddenly, they must be accounted for at their purchase price'. Once intangibles become assets, they risk being written down. As a result, a 'company that acquires a lot of goodwill is also acquiring a drag on future earnings'. The practice of pumping up the value of intangibles when promoting the issue of shares thus undermines the benefits promised from the acquisition of the stock. The escape clause is for the merging firms to pool their interests. Under pooling, 'companies simply combine their existing assets at their historical cost. Most intangibles remain valued at zero...In short, most of the cost of acquiring a knowledge-based company simply vaporises.'[65]

In the late 1990s, the scarcity of profits from IT stocks led their promoters to adopt gross revenues as the measure of worth. Some firms did not stop at this manoeuvre, but boosted their reported sales by means that the CEO of Internet.com branded 'fraudulent'. For instance, on-line travel firm Priceline reported revenue of $US152 million, which was the total value of airline and accommodation reservations handled. In fact, it would retain only a fraction of that sum. It went on to describe the $US18 million the firm retained as gross profits, despite an actual loss of $US102 million. Online companies have also boosted their reported earnings by including the nominal value of the advertising they barter with other IT servers. The result is a new style of double entry, or what *Fortune* disparaged as a 'revenue merry-go-round'. In addition, permanent marketing and delivery costs are booked as start-up expenses, making those charges appear temporary. In October 1999, Varsitybooks.com replaced KPMG with PricewaterhouseCoopers as its auditors after KPMG had declined to accept that marketing outlays were only initial expenses to establish brand recognition.[66]

These versions of 'now-you-see-it now-you-don't' were only some of the ways in which creative accountants drove up the prices paid during the pandemic of leveraged mergers and acquisitions from 1997, when Wall Street had more money to splurge than its brokers had good buys to spend it on. As *Fortune* complained: 'By inflating reported earnings and covering up the true cost of an acquisition, they can make even a dog of a deal look brilliant'.[67] Timid auditors and over-confident promoters muddied the valuation of stock and the calculation of economic well-being. After the Asian meltdown, Wall Street and the IMF demanded that firms in Thailand, South Korea and Indonesia adopt transparency in financial reporting. But was the time bomb in Bangkok or on Manhattan?

Even without the mysteries of the knowledge economy, the value placed on shares need have little relation to previous investments, physical assets or recent earnings. Coca-Cola stock dropped 25 per cent in the October 1987 market crash, a fall which encouraged Warren Buffett to purchase 7.7 per cent of The Company for $1 billion. Buffett has never accepted the wisdom of Wall Street that stock-market prices express the worth of a firm. Believing that many companies are overpriced while a few remain undervalued, Buffett sought out the latter and held on to them. From his studies of the 1929 Wall Street crash, Buffett had discerned that the stock market was a 'voting machine', not a 'weighing machine'. An investor therefore should look at the prospects of a business, not at its current popularity among share traders. Buffett established himself as the king of the market without ever owning a ticker-tape machine. Because he sought to determine where a stock would be in five years' time, hourly fluctuations were a distraction. He tracked dynamics, not snapshots, believing that a firm should be valued by how much will come out of it, not by the money that has gone in. He sought the capacity to add value, that is, its performance as capital.[68] Thus, he bought into Coca-Cola when its worldwide sales were expanding.

From a less scholarly perspective, Sam Walton also recognised the illusory dimension of share prices. When *Forbes* declared Walton the richest man in America between 1985 and 1988, the magazine based its computation on the price of the last share traded in Wal-Mart, multiplied by the number of shares he held. Walton never saw that $20–25 billion in cash. The only way he could have realised that sum would have been by selling out; and even then he would have received part payment in stocks in the new owner's business. After the 1987 crash wiped $US500 million from the stock price of Wal-Mart, Walton quipped: 'It's paper anyway. It was paper when we started and it's paper afterward.'[69] Wall Street took Walton's remark as further proof that he was a hick, yet he knew better than they did.

*

As invested capital came under more controls both within the corporation and from outside regulators, speculators invented new instruments for transferring wealth between corporate producers and financial agents. One investor's loss of a fortune is generally someone else's gain. When the stock market failed to supply the funds needed to expand business activities, capitalists developed alternative means to marshal capital.

CHAPTER 5 **A Capital Idea**

The world would still be without railways if it had had to wait
until accumulation had got a few individual capitals far enough to
be adequate for their construction.

Karl Marx, *Capital* (1867)[1]

As an army clerk during the US invasion of Cuba in 1898, Benjamin
Franklin Thomas envied the locals swigging their bottled pineapple
brew while he craved a glass of Coca-Cola. Desire and dissatisfac-
tion prompted the notion of bottling his favourite belly wash.
Returning to Tennessee, he enlisted his partner-at-law, Joseph
Whitehead, in a campaign to do just that.

On 21 July 1899, the owner of The Coca-Cola Company, Asa
Candler, transferred most of the rights to sell his product in bottles to the two friends, who became known as Parent Bottlers. After
paying a nominal dollar for the privilege, they had no money to set
up their own bottling plants. Instead, they had another idea. They
got Candler's agreement for them to sub-franchise to Actual Bottlers.
The pair then divided most of the United States between them.

Expansion was slow because, in most cases, 'the business of bot-

tling was started from the ground up, requiring investment of capital for real estate, machinery, equipment, et cetera'.[2] At the end of
1901, only five contracts had been awarded. The following year
brought twenty-nine more. By 1905, almost two hundred had signed
up. The Parent Bottlers were on their way towards a thousand
Actual Bottlers by 1919. Everywhere, the partners' operation was
simplicity itself. Although Thomas and Whitehead did not 'see or
touch' the syrup, they sold millions of gallons to the Actual Bottlers
for a 12.5 per cent take. For good measure, they added 25 per cent
to the price of the promotional materials they passed along from
Atlanta.[3]

Franchising provided Asa Candler with a means to secure credit
and garner investment at no cost. Actual Bottlers in effect lent their
plants and bottlers to the Parent Bottlers, and through them to The
Coca-Cola Company. Although bound by only a supply contract,
the network brought the advantages of a joint-stock company. No
sooner had the franchises been initiated than the bottling industry
underwent a technical revolution, which multiplied the costs of setting up plants. Had Candler not been handed this investment-free
route to growth, he would have been obliged to divert all his
resources into building hundreds of bottling sites, an effort which
might have brought his ruin.

This chapter examines how franchising marshalled capital and
why Candler let the bottling rights go for so small a sum. It goes
on to the franchise economy since 1950. The conflicts inherent in
that business method lead back to The Company's war of attrition
against its bottlers from 1919 onwards, culminating in the buy-back
of franchisees after 1980, the creation of Coca-Cola Enterprises in
1986 and the consolidation into 'anchor' bottlers.

A capital idea

The franchising of Coca-Cola coincided with the great merger movement in US business, which peaked at the beginning of the twentieth
century. Asa Candler did not merge directly with his distributors
but stumbled on to franchising as an equivalent to the stampede
into trusts and combines.

A revolution in the jurisprudence of commerce in the late nineteenth century made the franchise available for the co-ordination of capital. The franchise had been developed in the 1700s, when the British Crown granted privileges to chartered companies for the construction of public utilities. The new American Republic continued this procedure into the nineteenth century. For instance, in return for private investors' providing the public with a toll bridge, a State legislature would bind itself not to allow competing bridges to be built.

During the 1880s, lawyers refashioned the franchise to meet the needs of a new breed of monopolisers. This innovation placed the US Supreme Court in a dilemma. Its members were committed to the inviolability of contracts and the sanctity of property, but were becoming as opposed as Adam Smith to government-granted monopolies. Their way out was to ban exclusive franchises in the public domain while allowing private ones. The court ruled that restriction on trade was lawful, providing the franchise was agreed to by non-government concerns. Had Coca-Cola syrup been a public good such as river water, the justices might have invalidated Coca-Cola's exclusive dealing.

Heaven for capitalists is where they get equipment, raw materials, labour-power and their sales effort at no cost. Most firms must be content with limiting such outlays. Franchising offered entrepreneurs the opportunity to externalise several of those expenses. At first, economists assumed that franchising flourished because a patent-holder with insufficient capital could lease its brand-label and expertise to other small businesses, thereby organising other people's savings to expand its own capital. In 1978, economist Paul H. Rubin questioned whether this practice was of greater benefit than issuing shares:

> The franchisor would do better to create a portfolio of shares of all outlets and sell these shares to his managers. This would diversify risk for managers, with no [capital] effect on the franchisor.

This alternative would require franchisor and franchisee to have equal information, a condition denied by Rubin's own assessment that 'the franchisor has almost complete control over the behaviour of the franchisee'.[4] His assumptions apply only when the operators are adept at econometrics. What now seems obvious to a professor was not practicable for a businessman in 1899, when Candler sold the Coca-Cola bottling rights. Few owners understood cost accounting, and some confused net with gross incomes. That situation lasted into the early 1950s, when Sam Walton overcame discrepancies in the monthly accounts at his franchised store by adding 'ESP' to whichever side of the ledger was giving him trouble; 'ESP' stood for 'Error Some Place'.[5] In post-war Italy, the undercapitalised Benetton family franchised outlets on a handshake, exacting neither premium nor royalties, but accepting no returns of unsold stock.

Asa's folly

Instead of scolding Candler for surrendering the franchise for $1.00, we need to understand his agreement against his day-to-day concerns. Disposal of bottling rights was far from his most pressing problem in the summer of 1899. With his mother-in-law on her deathbed, he had to manage a national sales force, fill a 5000-gallon backlog and open another syrup plant. Three days after he signed with Thomas and Whitehead, Asa ran out of order books.[6]

Candler also lacked a managerial team who could set up and control hundreds of bottlers in a continental network. The Company's policy of offering a rebate of 5 cents per gallon on orders over 100 gallons a year made administration fiendish, since wholesalers were responsible only for the rebate on the 'quantity bought of them'. He chided his eldest boy, who was travelling as a salesman: 'You do not quite understand our contract' for soda fountains.[7] Candler illustrated the system—if it can be called one—with this example of a Kansas City retailer who was buying from two different wholesalers as well as from The Company:

> Mr Rogers gets from all sources 100 gals Coca-Cola. 50 of Loose Brothers, 25 Gals of Evans-Smith, and 25 Gals of The Coca-Cola Co. When he proves to us that he has bought and paid for 100

Gals we pay him 5c Gal. on 25 Gals. And the Jobbers either pay him the rebate on quantities bought of them or authorise us to do so, but we are not liable for rebate due from others than ourselves unless we have authority to assume liability.[8]

Lines of communication were knotted, causing conflict within the sales force. Asa counselled his son on how to deal with wholesalers:

Your habit will be of course to...do all the business that possibly can be done through them, letting nothing be done directly with the retailer that can be done through the Jobbing house, otherwise you will create an impression that The Coca-Cola Company wish to alienate the dispensing and retail trade for the wholesaler in its own interest. The wholesale men will make this claim any how, but let us give them no excuse for doing so.[9]

Candler continued to supply syrup to soda fountains through a miscellany of agents, some of whom were cotton buyers in the off-season. These 'drummers' gained access to a grab-bag of products to sell on to retailers for a commission. Their function, according to Asa, was to

make sales to retailers whose account none of the Wholesalers would accept...the men detailed to work these large cities by staying continually there, say for a month or more, shall have under their personal control goods and advertising matter and thus not be dependent upon any one dealer, which condition might bias some other dealer.

Drummers were already being replaced by commercial travellers, whose numbers rose from 7300 to 93 000 nationally between 1870 and 1900. Advertising tipped their task away from selling towards distribution.

Franchises and commercial travellers were but two of the novelties advanced to conduct mass marketing after the 1870s. Department stores opened in the cities and mail-order catalogues serviced rural districts. Swifts, Eastman Kodak, Pabst brewers and

United Fruit created their own marketing branches. Heinz agents no longer filled orders when placed, but sold from a sample box.

The principal innovation was the wholesale house, which handled thousands of items for hundreds of manufacturers. Candler's use of these jobbers, who bought in bulk and bore the costs of distribution, showed the same caution that led him to adopt the franchise. As he explained:

> It is much safer to let Georgia jobbers take Florida risks than ourselves and we prefer that the orders be given to the jobber direct by the retailer than we then have any loss to bear if the retailer fails to pay the jobber.[10]

Alone among manufacturers, Coca-Cola always dealt through jobbers. In 1931, The Company refused to sell syrup direct to the president of Loft Confectionery, who wanted a discount. On being rebuffed, he bought the bankrupt Pepsi-Cola and sold its beverage in his sweet-shops.

Candler had more trouble than enough supplying hundreds of salesmen, without also finding or funding a network of bottlers from coast to coast. His release of bottling rights for a dollar was more a necessity than a choice.

The disaster came with the detail.

Looking back, Candler's give-away is less puzzling than his agreeing to supply syrup at a set price. His confidence that costs would not increase had been formed during the late nineteenth century when commodity prices slid by 25–30 per cent. The 1893–97 depression reinforced his expectation; retail prices collapsed by one-third, with refined sugar falling from 9.6 cents a pound in 1880 to only 5 cents in 1899.[11] Deflation seemed more likely than inflation. When inflation did come, it exposed the flaw in the original contract and caused friction between The Company and the Parent Bottlers.

The perpetuity of rights became the other point of contention. Motor dealerships are not inherited, yet several Coca-Cola franchises passed through several generations; in Quincy, Illinois, for example, the Flynn family began bottling in 1905, and were still in charge in 1958. Candler perhaps had not meant the Parent Bottlers to hold the rights for ever; he had limited a previous arrangement for New England to twenty years. Moreover, firms were still not expected to outlive their founders. Anyway, the 600-word franchise agreement in 1899 was not the surest guide to Asa's intentions, since the 'laws at that time were in such a condition that it made little difference what was placed in a contract'.[12]

Asa Candler was reluctant to involve himself with bottling because in the 1890s bottlers were 'back-alley dumps' without 'proper means of sterilisation'; Dr Pemberton's attempts to bottle Coca-Cola had been 'typically unsanitary, dirty and antique'.[13] For self-protection, Candler inserted a no-liability provision in his contract with Thomas and Whitehead. In turn, those good ole Chattanooga boys had to decide how best to monitor their franchisees. Thomas favoured fixed-term contracts with Actual Bottlers in order to maintain standards. Whitehead prevailed with his view that perpetual contracts would secure the most dependable applicants, seized by a singleness of purpose. For the next twenty years, Candler 'was not happy over the indifferent performance of the Parent Bottlers in policing the quality of the product'.[14]

Other soft-drink makers were slower to franchise bottlers. Dr Pepper began in the mid-1920s, with Canada Dry and Clicquot Club following in 1938. When Pepsi revived around 1940, its executives could divide 'the country into much larger areas, equivalent to the distance a motor truck could go in a day for delivery and return'.[15] Because the Parent Bottlers had allocated many franchises when deliveries were by horse and cart, Coca-Cola still had 1000 franchisees in the mid-1950s, twice as many as Pepsi.

Bottle-O!

The pop in soda-pop was no marketing metaphor. The bottling of soda waters was a hazardous business. It had begun in 1783 when Jacob Schweppe put his mineral waters in an egg-shaped bottle designed to be stored horizontally to keep its cork moist. Benjamin Silliman manufactured soda water in New York from 1807 but, with no one in North America able to supply leak-proof containers, he sold in bulk or in imported bottles.

Consumption of bottled drinks across the USA increased eight-fold between 1850 and 1900. Hires, for instance, bottled their root beer from 1897, while the bottling of all soft drinks trebled in the thirteen years between Coca-Coca's creation in 1886 and Candler's deal with Whitehead and Thomas in 1899. Table 1 gives the data for all soft drinks.

Table 1: Soft-drink Bottle Production, USA, 1879–1899

Year	No. of Plants	Production (millions of bottles)	Per Capita
1879	512	227	4.5
1889	1377	626	9.9
1899	2763	930	12.2

In Chicago, the number of bottling plants for all carbonated waters grew from eighteen in 1890 to forty-four in 1900. The next twenty years saw a quadrupling of sales, up to one bottle of soft drink per person per week. A five-fold increase in the volumes of Coca-Cola sold between 1900 and 1905 shows that Candler could not have long avoided extending to home delivery and corner stores. Had he held out, Coca-Cola might have disappeared long before 1928, the year when its bottle sales first exceeded those at soda fountains.

Technical improvements after 1880 underpinned the bottling trade. The liquefying of carbon dioxide was followed by the invention of machines which made bottles, machines which washed 150 dozen bottles per hour and machines which filled 100 bottles per minute. The sticking point was the lack of an effective stopper. A Baltimore tradesman worked on a metal seal with cork inlay. He took out patents on his Crown Seal in 1892 and later patented a capping machine, which came into general use after 1900. The Crown Seal needed bottles with a particular lip, which made the 'changeover process...long and tedious,'[16] not to mention costly, because the bottlers had to replace their stock of bottles while financing the new equipment.

Between 1880 and 1900, the average investment in a US factory went up from $11 000 to $19 200. The establishment costs of plants in the industries connected with Coca-Cola ranged from $500 000 for a sugar refinery down to $5000 for a bottling plant. As soft-drink makers mechanised after 1900, bigger investments were required. To finance that expansion himself would have called for all Candler's resources, real estate, and then some debts.

Neither did Candler buy into sugar refineries or other raw-material producers. By contrast, the typical 'mass-production enterprises' to emerge from the 1890s became as vertically integrated as they were capital-intensive.[17]

For Candler to establish his own plants, he would have had to pay for the bottles. As soft drinks gained in popularity, the number of bottles in circulation grew sixfold between 1889 and 1919, reaching four billion. They were returnable for a fee, and each made as many as sixty trips. To reduce the purloining of one bottler's property by another, a Protective Association had been formed in 1882. The distinctive shape of the Coke bottle was one way of ensuring that Coke bottlers were not hobbled by the depletion of their stocks, especially during the summer months. In 1913, Coca-Cola commissioned a university researcher to devise a method of producing 'surface colorations on glass', in the hope of replacing paper wrappers with an embossed brand label. As a by-product of these experiments, the iconic bottle went into production in 1916 to make 'a proprietary statement through shape'.[18] The territory name was embossed on the base of the bottles to make sure they boomeranged to the right franchise-holder.

A franchised economy

Although The Coca-Cola Company was among the first mass producers to succeed with franchising, its early experiences differed from the eruption of franchising after 1950. The numbers involved were only 1000 on a single brand, against millions in every field of commerce. The perpetuity clause was exceptional, as was the cap on syrup prices. In general, post-1950 franchisees started from a position of weakness vis-à-vis the franchisors, an imbalance which did not overwhelm Coke's bottlers until the 1980s.

The verb 'to franchise' derives from an old French word, *francher*, meaning to set free from servitude. Franchising fulfilled that promise for most of those lucky enough to secure the rights to bottle Coca-Cola. Although no Coca-Cola bottler in Chicago made a profit in 1906, and three years later one of them was bankrupt, more typical was the bottler who acquired the franchise for New York in 1904, sold it for $160000 and retired to the West Coast. Few who took franchises with other companies after 1945 fared so well. The contract that freed them from wage drudgery often bound them to the franchisor. In 1966, regulators were worried 'about the highly exaggerated and sometimes fraudulent claims of concerns offering franchises to small investors'.[19] Although would-be entrepreneurs still desire to be free of corporations and dream of becoming the next Ray Kroc at McDonald's or Sam Walton at Wal-Mart, the franchise relationship is 'almost that of a firm and an employee'.[20]

Moreover, any promise that franchising would free individuals from servitude to big business has been cruelled by a concentration of ownership among the franchisors. Burger King, Burger Chef and Jack-in-the-Box had been taken into conglomerates by 1970. By 1988, all but two of the fifteen biggest restaurant chains operating in 1976 had gone bankrupt, been taken over, or were in danger of those fates.

Early in February 1960, forty hope-filled corporations had held the first meeting of the International Franchise Association, but they could not agree whether the number of franchise holders was 50000 or more than 100000. By 1976, the total was on its way to a million, handling 40 per cent of retail sales and a tenth of the US gross national product. That explosion was part of a renovation of merchandising through self-service at shopping centres and at the discount chains of Wal-Mart, Kmart and Target, all of which began in 1962.

The best-known of this post-war generation is McDonald's. For the first thirty-five years of Ray Kroc's working life he had ground out the American dream of one day becoming his own boss, keeping a step ahead of Willy Loman in Arthur Miller's 1949 play, *Death of a Salesman*. In July 1954, Kroc called on the McDonald brothers at San Bernadino, California, who owned eight of the multimixing machines that he was then selling. The brothers signed a contract with Kroc permitting him to use the McDonald's name and methods and to franchise additional outlets in return for a quarter of his 1.9 per cent of gross sales, a deal which wore a hole in his pocket until he bought them out. Even then he saw very little cash before he turned from food to property, selling off half the stock in his company to fund his purchases. By 1971, he had turned McDonald's from a hamburger chain into a real-estate empire, which he expanded during the 1974–75 recession by acquiring sites on the cheap. Franchise-holders became his tenants as much as they were his servants. He benefited from their fees, took a percentage of their turnover and charged them rent.

Franchise-holders in the US are protected by anti-trust regulations which limit a franchisor's power to be the mandated supplier. In 1971, one corporation rescinded all its franchises after the courts forbade it from entering into exclusive supply contracts for paper products. The law does, however, allow a franchisor to monitor standards by requiring the franchisee to obtain certain items from set suppliers. Thus, KFC may specify the source for gravy and spices but not napkins and buckets, a loophole that lets the franchisor provide key inputs 'at above market prices'.[21] McDonald's sells no products. Instead, it approves certain suppliers of equipment, foods and beverages in order to maintain quality. For instance, McDonald's has a contract to serve only Coca-Cola soft drinks. Kroc cancelled a franchise after its operator switched to Pepsi. A prime supplier of meat patties and sauce to McDonald's already had a Coke dealership to supply fountains. Representatives of those allied firms, including a former Coca-Cola president, sat on McDonald's board.

The Golden Arches came with leaden chains, dragging McDonald's into disputes with its franchise-holders. A 1997 internal survey revealed that only a quarter of franchisees believed the managers were on the right track. Unlike Coca-Cola, McDonald's allocates sites, not districts. Existing contract-holders complained that the company had roasted them by selling franchises into neighbourhoods that already had outlets. 'We are our own worst competitor', moaned a spokesperson for disenchanted franchisees, who accused McDonald's of having been taken over by 'lawyers and accountants and other bureaucrats whose primary focus is on building personal wealth at the expense of franchisees'.[22]

Mismanagement at McDonald's throughout the 1990s left Coca-Cola's largest single outlet vulnerable. While the stock-market leaders increased their share prices by two-thirds in 1995–98, McDonald's achieved only 3 per cent growth in its share price; investors would have been 'better off in an insured savings account'. During 1999, a new chairman and CEO, Jack M. Greenberg, lifted earnings by 26 per cent. He also expanded through parallel food outlets— Donato's Pizza and Mexican Grills—holding back on the sale of more McDonald's sites. [23]

The war of attrition

After eighteen years of amicable relations with its bottlers, in 1919 Coca-Cola became entangled in a series of disputes. As the new owners of The Coca-Cola Company, the Woodruff syndicate set out to break its agreement to sell syrup via the Parent Bottlers. A 250 per cent spurt in sugar prices in 1919–20 spurred attempts to end both perpetual rights and the fixed price. Even without that crisis, Woodruff senior was not a man to let anyone take 12.5 per cent for the effort of signing an invoice, as the Parent Bottlers were entitled to do, serving 'no useful purpose; simply buying the syrup at a fixed price and reselling same at a profit—not even seeing the syrup that is sent direct…to the Actual Bottlers'.[24]

If Coke could end the contract with the Parent Bottlers, the arrangements with the Actual Bottlers would also be void. The new owners were shocked to discover that their contracts 'in perpetuity' violated the Sherman Anti-Trust Act. In 1921, they beseeched the court to deliver them from their iniquities. The justices held firm that capitalists could take care of each other. Ernest Woodruff had to accept the perpetuity of the contracts in exchange for the bottlers' agreeing to a flexible pricing for sugar. During the next seventy years, conflicts between Atlanta and the Actual Bottlers simmered in the cauldron of that compromise. The Company used every innovation in product and distribution to claw back the concession forced on it in 1921, while the bottlers suspected that every deviation from the classic drink in the standard bottle was aimed at diminishing their inalienable rights to syrup, trademarks and the pursuit of profit.

Ernest Winslow Woodruff (1863–1944) was not a nice man. His son called him 'dictatorial'.[25] He was tight-fisted even for a banker. When he searched his pockets to tip a porter, the Negro advised him to keep looking: 'If you ever had it, Mr Woodruff, you still got it'.[26] Woodruff bought The Coca-Cola Company to make a killing on the stock market; he did not intend to waste his life in the lolly-water business. But the best-laid schemes of financiers 'gang aft a-gley'. Profits plummeted when the post-war boom drove up the price of sugar. Then came the slump of 1922. Costs fell, but so did sales and hence profits. Woodruff's syndicate had to borrow millions. By 1923, when Ernest installed his son Robert as president, The Company was tottering.

Robert Winslow Woodruff (1890–1985) was a nicer man than his father. He indulged his friends, to whom he sent a single rose on their birthdays, and was generous to his community, which he endowed with an arts centre, though he had no interest in high culture. What he loved was shooting small birds and driving big motors. Robert Woodruff became known as 'Mr Anonymous' because his gifts were so numerous, capped by $250 million to Emory University. He had made his own fortune by selling automobiles before his father made him place a portion in The Coca-Cola Company. He agreed to work at Coca-Cola only to redeem that investment. He added its management to his other full-time job as vice-chairman of White Motors.

Both Woodruffs recognised that the amended contract with the bottlers had left a 'fundamental weakness', while liaison through the Parent Bottlers was 'weak and ineffectual'.[27] Between the wars, Coca-Cola took control of Whitehead's territories through exchanges of stock. The Thomases, however, kept their distance. Coca-Cola reiterated its 'constant intention and fixed purpose' to buy the stock for cash, maintaining a war chest of more than $20 million to liquidate the last of the Parent Bottlers.

Robert Woodruff proved reluctant in the 1940s to allow the bottlers to become involved with the 'cup vending machine', which he wanted to treat as an extension of the soda-fountain business, an area where no long-term agreements applied.[28] A similar dispute arose in 1957 over whether pre-mix belonged to bottlers or wholesalers. Bottlers had just resisted the introduction of sizes other than the 6.5-ounce bottle from January 1955, suspecting that the simultaneous release of Coke in cans infringed their privileges.

In 1963, Thomas Bottlers condemned The Company's planned diet cola, TAB, as an 'imitation' which violated its 1899 contract. Coca-Cola retorted that 'the Thomas Company ha[d] no rights concerning the sale of "TAB" in its territory'.[29] Accordingly, the hold-out Parent Bottler would not receive the percentage of the sale price that it got for Coca-Cola syrup. After forty-one years in the business, a Mississippi bottler said that the TAB dispute made him feel as if 'my granddaddy and my pappy were feuding and fussing'.[30]

The Thomas Company retained a certain fondness for a contract which brought in 12.5 per cent of the value of Coca-Cola syrup from the wealthiest 60 per cent of the US population, a sentiment worth $7 million a year by 1970. Then, in the mid-1970s, fearful lest the Federal Trade Commission invalidate all exclusive supply agreements, the Thomas legatees sold out for $35 million. Henceforth, the surviving 700 Actual Bottlers would confront Coke head to head. At that stage, The Company had no thought of buying out local franchisees, who were useful to The Company because they could lobby on Atlanta's behalf at every level of government, saving it from the State and municipal taxes levied against chain businesses.

The franchise system that had cleared a path to growth around 1900 had become an impediment to Coca-Cola's expansion by the 1950s. By then, the behaviour of the Actual Bottlers had confirmed fears that family-owned and managed businesses would put their desire for dividend cheques above the need for reinvestment to sustain growth. Trucks were breaking down, as were bottling lines. Older plants were less profitable. A tight labour market meant that inefficiencies could not be patched over with more cheap labourers. The Actual Bottlers could no longer meet all the demands on them from unions, shareholders and competitors. The bottlers freeloaded on The Company's marketing to sustain their sales, yet resented promotional outlays that squeezed quarterly pay-outs. Pepsi dealers, by contrast, were fewer, leaner and thirstier, prompting Coca-Cola's chief operations officer to warn the bottlers: 'You'll lose share but in the meantime, you can draw out a lot of cash'.[31] One solution for the family bottler was to sell out for what amounted to lump-sum superannuation.

Buy-back

Coca-Cola's racing start had come from its not having to fund a large slice of its growth, but The Company could not escape investment costs for ever. A system which had sustained a thousand medium-size entrepreneurs for eighty years was overtaken by the monopolising to which it had been an alternative. Ownership was further concentrated in order to finance the marketing imperatives of oligopolistic competition. The publisher of the leading trade journal, *Beverage World*, commented that neither Coca-Cola nor PepsiCo had 'a strategy to eliminate smaller bottlers. But there is a strategy to grow the business, and the tools required to grow the business in some cases, will be more likely found in the hands of a larger, consolidated bottler'.[32]

Until the 1980s, The Coca-Cola Company had given no thought to becoming its own largest bottler. Indeed, it offered to get out of the bottling side if its rivals did so. In the late 1970s, Atlanta purchased a bottler, but only to prevent its passing 'into the hands of those particular type of people who are...well seeded with Mafia relations'.[33] Two factors put an end to this self-limitation.

First, the Federal Trade Commission in 1971 had argued that franchising, by definition, restricted competition. The dispute made its way through the courts until 1980, when it ended in favour of Coca-Cola. The Company also secured a Soft Drink Interbrand Competition Act to give Actual Bottlers exclusive rights over a territory. Once the franchises were safe in law, their value rose and a backlog came on the market. Coca-Cola now had an opportunity to strengthen its network by directing the resale of franchises towards contiguous bottlers of proven efficiency. Atlanta became a clearinghouse for bottling contracts, half of which changed hands during the early 1980s.

The second point in play was old news. Inflation had crept back. Bottlers were suffering a long-term cost squeeze. Between 1968 and 1973, input costs for all US manufacturing rose by an average of 11 per cent per annum, whereas the prices that processors received increased at less than half that rate. Then the oil price shocks of 1973 and 1979 brought the annual rate of consumer price inflation to successive 'peacetime records'. The return of inflation raised the prospect that The Coca-Cola Company would again be wholesaling its syrup for less than the cost of production.[34]

The barney over TAB flared again in 1983, when Atlanta proposed to call its new no-cal drink Diet Coke. The contract for its supply gave The Company greater control over the Actual Bottlers, because the more Diet Coke cut into sales of Classic Coke the stronger Atlanta's hand would be. One reason given in-house for introducing Diet Coke was 'to re-establish [The Company's] leadership as the prime mover of the company/bottler system'.

Confronted by a handful of franchise-holders resistant to amending their 1921 contract, Atlanta turned its thoughts to gaining control through purchase. Buy-outs during 1979 gave The Company ownership of 10 per cent of domestic volume. Its first leveraged buy-out was a move into Washington DC. Under that takeover method, the purchasers used the assets they were getting as collateral for their loan. The manoeuvre was an early sign of a stock-market boom. Although The Company itself never became an open target for acquisition, its bottlers were attractive to traders skilled at stripping assets or siphoning cash flows. Coca-Cola became its own white knight to prevent its bottlers from being bled just when Atlanta needed them to be injecting funds, not sucking them out.

Before 1980, The Coca-Cola Company had been a manufacturer of syrup and a marketeer of soft drinks. The Company's chairman, Roberto Goizueta, invested in Actual Bottlers, which brought debts which overloaded the balance sheet. To boost the rate of earnings per share, he split the bottling operations off in 1986 into Coca-Cola Enterprises. Two years later, he used the windfall profit from the resale of Columbia Pictures to buy out whole franchises. Coca-Cola Enterprises grew into a mega-bottler across thirty-eight States, responsible for 70 per cent of US volumes by late 1998. The number of bottler ownerships had fallen from 110 to 90 in the previous eighteen months. In the judgement of the president of Coca-Cola Enterprises, it is 'just a matter of time before the US will have one Coke bottler and one Pepsi bottler'. [35]

Before the 1990s, Coca-Cola had had little experience of multi-divisional management because franchising had externalised bottling and distribution. Once Atlanta became its own largest bottler, a redivision of its managerial functions proved essential. If it were obliged by law to reintegrate those assets, The Company would still need to divide control of its operations between production and marketing.

PepsiCo encountered similar pressures. Although the number of its independent bottlers had dropped by one-third to 120 during the 1990s, an industry analyst identified PepsiCo's 'fragmented bottler network' as its key weakness in competing against Coca-Cola.[36] PepsiCo renegotiated its bottling contracts in 1997 to become its own supplier to fountains. In 1999, it copied Atlanta by putting its bottling arm into a separate corporation, the Pepsi Bottlers Group, which sold 55 per cent of volume in North America and planned to take over 1–2 per cent of the franchisees each year.[37]

Consolidation among bottlers did not protect them from The Company's ambitions and failures. Coca-Cola's determination to increase volume by 7–8 per cent a year had meant an 'unprecedented rate of bottler investment in plants, trucks, machinery and coolers'. The levelling-off in demand from mid-1998 cut the rate of return on these funds. The consequent collapse in the share price of Coca-Cola Enterprises halved the paper fortunes of some bottlers. On top of these blows, The Company set out to lift its earnings and share price by doubling the annual rate of increase in the price of syrup.

Anchor bottlers

Coke contracts outside the USA had always allowed for flexible syrup prices. The Company's investment in overseas bottlers varied according to balances of power, from 100 per cent in France, where its partner would not agree 'on how to aggressively market our products', down to zero in Japan, where it is neither polite nor politic to upset cartels. For the old East Germany, Coca-Cola Enterprises decided on a total buy-out as the quickest way to breach the wall. Goizueta explained that the 'goal is not to own 10 per cent or 5 per cent or 40 or 52 per cent of bottling operations around the world, but to assure ourselves that—on a market by market basis and a country-by-country basis—we have the strongest Coca-Cola bottling network possible'.[38] This '49 per cent solution' made Atlanta dominant but held its shareholding below the mark that would trigger foreign investment and anti-trust regulations. The 'balance-sheet manoeuvres' from the buying and selling of Coke bottlers also helped Goizueta achieve 18 per cent annual growth.[39]

The concept of 'anchor bottlers' grew out of a 1981 purchase in the Philippines. The qualifications to be chosen as an anchor bottler were experience in marketing beyond one's home country, a background in bottling, and the funds to invest offshore. Between 1986 and 1999, Atlanta designated eleven anchor bottlers to cover forty countries, with six billion global consumers served at eight million outlets. Those eleven firms account for 70 per cent of volume outside the USA. Until 1998, the weightiest of those anchors was Coca-Cola Amatil (C-CA), based in Australia, but operating throughout Asia, the south-west Pacific and Europe.

Heading the fleet of pleasure boats that celebrated 200 years of the European invasion of Australia, the *Soren Larsen* entered Sydney Harbour in 1988 bearing a Coca-Cola emblem on its mainsail. The invasion by Coca-Cola had begun fifty-one years earlier. Atlanta's connection with Amatil began in 1966 when its predecessor, British Tobacco, acquired Coca-Cola bottlers in Melbourne and Perth. Between 1970 and 1994, the number of Amatil's Australasian bottlers fell from forty to two. The firm had marketed tobacco, beer and food until 1989, when Atlanta convinced it to drop non-soda products and focus on Coca-Cola lines. The Company then made its largest investment in an overseas bottler with $US476 million for a 60 per cent share, a sum which bought seats on the board and put Goizueta in 'control of the company's expansion program'.[40] As a fund manager pointed out in 1998: 'Anybody who is foolish enough to think that Coca-Cola Amatil isn't controlled by Atlanta is crazy—you buy them for that'.[41]

By then, fund managers were no longer rushing to invest in Coca-Cola Amatil, which had gone into debt and raised funds from shareholders to buy and build in Eastern Europe on Atlanta's behalf. An analyst with BNP equities concluded: 'To prop up their Earnings Per Share they're having to sell assets and do deals so other bottlers pay for the capital expenditure, take the depreciation on their profits and wear a political risk'.[42]

Later in 1998, Atlanta oversaw a de-merger, which left Amatil with Australia, Fiji, Indonesia, New Zealand, the Philippines and Papua New Guinea, and only half of its market capitalisation. Amatil bought the bottler South Korea, where losses seemed inevitable after annual growth of only 1 per cent. Amatil ended up with an acquisition worth barely a third of the $1 billion price it paid. The sacked chief executive of Coca-Cola Amatil abused his erstwhile employers for their 'interference', which he alleged had prevented him from serving the interests of the other shareholders.[43] Early in 2000, C-CA wrote down its investment by $1.2 billion, a loss confirmed a year later when it sold its Philippines operation to its partners in Atlanta and Manila.[44]

Around 1900, franchising had been an alternative to a vertical integration of syrup-making with bottling. Today, the bottlers are few, and those that survive are in thrall to their supplier. The drive to oligopolisation could be re-routed, but never road-blocked.

PART THREE **To the Power of One**

One capitalist always kills many.

Karl Marx, *Capital*[1]

CHAPTER 6 In Rockefeller We Trust

People of the same trade seldom meet together, even for meriment and diversion, but the conversation ends in a conspiracy against the public, or in some contrivance to raise prices.
Adam Smith, *The Wealth of Nations*, 1776[2]

Monopolisers could not foretell the steps through which their concentration of capital would advance. Businessmen had to teach themselves how to manage branch offices, bankers how to supervise manufacturers, judges how to reach apt precedents and chemists how to synthesise materials. Capitalists tested cartels, combines, mergers, pools, rings and trusts as ways of fixing prices, dividing market territories, excluding entrants or driving down the cost of inputs.

Manoeuvres by US whisky makers illustrate how capitalists had to learn the monopolising trade. Around 1870, the New York whisky ring bribed politicians to reduce excise for existing manufacturers and thereby secured themselves a permanent price advantage over newcomers. The distillers formed a whisky trust in 1887; it collapsed nine years later, only to reappear around 1898–99, by which time it included almost all the US spirit makers. Such goings and second comings were marks of the anarchy of overproduction that caused businesses to cast around for ways of rolling back a free market.

Expropriation governs relations among capitalists, the failure of one firm flagging an opportunity for another. This contest leads 'to a centralisation of capital, and thus to expropriation on the most enormous scale. Expropriation extends here from the direct producers to the smaller and the medium-sized capitalists themselves'.[3] Of the corporations listed in the *Fortune* 500 for 1970, only eighty were more than a hundred years old, and fifty of those were banks or insurance companies. The first fifty years of monopolising to 1923 had been tumultuous, but once that round of concentration had reduced 'the risks of doing business in a "competitive" economy...the industrial structure established by the end of the First World War' continued to the 1970s.[4]

Consolidations moved in three directions:

- *horizontal integration* through arrangements among direct competitors such as the sugar refiners' trust;
- *vertical integration* of manufacturers with suppliers and merchandisers, as when the chain-store grocer A&P bought coffee plantations in Brazil; and
- *diversification* into conglomerates, as in James B. Duke's decision to add power generation to his tobacco investments.

These moves were not mutually exclusive. The du Ponts, for example, had engaged in horizontal integration since the 1870s, when they consolidated the gunpowder trade, which was oversupplied after the Civil War. Around 1907, they vertically integrated some of their supplies. By then, they were also on their way to becoming a conglomerate, with an interest in General Motors alongside their chemical concerns.

This chapter looks at monopolising since the 1870s from several perspectives which will provide the context for the cola wars explored in the next chapter. The phrase 'monopolising capitals' is used throughout because 'monopolising' points up the ceaseless nature of the process, while the plural 'capitals' indicates the persistence of competitors, albeit of a new kind.

Monopolising competition is no oxymoron. Far from disappearing in the age of monopolisers, competition became more ferocious as resources became more concentrated. Joseph Schumpeter recognised in the 1940s that monopolising had intensified capitalism's gale of 'creative destruction'; the processes that monopolisers had invented to shore up their power were reducing their individual chances of survival. Anti-competitive devices, Schumpeter wrote, are like the brakes on an automobile, which encourage motorists to drive faster than they would dare if their only means of stopping were to crash.[5] If capitalists did not manage prices and restrict entry to their markets, they would not accumulate the funds for the next round of investments, which will in turn strip value from their existing properties.

The firm

Firms have star billing in most economics textbooks, which often begin with a firm rather than some Robinson Crusoe consumer. Yet the firm is no more natural than a Crown monopoly. Both were invented by human beings to cope with capital expansion.

The godfather of free-market economics, Adam Smith, delighted in the novelty of the division of labour. His archetypal pin-maker bought steel from one agent for his workers to turn into pins, which he then sold to a second agent, who sold that commodity on to a wholesaler. Such specialisation, Smith believed, would reduce the costs of production. Smith drew his ideas from tradespeople and shopkeepers, and supposed 'that eighteenth-century England will remain unchanged forever'.[6] He could not conceive that the economic developments he favoured might undergo an even greater transformation.

Between Smith's individual entrepreneur and today's global corporation came the firm. Instead of specialising in one branch of production, the firm forged a chain of related activities and services. The creation of the firm shifted the cost of buying the steel—as distinct from the price of the steel itself—from fees for an outside agent to wages paid to an employee. At its best, 'vertical integration converts external economies to internal profits'.[7] Thus, every firm is an oligopoly in embryo. Smith himself opposed all business combinations, including the joint-stock company, as incipient monopolies.

The separation of production from circulation persisted into the 1870s, when 'nearly all American industrial enterprises only manufactured. They bought their supplies and sold their finished products through commissioned agents, wholesalers, and other middlemen'.[8] During the 1890s, however, firms such as Carnegie's steel and McCormick's harvesters internalised their marketing. By 1904, 54 per cent of food makers had established forward links with wholesalers and retailers. The less that firms relied on outside suppliers, the greater became their control of inventories. Du Pont 'began to acquire ownership of many supply sources' in order to manage its stocks after the 1907 financial crisis had left it with surplus products.[9] In the 1920s, the du Ponts set up a hire-purchase arm to smooth sales of General Motors vehicles and thus avoid the costs of holding excess inputs or finished cars.

In the late twentieth century, a strand of free-trade economics revived Smith's objections to the firm *per se*, condemning it as anti-competitive. The manufacturing firm that uses its own staff to prepare advertisements can only guesstimate how much an outsider might have charged, since 'one can only establish a price by making a trade'.[10] Otherwise, the figures are like quoting the price of cheese on the moon. Some dismantling of the firm commenced in the 1980s and 1990s, with tasks being outsourced and in-house suppliers forced to bid against non-affiliates. The argument against this disaggregation is that reliance on others can leave a business short of essentials or subject to volatile prices, both of which can add as much to costs as any inefficiency from internalising those trades. Another negative is that training regimes break down, resulting in shortages of skilled labour. This loss of expertise requires firms to share knowledge, a version of monopolising glossed as 'alliance capitalism'.[11]

The impoverishment of theory

An economist who accepts monopolising capitals as the norm is as rare as a market free of oligopolies. Many experts cling to a model of 'perfect competition', though a few scholars in the early 1930s conceptualised 'imperfect competition' as more typical. After humming and hawing, the profession absorbed the presence of oligopolies by turning them into special cases. The new ideas

> affected relatively little of the general corpus of economic theory as an analytical and conceptual framework...At first attention was focussed on imperfect competition as a theory of price at the microscopic level of particular industries and product markets. Little attention was paid to its significance on a macroscopic scale.[12]

Joan Robinson's 1933 chapter 'A world of monopolies' remains exceptional in placing monopolising competition 'at the very centre of the analytical effort'.[13] Rather than replace talk of 'perfect' or 'atomistic competition' with 'imperfect competition', analysis should start from imperfect monopolisation, also known as oligopolisation. To do so would reveal 'a more perfect, purer form of capital than that found in its historical infancy'.[14]

Monopolising takes a variety of forms: duopolies, monopsonies (where there is a single purchaser) but, above all, oligopolies, the testy few. Monopolising is as difficult to compute as it is to regulate because it is hydra-headed, and is never simply a matter of price-fixing, or market sharing, or dominance over suppliers and retailers. Monopolising calls for some of each, varying like the parts in a sung canon, where each voice takes up the tune as called upon. The academics and lawyers who evade the import of monopolising prance from one criterion to the next to show that, since none proves near-total dominance, monopolising does not exist, has never existed, and cannot exist. The US Supreme Court was beside every point when it declared in 1945 that a 64 per cent market share was 'not enough for a monopoly'.[15]

Business historians have been so defensive about monopolising that it is a surprise to find one concluding that 'market control was and is a major element of corporate purpose'.[16] Alfred D. Chandler Jr, on the other hand, was content to claim that the modern corporation 'replaced small traditional enterprises when administrative co-ordination permitted greater productivity, lower costs, and higher profits than co-ordination by market mechanisms'.[17] His choice of the term 'permitted' denies his own thesis that managers were active organisers. In directing his attention from the 'why' to the 'how', he misjudged a means of oligopolisation for its cause. Chandler thus contributed to the rehabilitation of big business by offering a value-free excuse for monopolising. This version of objectivity was necessary because, as one public-relations man admitted in the late 1940s, while '"capitalism" might be a logical brand name' it had become 'a brand name of demonstrated ill will'.[18] Chandler's Harvard colleague, Richard S. Tedlow, sank into apologetics after it was revealed to him that business 'became big when it delivered value to the customer'.[19]

The first wave

As two plus two began to make one, the number of firms capitalised at more than a million dollars swelled from eleven in 1887 to thirty in 1890. Then came a pause during the 1893–97 depression. Monopolising again erupted in 1899 with 129 million-dollar mergers. Two-thirds of those consolidations created single companies with more than 60 per cent of their industries' capacity. By 1904, 318 corporations had integrated 5200 plants, or 40 per cent of the nation's manufacturing assets; almost one sixth of investment in that sector was held by Carnegie's US Steel. Comparable processes were occurring in Britain, Europe and Japan; monopolising tendencies were not peculiar to the USA, but inherent in capital's expansion.

The urge to combine percolated into every recess of the economy. Soon there were trusts for window glass, straw board and soda fountains. Industrial stocks boomed during the merger mania of 1898–1902, which gave prominence to brand-name firms in which investors felt more confident about placing their funds. In January 1890, the five largest US cigarette-makers—controlling over 90 per cent of national output—incorporated as the American Tobacco

Company, with James B. Duke as president. Duke extended his reach in 1898, when he headed a chewing-tobacco trust. After brief and unhappy exposure to international competition, he divided the global market with British firms through the creation of the British-American Tobacco Co. in 1902.

From 1885, oatmeal millers made several attempts to form a cartel before the Quaker Oats Company set up a voting trust in 1901 to manage their collective interests. Ten years later, Quaker bought out its only serious rival. The Biscuit Trust, which survives as Nabisco, was formed in 1898. These cases indicate the variety and density of the transformation which monopolising brought to every aspect of daily life.

The agglomerations fired political fantasists. When Edward Bellamy published *Looking Backward* in 1887, he envisaged the government of the United States in the year 2001 as a benign Great Trust, controlling every aspect of economic life. Some socialists hoped that once individual ownership had been dissolved into the trusts a takeover by the state would be the next step. Before 'King' Gillette perfected his safety razor, he spent the 1890s promoting shares in his Twentieth Century Company, which would eradicate the evils of competition by buying up the entire planet.[20]

Businesses could not always afford to be so utopian. H. K. & F. B. Thurber were the largest wholesale grocers in the USA, stocking anything edible, with sales for 1879 in excess of $2 million. Under pressure from the railroads over freight charges, the Thurbers announced that, although they were 'opposed to the centralisation of power either in the hands of Government or of corporations', they accepted that 'centralisation is a <u>fact</u> staring us in the face and we must see if we cannot make one form of centralisation neutralise the other'.[21] Their solution was to make their big business even bigger. Few citizens had that opportunity. Most looked to the government to provide relief by breaking up the trusts.

Anti-trust laws

Anti-trust laws came into being after farmers, workers and small to medium businesses pressured the US Congress to pass the Sherman

Act in 1890. The vote in favour of the Act was almost unanimous, a sign that it would be ineffective, other than as a sop to the protesters. By making cartel arrangements illegal among independent firms, the Act redirected monopolisers towards mergers, which were allowed, providing they did not establish absolute control. In the words of George Stigler, 1982 winner of the *faux* Nobel Prize for Economic Science, 'the ghost of Senator Sherman is an ex officio member of the board of directors of every large company'.[22] In the same vein, an 1898 judgement outlawing price-fixing between competitors stimulated their consolidation into single firms.

In the 1930s, some States tried to protect their corner shops by taxing stores according to the number in their chain. This regulation too had unanticipated consequences for it encouraged fewer but bigger outlets, quickening the shift towards the supermarket. At the same time, Congress legislated to stop wholesalers offering extra discounts to their biggest customers, who would then cut their selling prices and put the small retailer at a disadvantage. The chain stores responded by setting up their own suppliers: 'Designed to cripple big business through indirect means, [the Act] succeeded only in encouraging further vertical integration'.[23] Hence, one effect of laws against monopolistic behaviour has been to stimulate new forms of combination. The USA has a tradition of trust-busting, while governments in Australia did next to nothing. The outcomes have been much the same. Oligopolies arise from the dynamics of capital expansion, irrespective of the laws of the land. To prevent monopolising would have stymied capitalism.

Even where the law had some effect, the remedies proved partial and temporary. In 1911, the Supreme Court upheld the dissolution of Standard Oil (New Jersey), obliging Rockefeller's trust to disgorge properties among the confidants who had set it up. Nothing much changed until the 1920s, except that the stock-market value of the parts was greater than it had been for the whole.[24] Around the same time, federal authorities busted Duke's Tobacco Trust into sixteen companies. Yet, within thirty years, the three market leaders held more than three-quarters of US cigarette output. The trio were then convicted and fined under the Anti-Trust Act, but were not made to divest themselves of their gains. Oligopolies are like starfish. Rip them apart and they regenerate their tentacles.

Pre-trial manoeuvring has been more successful than logic in warding off anti-trust suits. In the early 1940s, Coca-Cola lawyers warned Woodruff against keeping incriminating files, because when the anti-trust division moved in

> the documentary evidence [it] turns up on competitive relations usually amazes executives and their attorneys. It is seldom that members of a trade association know what its employees do though often their blindness is deliberate.[25]

Hit by one such suit, A&P stores adopted 'a strategy that has since become traditional...that of delaying until the advent of a more sympathetic administration'.[26] IBM's lead advocate reflected that he had 'quickly realised in my early days at the bar that I could take the simplest anti-trust case...and protract it for the defence almost to infinity'.[27] Lawyers later instructed IBM executives to 'avoid such phrasing as "containment of competitive threats" and substitute instead "maintain position of leadership"'.[28]

Technology

To explain why monopolising takes place, its apologists have focused either on technologies or on the firm. These developments cannot be cut off from each other, since they are strands of the one process. Machines are designed so as to constrain worker resistance and to lock in customers. Equally, the firm is a soft technology, managing relationships between capital and labour, manufacturers and merchandisers, marketeers and consumers.

Technology is one excuse monopolisers offer for their pursuit of market dominance, as in this imaginary cross-examination:

Q. How did you become an oligopoly?
A. We're innocent. Our machines did it.
Q. Did what?
A. Made our products cheapest and best.

Q. What can be done about your power?

A. Technology will take it away.

Q. Where will it go?

A. To another oligopoly.

Such a defence represents technology as neutral in terms of social power. 'Technology happens', declared Intel's Andrew Grove. 'It's not good, it's not bad.'[29] We are told that the world will beat a track to the inventor with a better widget, but we rarely hear how crooked that mile is. No single or straight track runs between the upgrading of machines and the survival prospects of a firm. Some innovations favour entrants, others strengthen existing oligopolies. The powerful adapt innovations to their own interests as often as technology reallocates power.

The food cartels that rolled out along the US railroad tracks as they trebled between 1880 and 1900 were not simply the consequence of that vaster transport service. The commodity trusts depended on how the rail network affected merchandising, which was being promoted by national magazines and catalogues delivered almost free by the postal service. Moreover, expanding the railroads did not initiate competition between the biggest firms, because most of the processing works were already in the same city. In the case of meat, the regional slaughterhouses suffered once the four meat-packing giants of Chicago could send fresh beef thousands of kilometres in refrigerated railcars. The 'small business problem' appeared only after the economy developed 'a leading core of oligopolists'. Coca-Cola was one of the few from the 'small-firm fringe' to make its way to the top. [30]

The social dimension of technology was apparent with the introduction of cigarette-rolling machines. When James Duke halved his wages bill by replacing his skilled workforce, he could undercut his competitors. No less importantly, he made a deal to hire the fastest machines at prices 25 per cent cheaper than those that would be charged to any other cigarette maker. Technological innovation reduced Duke's labour costs, but a restrictive trade practice raised the start-up costs for anyone hoping to follow. Thereafter, Duke could cut prices if necessary and could afford to advertise extensively, advantages which encouraged further concentration. Between the wars, US bottle-makers had a similar deal preventing the manufacturers of their equipment from selling machines to newcomers.[31] Much the same happened in the tobacco industry during the mid-1970s. Philip Morris ordered all the available electronic cigarette machinery, while R.J.Reynolds dithered. The result was that Philip Morris's Marlboro replaced Reynolds' Winston as market leader. The reversal arose from poor management at the latter company as much as from improved equipment at the former.

A new technology can undermine an oligopoly by superseding its products. Technical changes contributed to the demise of all but two of the top twenty-five firms listed in Moody's 1900 Industrial Manual. At the turn of the twentieth century, half of the largest industrials were cotton mills; other leading companies manufactured buggies and bicycles, harnesses and wagons, gas mantles and ice, all of which were being displaced by automobiles or electricity before 1930. A mix of social, cultural and financial factors prevented the established leaders from switching to manufacture of the new equipment.

Three aspects of Coca-Cola's history illustrate this substitution: plastics replaced glass in most bottles; advertisements went beyond print, first to radio and then to television; and sweeteners switched from cane or beet to corn or synthetics. In each case, the replacement technology has been taken into an oligopoly, if it was not already owned by one. No matter how rapidly technologies advance, the oligopolisers march on as before.

Nowhere has praise for the liberating power and neutrality of technology been more raucous than around business machines. To explain IBM's 'dominance of the industry' as the consequence of its research and development, its overseas marketing and its investment in managerial skills is to ignore the restrictive pricing practices that have been demonstrated by anti-trust convictions.[32] Far from securing their clout with excellence in design, the large purveyors of business machines have bundled technologies and pricing with marketing to defeat superior products. IBM's president acknowledged in 1966 that to block possible rivals, his company had promised customers a programming system which it had 'not yet invented'.[33]

Even by the standards of the late nineteenth century, John Patterson of National Cash Register (NCR) was a buccaneer, grabbing at every niche for fear that it 'might some day provide ground for an attack on the core business'.[34] Thomas Watson Sr, who founded IBM in 1924, learnt market manipulation as Patterson's offsider. In 1912, they were sentenced to a year's imprisonment for price-fixing, a verdict overturned on technical grounds.

In the 1930s, the Supreme Court upheld a judgement against IBM for conspiring with its chief competitor, Remington Rand. IBM made the transition from dominating punch-card machines to controlling computers in the 1950s and 1960s because the long overlap in technologies let the Watsons steer customers of its earlier systems towards the new products that returned IBM the biggest earnings. IBM held almost 95 per cent of the market in 1959. New technologies and anti-trust suits brought its share down to two-thirds before it again rose to three-quarters in 1972. In addition, IBM controlled 70–80 per cent of peripherals. By setting 'numerous industry standards', it made rivals 'all dance to the IBM tune'.[35] According to Thomas Watson Jr, servicing a system was four times more important than inventing it, because services locked customers into ever more expensive models, and for the next generation. IBM benefited from the fact that half of the *Fortune* 500 had recruited their chief information officers from IBM. Its board members also enforced the IBM-only rule at other corporations where they were directors.[36]

Despite a string of failed products in the 1980s, Bill Gates prospered because the cash flow from his 1979 exclusive agreement to supply MS-DOS for IBM PCs allowed him to buy up innovators and outspend rivals. Peter Drucker dismisses Gates as a 'celebrity'.[37] That Gates's leadership is not in technologies became obvious when he did not mention the Internet in the first draft of his book *The Road Ahead*. After a staff member raised the potential for the Net's computer language, JAVA, to render Windows irrelevant, Gates called him a 'communist'.[38] At the last minute, Microsoft tacked Internet Explorer onto Windows 95 and Gates revised his computer manifesto to praise the Internet, not as an ocean of knowledge but as a 'river of gold'.[39] As with NCR and IBM, technology at Microsoft has been a tool for monopolising.

Tsunami

Deregulation is today's highway to ever more monopolising. According to *Business Week* in 1991: 'The idea that you can compete by buying your competitor is allowing the concentration of vast market power in the hands of just a few companies in many industries. You might call this the Age of Consolidation'.[40] Freed from many governmental controls in the 1980s on the pledge of increased competitiveness, Australia's seven major banks combined into four. The quartet would be happy to become a duo were the government ready to risk further electoral wrath at the loss of services. In the US airline industry, no 'post-deregulation start-up of significant size has avoided merger, bankruptcy, or outright failure'. Instead, airlines formed global alliances, with the four biggest controlling more than half of the business by 1995. After Brazil deregulated, the number of mergers and acquisitions there went from fifty-eight in 1992 to almost 400 in 1997, with its free-market government subsidising the administrative costs.

Concentration among clients has encouraged consolidation by their advertising agencies. Three of the biggest billing firms combined as Omnicon Group in 1986. From London, Saatchi & Saatchi went global by taking over a Madison Avenue leader. A year later their financial manager turned freelance for a hostile raid on J. Walter Thompson. This round of oligopolisation was spurred by the prospect of bigger profits out of the deeper discounts from more massive buys of TV time. Saatchi & Saatchi also absorbed all the services that their clients might need—consultancy and public relations—in a mix of vertical and horizontal integrations. By 1999, three agencies had half the global billings and the next nine held another 40 per cent, leaving 10 per cent for the rest.

The lowering of trade barriers across Europe has encouraged greater levels of concentration, liberating 'more capital by exposing over-capacity that used to be protected'.[41] At first, mergers and acquisitions within nation-market-states strengthened locally based firms against those elsewhere in the EEC. After those combinations were completed, cross-border integrations trebled in the decade to 1996. Meanwhile, outsiders bought into European firms to gain a foothold in the continental market.

The tsunami of mergers and acquisitions in the USA during 1998 totalled $2.4 trillion. That year saw 'eight of the ten biggest deals of all time—and all of the seven biggest'. The immensity of those consolidations is apparent when compared with US Gross National Product. While the 1900 merger wave reached 13 per cent of GNP, that of 1998 hit 20 per cent. These mammoths did not cobble together disparate industries, like the flops of the 1960s, but instead set out to integrate rivals in banking, oil, communications and automobiles. One of the biggest of these horizontal integrations was CitiCorp with Travelers Group at $73 billion. [42] In the vehicle industry, Ford acquired Volvo while Daimler merged with Chrysler, and Renault with Nissan. The plunge into mergers and acquisitions continued through 2000, when J. P. Morgan Chase was formed with assets of $667 billion, revenues of $31 billion and profits of $7.6 billion. GE bought Honeywell for $45 billion. Time-Warner closed with America Online, combining the world's largest Internet provider with the world's largest supplier of media. Rothmans and British American Tobacco joined forces, as did Philip Morris and Nabisco.

Monopolising has marked the entire biochemical sector. Two Swiss firms, Sandoz and Ciba-Geigy, completed a $27 billion merger in 1998 to form Novartis. Hoescht and Rhone-Poulenc came together as the world's biggest supplier of agrochemicals. Mergers among the oil majors—BP with Amoco and Exxon with Mobil —had flow-on effects in petrochemicals. Du Pont began selling its oil business to fund a move into biotechnologies under the motto 'Miracles from Science'. Already the fifth-largest agrochemical company, it bought out the world's largest seed producer. Pfizer took Warner Lambert for $80 billion. SmithKline-Beecham joined GlaxoWellcome to become the world's largest pharmaceutical corporation.

Around the periphery of these mega-moves, the usual run of consolidations proceeded. The number of independent confectioners in the USA continued to slide from 6000 in 1945 to a projected 150 by 2010. In April 2000, Unilever paid $326 million to the socially conscious owners of Ben & Jerry's for their all-natural ice cream company.

Timing

To accept that capitals must become concentrated is not to explain why that process intensifies at particular times. Nor can any one factor account for every node. The specifics of capital growth are revealed in the differences between the monopolising at the close of the nineteenth century and its resurgence a hundred years later, just as its immanent character is exposed through the century of concentration.

Monopolising capitals emerged from the 1870s when the size of the investments involved for mass production required enterprises to run their machinery at close to full capacity. The resulting excess produce swamped the market, driving out small concerns; by the late 1880s, industries were dominated by 'a dozen or more large firms', equally efficient and hence incapable of wiping each other out.[43] Fiercer competition between these producers drove the price-cutting of the 1890s depression, when the 'value of finished perishable commodities destined for domestic consumption' went up and down like a yo-yo.[44] Firms thereafter merged to restore profitability by containing price competition.

Those mergers became possible because more finance was available: 'the gradual increase of capital by reproduction...is clearly a very slow procedure compared with centralisation', which has only to realign its constituent parts.[45] Before the 1890s, excess funds had favoured real estate or railroads. Yet even the House of Morgan had failed to install a single railroad cartel, because the bankers could not muster sufficient funds to buy out the non-compliers. Some owners of merged corporations found a way around such shortfalls by selling stock to the public. 'Industrials' did not become a financial term until 1889, and several more years were to pass before Dow Jones issued an industrial stock average. The subsequent inflow of investors funded a wave of mergers until the bankruptcy of National Cordage, a combination of thread manufacturers, triggered the 1893 panic. In spite of this inauspicious start, industrial listings recovered; two hundred companies were traded in 1897, as against only thirty in 1893. 'Without a ready market for industrial securities...the creation of a big industrial merger would have been made very much more difficult'.[46]

During the twentieth century, corporations generated their own investment funds or relied on their banking allies. The stock market supplied some new capital but mostly transferred wealth between speculators. Very little of the trillions of dollars at which the market valued the top 500 corporations was available in ready cash.

When the chief executive of RJR Nabisco was plotting a leveraged buy-out in 1988, he feared that there would not be enough takeover funds in the world to pull off his plan: 'Fuck. I'll be going around on my hands and knees like a monkey with an organ grinder to find seventeen billion dollars'.[47] Since then, the situation has changed yet again. The world now has more financial capital than it knows what to do with, partly because of the securitisation of retirement savings from the baby-boomers.

To attract investors, portfolio managers had to keep ahead of the Wall Street average, which meant constantly buying and selling stocks. The 'ratio of the volume of shares traded annually on the New York Stock Exchange to its total shares listed 'grew' from no more than '16 per cent in the early 1960s...to over 50 per cent by the mid-1980s'.[48] By the 1990s, the growth of mutual funds made a new ocean of money available for takeovers. Three-quarters of the shares of the average US company listed on the New York Stock Exchange turned over in 1998, up 50 per cent in twelve years. By late 1999, the average time a share in Amazon.com was held was seven days, and in Microsoft seven months. Coca-Cola was exceptional at twenty-six months.[49]

The availability of funds explains why corporations could afford to acquire their rivals, but those flows cannot explain why gigantism is necessary. The answer has to be sought in the demands placed on firms through their competition to control ever wider markets.

The 'highest stage of capitalism' was how Lenin in 1916 described the monopolising that spread after the 1870s. Has there been a qualitative bound to an even higher stage since the 1980s, or just a quantitative blip? Either way, more than an e-commerce program will be needed to convince the shade of Adam Smith that 130 years of monopolising has been an exception to the norm of perfect competition.

CHAPTER 7 What Challenge?

We have to have it all.

Don Kendall, PepsiCo president

I want it all. I don't want them to have even these niche products.
Roberto Goizueta, Coca-Cola chairman 1981–97

The only business we don't want is the business that doesn't exist.
Doug Ivester, Coca-Cola chairman 1998–2000[1]

A beverage can be the essence of capitalism only in a metaphoric sense. The reproduction of capital cannot be read from the curves of a bottle, or from the sales curve for lolly-water. It must be a coincidence that, for 160 years, economists have modelled monopoly pricing around a fable about the owner of a natural spring with unique curative properties, who adjusts his price per litre until he attracts the largest volume of customers and so brings in the largest possible profit.[2]

In 1886, when Dr Pemberton began to sell his cola through one of the six soda fountains in the State of Georgia, thousands of other small businesses were peddling their cure-alls and soft drinks across the United States. Few competed against each other because their distribution did not extend much further than a horse-drawn cart could travel in a day. The competitors for branded soft drinks were home-made ginger beer and lemonade, although Hire's Root Beer dry compound came halfway between the kitchen and the factory.

The United States was abuzz in the 1880s with chemists concocting nostrums. In 1885, a pharmacist in Waco, Texas, brewed phosphorescent water, fruit juices and sugar into a sharp yet sweet soft drink, soon named for a local identity, Dr Pepper. Nehi Inc. did well with its Chero-Cola before Coca-Cola prevented it from registering a trademark in 1921; Nehi then sold fruit flavours until it developed Royal Crown Cola in 1936. Older than Coke, Moxie was a bitter herbal drink favoured by New Englanders into the 1930s, its brand name entering American English as slang for energy and smartness. From his pharmacy in North Carolina, Doc Bradham relaunched Brad's Drink as Pepsi-Cola in 1898. Only a handful of brews have survived to compete against the essence of capitalism.

Until the 1880s, almost anyone could enter the business. Then the rules changed, so that now the few rule. During 1986, the US Federal Trade Commission prevented The Coca-Cola Company and PepsiCo from absorbing Dr Pepper and 7-UP respectively, although 80 per cent of the latter's products was distributed by Coke or Pepsi bottlers. The targets themselves then combined before being taken over by Cadbury–Schweppes in 1995. Four years later, Cadbury–Schweppes had integrated with Coca-Cola in 155 countries.

In place of thousands of exclusive territories, the US marketplace is dominated by three firms. Coca-Cola took 44.1 per cent of 1999 sales, up from 40.5 per cent in ten years. PepsiCo stayed at 31 per cent and Dr Pepper–7UP (DPSU) had 14 per cent. A duopoly held three-quarters of the market, and the top three took nine out of ten sales. How that contraction has come about is the subject of this chapter.

Beneath the three majors, hundreds of local operators still provide speciality flavours, often root beers. Their share of the shelves is the target of the Cott Corporation, which supplies private labels such as Sam's Club to Wal-Mart. Cott's uses the cash flow from its supermarket sales to squeeze the moms & pops, just as Coca-Cola did in earlier decades.[3] The pressure is felt all the way down the line from Coke and Pepsi to DPSU and Gatorade to Cott's and the neighbourhood brands.

Free entry

Were Coca-Cola to supply 100 per cent of the world's soft drinks, some economists would tell us not to worry, so long as other firms could enter the market freely. These cheery optimists argue that the monopolisers' fear of emerging competition is sufficient to keep prices down, quality high and service satisfactory. This situation is called a 'contestable market'. A market is deemed 'perfectly contestable' when the entrant 'faces no disadvantages *vis-à-vis* the incumbent'.[4]

The force of this account depends on how one understands 'free' and 'enter', just as its persuasiveness increases the further one is from actual existing capitalism. 'Free' surely means more than 'without a government permit', since entry can never be free of start-up costs. I am not allowed to set up a lemonade stall on my footpath without any number of government approvals. These limitations are nothing compared with the commercial barriers to my gaining even 0.1 per cent of Australia's soft-drink sales. So 'enter' must mean more than a raid; the newcomer must be able to stay long enough to secure a niche. Reluctant exiting is more common than free entry.

The fairytale nature of 'perfectly contestable markets' is apparent in the failure of attempts by already large firms to move into the soft-drink industry. Proctor & Gamble spent the 1980s building up its soft-drink line, Crush, and still achieved only 2 per cent of total sales. Such is 'the overwhelming might of cola kings Coca-Cola Co. and Pepsi-Cola' that 'the odd innovation becomes an overriding trend only if it's implemented by those titans'.[5] Coca-Cola's Minute Maid so dominated sales of fruit-juice concentrates that it kept sales of Proctor & Gamble's Citrus Hill to less than one gallon in ten. P&G discontinued the line in 1992 because it 'couldn't even find a buyer' for its failed brand.[6]

To enter a market freely, a firm must also be familiar with the marketing of each particular product. A newcomer can obtain those skills with long experience and deep pockets, but it may prove more profitable to buy that knowledge by taking over an established producer. The consolidation of franchised bottlers has made it even harder for entrants to find distributors, so that entry to this market is becoming less free in every sense. Proctor & Gamble failed with Crush because its shipment methods were not adapted to the task. Quaker Oats bungled its 1994 purchase of Snapple by bundling its distribution with Gatorade, to lose nearly $1.5 billion in four years.

Realignment in the European beverage industry illuminates who has the freedom to enter a market. In 1990, the contretemps over benzene contamination in Perrier water left its French owners willing to sell their soft-drink arm to Cadbury–Schweppes. Eighteen months later, a tussle developed for control of Perrier's core business. From north of the Alps came the Swiss conglomerate Nestlé, which already controlled the Vittel brand. To the south stood the Agnelli family, owners of Fiat, who purchased a third of Perrier in November 1991, backed by an ally with another 14 per cent. The Agnellis had been moving away from the automotive industry into food and beverages through an arrangement with France's BSN, purveyors of Evian water. Perrier's minority investors, mostly banks, called in one giant to protect their share from another predator.

The takeover of the Perrier company was one more step towards the concentration of Europe's food industry as part of the creation of a continent-market-state. Although Nestlé's Perrier bid was mounted from Switzerland, which is outside the European Union, the expanded sales territory allowed greater concentration among the suppliers of bottled water. After 1991, a duopoly operated between Nestlé, with 40 per cent of sales, and BSN, with 33 per cent. Nestlé had sold a segment of Perrier's operation in order to avoid an anti-trust action—as if the duopoly's grip on three-quarters of the market were not restrictive enough of free entry.

Survivors

Most small businesses go bust, are in debt to the banks, or sell out to one of the oligopolies. The Coca-Cola Company skirted all three possibilities before becoming a monopoliser in its own right.

Blasphemous though it sounds, the holy water of the South might have gone the way of Kickapoo Indian Sagwa, or been merged with Dr Pepper, during one of the crises through which The Coca-Cola Company has passed. Until the early 1900s, Asa Candler ran the kind of small business that Sherman's anti-trust legislation was supposed to preserve. Yet it was not the law that maintained Candler's independence through the 1899–1901 merger wave. Coca-Cola survived because its most likely purchasers had more pressing concerns. One conceivable buyer, the American Sugar Company, was caught up in anti-trust cases and battling to hold its members together.

Given the nature of Coca-Cola's outlets, four other kinds of companies might have added Coke syrup to their jobbers' range of merchandise. The American Soda-Fountain Company, formed in 1891 out of the nation's four leading manufacturers of soda-water apparatus, made no attempt to extend its product range because it was a disguised cartel, managing prices and allocating territories. Other possible buyers included pharmaceutical manufacturers such as Drugs Inc., which was rumoured much later to be moving on Coca-Cola. A third candidate could have been one of the patent medicine firms, which were spending more on advertisements during the 1890s than Coca-Cola earned. Candy-makers were another possibility, as shown by events at Pepsi in 1931. For a long time, Coke's competitors were not other lolly-water firms but 'ice-cream and confectionery and chewing gum, and...most things that clamour for a nickel'.[7] Combined US spending on those treats in 1935 was three times greater than for all soft drinks.

When Coca-Cola did change hands in 1919, its new owner was not a rival soda-pop maker but a syndicate of financiers. Without support from bankers and sugar oligopolists, The Coca-Cola Company might not have survived the 1921 slump. It experienced strong growth and profits from rising sales and falling costs during the later 1920s, but again looked ripe for takeover with the ending of Prohibition after 1932. Brokers supposed that sales of all soft drinks would fall once alcohol returned to open sale.

A company is never too famous to be merged or acquired. In the 1980s, Proctor & Gamble 'evaluated whether to buy Coke or Pepsi'.[8] The fiasco of New Coke could have exposed Atlanta to a raider in 1985 had Goizueta not backtracked so totally and quickly. Even so, he had to admit that Columbia Pictures 'carried the earnings of this company' from its purchase in 1981 until about 1986.[9] Coca-Cola managers thereupon restructured their company through what could be called an insider takeover. First they bought back franchises, then they spun the bottlers off into a quasi-subsidiary, Coca-Cola Enterprises. Their third and simultaneous step was to give themselves share options. By those means, Coke's management got the benefits of a buy-out without the risks or opprobrium associated with the botched insider bid for RJR Nabisco in 1988, a deal documented in the aptly named book *Barbarians at the Gate*.

Despite Coca-Cola's dominance in the soft-drink industry, it remains a medium-sized corporation in terms of earnings, at around seventieth place in *Fortune*'s 500. Corporations larger than Coca-Cola continue to stumble. Since 1997, Coca-Cola executives have had to cope with a run of difficulties: calls for accounting reforms which would slash capital and revenue valuations; ructions inside McDonalds, Coke's largest customer; a jolt to growth from overseas revenues as the Asian crisis and its aftershocks hurt sales from Russia to Brazil; setbacks to its program of takeovers; and the largest health-scare recall in its history. In the final quarter of 1998, total sales volumes fell for the first time since 1954, and earnings were flat for two years from mid-1997. The Company then reported a $45 million loss for the final quarter of 1999 after writing down assets by $813 million. The Coca-Cola Company has no guarantee of survival as a stand-alone corporation. The 1999 departure of its CEO, Doug Ivester, demonstrated that its managers are secure only as long as their decisions mesh with the needs of monopolising capitals to get the price right.

The price of everything

Monopolising does not eliminate price competition. Rather, the rival monopolisers position their prices to sharpen other marketing tools to improve market share through differentiation, fixing and cutting.

Differentiation

Car makers were early in discovering the benefits of price differentiation. From the 1920s, General Motors offered a 'car for every purse', from a Chevy up to a Cadillac. In 1931, GM's president, Alfred P. Sloan Jr, comforted his finance committee: 'No prospect [buyer] is intelligent enough to definitely determine the weighted value of all the elements that enter into any particular car'. GM's price pyramid, allied with promotions for a new model each year, encouraged drivers to trade up one or two notches during a lifetime, chasing chrome as a status marker. [10]

IBM constructed its pricing pyramid to entomb customers and extract higher returns over time. The prototype of this trap was a 1920s printer designed so that its speed could be doubled by moving a belt from one wheel to another. For making this five-minute adjustment in secret, IBM doubled the rental.[11] This procedure set a pattern for the marketing of its electronic data processing. By the 1980s, IBM was shipping machines that were more powerful than the client had ordered; when the customer needed extra capacity, a technician would arrive to erase a couple of lines of software. A bill for a few million dollars would follow. The tactic was 'referred to internally as the "golden screwdriver"'.[12]

A lawyer working on the 1970s anti-trust case against IBM compared its pricing policies with a knife:

> Just as the part of the blade that starts the cut must be sharpened to as thin and as narrow an edge as possible, IBM's entry-level prices and profits were similarly honed down to get a wedge into the customer's data-processing room. Behind the sharp edge of the deeply cutting knife follows the broader and stronger body of the blade. Similarly, IBM's follow-on prices—and profits—for larger systems were greater.[13]

IBM's financial officer acknowledged that 'the optimal feature prices were established so as to yield substantially higher profit margins than the basic machines'.[14]

From 1960, Coca-Coca added to its range of soft drinks in order to build volumes and maintain price. Once soda fountains installed dispensers with three spouts, Coca-Cola needed its other flavours, Fanta, Sprite and Fresca, to make sure that Pepsi did not gush from those extra taps. 'This drive towards line proliferation ... was probably an attempt to escape direct product to product comparisons and, hence, lessen direct price competition'.[15]

Andy Warhol was wrong to claim that all Cokes are equally good. They are not all equally good for The Coca-Cola Company, where profits per litre differ according to the point of sale and the container size. The 600 ml (20-ounce) bottle is the most profitable, retailing at about three-quarters the price of a two-litre bottle. 'Coca-Cola ushered in our current packaging era away from lowest cost to highest value added—with its 1993 debut of the 20-ounce contour PET bottle'. A bottler found 'the best margins in 20-ounce', which it 'sold for 75 cents to $1.00 as opposed to about 50 cents on cans'.[16] Margins could be 15 per cent at fountains and as much as 30 per cent on vending machines; on supermarket sales they headed towards zero.

Sometimes Diet Coke will be on special in the supermarket. At other times it is be Coke Classic. These variations are aimed against Pepsi, not at each other. If an independent firm were marketing Diet Coke, its prices would not be linked to promotions for other Coca-Cola lines. The same goes for New Coke, which is not priced against Classic Coke but put up against Pepsi in the US Midwest, where its added sweetness appeals and drinking Classic Coke was not a religious observance.

Price-fixing
Input costs

A corporation which owns its raw materials can stabilise expenses, a reason for vertical integration. Because Coca-Cola did not take that route, it has had to defend itself against the possibility of predatory pricing from a monopoly supplier. In the 1930s, The Company

paid '40c a pound more to certain manufactures for certain ingredients to keep two sources of supply open'.[17]

In 2000, Coca-Cola joined Proctor & Gamble, Nestlé and 46
other manufacturers of consumer goods to operate an online marketplace to get bargains for the $300 billion they spend each year
on resources and services. The project promises a virtual monopsony across the US economy. Wal-Mart already exerts a similar
purchasing power by obliging its suppliers to absorb increased production costs.[18]

The sale price

Monopolising does not require one firm to buy up all its competitors. Just as often, a few large firms will agree to smooth movements
in their selling prices, the largest firm acting as market leader because
it has the resources to defeat any outsider selling below the approved
levels. The US Federal Trade Commission warned in 1960:

> When any two businessmen get together, whether it is a Chain
> Institute meeting or a Bible class meeting, if they happen to belong
> to the same industry, just as soon as the prayers have been said,
> they start talking about the conditions in the industry, and it is
> bound definitely to gravitate, that talk, to the price structure of the
> industry. What else is there to talk about?[19]

Throughout the 1950s, the managers of the heavy electrical equipment industry in the US engaged in what *Fortune* called a
'conspiracy' of price-fixing. On his way to prison, one of the executives protested that such arrangements were 'the only way a business
can be run. It is free enterprise.'[20] In 1973, a former executive with
the Swiss pharmaceutical giant Hoffman-La Roche, Stanley Adams,
reported the corporation to the European Commission's anti-trust
regulators for promoting 'fidelity contracts' under which retailers
received the most popular vitamins at competitive prices, but only
if they bought 90 per cent of their supplies from the firm.[21] In the
1990s, Roche returned to its malpractice in cahoots with six other
vitamin suppliers to apportion markets and set prices.[22]

One objection to monopolising is that it helps firms to put up their prices, and thus to keep profit rates above the average. Recently, free-trade economists have argued that corporations compete by reducing their costs rather than by raising their selling prices. In 1981, President Reagan's Assistant Attorney-General for anti-trust matters contended that profits went up, not because oligopolisation allowed firms to increase their prices, but 'because costs go down'. [23] According to the deregulators, monopolising contributes to the general welfare because its economies of scale are passed on to consumers in the form of keener prices.

Do these benefits flow to the consumer? When increases in productivity deliver a lower unit cost, the saving can be used to finance additional marketing, not to lower the selling price. With more than three-quarters of the fountain market in the 1950s, Coca-Cola raised prices at those outlets to accumulate funds 'to escalate the price wars' in supermarkets, and wrest sales leadership back from Pepsi.[24] The market leader for instant coffee, Nestlé, did not pass on the price benefits of 'increased efficiency' in the early 1990s but directed its higher rates of return into more marketing to stay in front.[25]

Lower costs improve services only for the big spenders. In a survey headed 'Why Service Stinks', *Business Week* explained that companies would rather lose custom than fix a problem. One utility company assigned six consultants to its top 350 customers and two to its 30 000 middle-ranking clients. The 300 000 domestic purchasers got a toll-free answering machine. Technology allows corporations to channel incoming messages according to the caller's spending profile, bought from a credit-rating agency. An operator will intercept a travel inquiry from a platinum card-holder within seconds. The expense of this service is recouped by not listening to the also-rans. Far from e-commerce providing buyers with the signals needed for the best choice, computers set up 'consumer apartheid'.[26]

Price cuts

Price cuts are only one tactic in a marketing strategy. A few are genuine fire sales, but most are ploys, like the clothiers who maintain a year-round table of specials to entice passers-by. Other perennial devices include the 'loss leader', where all the profit is sacrificed on one item to secure greater turnover for the rest of the stock. Around 1900, Sears led the way with 'penetration pricing' on its sewing machines and cream separators. The aim was not to get repeat orders for those durables but to attract their buyers back for the cornucopia of goods in succeeding mail-order catalogues, known as 'wish books'.

Free samples are the extreme end of price cuts as a sales pitch. The creators of Coca-Cola used this ploy. Asa Candler encouraged druggists to stock his product by distributing tickets to be redeemed at soda fountains. This approach reappeared in a 1950s promotion of six-packs, when supermarkets received bottles for resale at a fraction of a cent each. Coca-Cola passed around samples in East Germany to build a customer base in 1990, while PepsiCo was giving its product away on Rio beaches. Quaker Oats' isotonic Gatorade had 90 per cent of the fitness niche until Coca-Cola countered in 1993 with give-aways of Powerade.

When oligopolies dip into their reserves to sell at or below cost, the price reductions can be immense. Oil majors underwrite their outlets with cut-price petrol to punish any lowering of prices by independent suppliers near by. In 1998, Coke offered a 12-pack for $1.99 retail in order to penetrate Pepsi heartland in Kingston, North Carolina, where a 24-pack of Pepsi was selling for $6.99.

During 1998, Coca-Cola transferred $1.84 billion into its affiliated bottlers in Latin America to ward off price increases that would have cut volumes, lowered demand for concentrate and lost prospective lifelong consumers. Such losses are affordable in one territory for a short time because they are subsidised from the rest of the company's operations: 'If this process continues, the value of the advanced capital disappears'. [27] The end comes sooner to the small, the local and the new.

As a device for distributing profits within the soft-drink industry, price cutting operates differently at the three stages of distribution: wholesale, retail and consumer.

First, lower charges to wholesalers encourage them to push sales. In December 1999, Italian authorities fined Coca-Cola Enterprises $16 million for blocking its rivals' access to Italian wholesalers by offering them 'rebates and bonuses for stocking only Coca-Cola products'.[28] PepsiCo filed a suit against Coca-Cola, claiming that in the US The Company was 'threatening food service distributors with the loss of Coke if they dare to carry Pepsi…and by cutting off any distributors that decide to carry Pepsi anyway', making examples of them.[29] Not surprisingly, Coke had two-thirds of all fountain sales and PepsiCo less than a quarter. The Company plans to increase returns from sites where Coke is already sold by getting more of the customers to buy drinks, to choose larger sizes and to purchase a wider range of products—a campaign summarised as 'incidence, ounces and valves'.[30]

Secondly, discounts to retailers buy visibility and space. As the publisher of *Beverage Digest* explained: 'This is a distribution business. The bottler decides what goes on the shelf, and all the rest is just conversation.'[31] Some storekeepers have to be bullied, but more are enticed with up to $10 000 worth of Coke equipment and a free refill. Stores that accept this bait must then participate in a set number of promotions each year. The area sales manager might vary the price charged for two-litre bottles, from 89 cents up to $1.49, as a reward or punishment according to how co-operative the retailer has been. An Italian supermarket chain complained in 1999 that Coke's 'supply contracts require minimum display space and a certain number of refrigerators in stores. Such conditions have forced [the chain] to sell Coke products at a loss.'[32]

While a good price is a reason for drinkers to buy, 'too good a price may offer little reason to sell', since the margin for the retailer will be too small.[33] Retailers accept this burden because marketing has made Coke Classic an essential line in their shops. A court in Texas ordered The Company to pay for arranging with store-owners to promote only Coca-Cola products. Evidence showed that the aim was to make 'rival brands all but invisible'. One agreement signed in 1998 stated: 'Coca-Cola products will occupy a minimum of 100 per cent of total soft-drink space'. Coca-Cola called the verdict of anti-competitiveness 'incorrect' because there had been 'too much competition'—the monopolising competition that kills competition.[34] Coca-Cola has adapted the block-booking tactic developed by

Hollywood studios to push the rest of its beverages: '"You want Coke? Okay, but you'll have to take some Sprite, too".'[35]

Resistance from retailers has grown until they have become big enough 'to force better prices from manufacturers'.[36] In 1980, Nabisco's top ten customers took one quarter of its sales; ten years later the share going to the majors was up to 44 per cent. A comparable shift overtook soft-drink retailers when the proportion taken by the top five chains rose from 30 to 50 per cent between 1993 and 2000.

Mega-retailers extract concessions from manufacturers. Since the mid-1980s, they have demanded payments of $9 billion a year for shelf space, known as 'slotting fees'. Nine out of ten stores impose these charges, which bring in 20–40 per cent of the profits for some chains. According to *Beverage World*, this marketing expense can 'raise consumer prices, "squeeze" small manufacturers out of the marketplace and enable large competitors to "purchase" an economic advantage'.[37] A few stores also demand 'failure fees' for giving shelf space to a new line which has not sold as well as promised within ninety days.

The third truth about monopoly pricing is that no firm cuts its prices to enrich its customers. When executives at Coca-Cola Enterprises speak about customers they mean the retailers, not the drinkers. We consumers are the last to be considered. Coke sales managers think of their consumers as pussycats. 'Partnering' is the new buzzword for the deals between suppliers, bottlers, wholesalers and retailers to pass costs on to consumers.[38]

Consumers are striking back, learning how to take advantage of the concessions aimed at retailers. Many consumers delay purchases until goods are on special. Their canniness led Sears to abandon 'rebates' in favour of 'everyday low prices', as General Motors and P&G had done.[39] The volatile mix of promotions with price cuts has posed 'a problem for...brand loyalty' among consumers, creating the 'disloyal drinker'. [40] Half the cola-buying population will switch brands to get the weekly specials. To stem this leakage, PepsiCo introduced frequent-guzzler points to be traded for $300 million worth of Pepsi Stuff—T-shirts, hats and jackets—which turn loyal customers into perambulating billboards.

The marketing package is more profitable than bursts of price competition. An in-store price cut will lift sales by 49 per cent; a price cut coinciding with print advertisements draws 79 per cent extra custom; a combination of lower prices and in-store displays brings a 193 per cent boost. In the mid-1990s, the cola giants chased supermarket share by deploying all three at once. In combination, they attracted a 350 per cent increase.[41]

Lower prices and higher marketing costs reduced Coke's unit return, reviving Asa Candler's 1899 problem of costs rising faster than volumes and depressing the rate of profit. Coke sought to compensate for the souring of Third World markets from 1997 by lifting syrup prices to US bottlers. PepsiCo was not far behind. The rivals were also united in balancing these hikes with 'more aggressive marketing support' for retailers. The immediate effect was to slow sales, but the contraction of effective demand reduced the pressure to invest, thereby delivering higher revenues per unit from existing production and distribution systems over the short term.[42] Another effect was to force smaller bottlers to sell out to Coca-Cola Enterprises or Pepsi Bottling Group. The CEO of DPSU bottling recognised that concentration among retailers would 'cause more consolidation on the bottler side'.[43]

Hitting the spot

Pepsi provides a case study in the uses and limits of pricing. Until confectioner Charles Guth took Pepsi out of bankruptcy in 1931, it had 'for nearly thirty years...been one of the 1000 also-rans'. Guth had the brew reformulated to give it a 'competitive resemblance' to Coca-Cola, and sold it in 12-ounce beer bottles at 10 cents. [44] He then halved his price, while Coke stayed at 5 cents for 6 ounces. Through the depressed 1930s, Pepsi's sales improved behind the slogans 'Two large glasses in each bottle' and 'Twice as much for a nickel, too'. A 1938 survey itemised why some consumers preferred Pepsi. Housewives on a budget 'can serve two glasses from one 12 oz bottle'; the working man 'requires more liquid than he gets out of a 6 oz bottle'; children 'want all they can get for a nickel'; and 'coloured people...want sweet drinks in quantity'.[45] Nonetheless, price-driven promotions never moved more than one gallon for every ten of Coke.

After 1946, Pepsi's reliance on price as a selling strategy had less appeal to cashed-up consumers. By not increasing its bottle price, Pepsi was also caught by the post-war inflation, which dragged profits down by two-thirds to $2 million in 1949. Its share price dropped from $40 to $8. The bottlers rebelled and installed an erstwhile Coca-Cola executive, Al Steele, as Pepsi president.

Steele knew that Atlanta's weak spot was its arrogance. Woodruff's coterie refused to mention Pepsi by name, having convinced themselves that there was no other cola but Coke. Coca-Cola was about to encounter what *Fortune* had said in 1938 it needed most, namely, competition.[46] Steele agreed with Woodruff that what existed at Pepsi deserved to perish. He reinvented the product by reducing its sugar content, reformulating its flavours, shedding its scruffy label, standardising its image on packages, trucks and signs, and introducing 6 and 8-ounce bottles. His next step built on Pepsi's strength in take-home sales from the supermarkets, which were following car-owning families to the suburbs. 'Shoppers wanted more, but they wanted to carry it home with ease', which was difficult with Coke's trademark small bottle.[47] Then Steele went after the young who had not yet taken the oath of allegiance to Coke as the essence of all that America stood for.

Results were uneven but strong enough to rattle Coca-Cola. Its sales and profits dropped in 1954 for the first time in twenty years. In the six years to 1955, Coke's share of the carbonated market slipped from two-thirds to a half, while Pepsi's doubled to a third. Thus, when Coke met its first substantial competitor, it lost on every measure. From operating a near monopoly, Atlanta had to learn how to lead in the duopoly waltz. Coca-Cola increased sales by 10 per cent in 1959, copying the methods of its chief imitator with a range of bottle sizes. Advertising remained a major expense, with Coke spending $50 million in 1961 and Pepsi $34 million. The battle has been on ever since.

Pepsi's move into salted snacks and fast-food outlets after 1960 led Atlanta to sneer that this upstart was not really in the beverage business. In 1965, the US Federal Trade Commission had approved Pepsi's acquisition of Frito-Lay with ten-year bans on tie-in advertisements and on further PepsiCo takeovers in that sector. In the 1990s, PepsiCo began linking its marketing of soft drinks with salty snacks to cut better deals with fountains and stores, exercising what its chairman Roger Enrico called 'the power of one'.[48] In practice, that means positioning PepsiCo beverages beside the more popular Frito-Lay chips, and using the high retail margins on the latter to leverage shelf space. In 1999, Frito-Lay held 60 per cent of US crisp sales, having fulfilled PepsiCo's original offer to its previous owner: 'You make them thirsty, and I'll give them something to drink'.

Enrico needed every advantage by then, because PepsiCo no longer had a major national market to call its own. In the early 1980s, the firm had lost the Philippines, where it had been outselling Coke by three to one; by 1998 the balance had reversed. Its venture into post-apartheid South Africa also flopped in the face of what its spokesperson called Coke's 'entrenched monopoly'.[49] Pepsi lost Venezuela in 1996 when Coke seduced its bottler away, a manoeuvre for which an arbitrator penalised Atlanta $94 million.[50]

The loss of Venezuela spurred PepsiCo to seek revenge in Japan, which contributed a sixth of The Coca-Cola Company's profits. Coke had 90 per cent of Japan's cola sales. In 1998 PepsiCo joined with Suntory Brewery, so that its entry was freed up by a local oligopoly. Supermarket sales of Pepsi doubled by mid-1999, as did the number of convenience stores stocking its products.[51] Atlanta reacted by amalgamating its Japanese bottlers. Once again, intensified competition resulted in greater concentration.

Because beverages contribute only a quarter of PepsiCo's sales and profits, the US soft-drink industry is becoming less of a global duopoly, and more like a set of niche monopolies. In the late 1990s, Enrico abandoned any attempt to dislodge Coca-Cola from its dominant territories, at home or abroad. Instead, be bought Tropicana in 1998 to consolidate PepsiCo's grip on US supermarkets. Late in 2000, Quaker Oats accepted PepsiCo's offer to exchange $14 billion worth of shares. The deal gave PepsiCo control of Gatorade, which holds 84 per cent of the sports-drink category. The merger had flow-on benefits to the distribution of PepsiCo's Tropicana's fruit juices, while Quaker Oats' sweet snack lines complemented the merchandising of Frito-Lay's salty ones on supermarket shelves.

Enrico has focused on countries that can still be entered freely, including India, where PepsiCo sales overtook Coca-Cola's in 2000. But with PepsiCo earning only a 3 per cent return on investment overseas in soft drinks, its impact on that global marketplace will remain marginal.[52]

Store-to-store fighting

In the USA, Coca-Cola's strengths have always been regional. By 1931 its per capita sales in the South were twice the national average.[53] In 1998, consumption of all soft drinks ranged from a low of 39 gallons per capita in the Pacific Coast to a high of 70 gallons in West Central.[54] The goal for Coca-Cola therefore is to get its national averages closer to its regional bests.

The US market is also segmented between off-the-shelf sales in grocery stores, cold drinks for on-the-spot consumption, and sales at fountains—or what is known as shelves, coolers and counters. The purchase-triggers for the buyer of large warm bottles are price and in-store display. In the other two domains, price is less potent than location, which is everything if it can be an exclusive arrangement.

To secure exclusive deals with the fast-food chains, Coke took losses on its fountains until the early 1990s; since then, returns have been slightly better than break-even. Recent offers from PepsiCo have helped McDonald's and Burger King to wring more concessions from Coke. For instance, Atlanta struck exclusive deals with McDonald's by offering franchise-holders enough free syrup for as many as 90 000 drinks.

The front line in the cola wars is now over the positioning of visi-coolers and vending machines, which gave material form to Woodruff's precept of keeping Coke within arm's reach of desire. In 1999, Coke added 300 000 vending machines to PepsiCo's 150 000. Competition for these sites is fierce, with both companies offering concessions to retailers. How widely the machines can be distributed also depends on the culture: they can stand in the back alleys of

Oosaka and never be vandalised, whereas in parts of Brooklyn the refill trucks get hijacked. The vending machine is another reason why the soft-drink industry cannot 'freely be entered'. Newcomers have neither the capital to install their own machines nor the range of products to fill the slots.

Potent brews

In the late 1930s, US Assistant Attorney-General Thurmond Arnold put many corporate executives in the dock for anti-trust violations. In 1941, he praised Coca-Cola for maintaining 'its predominant position through advertising to convince the public, not to coerce dealers or control distribution'.[55] Coca-Cola could afford cleaner hands than other firms, because it had not faced a nationwide competitor before the Pepsi revival. Arnold might have revised his opinion had he read the correspondence that preceded Coca-Cola's 1963 merger with the coffee-maker Duncan Foods. Those documents supply the collective wisdom of a monopolising competitor.

The coupling of Coke with Duncan's did not reduce competition among coffee merchants. Although The Company already owned an instant coffee line, that segment of the market was where Duncan's was weakest. Hence, their deal was neither a vertical nor a horizontal integration but more a parallel investment on which Coca-Cola would make small savings in distribution and promotion. Yet the move was predicated on monopolising tendencies within the coffee market. Coca-Cola had decided to purchase Duncan Foods after 'careful investigation' indicated that Proctor & Gamble's purchase of Folger, another coffee-maker, would 'strengthen and stabilise the national picture instead of creating even more competitive drives than now exist'.[56] Thus, Atlanta did not see expansion by P&G as a threat, but welcomed it as a move which would suppress wildcats, with their erratic pricing. The entry of bigger players into the coffee market promised much the same results that Coca-Cola and Proctor & Gamble would have achieved had they formed a trade association to stabilise prices.

Atlanta encouraged Charles Duncan to merge by emphasising how vulnerable his profits would be if he continued to stand alone.

In sharing its expertise on predatory competition, Coca-Cola exposed the mechanisms of restrictive trading. The following extract from its advice to Duncan speaks of how a major supplier can keep itself the market leader.

According to Coca-Cola:

1. A Regional Coffee Roaster has a certain vulnerability—market-wise. The more powerful National Brands can move against him at will with 'off-Labels' and other promotional schemes designed to capture a slice of the Regional Roaster's business.

2. In periods of rising coffee prices the 'Bigs' can, by their greater purchasing power, 'squeeze' the Regional Roaster by either pur-chasing more advantageously or actually 'holding prices' down in the Regional Roaster's area, thus denying the Regional Roaster a higher price—or forcing him to give the 'Big' a competitive advantage if he moves up in his prices.

3. The highly competitive nature of the coffee business makes it very costly for a given Brand to consistently gain an increasing share of the market from his competitors. This would appear to be particularly true of the Regional Roaster versus the 'Bigs'.[57]

This catalogue of perils points to why competition was less than perfect far beyond the realms of coffee and cola.

Coca-Cola has been proved right about how the coffee Bigs would behave. After twenty years, Coca-Cola's own lines still had only 2.5 per cent of the market in 1998: 'As Coke and Pepsi have done to their competitors in soft drinks, so General Foods and Proctor & Gamble have done to coffee, increasing their combined shares in the USA from 57.8% in 1983 to 65.8% in 1987'.[58] Globally, Nestlé dominates, leaving P&G in fourth place with only 8 per cent. Nestlé defends the market leadership of Nescafé 43 through price differentiation, selling International Roast into the cheaper end of the market and promoting Gold Blend for candle-lit occa-sions. To get into supermarkets, Starbucks has allied itself with Number Two, Philip Morris–Maxwell House. Coke's experience gives little sign that the coffee market is contestable even by another beverage titan.

Market entry is free only if you can afford the sales effort, as advertising executive David Ogilvy spelt out in 1964:

> It is becoming progressively more difficult for small companies to launch new brands...If you don't believe me, try launching a new brand of detergent with a war chest of less than $10 000 000. Furthermore, the giant advertisers are able to buy space and time far more cheaply than their little competitors, because the media owners cosset them with quantity discounts.[59]

That analysis is truer today, when Ogilvy's $10 million is more likely to be $100 million. When two Japanese Coke bottlers merged in 1999, the new chairman explained: 'We will also be able to get a great deal more for our sales-promotion budget and better terms on production and materials procurement'.[60] Under the aegis of marketing, advertisements and brands are lions in the path of every firm's entry to any market.

Sale of the Century

It is only consumption which, by destroying the product, gives it the finishing touch… Consumption is thus a phase of production.

Karl Marx, 1859.[1]

PART FOUR

Sale of the Century

CHAPTER 8 # The Force of the Market

Let us face it; we don't want a free market economy either.
James B. Farley, president, Coca-Cola Export Corp., 1959[2]

Marketing was an unexplored area before the late nineteenth century, when universities began courses in 'distribution'. Few of the professors knew of each other's existence; they had no textbooks, and their examples were often rural products. The Harvard Business School in 1914 defined marketing as 'a way of emphasising that more than salesmanship is involved in getting a firm's products and services sold'.[3] Practitioners formed national organisations in 1915, taking their name from a market economy, although their prescriptions were in conflict with the ideology of an invisible hand guiding the market towards equilibrium.

Free-trade economists attribute superhuman powers to market forces, picturing them as natural elements against which resistance is futile, indeed counterproductive. Such reverence neglects history. The market-directed economy is not a universal phenomenon but another creation of the recent past. To equate the exchange of an amulet for a bushel of grain in an Indian village 4000 years ago with the trade in copper futures that rocked the Sumitomo Bank in 1996 is to exorcise capitalism of its spirit. Only wishful thinking can transform a 3800-year-old beer container from Canaan into a prototype for the Coke bottle. The gulf between a marketplace and a market economy becomes blatant when we contrast haggling over a hand-woven prayer rug in Qum with meeting the price set for ten metres of broadloom in a carpet emporium today. Negotiations over price as the essence of the marketplace began to fray with the introduction of recommended retail prices in the 1850s.

Managing demand

The market-directed economy gathered force from the late nineteenth century through the management of demand as well as of supply. Alfred D. Chandler Jr has challenged free-trade fantasies by documenting how the visible hand of managers co-ordinated production and distribution, yet he made his obsequies to the dogma he had interred:

> The new bureaucratic enterprises did not, it must be emphasised, replace the market as the primary force in generating goods and services. The current decisions as to flow and the long-term ones as to allocating resources were based on estimates of current and long-term market demand.[4]

Who supplied those estimates if not managers and their market researchers? Indeed, Chandler himself acknowledged that:

> By the middle of the twentieth century the salaried managers of a relatively small number of large mass producing, large mass retailing, and large mass transporting enterprises co-ordinated current flows of goods through the processes of production and distribution and allocated the resources to be used for future production and distribution in major sectors of the American economy.[5]

If so, what was left for the market to generate?

More fundamental is why mass marketing attained its importance for the era of monopolising capitals. Corporations must counter two pressures bearing down on their rate of profit. First, workers strive for higher wages, shorter hours and better conditions. Secondly, other firms offer competing products. In the hope of at least maintaining profit rates, capitalists introduce machinery to make more goods more cheaply. Meanwhile, their rivals are doing the same. Because each firm looks forward to a growing share of the market, they collectively produce more than the total buying power. The additional commodities must be sold if any profit is to be realised from their production. Marketing tries to take up the slack. Across the twentieth century, the sales effort has involved a broader range of tactics beyond advertising to brand logos, merchandising, packaging, product placement, public relations.

This phenomenon, which some call overproduction and others under-consumption, further distinguishes the Crown monopolies of the eighteenth century from the corporate monopolisers who emerged after 1870. In 1776, Adam Smith accused the Crown monopolies of 'keeping the market constantly under-stocked' in order to 'sell their commodities much above the natural price'.[6] That option narrowed as investments boosted production far beyond Smith's imagining. Moreover, sales estimates are not neutral. When Stanley Adams reported the price-rigging of vitamins, he explained how such figures were used to set a level of production 'always slightly below world needs in order to keep demand and therefore prices high, even if it means factories not producing at full capacity'.[7]

Supply instigates demand as often as demand summons supply, in a cycle as unstable as it is self-perpetuating. More products require more sales; more sales require greater consumer spending; greater spending depends on higher incomes; improved wages provoke the installation of more productive machines; those machines make more products; and round they go, the expansion of each corporation running counter to the stability of the economy as a whole.

Competitors and workers disrupt this cycle in ways which marketing cannot prevent. The investments required to cope with these twin disturbances can push down the rate of return even when the volume of profit is maintained. Such a fall does not 'manifest itself in absolute form, but rather as a tendency'.[8] The decline is best understood, not as an irreversible obstacle, but as a 'barrier' to be 'constantly surpassed'.[9] Indeed, 'the same factor which brings about [that] tendency in the rate of the profit to fall, again produces a counterbalance…and more or less paralyses its effects'.[10] That capitalism survived the booms, wars and depressions of its monopolising era indicates how effective its self-defences are.

No single means has been found to end the conflicts built into capital's expansion. Wars, monopolising and marketing play their contrary parts in keeping the system going, but at some risk to its prospects. No matter how effective the sales effort becomes, it chases the rise in production. Marketing is never more than a temporary and marginal solution to overproduction.

Demand is more elastic than many economists allow, but not as elastic as marketing executives pretend when they suggest that consumers can be persuaded of almost anything. Marketing executives argue that economic downturns can be overcome by 'demand management', including more advertising and sharper selling. Firms are not readily convinced. Their financial officers see marketing as a cost. The marketing department stresses its power to increase sales, boost profits and add value to the brand. The expense is immediate and actual, the benefits hypothetical. Management failure is as prevalent in selling as in manufacture.

At issue is the extent to which marketing can alter demand. Its success is in moving buyers from one product to another, whether among brands—from Coke to Pepsi—or between near substitutes—from rented videos back to movie tickets. Marketing can also encourage consumers to realign their spending between categories—from food to gambling. To demonstrate that consumer preferences are malleable at their margins, however, is not to prove that total demand is elastic.

Mass marketing could do very little to lift industrial capitalism out of a depression, because such a turnaround required a demand for the machines that made consumer goods. By encouraging consumer demand, mass marketing could eventually stimulate some extra production, which would help wear out existing machines and so bring nearer the day when new capital investments were required. The making of that equipment would, in turn, help to wear out the machines that make machines and—in the long run, *ceteris paribus*, and other clichés—the economy would begin to grow again. Such an indirect effect, however, was too slow and too slight to be of much use in overcoming a protracted slump, such as in the 1890s or the 1930s. In general, mass marketing followed the rhythms in the great transformation towards over-consumption in the West.

Mass luxury

From the late nineteenth century, US corporations expanded by increasing the volume of sales per capita, by entering new territories, and by penetrating additional social groups. Once the railways, the express companies and the postal service had installed continental delivery networks, the *Ladies' Home Journal* (c. 1883) and *Saturday Evening Post* (c. 1897) could carry word of branded commodities to millions of homes. Yet most US families spent the bulk of their incomes on basics: food, not dining out; clothing, not fashion; shelter, not décor. Before 1900, chocolate bars were a luxury, with only three small makers.

Other forces veered beyond the control of any sales manager. Between 1890 and 1910, the US population increased by a third to 88 million, but the increase slowed after 1920 with the imposition of immigration quotas. Meanwhile, the more prosperous reduced their family size, leaving more pocket money for each child.

The number of automobiles almost trebled during the 1920s. General Electric promoted domestic appliances to spread demand for its power across the day. Those brief boom years were based on mortgaging future incomes to instalment purchases. At a time when 'real wages rose very slowly', debts soon 'checked the rate at which consumption expanded'.[11] Once most farmers had their Model-T's, the fall in new orders deepened the Great Depression.

In the 1930s, spending on advertising collapsed, both in absolute terms and as a percentage of disposable personal income. Gross advertising revenue for the *Saturday Evening Post* and the *Ladies' Home Journal* dropped by two-thirds over the decade. Meanwhile, the number of radios went from 13 million to 45 million, including 7 million installed in automobiles. Radio carried advertisements into homes newly connected to electric power. In the 1930s, the number of domestic refrigerators leapt from 2 million to 20 million, allowing families to keep more perishables at home. After the economy slumped again in 1937, New Dealers pursued hundreds of anti-trust suits to crack the monopoly pricing which, they believed, was limiting sales, and hence employment.

In the post-war decade, the share of income spent on food fell from 45 to 25 per cent, while the proportion needed to pay off durables increased. Early in 1955, *Life* proclaimed the arrival of 'Mass Luxury' for the USA; discretionary household income 'rose nearly sevenfold from 1941 to 1958'.[12] General Motors led the way to 'dynamic obsolescence'.[13] As a measure of this growth, the Fuller Brush Men, who began their rounds in 1906, sold a million brushes and mops in 1919 but 109 million in 1960. Between 1945 and 1959, the number of air-conditioning units went from 100 000 to 11 million. US spending on sport and recreation grew from $1 billion in 1950 to $265 billion in 1990. The number of US residents making overseas trips took off from fewer than a million to 45 million.[14]

The upsurge in sales inside the USA in the 1950s compensated for the fact that its corporations were cut off from half the world by the Iron and Bamboo Curtains. That loss was also balanced by renewed opportunities in Western Europe and the opening up of Japan. After a slow start, the Japanese trebled their national income during the 1960s. Although policy-makers had absorbed Keynes's stress on the need to manage investment to keep up effective demand, few predicted the length or strength of the boom that charged into the early 1970s. Experts were still suspecting a depression in every slowdown when J. K. Galbraith published *The Affluent Society* in 1958.

During the last fifty years, personal, corporate and government debt has expanded to boost total effective demand. The marketing of credit by finance houses, retailers and manufacturers has resulted in many households, firms and governments owing more than they earn each year. By 2000, US householders had borrowed the equivalent of 165 per cent of private disposable income, a third of the loans stoking the stock-market boom. Corporations owed three-quarters of their combined gross product. Meanwhile, the US economy in effect borrowed $300 billion a year to finance its way of life.

Standardisation

To say that capitalism needs marketing to stimulate demand is one-sided. Because capital expands through cycles of production and consumption, marketing has to be merged into the technical aspects of manufacture. In the 1760s, Josiah Wedgwood integrated product development with marketing after he learnt that 'selling from samples and catalogues required the products to be completely uniform in quality'. To that end, he strove 'to make such *Machines* of the *Men* as cannot err', and switched to cream-glaze because it showed fewer variations than green-ware.[15] Across the intervening centuries, production has been arranged to facilitate sales.

Standardisation applied to both selling and production. The rule book had been written at National Cash Register, where John H. Patterson believed salesmen were made, not born. In the same spirit of regimentation, Sears Roebuck broke its mail-order procedures into twenty-seven steps, while Proctor & Gamble imposed its distribution network on its retail customers. 'Reputation is repetition', Bruce Barton never tired of reiterating to staff and clients at his advertising firm.[16]

At Rowntree, the English confectioners, a financial director proposed emulating rival Cadburys by moving away from 'a wide and constantly changing range' of sweets, each needing its own sizeable promotional budget. Instead, the firm should reduce its varieties, standardise its packaging and focus its advertising to profit from 'a larger, individual turnover'.[17] Standardisation would also reduce the investment required to meet demand for the most popular lines. Unable to decide between quality and quantity, the Rowntree board pursued both, thereby achieving too little of either.

Uniform marketing was easier for The Coca-Cola Company with

its single product. The Candlers went some way towards standardising Coke's look and taste. Brand names and trademarks were
patented, and typefaces and colours on Coca-Cola's advertisements
fixed. Asa Candler enforced exact measures and temperatures for
every glass. Yet his sales manager recognised by 1909 that The
Company needed more than brand names, logos and point-of-sale
advertisements to push up Coca-Cola volumes. It needed to take
selling seriously:

> No man who isn't a salesman has any right to direct the advertis-
> ing policy of any concern...I travel approximately thirty thousand
> miles a year feeling the pulse of the country, carefully studying con-
> ditions, meeting the trade with our salesmen, seeing and studying
> their problems, and endeavouring to meet and know the difficul-
> ties they are up against.[18]

When the Woodruff syndicate arrived in 1919, The Company still
'lacked a sales organisation in the modern sense of the word':

> Between Sales Manager Dobbs and a salesman in, for instance,
> Seattle, there was hardly anything except large stretches of geog-
> raphy. If the Seattle man concentrated on decorating hotel lobbies,
> it took a long while for his dereliction to show in sales.[19]

The Company's secretary—a Mr Rainwater—assured the Bottlers'
Association in 1924 that the new management was having 'a won-
derful effect in the uniformity of things'.[20]

In 1926, Robert Woodruff sacked all the salesmen, then re-
employed most of them as servicemen. His attention to service drew
on his experience with auto dealerships. Woodruff's servicemen
were more regimented than Coke salesmen had been. In 1930,
Atlanta produced a training film for soda-fountain operators. The
D'Arcy Advertising Agency in 1938 laid out thirty-five rules for the
promotion of Coca-Cola, starting with 'Never split the trade mark
"Coca-Cola" in two lines', and ending at 'Approval on sample
posters should be obtained from Atlanta before releasing from
lithographer'.[21] Conformity overwhelmed the look, content and

promotional treatment of major brands. Coca-Cola did not invent our image of Santa Claus out of nothing, but it did standardise his appearance in its 1930s advertisements by reducing his livery to its own red-and-white.

Woodruff knew that codifying advertisements would not sell another gallon unless Coke the product was put within 'arm's reach of desire'. Gas stations had to be induced to display the product prominently, thereby placing two iconic fluids side by side. Coca-Cola also needed coolers in confectionery shops if it were to compete for impulse buying against Wrigleys and Life Savers. Twenty years elapsed between 1909, when a 21-year-old from Georgia Tech offered his vending machine to Coca-Cola, and the mass distribution of a top-opening version. In the mean time, the Coke bottle had been shaped to help shopkeepers find a Coke in the dark of their ice-boxes and cupboards. Even so, one Canadian bottler complained:

> Where is Coca-Cola all of this time? Back in the dark with the liver and the tripe. Our sales methods have put it there, and they will keep it there if we don't change them…[M]ore likely it is catching dust in the back room, waiting to disappoint some customer who expected a cold one, or acquiring a coat of filth and smells in the ice box—or it may be serving as an island refuge for a cockroach who went astray in the ice tub.[22]

A dedicated icebox became the solution. In the 1930s, Coke's automatic coin machines were priced between $55 and $325, while factories and offices paid $15 for coolers. In the 1950s, the closure of soda fountains gave even more importance to vending machines.

Consumer sovereignty

To conceal the coercive consequences of mass marketing, its champions trumpet consumer sovereignty. Yet the objective of marketing is to sap life from that phrase. The more marketeers boast of fashioning consumer preferences, the more evidence they provide that marketing is propaganda for capital's expansion. To escape from the charge of brainwashing consumers, marketing practitioners concocted the notion of latent demand, in which the unconscious turns out to be a treasure chest of branded commodities.

Marketing awakens the consumer to the truth that we were born to shop. Instead of being responsible for inducing us to want a warmed toilet seat, the marketeers claim that they have articulated a desire which had remained latent for millennia, when our species had not realised that we were genetically programmed to perch on porcelain bowls. Far from being guilty of implanting the needs of capital in the brains of consumers, marketeers are freeing us from the restraints of a Puritan superego. Although claims about a pre-existing catalogue of wants do not square with the behaviourists' proposition that advertisements can inscribe human preferences, the contradiction hardly matters. In the halls of marketeering, consistency rests in the massaging of business confidence through the power of positive thought.

Who knows what is best for the consumer—the marketeer or the consumer advocate? Confronted by their critics, marketing managers accuse environmentalists and feminists of interfering with free choice, and assert that consumers know what is best for them. Corporate clients, of course, are sold the opposite.

The marketeers want consumers to be passive in accepting their advice on how to be active when shopping. They flatter us as discriminating when we buy as we have been told, but insult us behind our backs by treating us as just another product to be marketed. The publisher of the *Ladies' Home Journal*, Cyrus Curtis, explained why he published that monthly:

> The editor thinks it is for the benefit of American women. That is an illusion, but a very proper one for him to have. But I will tell you; the real reason, the publisher's reason, is to give you people who manufacture things that American women want and buy a chance to tell them about your products.[23]

Curtis had earlier doubled his subscription price to attract better-off readers who would draw in better-paying advertisers.

Similarly, in 1994 Rupert Murdoch's newspapers assured the marketing trade that their pages would 'Deliver more "Purchase

Active" Readers' than their rivals.[24] That self-promotion revealed two connections between the mass media and the market. The first is that the media deliver audiences to marketeers, not advertisements to audiences. Secondly, what the media promise to deliver are the 'Purchase Active', not just the largest number of us. A US national weekly proclaimed 'We spare our advertisers unimportant readers'— that is, those who will not or cannot spend.[25]

The failure of New Coke in 1985 was not proof of consumer sovereignty but a testament to the previous ninety-nine years of promoting the classic version. Gatorade could win a greater share of US soft-drink sales than New Coke because it did not offend conditioned responses. PepsiCo's Roger Enrico narrowed our right to choose when he enthused over one of the 'great consumer-products truths':

> Companies are in business to fulfill the desires of consumers. We're not in business to dictate those desires. Consumers have the right to a voice. If people want a caffeine-free drink and we know they like the taste of Pepsi, then if we just make a Pepsi without caffeine, how the hell can it fail? It's impossible.[26]

Had PepsiCo executives operated according to this account of how a product succeeds, they would have been fired for incompetence. Every marketing manager knows that without promotion, distribution and merchandising, any reformulated product will flop. Or, as the publisher of *Beverage Digest* advised, 'No matter what else you do...you have got to have the display in the store'.[27]

Although marketeers cannot dictate our desires, they do affect what is available to fulfil our needs. My preference in soft drinks is for a sparkling mineral water because it limits my intake of calories and I enjoy its tingle in my mouth. Yet for every chance I have to pay for my favourite beverage, I end up buying ten Diet Cokes, because that is the only low-cal drink in visi-coolers or vending machines. Advertising has not drawn me to Diet Coke, but its maker's dominance of retailing channels means that I either take it as the best of a bad lot, or go without a cold drink on a sweltering afternoon.

Marketing expands some choices by restricting others. The limits on our choice are disguised beneath a proliferation of styles and brand names. When chain stores opened in 1886 they stocked six categories of product; by 1911 they were carrying 25 different categories, with 270 varieties, including 23 teas. Since 1980, the number of items stocked by grocery stores has trebled. A few of these new lines offer new uses, but most of the changes have been to the sizes and shapes of packages, or to the flavourings and colourings added to otherwise interchangeable formulae.

Coca-Cola is no longer just a Coke, but a Sprite, a Fanta, or a Powerade. A Coke can be New, sugarless, caffeine-free or cherry-flavoured. Variants of Gillette razors, M&Ms or Colgate toothpaste occupy shelf space to lock out rivals, not to fulfil our latent needs. In response to Crystal Pepsi, Coke launched Tab Clear to contain choice: 'we wanted it to die' to kill the category so that clear colas would not weaken existing brands. According to Coke's marketing *honcho* Zyman, 'The consumer has too many choices'.[28]

Information-free

In advancing their doctrine of consumer sovereignty, economists contend that advertising supplies information we cannot gather for ourselves. Advertising, its apologists assert, is a charge on consumers for knowledge that we could not afford to acquire individually, because the time required to become our own experts, like the expense of hiring a consultant, is prohibitive.

The founding professors and practitioners of marketing had no such delusions. In the 1920s, W. D. Scott relied on suggestibility rather than the power of reason. In his eyes, the customer-cum-audience was equivalent to the mob, a rabble to be tamed by being inculcated with a desire to spend. Edward Bernays, the founder of public relations and nephew of Freud, agreed in 1928 that 'the group mind does not think in the strict sense of the word. In place of thoughts it has impulses, habits, emotions.'[29]

The continuing absence of the knowledge needed for markets to operate competitively prompted Bill Gates to promise that his products would bridge the chasm between high theory and retail practices by supplying consumers with all relevant information regarding prices and quality. We would then make instant bids on our credit cards. Meanwhile, marketeering—including Microsoft's—strengthens the oligopoly of knowledge that blights our ability to make informed choices.

George J. Stigler recognised that consumer knowledge approaches perfection as choice approaches zero.

> [A] perfect market is one in which the traders have full knowledge of all offer and bid prices...[so that] a perfect market may also exist under monopoly. Indeed, in realistic cases a perfect market may be more likely to exist under monopoly, since complete knowledge is easier to achieve under monopoly.[30]

Stigler was 'more impressed by the ignorance of economists than by the ignorance of consumers'.[31]

Marketeers also set about confusing price signals. When Coca-Cola in Japan had to ward off lower-priced unlabelled soft drinks during 1995–96, it did not resort to price-cutting but relied on packaging and advertising: 'Almost each week we gave consumers a new contour option of a different price so that they could never figure out Coke's real value against cheap imports'.[32] Such marketing violates the assumption that the market operates on price signals, and is another instance of the disinformation that refreshes capital.

Evidence to back up textbook assumptions about informed choice from marketeering remains meagre, while documentation for capital's fostering of ignorance among consumers is abundant. E. H. Chamberlin's 1933 admonition stands:

> Selling methods which play upon the buyer's susceptibilities, which use against him laws of psychology with which he is unfamiliar and therefore against which he cannot defend himself, which frighten or flatter or disarm him—all of these have nothing to do with his knowledge. They are not informative: they are manipulative.[33]

The 1950s hope that advertisements would become more informative and less manipulative has never been fulfilled. Instead of seeing more of the fact-heavy copy that distinguished a David Ogilvy advertisement, we have had a mountainslide of content-free claims in the manner of 'cleans your breath while it cleans your teeth'. With the triumph of television came the drift of advertisements from 'the verbal and literary to the audio-visual', which emphasises mood over information.[34] A 1992 report on the marketing of instant coffees in Australia found 'little factual information relating to the product...Factual information on important decision-making variables (such as price, quality, bean mix and taste) that might reduce buyer and seller search costs is often distorted.' For example, the campaign for 'the Nescafé premium range contains attractive shots of Kenyan landscapes and wildlife with a background of harmonious tribal music'.[35]

For all the billions that Coca-Cola spends on marketing each year, its promotions never tell us what we are drinking. Instead, The Company lobbied for an exemption from a 1938 law requiring that ingredients be specified on its bottles. Atlanta was allowed to say merely that they contained Coca-Cola Syrup—which was a trade secret. When did a Coca-Cola TV commercial last tell you how much caffeine, sugar or phosphorus you will consume if you choose Coke? Similarly, Pepsi's taste test does not address these matters. The Ray Charles commercials for Diet Pepsi perpetuated this vacuity by assuring the viewer 'You've got the right one, baby, uh-huh'. Coca-Cola's slogans—'Delicious Refreshing', 'The Pause that Refreshes', 'The Real Thing', 'Always Coke' and 'Just for the Taste'—defy the analysis available from consumer-advocacy publications. Semioticians may discern signs as wonders among the Coke neons above Times Square and Tokyo's Shibuya station, but even those magi cannot read Coke advertisements as product specification sheets.

Much of the information offered in advertisements could not matter less. One tactic is to highlight a property common to all brands. Another is to play up an irrelevant difference. In the early 1950s, the marketing agency for Minute Maid grabbed at the fact that juice from fresh oranges contains traces of contaminants from the peel: 'Doctors prove Minute Maid is better for your health than oranges squeezed at home'. Definitions of 'pure' and 'fresh' have become marketing niceties. Minute Maid had to withdraw a 1988 advertisement promoting its 'Premium Choice' as coming 'Straight from the Orange' because its juices had been pasteurised.

Secret formulas are not peculiar to Coca-Cola, but remain the norm for every commodity. Capital-induced ignorance is rife in Monsanto's reluctance to let us know which foods it has genetically engineered, a hesitancy shared by the Soft Drink Association. Regulation is the source of such knowledge as we receive about most products, even if it is in tiny print.

Freedom from the market

The illusion that the force of the market carries the economy towards competition is replicated in the identification of market-directed economies with political, cultural and social freedom. This association is as false historically as it is misleading about contemporary life. For a start, the impact of marketing on the media contravenes the 'primary freedom of the press', which rests in its 'not being a trade'.[36] Marketing executives shy away from sponsoring anything controversial—even sedate radio discussions on abortion, with all sides represented. Although James Twitchell celebrated *Adcult USA*, he was scathing about its subversion of free speech; editors killed stories to satisfy the advertisers who pay for 80 per cent of print media and for all of so-called free-to-air radio and television. These market-driven interventions are as authoritarian in their effect as any censorship by the state.

The *Wall Street Journal* reported in 1997 that 'major advertisers are wielding their economic clout to change the rules of magazine publishing' with companies 'demanding advance notice about stories'. *Esquire* killed a short fiction about a gay man after Chrysler warned that it might pull advertising if the story were published.[37] PepsiCo paid $5 million to Warner Brothers and Madonna to associate its soft drink with her 'Like a Prayer', but never screened the commercial because of complaints about its sacrilegious imagery. The point is not to offend. Because of the backlash provoked by

NYPD's nudity and language, its first series 'carried no spots from any of the mainstays of prime-time drama...No fast-food restaurants...No soft drinks'.[38]

At Coca-Cola, marketing as censorship included discrediting researchers who found that sugar was bad for children's teeth. By 1951, San Francisco schools had banned soda pops in canteens, and The Company feared that if more school districts followed suit 'the loss to us may well be in excess of a million gallons of syrup a year', not to mention the lost opportunity to condition children's palates.[39] The Company knew it had to respond with care. To deny all responsibility for tooth decay might provoke further attacks, and any defence that stressed multiple causes would be an admission of partial guilt. The same caveat applied to shifting 'the spotlight off sugar and...on such preventive measures as fluoridation of drinking water'. In particular, Atlanta had no desire to inflame anti-fluoride campaigners. Expert evidence was another dilemma; science had to appear independent, which meant that it 'could not be completely controlled'.[40]

Silencing critics had the virtue of being straightforward, even if the tactics needed to be indirect. When the *Journal of the American Dental Association* suggested that the *Boy Scouts Handbook* caution members about sweets and soft drinks, it faced opposition from the vice-president of the Georgia Institute of Technology, a Scouts board member, who warned against any 'attempt to influence the next revision of the Handbook for propaganda purposes'.[41] A Los Angeles bottler had fellow Rotarians persuade their program chairmen not to invite anti-sugar speakers. The most pestiferous critic was Cornell Professor Clive M. McCay, who publicised findings that Coca-Cola rotted rats' teeth down to the gum line. Woodruff talked with Cornell's president about McCay 'many times' after the university's vice-president had failed to 'soften' McCay's stance. The chancellor of the University of Kansas volunteered the suggestion that 'chloroform was in order'.[42] In the 1950s, McCarthyism allowed businesses to brand their critics un-American. When the communist *Daily Worker* reported McCay's complaints against Coca-Cola, Coke's public relations people decided that 'somebody is following the party line'.[43]

More to Atlanta's taste was nutritionist and Harvard professor Fredrick J. Stare, who recommended Coke by name in his 1954 ideal teenage diet, and who plied Woodruff with copies of his journalism and requests for research funds.[44] Closer at hand was a professor of dental hygiene at Emory University, John Haldi, who had co-authored a 250-page book arguing that 'sugar can be consumed in large amounts without causing dental caries'.[45] The Coca-Cola Company honoured Haldi for having 'served so well as our scientific adviser for many years'. In 1964, he 'handled another situation for us in a most capable and effective manner', convincing 'The Macmillan Company ... to delete a very damaging reference to "Cola" drinks from their elementary science texts'.[46]

As a relentless advertiser itself, The Company knew that rebuttals in one-off articles were not enough:

> We must find some way of presenting our case over and over and over again at frequent intervals. The most effective way of accomplishing this would be first of all to find an *entrée* into the good graces of some influential people in Associated Press, International News Service, and United Press.

The Company therefore set up a fund in collaboration with the National Confectioners' Association to arrange for the press to interview experts every two weeks.[47]

Orphaned

Marketing to children confirms the hollowness of a sovereignty under which the consumer is considered an object. As PepsiCo's Enrico put it: 'Tomorrow's kids nobody owns yet'.[48] Pre-school children have little knowledge of comparative prices or product qualities. Marketing encourages them not to discriminate but to want it all now. Because few pre-teens in the West work for their spending money, they lack one essential that alerts adults to marginal utilities.

The determination to catch consumers as young as possible has never been confined to the tobacco industry. For Coke, the aim has been to capture drinkers before they settle on an alternative cola. The Company long ago recognised that a child 'probably enters the Coca-Cola market about five years after entering the soft-drink market'.[49] The mission has been to educate the palate from a sweeter taste towards the astringency of the Real Thing.

Because elementary-school pupils are becoming aware of environmental threats, food values and advertisers' ploys, Coca-Cola has sought to capture these smart kids through exclusive deals with their schools. As one Coke bottler admitted: 'You don't want to be locked out of an institution like that for that long'.[50] A student's choice is thus limited to Coca-Cola lines, which means no milk. Although US federal laws forbid the sale of soda pops from lunchrooms, the ban does not extend to vending machines in corridors and gyms. The promise of corporate funding if the school sells a set number of cases in one year has encouraged administrators to bend their own rules prohibiting vending machines being on during lunchtime.[51] These sponsorship monies are not a gift but come out of the students' pockets when they pay for their drinks. With a captive market, The Company pushed up the can price from forty cents to a dollar.[52] The number of school districts with exclusive marketing deals rose from 46 to 140 in the year to May 1999, but to only 175 a year later, following parent and teacher disquiet.

Other US high schools have accepted company promotions as pedagogy rather than propaganda. During a 1998 'Coke in Education Day' in a Georgia school, the economics lesson became a tutorial on Coke's marketing, while social science classes heard about the benefits of Coke's globalisation. Afterwards, students in red or white tops formed the word 'Coke' for a photograph. A 19-year-old who had worn a Pepsi work shirt received a one-day in-school suspension for being 'rude and disrespectful'.[53] Company spokespeople sounded relaxed, but the principal knew better than to joke with a sponsor dangling millions of dollars. Retail is becoming the most prominent of the three Rs. As a promoter put it: 'If you have no advertising in schools at all, it doesn't give our young people an accurate picture of our society'.[54]

Generation why

With the abolition of almost universal child labour in the West came the specification of stages to maturity between infancy and adulthood. Adolescence appeared as a term around 1900. In the 1930s, the words 'teenager' or 'adolescent' were applied only to high-school students, not to those who worked. In 1910, only 15 per cent of US 14 to 17-year-olds were in school; the figure reached 70 per cent thirty years later. Segmentation of the market by age could not gain sway unless students had money to spend, which they earned after school or in vacations. The publication of *Seventeen* and *Ebony* from 1944 provided vehicles for targeted marketing by age.

Marketing to younger customers was also stimulated by changes in the methods of production. As technological turnovers accelerated, experience could be a liability as much as a fount of wisdom or profit. The young in years were better able to operate the newest equipment, an advantage which continues through the echo boomers of the 1990s, with their skills on the Internet. Ownership remained with their parents and grandparents, but the creative power from new technologies slipped towards younger adults. The emergence of this filiarchy underpinned the youth culture of the 1950s, rock 'n' roll, and the student rebellions of the 1960s.

Coca-Cola had recognised in 1947 that although 15 to 19-year-olds made up only 10 per cent of the US population, they were buying 21.5 per cent of its product. Coke associated itself with that age band through a radio show featuring comedian Spike Jones. Then, in 1950, The Company made a flat-footed attempt to tie Coca-Cola to back-to-school fashions. The debacle foreshadowed how much difficulty Woodruff's generation would have in dealing with customers a quarter their age. Selling the universal beverage had not prepared Atlanta for any segmentation of its market, other than along race lines. Pepsi had nothing to lose by attaching itself to the young.

In the 1950s, only a rebel without a cause would have worn the wrong shirt to a school parade. By the early 1960s, the young ones were becoming restless. The television commercial for the campaign included a shot of a helicopter delivering a vending machine to the top of a mountain, an image adapted from Federico Fellini's 1960 film *La Dolce Vita*, where a helicopter transports a statue of Jesus over Rome. The Pepsi Generation in the USA of the 1960s was enjoying even more of the sweet life.

The background document for the Pepsi Generation concept is treasured as the 'Necktie memo':

> [The memo] never mentions soft drinks. It's all about neckties…
> Are ties essential? Not at all. The only purpose they serve is to express the personality of the buyer. Which leads to the point of the memo: The necktie doesn't make the buyer feel good about the manufacturer of the tie; it makes him feel good about *himself*. So don't extol the virtues of your product. Extol the virtues of the consumer who selects your product. Find out who he is: then praise him for being himself.[55]

This selling of the 'self' got away from the marketeers. If Frankenstein's monster turned nasty because he was denied love, the 'Me' generation became ungovernable because marketeers inculcated self-love to the point of narcissism. Resisting conscription for Vietnam proved central to 1960s dissent because the cohorts who had to fight that war had been softened up to expect a Pierre Cardin suit, not a body bag. Revolutions come when rising expectations are cut short, not from the persistence of misery.

Marketeers jumped on board the Sixties with counter-cultural ads. Even Coke had its 'I'd like to buy the world a Coke' from the flower-powered throng. Radicals have complained that protest was commercialised when mass marketeers discovered that 'hip is the cultural life-blood of the consumer society'.[56] Thomas Frank has gone some way to show that the commercial drive had come first. Throughout the 1950s, Madison Avenue had been split over the value of its Men in Grey Flannel Suits. A Now Generation had to speak against the majority of Then people before 'admen looked at the counter-culture and saw…themselves'. Although the Pepsi Generation is now confused with baby-boomers, the pitch was to all 'Those Who Think Young'. Creativity in advertisements and male fashion sparked attitudes which could be expressed by angry older men.[57] Dr Dichter, the bogeyman of Motivational Research in Vance Packard's *Hidden Persuaders*, slipped across to the psychedelic to apply depth psychology to the style of advertisements rather than to their content.

Today's marketeers must strive to package generations which are more fissiparous than ever. Niche markets that differ in income, gender, locale and ethnicity have been further fragmented along age lines, so that a 12-year-old will be turned off by what fascinates an 11-year-old. Marketing executives discovered that the audiences for Madonna were as polymorphous as their idol:

> Marilyn Monroe...had an image that was...unique and well defined. She was luscious as a Hershey's bar, shapely as a Coke bottle. But in a world where Coke can be sugar free, caffeine free, and cherry flavoured (and Pepsi can be clear!), just one image isn't enough for a superstar. Madonna is available as Marilyn or as a brunette, a Catholic schoolgirl, or a bondage devotee.[58]

Madonna's representations of sexuality were just as fluid as her fans' self-identification. This girl was as materialistic as any marketing machine could desire. The problem for those using her to sell was that her sisters, clones and admirers did not all desire the same commodities at the same time, or for long enough to mount a profitable campaign. The organisation person now assembles a career from a jigsaw of jobs. Consumers, like corporations, are using multiple brands to construct such identity as remains possible.

The anxieties that US marketeers exposed when they pinned the label Generation X on 17 million youngsters were mild compared with the panic induced by the arrival of their successors, the 60 million born into Generation Y between 1979 and 1994. In the USA, only two out three members of this age bracket are Caucasian, one in four lives in a single-parent home, and three out of four have working mothers. This cohort not only continued to influence their parents' choice of drinks for the fridge, but also doubled their own spending between 1987 and 1994. Generation Y found their way to Pepsi's high-caffeine Mountain Dew by word of mouth, just as they enjoyed the Sprite ads that mocked celebrity endorsements to proclaim 'Image is nothing. Obey your thirst.'[59]

Since 1992, the teenage segment of the market has grown twice as fast as the total population. By 1994, they were spending $90 billion annually and influencing as much again in their parents' choices. Teenagers are responsible for a rise in sugared sodas against diets. In 2006, their numbers will exceed the boomer peak of 1976, and their effective demand will be far greater. This Millennial Generation is talking small, hoping to become better parents than their own, yet flashing like fireflies with electronic gadgets.[60]

Coke switched its approach to the young. Yo-yos are out. In three months of 1987, the computer-generated geek hero Max Headroom 'doubled positive feelings towards Coke among 12–19-year-olds'. Pepsi attempted to do the same with XL as a half-diet version for Gen-X-ers. To profit from the current attitudes, Coca-Cola sends youngsters onto the streets to hang out for informal focus groups. 'We can't make ads for them that have people jumping up and down singing', admitted Coke's Zyman. Pepsi has the advantage of being accepted as a tradition of the new, its set image being to change with the times. Still, as PepsiCo's senior vice-president for brands acknowledged: 'We have a dual challenge. We have to keep the original Pepsi Generation involved with the franchise, and we have to enrol the new generation'.[61] Meanwhile, Coca-Cola hopes that, with advertainments and brand loyalty, 'all ways' will not rule out 'always'.

CHAPTER 9 # Adtopia

The Fruit Label Company...worked with Universal Home Video
to stick ads for *Liar, Liar* on six million apples.

New York Times, 26 February 1998

The British newspaper proprietor Lord Northcliffe overturned the
economic organisation of the press in 1896 with his halfpenny *Daily
Mail*.[1] In the USA, *Munsey's Magazine* was already billing advertisers per thousand copies instead of a flat fee for each column
inch. From then on, print could become mass because other businesses subsidised its cover price with advertising.

Around 1880, barely a dozen US companies—most of them
patent-medicine makers—outlaid more than $100000 on adver-
tisements. Within ten years, about a hundred were spending that
sum. In Britain, Lever Bros spent £50 on advertisements for its
soaps in 1886; under pressure from an adversary, its marketing bills
over the next twenty years amounted to £2 million.

This flood of cash transformed the appearance of publications.
Typeset classifieds gave way to illustrated displays. News layout was
also altered; newspapers introduced the 'jump', in which a story

would begin on one page and conclude several pages on, obliging the reader to churn through wads of advertisements.

These changes to the look and quality of advertising indicated its new purpose. Whereas old-style advertisements had sought to sell what had been produced, corporate advertising hoped to alter what was being sought. Corporate advertising has only a nominal connection with the hustling that has brightened marketplaces for thousands of years. Until the 1870s, print advertisements had come from shopkeepers or auctioneers drawing attention to other people's produce. Monopolising added three features: placement by manufacturers, brand names, and marketing.

This monopoly-era advertising did not plop out of capitalism fully formed, but registered the rhythms of that system. Total outlays in the USA grew from $200 million in 1880 to $542 million in 1900; they thereafter increased at about the same rate as consumer spending until the Great Depression, when the ratio fell by half. The rate of growth stayed low until after the Second World War, having reached its nadir in 1945. Then it soared. Expenditures in the USA went from $5.7 billion in 1950 to over $200 billion in 1999.

Mind control

For firms to expand by creating new markets, they had to colonise the minds of their domestic populations. One prerequisite was to overcome people's faith in thrift by advancing debt and indulgence as virtues. The promotion of each branded commodity stimulated a generalised appeal to want more. Buying a Chevrolet on hire purchase nourished the mentality in which it was right and proper to enjoy more Cokes. The 1950s master of Motivational Research, Dr Ernest Dichter, advised:

> In the promotion and advertising of many items, nothing is more important than to encourage this tendency to greater inner freedom and to give moral permission to enjoy life through the use of an item, whether it is good food, a speedboat, a radio set, or a sports jacket.[2]

To convince people to buy what they had never thought of needing, advertisers at first replaced religious inhibition with secular guilt. Once customers felt the lack of something other than Jesus in their lives, advertising could offer them redemption. In the 1920s, soap manufacturers had funded a Cleanliness Institute, which reinterpreted the maxim that cleanliness was next to godliness as meaning that families should bathe more often than on Saturday night. Listerine had been sold only to hospitals until 1926, when its owner diagnosed halitosis as a social disease. One of the founders of behaviourism, ex-professor John Broadus Watson, joined the J. Walter Thompson advertising agency where he devised a campaign for Johnson's baby powder. In a 1925 lecture, he explained how he had increased its sales by making the mother who did not use it 'feel bad, that she was less of a mother, not really a good mother'.[3]

Advertisers raided every school of psychology. Freud's *Introductory Lectures on Psychoanalysis*, published in New York in 1922, diffused the idea that humans were not wholly rational and so were amenable to suggestion. Had Freud analysed the good life as portrayed in corporate advertising, he would have recoiled from its embrace of instant gratification. A young Marshall McLuhan decried the infantilism of a 1950 *Time* cover of 'the globe sucking a Coke'.[4] The zones of arousal in the pleasure palaces of commerce have never been confined to the oral; advertising penetrates every orifice and all five senses to profit from what Freud called 'polymorphous perversity'.[5] Advertising has suffused every layer of consciousness with encouragements to consume until we inhabit a super-saturated solution of purchase signals. Advertisements alter consciousness, yet leave each generation believing that its appetites are natural.

As part of the post-war swing towards in-depth psychology, both industry and academe repackaged Freudianism as Motivational Research. This conversion helped James M. Vicary to sucker Madison Avenue with its own pseudo-science when he claimed that his projection of the subliminal message, 'Drink Coke', onto a movie screen had increased fountain sales. The eagerness with which advertisers bought Vicary's scam exposed how they saw their tasks.

In contrast to the Freudians, the Behaviourists developed an ideology for the exploitation of both consumers and producers. Marketeers became the school's field workers and factory managers its laboratory assistants. Advertising agencies took techniques developed to calibrate the attentiveness of workers by measuring the dilation of their pupils and turned them into a means to quantify the appeal of commercials. Corporate advertising was also linked to industrial psychology through research on labour discipline. Within those jaws, it became easier to sell people a sense of personal inadequacy.

Few of us are so stupid that we respond to the 'brazen wink of untrue propaganda', unless it accords with some strand of our experience.[6] Persuasion will not succeed unless we are susceptible to its blandishments. Only in that sense, we are agents in our own subordination as much as in our resistance, whether to particular brands or to the entirety of Admass. Which chord do advertisers strike?

The lost chord

Throughout the 1920s, more employees were becoming dissatisfied with their work as companies standardised manufacturing, selling and administration. Workspaces were redesigned to 'supervise every movement' as a means of quickening the throughput.[7] Steel chairs gave offices the look of factories; clerks went from nibs and ledgers to typewriters and adding machines. Advertising fed off the sense of inadequacy induced by this standardisation. More than ever, workers lost the sense of fulfilment from seeing a product or service through to completion. The particularisation of labour made their achievements appear ever more alien. Shopping for mass products promised liberation, but also intensified the need to work harder and longer to afford them. Consumption became a snare in which to reclaim the product of one's labour. To make this surrogate acceptable, advertisements ceased to scold, and emphasised the positive in every purchase.

In Wagner's *Ring*, the giants are promised a goddess as payment for their constructing Valhalla, but Wotan breaks his contract. The giants then demand a mound of gold high enough to block their view of the beauty they are forgoing. Under monopolising capitals, workers are offered a pile of commodities to conceal their loss of fulfilment at work.

Advertising propagates this promise as an ideal society, Adtopia. Critic Richard Simon located Adtopia as following on from Karl Mannheim's schema of four overlapping phases of Utopian thought: first, two millennia of religious enthusiasm for the end of the world; secondly, celebration of reason by liberal humanists; thirdly, a conservative reaction by reliance on the *status quo*; and, fourthly, revolutions for social equality. Then came 'Adtopia' as a Cold War reaction against 'communism and socialism'.[8]

Although Soviet imagery idealised the producer while advertising glorified the consumer, both required their creative artists to picture life not as it is, but 'as it should become'. Advertising pivots on a contrast between 'before' and 'after': 'after' you have bought you will be happier than you were 'before'. The thousands of commercial messages that we encounter every day constitute a serial sermon on how to achieve an earthly paradise. Michael Schudson identified the aesthetic style of advertising as 'Capitalist Realism', the counterpart of Socialist Realism. Capitalist Realism 'is thoroughly optimistic', offering to solve every problem with 'a particular product or style of life'.[9]

When advertisements became 'the official art of modern capitalist society', post-1945 painters struggled to see and be seen through a blizzard of commercial imagery.[10] Minimalism and pop were not antithetical but alternative ways of resisting the snow jobs. Abstractionist Mark Rothko eschewed figuration for fear that any object he depicted would turn itself into 'merchandise', as happened to his canvases in the hands of his dealers.[11] Andy Warhol mimicked the repetitiveness of Admass in his *Green Coca-Cola Bottles* (1962), which showed seven rows with sixteen bottles each. Claus Ollenberg parodied the gigantism of affluence with his soft sculptures of mammoth burgers.

Monopolising

Controversies persist over how advertising aids the concentration of ownership. The *Saturday Evening Post* editorialised in 1910 that advertising 'is the small man's chance to win on the sheer merit of his goods and the brains that he puts into pushing them, against the brute strength of the most powerful trust'.[12] Two years later, after the US Supreme Court ordered the break-up of the Standard Oil Company, Harrison King McCann, co-founder of the McCann-Erickson advertising agency, held the sales effort of the various Standard Oil companies together by directing of all their publicity. In 1930, McCann promoted his services under the heading "Fascisti All!':

> The bundle of rods which is on the US ten cent piece; the red-strapped fasces that lay over the left shoulder of the Roman Lector; the name of the Italian Fascisti—all these registered names say strength is in union. This is the kind of strength acquired by an advertising agency of many offices... of many accounts widely diversified.[13]

At the same time, the J. Walter Thompson agency promoted itself to corporations by quoting the president of the Guaranty Trust of New York, who welcomed advertising for its acceleration of 'the process whereby the world's productive activity is becoming centralised in the hands of those who are best equipped to carry it on'.[14]

Few any longer pretend that advertising favours the small. Rather, a constant complaint has been that the expense of advertising erects a barrier against entrants and allows incumbents to extract higher prices. The abundance of evidence for those outcomes does not close off debate on the connection between monopolising and its advertising because the barriers to entry are constructed out of the entire armoury of marketing. Economists find expenditures on advertising easier to compute than the varied and concealed outlays on marketing. Hence, the experts have satisfied themselves that advertising has a minimal effect on concentration. Such research neglects the sales effort as a whole. For example, in 1982, when both Proctor & Gamble and PepsiCo attempted to enter the soft cookie trade, Nabisco defended its leadership by price cuts and reclaiming shelf space. The two well-financed oligopolies failed because they did not have the manufacturing capacities or distribution networks to keep up the quantities needed to dominate the supermarket aisles. The entrants could afford to advertise but not Nabisco's panoply.

As one prong for monopolising competition, advertising is sharpest when products are distinguishable primarily by their packaging and promotions, notably for soap and detergents, where manufacturers offer almost identical products under a variety of brand names. Two Australian government reports found that these practices lead to further concentration:

> Substantial retail shelf space is taken up by the different brands of those two dominant companies in the industry thus 'drowning out' the products of newcomers. The practice acts to complement high advertising budgets of these concomitant companies to prevent efficient new entrants obtaining a significant share of the market.[15]

> A ban on advertising and promotion...in these circumstances would not assist the entry of new sellers into the market. Indeed, in the absence of advertising, new entrants whose products would be relatively unknown would be at a significant disadvantage when competing with the previously established and heavily promoted brands of the two main manufacturers.[16]

The detergent duopolists in Britain in the early 1960s had 80 per cent of cleanser sales between them, and were spending 10 to 15 per cent of their revenues on advertising. No sooner had they agreed to restrict promotion of laundry powders than their truce broke down because of 'uncertainty in the minds of each company about the competitive intentions of the other, particularly with regard to new products'.[17]

Contenders have to spend more to catch up with the reigning champions, whose brands have acquired recognition through decades of promotion. No conclusion about the effect of advertising on market share can be drawn by comparing the budgets of an oligopolist and a newcomer, because the existing firm usually has the advantage of being a known quality. The incumbent will also have tied up the best positions and timeslots in the media, where larger outlays attract discounts. After Philip Morris bought the American

Safety Razor in 1960, for example, its 'television advertising was "piggy-backed" on Philip Morris's cigarette commercials to gain lower media rates'.[18]

Advertising can shield oligopolies against new contestants, but cannot protect the majors against each other. Indeed, advertising became more important as monopolising made competition ever fiercer. When the burden of fixed capital costs prevents prolonged price-cutting, the sales effort becomes 'the principal weapon of competitive struggle' between corporations.[19] The advertising director of Pepsi in 1960 explained: 'Our sales are going up and up, and not because we "offer twice as much for a nickel, too". As a matter of fact we are giving less for a nickel. Sales increase because we have advertising that gets people into our ads and gets them to buy our product.'[20]

Advertising, therefore, is not an excrescence to be cut off an otherwise healthy body of monopolising capitals. As the chairman of the British group of J. Walter Thompson put it: 'One may dislike advertising and wish it didn't exist: but it is a vital part of the modern capitalist system and you cannot have one without the other. You can, of course, have neither.'[21] Capital can expand only after commodities have been exchanged for money. If capital cannot be produced by circulation alone, 'it is equally impossible for it to originate apart from circulation'.[22] Hence, the sales effort is vital. The waste is in the overproduction that makes mass marketing necessary. How necessary is advertising for mass marketing?

Effectiveness

The advertisers' power to make us respond to their entreaties has stern limits. Most decisions to buy are on the necessities that replenish our capacity to labour for next week's wage. A New York congressman observed in 1929 that the titans of industry and banking could hardly improve on 'the financial genius' of women who raised 'five or six children on a weekly envelope of thirty dollars'.[23] Workers must still manage their preferences according to the reality principle if they are to pay for the next round of goods and services. If advertising is omnipresent, it is far from omnipotent, because it is a bit player in the individual and corporate struggle for survival.

Despite the millions spent each year researching the impact of advertising, the causal link between a commercial and a sale remains elusive. In 1988, for example, Coca-Cola's Max Headroom commercials for New Coke ranked first in audience recall, but the cartoon robot could not slow the product's decline. Five of the seven consumer products with the most popular advertisements recorded static or depressed sales in 1993. Pepsi advertisements usually beat Coke's in recall tests, but Classic Coke retained its wide sales lead. In snapping up show-business names, Pepsi forgot that 'advertising that's entertaining doesn't always sell'.[24] Cigarette advertisements are more successful at stopping smokers quitting than at getting people started. As a Pepsi bottler explained: 'advertising claims alone never made the first sale'.[25]

Worse still for the advertisers' self-esteem, demand for some commodities expands without their inventiveness. Illegal drugs flourish on word of mouth, free samples and the quiet desperation of everyday living—forces more persuasive than official anti-drug campaigns, zero-tolerance policing or media reports of infection and overdosing.

The effect of advertising on sales is misjudged whenever it is isolated from the rest of marketing. Hersheys did not advertise their chocolate bars until 1970, fighting instead for primacy on the candy counter. Similarly, Life Savers flourished after 1915 once their new cylindrical packaging put them beside the cash register. Marion Harper, who won the Coca-Cola account for McCann-Erickson in 1955, spelt out the limits to what even his integrated organisation could provide:

> Advertising, for example, cannot produce a desirable product. It cannot establish an optimum price. It cannot acquire the best retail outlet. It cannot provide a convenient, saleable package, it cannot put the product in the best shelf position. It cannot maintain inventory. It cannot train a sales force. It cannot report on the product or on its own performance in the market. Advertising can affect

some of those but it cannot cancel their influence as roadblocks to sales.[26]

Yet the publisher of *Beverage Digest* went too far when he dismissed advertising as 'only the stitching between pieces of fabric'.[27] Without that thread, the garment of marketing would be unfinished.

Coca-Cola has been exceptional in spending more on promotion than on production. In 1930, The Company had made profits of $13 million on sales of $35 million and spent $5 million on advertising, prompting *Fortune* to remark on its 'virtually unique position in the manufacturing world'.[28] Most of Coke's outlays were 'incurred in order to alter the position or shape of the demand curve' for its products.[29] Between the wars, each increase in spending on advertisements 'added more to sales than to total costs'.[30]

Advertising as a proportion of earnings fell from 10 to 4.8 per cent between 1955 and 1970. By late 1997, however, The Coca-Cola Company was 'struggling to get earnings per share growth. Every dollar they spend in marketing [was] returning less and less in terms of revenue.'[31] For Coke to maintain its growth rate of the previous decade, profit margins would need to 'balloon in 10 years from 26.5 to 40 per cent—an improbable feat'.[32] The Company was again in the grip of diminishing returns, with its profit rate falling against its largest item of expenditure, the result of ever more extravagant campaigns.

Advertainment

The impact of Coca-Cola advertisements is sapped by their omnipresence: 'ubiquity becomes wall paper, and wall paper can get dull'.[33] PepsiCo's Enrico rated untruthful advertising and quality failure with 'being bored' as the 'three things American consumers won't forgive'.[34] He therefore chased 'calculated risks so massive, so attention-getting, and so well executed that the consumer's imagination is completely captivated—and business responds like gangbusters'.[35] John Sculley's years at PepsiCo had taught him that 'Marketing, after all, is really theatre... The way to motivate people is to get them interested in your product, to entertain them, and turn your product into an incredibly important event.'[36]

In that spirit, Goizueta gave Diet Coke a $1.5 million Hollywood-style opening night for its 1983 launch at Radio City Music Hall with a regiment of Rockettes. Promotions for the new line ran up $100 million in its first year. Similarly, McDonald's announced its arrival to the world by paying $20 million for a 'billboard location' opposite the Star Ferry terminal in Kowloon, and gave comparable sums for sites on the Champs Elysées and Tokyo's Ginza district. The marketeers were venturing into Advertainment, blending product promotion into amusements, with an emphasis on spectacle. Enrico admitted PepsiCo seemed to be 'a company that creates advertising' and makes soft drinks as a secondary interest.[37] At the farthest edge of event marketing, Coke contemplated laser-beaming its trademark onto the moon.

Some Coke addicts need to believe that New Coke was a ploy to energise support behind the Classic product. This explanation is a rural myth, but Enrico's 1986 book in response was part of Pepsi's marketing campaign. Its title, *The Other Guy Blinked*, was the ultimate challenge from a generation guying conventional wisdom. As the underdog, Enrico welcomed any publicity for soft drinks in general: 'Consumer interest swells the market. The more fun we provide, the more people buy our products—*all* our products.'[38] Pepsi's public relations manager confirmed: 'our advertising is really to create a hip, younger, more cutting edge, more fashionable [image]. It all goes back to entertainment and that kind of thing—and fun—it's really about having fun.'[39]

During the 1960s, television abandoned the thump, thump, thump of 'buy, buy, buy' that was driving viewers from the room. Instead, the commercial became another amusement. Audiences stayed 'glued to the tube so that they could watch a gorilla manhandle American Tourister luggage'.[40] Video players allowed audiences to skip to the commercials they enjoyed. To join that select band, agencies larded their commercials with high-tech. Payouts to 'sellebrities' were intended to make commercials zap-proof, to freeze the finger on the remote control so that the sales pitch at least got a viewing.[41] PepsiCo spent $3 million to make a

1996 TV spot which morphed a Harley, an Apple Mac and Ray Bans. Coke has tried 3-D. Once the commercial is seen, the after-glow of its star performer or gadgetry is supposed to leave the watcher feeling good about the product. Benetton's catastrophe ads broke through the tedium barrier but kept their horrors stylish, framing them with artistic references. To amuse and grab viewers, commercials have to turn over more frequently, placing a premium on novelty. The danger for the advertiser is that spectacle will offer 'a self-contained experience', resulting not in a sale but in 'virtual consumption'.[42] To limit that risk, marketeers turned advertisements into advertainments using two of the props of commercialised culture: screens and sport.

Screens

In 1981, Goizueta went looking for a takeover to boost Coke's earnings inside the USA. After buying Columbia Pictures for $700 million, he realised that screens large and small could promote his beverages to the world.[43] Columbia and Coca-Cola executives argued over whether pushing soft-drink sales on videos would add more to revenues than it would lose by annoying renters. The movie men pointed out that when Pepsi had attached commercials to the start of the *Top Gun* video, viewers pressed their fast-forward buttons. To avoid giving offence, Atlanta revived the practice of product placement used in films of the early 1930s, where Coca-Cola had appeared 'as part of the natural American environment...introduced in the most natural, simple way possible'.[44] At that time, screen advertising involved little more than a few slides, making placements the way to attract audiences. Even without such subventions, films are always a catwalk for the latest in dress, music, furnishings and food—spot it on screen and see it in the shops.

In the 1980s, a Columbia production, *Mac and Me*, starred an alien (not ET) who lived on Coca-Cola. In Brazil, Coca-Cola paid TV Globo to showcase its beverages on soap operas. PepsiCo paid to have its Taco Bill restaurants 'the only fast-food survivors' in the 1993 movie *Demolition Man*. Other corporations also funded producers to display their products. An executive handling these trades explained: 'We break a film down and tell the producers exactly where we want to see our clients' brands'.[45]

Marketing did not stop with the insertion of branded commodities. Coca-Cola forbade Columbia from decorating film sets in Pepsi's shade of blue. Producers had to ensure that the mood of their movies associated a Coke with pleasure as the film rolled to a happy ending. Television programs are structured so that their dramatic rhythms synchronise with the commercial breaks. 'In the future', according to Bill Gates, 'companies may pay not only to have their products on-screen, but also to make them available for you to buy...if the film has been tagged with commercial information'.[46]

Goizueta sold Columbia to Sony in 1989 for a capital gain of more than a billion, but he kept Coke's advertising oriented towards Hollywood. He shifted the account from McCann-Erickson to Creative Artists, which he felt was closer to the US pulse because its staff freelanced from the dream factories. In keeping with this approach, Coca-Cola forged a $100 million five-year alliance in 1999 with Universal Studios for 'extensive tie-ins' for music and movies, as well as agreement to replace Pepsi at theme parks to reach teenagers and young adults.[47] Meanwhile, PepsiCo struck a $2 billion six-year three-film deal for *Star Wars* 'co-branded soft-drink cans'.[48] These campaigns expanded on the thinking that had led Enrico to put up $5 million for Michael Jackson in 1983: 'You've got to do big things to keep the image of the product out there. Big news is what it's all about.'[49]

Sport

The biggest news for Coke has become sport, which it treats as a crossover to Advertainment. The Company adopted surfing as its third globally sponsored sport after champion Kelly Slater appeared in *Baywatch*.

'Biz-Ball' is the collective noun for business-powered ball games.[50] The rules of sponsored sports are adjusted to insert more advertisements into telecasts, on top of the brand names that smother the fences and players' uniforms. The value of this connection became clear when Gatorade signed up Michael Jordan. Revenues shot up by almost a billion to put Coke's Powerade back in second place. Gatorade's marketing chief said of Jordan: 'We manage him as if he were a brand'.[51]

Until the 1920s, Coca-Cola had been happy to have lads carry its bottles through the stands. The next step was to secure exclusive fountain and signage rights at sporting events. After 1945, Coca-Cola encouraged bottlers to back their hometown teams. The strategy went global in the 1970s when The Company provided $8 million for the World Cup in order to penetrate market-territories where soccer was tops. The chairman of the Atlanta venue for both the Braves and the Falcons happened to be the city's franchised Coke bottler, and The Company's theme pavilion at Atlanta's new ballpark has a huge Coke bottle on top.

Goizueta treated sporting deals just like any other investment: would they yield 20 per cent? His successor, Ivester, did his equations in terms of how many extra cases were sold. In 1998, Coca-Cola walked away from the Yankees after its managers demanded a five-fold increase in sponsorship fees, with no guarantee of a 500 per cent lift to profit. Once Atlanta allocates its millions, it demands every inch of coverage. It therefore dropped the Lakers when the team recruited a star player who was a high-profile Pepsi endorser. Coca-Cola was not going to put up a cool million to have someone pull out 'a Pepsi in the locker room during an on-camera interview'.[52]

The biggest sports news became the Olympics. The Company claims that its involvement dates back to 1928, when it did little more than pass drinks around the US team. Selling cases at the events has given way to using the venues and athletes as billboards for television coverage. The commercialisation of the Games at Los Angeles in 1984 saw The Company provide the local organising committee with $30 million; it also sponsored thirty national teams and the Torchbearers Program.

When Atlanta won the 1996 Games, Coca-Cola had to appease the Greek activist actress Melina Mercouri, who raged: 'Coca-Cola defeated the Parthenon'.[53] The Company's defence against allegations that it had bought the Olympics was that it already owned them. Coke turned from associating itself with gold medallists to linking 'the emotions of the fans—their pride, their passion, their patriotism—to Coca-Cola'.[54] The outlays needed to saturate Atlanta with Coca-Cola neared $350 million, including $60 million for NBC coverage. The ordinary running of The Company was left to one-third of its usual workforce. A Coke spokesman observed: 'The Olympics is our business'.[55]

CHAPTER 10 **Drinking the Label**

...alleging that in devising the trade name Pepsi-Cola the defendants had deliberately contrived an obvious and infringing anagram of Episcopal hoping to profit from some subliminal confusion in the minds of the consumer public, thus enhancing the value of their worldwide bottling franchises and their marketing skills by exploiting the plaintiff's historical success in proselytising its spiritual wares honed down through the centuries thereby defaming the venerable image of the church...

William Gaddis, *A Frolic of His Own*[1]

Six months after Asa Candler invested in Coca-Cola he was still misspelling its name as Coco Cola. His inclusion of a hyphen would remain spasmodic.[2] Standardised spelling was only just coming into vogue and so annoyed Harvard psychology professor William James that he proposed getting 'a dozen influential persons to agree each to spell after his own fashion and so break up this tyranny of the dictionary'.[3]

More influential than lexicons in imposing uniformity on commercial writers were US statute books and judgements dealing with trademarks. To gain protection from the law, trademarks required long and repeated use. The courts distinguished between the sudden discovery granted by a patent and the protracted usage needed to establish the worth of a trademark. A patent was vested in an individual, whereas trademarks recognised that joint-stock companies were taking over from the inventor-cum-entrepreneur. The defence of trademarks had relied on common-law property rights until the emergence of the corporation called for legislation.

The United Kingdom parliament passed a trademark bill in 1875. British tea merchants shifted from campaigns to 'Drink More Tea' to 'Drink Ours'. Brand names for teas became universal from the 1890s, when Thomas Lipton established a vertically integrated empire covering every stage of production and distribution, from plantation to grocer.[4] As a sign of the times, the organisers of the 1893 Chicago Exposition divided the national courts according to brands such as Westinghouse rather than product groups, such as gas stoves.

Edison's maxim that a patent was an 'invitation to a lawsuit'[5] applied to the 1870 US Trade Mark Act itself. The Supreme Court ruled it unconstitutional, and Congress re-enacted it in 1881. In overturning the original Act, the justices recognised the importance of brands as

> instrumentalities, aids...by which trade, especially in modern time, is conducted. They are the symbols by which men engaged in trade and manufacturers become known in the marts of commerce, by which their reputation and that of their goods are extended...and as they become better known, the profits of the business are enhanced.[6]

The number of trademarks registered with the US government rose from 800 in 1870 to 10568 in 1906. The latter figure was exceptional because until 1905 the federal law would accept only trademarks involved in overseas commerce, a stimulus to export.

A case of Koke

Asa Candler could not apply for a patent on the formula for Coca-Cola without dissolving its cachet of secrecy. Coca-Cola had begun life as a patent medicine and, like most purveyors of nostrums, Candler sought title over its name, not its ingredients. Protection of his trademarks became crucial, leading to scores of court cases.

In 1920, the Coca-Cola Company triumphed in a six-year lawsuit against the Koke Company of America, owned by Dr Pemberton's sometime partner, who claimed to have his original recipe. Supreme Court Justice Oliver Wendell Holmes penned a judgement for which Atlanta might have paid its advertising agency a million dollars:

> The name now characterises a beverage to be had at almost any soda fountain. It means a single thing coming from a single source, and well known to the community. It hardly would be too much to say that the drink characterises the name as much as the name the drink. In other words Coca-Cola probably means to most persons the plaintiff's familiar product to be had everywhere rather than a compound of particular substances.[7]

Thereafter, The Company spent $200 000 a year protecting its trademarks. By 1940, it had won 240 suits to uphold its exclusive use of 'Cola'. During 1949 alone, Coke was involved in 163 hearings, including three in Algeria and two in Venezuela, with 630 others pending across an alphabet of countries.

As Coke expanded offshore, trademark battles had to be waged in each new jurisdiction. In the United Kingdom, The Company had registered the rendering of its name in its characteristic script by 1922. Seven years later, it conceded that it had no rights in Britain over Coca or Cola, however spelt, when they were used separately, but asserted an absolute claim on them in combination. In 1941, the British Registrar of Trademarks rejected Coca-Cola's objection to the trademark Vitacola since there was no prospect of the latter's confusing the public.

Coca-Cola's arrival in Australia in 1937 saw several imitators including a Cocoa Kola. Coca-Cola's local manager demanded that the Melbourne upstart change its name and surrender all labels and showcards for destruction. The rival replied that 'cocoa' and 'kola' were generic terms, which was why he had not been able to register them. But Cocoa Kola was small and Coca-Cola huge. The prospect of paying lawyers all the way up to the Privy Council put paid to this antipodean ambition. The Australian press asked whether its courts would have defended the local drink had it been called 'Coca Koala'.[8]

The resurgence of Pepsi stimulated Atlanta's vigour against interlopers around the British Empire. In 1938, Woodruff sanctioned a flanking action by challenging Royal Crown Cola. Coke lost the case because it had waited four years to lodge its complaint, during which time Royal Crown had spent $3 million on advertising its cola and sold a billion bottles. After Atlanta challenged Pepsi in Canada, their dispute went on appeal to London, where the Lord Chancellor, less a man of affairs than Mr Justice Holmes, reflected that cola 'to me at least, has no particular meaning. I know nothing about trees growing in Africa, I am afraid. I assumed that the two words were just pretty well fancy words'.[9]

Judicial ignorance might be a trademark of the English bench, but in this instance his lordship spoke truer than he knew. Coca and cola were 'just pretty well fancy words' when used to represent the contents of Coca-Cola. Asa Candler had appreciated that he needed to retain just 'enough Kola and Coca to keep us from being charged by the Government with being frauds'.[10] As Justice Holmes had noted in 1920, the Koke case had reached the Supreme Court because the Circuit Court of Appeals had decided that Coke's 'trade-mark in itself and the advertisements accompanying it made such fraudulent representations to the public that the plaintiff [Coca-Cola] had lost its claim to any help from the Court'. Holmes accepted that 'the very thing sought to be protected is used as a fraud', but reasoned that, because Coca-Cola was no longer a patent medicine but a popular drink, its decades of deceit should not weigh against it. Any 'ignorant' consumers buying Coca-Cola in 1920 'with the hope for incipient cocaine intoxication' had only themselves to blame.[11] Holmes's indulgence left the lawyer responsible for defending Coca-Cola's good name 'just as appre-hensive' of its 'being held deceptive as I am of its being held descriptive... Neither position I think is correct. The correct posi-tion is that Coca-Cola simply means... a soft drink manufactured by The Coca-Cola Company'.[12]

Any use of the brand name on another product, even one that was not a beverage, threatened the reasoning on which Coca-Cola had won in the courts—to wit, that it was 'a single thing coming from a single source'. In 1903 Candler had endangered his com-pany's case by selling the right to use the Coca-Cola name for a chewing gum. So literally did The Company's attorneys take Mr Justice Holmes's wording that in 1941 they warned against includ-ing phrases such as 'Coca-Cola man' or 'Coca-Cola crowd' in advertisements, because those expressions implied that Coca-Cola could mean more than 'a single thing'. They got Life Savers to drop its Cola flavour, and made a fashion house delete Coca-Cola brown and Cola beige from its catalogue.[13]

A formula for success

Coca-Cola also made its name by maintaining the quality of its product through action against slovenly soda fountains and bot-tlers. Decades of police work went into standardising the taste. Candler's first imitator had been Dr Pemberton himself, who was offering 'a very poor article at a less price' shortly before his death in 1888.[14] By 1899, jobbers in Nebraska, Missouri and Minnesota were 'complaining bitterly of substitutes and frauds'.[15] Quality was as elusive as it was expensive. Although Atlanta spent a million dol-lars a year on control throughout the 1930s, soda fountains across the USA remained substandard, with only one in three operating the dispensers that The Company recommended. By the 1960s, The Company had twenty-eight test laboratories moving around the United States, and forty abroad.

As testimony to Atlanta's success in associating its brand name with consistent quality, people would decant the much cheaper Pepsi into Coke bottles before serving it to their guests. To counter this deceit, The Company's counsel suggested a series of advertisements 'giving voice in a subtle way to the guest's protest for this treatment'. He also cautioned that 'the word "genuine" in no event should appear before "Coke". The use of the word indicates that there is more than one "Coke".'[16]

The Company's concern to hide behind Holmes's 1920 ruling discouraged it from extending the Coca-Cola name in 1963 to its diet version, which was known for twenty years as TAB. One reason for switching from TAB to Diet Coke was that 'the only logical extension of the brand name Coca-Cola is in the diet category; to fail to preclude a competitor in this category would endanger future implementation of the project'.[17]

Holmes had further ruled that anyone who could brew Coca-Cola essence was at liberty to sell it. It was thus essential for Atlanta to keep its formula secret. Because public belief in a secret formula had become part of the brand image being defended, The Company obtained exemptions from laws that required the listing of ingredients. 'Coca-Cola syrup' was treated as explanatory, like 'shortening' on a packet of pastry. To print 'Contains Coca-Cola syrup and carbonated water' on the label became '100 per cent compliance with the statute'.[18]

The secret about the formula is that it has been a moveable feast. Little remains of Dr Pemberton's 1886 concoction. Anyone who brewed syrup according to that recipe today would offend more addicts than Goizueta did by scrapping the so-called Classic in 1985. The kola has been replaced, the trace of active cocaine eliminated, and the confectioner's sugar replaced by High Fructose Corn Syrup-55 and artificials. During Prohibition, The Company abandoned alcohol as the emulsion for another ingredient. In addition, the formula for the fountain mix differed from the bottled drink, which 'contains more sugar, has 10 per cent more caramel for colouring purposes, contains more phosphoric acid, and less caffeine'.[19] The taste also varied with bottle size, 'not because the mixture is different. It's the carbonation. The same three and one-half volumes of carbonation are put in a twelve-ounce bottle as are put in a six and half ounce bottle'.[20]

Coca-Cola became the victim of its own success in 1985 when it responded to the Pepsi Challenge with the sweeter New Coke.

In blind tests, Coke devotees had preferred the new blend, but they had gone ballistic at the suggestion that Coca-Cola be replaced. They, and millions like them, raged when New Coke went on sale: 'the cognitive characteristics of brand name...overrode any true sensory preference'.[21] Had The Company merely gone on adjusting its formula without any fanfare, New Coke might have won over drinkers who preferred Pepsi's slightly sweeter flavour without offending those who could not tell the difference, no matter how fervently they declared they could. Pepsi knew that 'consumers overwhelmingly chose Coke over Pepsi when the brands were identified before the sip test. Coke had invested millions of dollars and many years to build a positive quality image. That work was enough to make people choose Coke over Pepsi regardless of taste.'[22]

The fifth element

'If it is true that we live by symbols it is no less true that we purchase goods by them.'[23] This opinion, given by Mr Justice Frankfurter in 1942, pointed to what has been called 'the Fifth Element' in design—namely, the ambience around the four elements that a company can register for a trademark: name, colour, typeface and image. These elements are not divisible in practice but have to be considered in turn.

Names

Even the best product is likely to be scuttled by a cacophonous name. Kroc Burgers would never have made Ray Kroc the multimillionaire he became with McDonald's, which evoked the homeliness of the old farmer from the children's song. A drink called Coca-Cola surely would have outsold Kickapoo Indian Sagwa, irrespective of taste and promotional budgets. At first, The Company had been chary of the nickname 'Coke' because of its association with cocaine, but after 1940 it laid claim to the shorter version as well. Advertisements encouraged customers to 'Ask for it either way...both trade-marks mean the same thing'.[24] Before The Company went into China it sought pictograms for its name that sounded like Coca-Cola while meaning 'tasty and happy'.[25]

A brand name can become so well known that it turns generic, as has happened with cellophane, escalator, aspirin, Xerox and Band-Aid. Some firms present themselves as the way to ask for that product. For example, tea breaks in Australia became 'Time for a Bushells', no longer 'Time for a cuppa'. By 1940, nine out of ten college students in California regarded cola and Coca-Cola as synonymous. At that time, The Company pressured the Church of Latter Day Saints to apologise for using 'cola' as a generic. One entrepreneur contemplated taking out copyright over the popular term for the oral contraceptive: 'After all, if you could patent the word "Coke" for Coca-Cola, why not "The Pill".'[26]

Yet, as Coca-Cola has discovered, there are costs as well as benefits in becoming a generic. Bar staff still assume that anyone asking for a Coke wants a mixer and will serve a Pepsi if that is all the house carries. Less often Pepsi is the generic. Struggling to crack the Venezuelan market in 1961, Coke executives lamented that their chief imitator

> had built such a strong brand image that the word 'Pepsi-Cola' signifies all soft drinks. We sampled children with ice-cold Coca-Cola, showed them a Coca-Cola movie, gave them a Coca-Cola ruler or pencil and they would say 'Thank you for the Pepsi-Cola'.[27]

This identification remained rare, as the head of advertising at PepsiCo admitted: 'The word Coke had practically become generic'. A PepsiCo executive trying to break into Texas recognised that 'people were drinking the trademark'.[28]

Protection of Coca-Cola's trademarks verged on the metaphysical. In 1941, The Company's legal counsel quoted the definition of a sacrament as the 'outward and visible sign of an inward and spiritual grace' before comparing the Coke label with the Red Cross, the crucifix and national flags. Similarly, McDonald's rounded arches are described as being as safe as a womb, 'which is advantageous if you're replacing home cooking'.[29] On the death of Sam Walton in 1992, his business, Wal-Mart, changed its name to Wal*Mart, the star indicating that the founder had gone to his reward. Such connections are not just the hyperbole of marketing department's but stem from the fact that, while the trademark has to be made flesh, the property rights at stake remain intangible.

Typography

When Dr Pemberton's bookkeeper first wrote out the words coca and kola in 1886, he felt that two capital Cs looked more harmonious. His handwriting was based on the 1855 copybook of Platt Rogers Spencer, who taught generations of grocers to pen their accounts with 'curves neatly shaded and capitals embellished with mazy whorls'.[30] The flowing script that has become Coca-Cola's trademark was not used during its first year, and was standardised only when the trademark was registered in 1892. Nowadays, the fluid Coca-Cola and the block Coke offer consumers a choice: grace for the old-fashioned and abruptness for the modern-minded. 'Coca-Cola' or 'Coke' can be recognised from a segment of their letters, or even from an abstracted version such as 'the dynamic ribbon' that flows along the side of the delivery vans, an instance of 'The Fifth Element'.[31] The curved lines of the bottle repeated the flow of the script. They stand out so clearly that billboards could caption those contours in 1993 with 'Quick. Name a soft-drink.'

With this level of recognition it is difficult to tell how little of a trademark has to be depicted for rights to be infringed, a matter which dogged the designers of the cover for this book. A Scottish judge in 1961 grappled with this problem before concluding that 'there was a *prima facie* case of passing-off in respect of bottles the same size and shape as Coca-Cola bottles if they were filled with brown liquid, but not if the contents were another colour'.[32] What would his honour have made of the de-caramelised TAB Clear?

Colour

The connections we draw between colours and brands are not consistent. A US study reported that six out of ten respondents associated red with danger; yet when asked to associate red with a product they named Coca-Cola, which they liked. In China, Coke benefited from the association of red with good fortune; Pepsi blue evoked cold or evil. McDonald's arches had to be golden, not cheap yellow.

By 1960 Pepsi had become the fifth-largest spender on colour in printed advertisements to 'escape from [the] poverty' of black-and-white images and move from the kitchen to the living room around the slogan 'Be Sociable—Have a Pepsi'.[33] To distinguish itself from Coke's red and white, in 1996 PepsiCo went from red, white and blue to electric blue: 'It's more than a colour change. It's about Coke being red and us being increasingly different to Coke', a marketing director commented. 'We wanted a visual statement to say that'.[34] Contrariwise, in 1988 Goizueta attempted to rescue New Coke from oblivion by relaunching it with a blue swirl to suggest that it was as sweet as Pepsi.

Imagery

The practice of branding began less ethereally in ports and freight yards. Because so many stevedores were illiterate, firms stamped bales of goods with designs to identify their dispatcher. Proctor & Gamble developed the star and moon as its motif, so that by the time it registered its trademark in 1882 the image had a history as long as the firm's. A century later, P&G abandoned its symbol after salespeople from the rival Amway alleged it was a mark of Satan.[35]

The popular misunderstanding of schizoid is a case of multiple personalities. The clinical definition, however, is one person's alienation from social realities. Those conditions coalesce in commodities branded with a personality. The millions who buy 'Michel Jordan' shades, sneakers and perfumes in order to feel special are losing their identity and their socialisation to a corporate trademark.

Brand identification relies on the image of a personality more than on a real person. Even a Finger-lickin' Honorary Kentucky Colonel could split into multiple selves in the service of capital. Before Harlan Sanders was known at all, he had replaced his all-black suit with the all-white one that we associate with his fried chicken. Sanders was a better cook than a salesman, but proved a success as a front for the men who bought him out for $2 million in 1964. Under contract to the new owners, the septuagenarian Sanders became the creature of a New York public-relations agent. In trading his personality to be used as a corporate logo, the Colonel became a two-dimensional cut-out in front of franchised outlets.[36]

Aunt Jemima, who continues to sell $300 million worth of products on behalf of PepsiCo, had a protean career:

> [She] began as a whiteman, in drag, wearing blackface...She became a face on a bag on pancake flour, then a real-life ex-slave...who entertain[ed] the crowds of the 1893 World's Fair. Next, advertising...brought her to life in the pages of ladies' magazines... shadowed by a succession of real-life Aunt Jemimas who greeted the curious public at country fairs and club Bake-Offs.[37]

On the other side of the racial divide, General Mills conceived 'Betty Crocker' as no more than an easy-to-read signature. The Betty Crocker of the cookbook years was never a 'living person', but forty-eight women in the corporation's Home Service Department. In 1936, her manufacturer invented her as an 'ageless 31', fixed a smile on her in 1946, then reformulated her as a mother figure in 1955. She 'was only a head, a graceful bust'. [38]

A 1990 survey of 10 000 people found that in the previous ten years the number of globally recognised brands had grown from one to ten. Investigators attributed this increase to the spread of homogenised sport and entertainment, particularly among the young, which suggests that consumers will increasingly identify their own worth with brands. This reification already had Filipino women visualising 'a well proportioned female' as a 'Coca-Cola body'.[39]

The waisted bottle became as much a part of the Coca-Cola trademark as its name. Coca-Cola lawyers in 1910 had turned the search for a distinctive container into another means to protect their product against imitations: 'The Coca-Cola bottle should be so shaped that, even if broken, a person could tell what it was'.[40] Its design could be protected by both patent and trademark. After 1910, the Coca-Cola trademark was put on bottle caps to stop their being used on surrogates.[41]

This quest for the unique took place in an industry heading towards standardisation. Until the 1900s, almost all bottles had been made by hand, but by the time the Root Glass Company of Indiana patented the Coca-Cola bottle on 16 November 1915, nearly 200 mechanised systems for glass blowing were in operation. To gain the lower costs of mass production, bottle manufacturers reduced their range, so that by 1930 the number of heights in production had fallen from seventy-eight to six. Atlanta resisted the introduction of ten and twelve-ounce bottles in the 1950s for sentimental reasons: 'Bringing out another bottle', one executive admitted, 'was like being unfaithful to your wife'.[42] To defend all its trademarks, Coca-Cola put TAB into a distinctive bottle with a textured surface. The 1963 specifications for this new container spelt out the conflict between creativity and standardisation:

> The package must be completely new, it must be a shape with a high remember value, it must have an identity all its own, it must be a new concept in glass packaging. And, most importantly, it must have the same dimension as other packages used by our bottlers and fit all existing machinery for bottling and vending these products.

The conclusion indicated how little remained of individuality in the era of monopolising capitals: 'In other words it must be unique but the same'.[43]

Under pressure from two big customers, The Company introduced cans. In the 1940s, US Steel told Coca-Cola that to keep its vending machines in plants, The Company would have to match Canada Dry in using metal. A few years later, the US military insisted on cans because they were lighter and unbreakable. A waisted twelve-ounce can had been tested, but its price premium and intractability inside vending machines sent it to the recycle bin. Printing the image of the bottle on cans is as close as designers have come to contouring the cylindrical.

In the late 1990s, Coca-Cola turned its vending machines 'from transactional appliances to marketing machines'.[44] The dispenser became another layer of the package, proclaiming the brand and the trademark, the front aglow with the life-size picture of one of the sporting stars who endorse the product. Similarly, McDonald's arches and buildings are part of the meal's packaging.

Goizueta scrapped the classic Coke formula in 1985 but was never so wrong-headed as to alter names, scripts, colours or shapes.

Indeed, he took Coca-Cola's marketing back to the curved shape. In 1991 he travelled to the site of the Root factory in Indiana to introduce the twenty-ounce plastic contoured bottle, which is credited with adding 2 per cent to market share.

Monopolising brands

Brands help to make and preserve monopolisers. When prices collapsed in the depression of the 1890s, some firms intensified their 'product differentiation' through brand-labelling. Quaker Oats, which registered its black-and-white garb as the first trademark for a breakfast cereal in 1877, improved its returns despite the slump in the bulk trade. Its success was an indication that branding could assist a firm to achieve market share and thus increase its prospects of surviving the great shakeout to join the ranks of the oligopolists.[45] The brand became another obstacle to newcomers entering a market. A patent expires but a trademark goes on and on, so that its possessor can expect to retain an advantage long after its inventor is no longer the sole provider.

The 1946 US trademark law excused the violation of a brand if its holder had used it to limit competition. That amendment treated the monopolising impact of trademarks as exceptional. Nowadays, free-market apologists hold that the brand, by drawing in extra customers, delivers economies of scale, and hence lower unit costs. This benefit is likely, but whether those reduced expenses ever turn up as cheaper prices to the consumer depends on how a company fits the advantage from its brands into its sales strategy.

A century after the first trademark Acts became law, the requirements of corporations had grown. To cover the lag time between market research and availability, the US Congress amended the law in 1988 to protect brands for the three years before the product went on sale. The distinction between patent and trademark was overturned. The latter is now protected even before it has earned a place through its association with quality. 'Which are the countries that do benefit from free trade?' the managing director of KeyCorp asked. 'Understand it', he replied, 'it is the countries which have already established their global brands'.[46]

Coca-Cola has a marketing need to be seen to be first in every niche and segment. In 1987, one of its executives drew out this link between brand image and market domination: 'You simply cannot allow the leadership, which is part of the specialness of the product, that has been built over years and years, to deteriorate'.[47] Being the biggest is the hallmark of a monopoliser. Brand recognition gives The Coca-Cola Company an advantage, even over an entrant with the same funds for plant and promotion. Warren Buffett decided that if you gave him '$100 billion and said take away the soft-drink leadership of Coca-Cola in the world, I'd give it back to you and say it can't be done'.[48] The Company spends its billions to protect that leadership position in the belief that, without a Coke sign in every milk bar, 'other brands would try to upset consumers' mental agendas by "jumping the cue"—by inducing us, at the point of sale, to consider them...So Coke tries to dominate the clutter of mental alternatives'.[49]

Semioticians who claim expertise in reading labels and brands fall victim to their seductiveness by failing to grasp that trademarks are but one tactic in a marketing master plan. This blind spot diverts cultural analysis away from 'the productive structures of goods and services to those of the sign and subjectivity'.[50] The result is not subtlety but sophistry. No marketing agency would dare rely on the symbolic aspects of packages in the tussle to secure salience in the store.

From the early 1960s, Coca-Cola worried about 'what appears to be a substantial increase in "Off-Label" pricing, which it feared might eventually have a seriously undermining effect upon Brand loyalty'.[51] Putting a can of no-name cola on the shelf at half the price of Coca-Cola had almost no impact on its sales, but when a cheap lemonade appeared beside Sprite the drop-off was considerable. No-name, no-frill packages appeared in the US around 1977, gaining 5 per cent of grocery sales within five years. Food giants such as Heinz produced their own no-name lines to ward off the smaller suppliers. Coca-Cola used its financial and marketing resources to carry on price wars wherever the cheap alternatives grabbed share. The principal effect of no-brands on Coca-Cola was the fallout from Marlboro Friday, the day in April 1993 when Philip

Morris buckled before the no-brand cigarettes and reduced its packet price by 25 per cent. The share price of Coca-Cola dropped one-tenth as brokers pondered whether brands had a future. They did, but in ways remote from a desire to protect what had existed for a hundred years.

Assets

On its debut, a brand is only as valuable as the product to which it is attached. The inventors of the zipper failed to secure repeat orders for their Plako brand because the product was such a tangle of technical hitches that one haberdasher chased the salesman away with a meat cleaver.[52] A trademark can guarantee a higher price or extra sales if its quality is maintained. Rockefeller chose the name Standard Oil to emphasise that his fuels would never blow you up when you lit your kerosene lamp. The SOC brand had become so pervasive by 1895 that comedians could raise a laugh by suggesting that Rockefeller owned the recently instituted standard time.[53]

Investors and lawyers took their time in accepting that brands could be assets. In 1888, when H. J. Heinz wanted 20–25 per cent over the book value of his family firm for goodwill, the buyers refused. By 1905, Royal baking powder valued its name at $1 million a letter. In the same year, the tobacco trust paid $3.5 million for a competitor with physical assets worth only $500 000. The trust pretended that the other $3 million was for goodwill and trademarks; in fact, the premium was paid to shut the rival down without being seen to violate the anti-trust laws.

Ferocious as firms have been in defence of their brands, their accountants remained reluctant to factor such intangible assets into balance sheets. In the 1960s, the head of Quaker Oats still sounded eccentric when he asserted: 'If this business were to be split up, I would be glad to take the brands, trademarks, and good will, and you could have all the bricks and mortar—and I would fare better than you'.[54] Twenty years later, his view had become conventional wisdom. Wriggles valued its brand at $1.6 billion, while General Electric's 'meatball' of its initials GE had become such a plus in the sale of domestic items that, when Black and Decker bought the small-appliance division in 1984, it sought rights to the logo.

On 1 January 1890, when Asa Candler approached the Merchants Bank for a line of credit, he put the 'Coca-Cola Patent Trade Mark etc etc' into his assets at a valuation of $2000, whereas his family home was given as $6000. At the same time he wrote down the value of the patent and trademark for his De-Lec-Ta-Lave dentifrice from $3750 to $1000.[55] He waited twenty-five years before again capitalising the Coca-Cola brand as an asset. In the interim, its worth had been threatened in 1906 when the Food and Drug Administration tried to declare Coca-Cola poisonous and its name misleading. If Candler had lost, the verdict would have demolished the $8 million book value of Coke's real properties, let alone its intangibles, which were valued at twice that sum. After the dispute was settled in Candler's favour, the annual stockholders' meeting in January 1917 authorised a new charter to capitalise 'good-will' at $25 million. When the Candlers sold in 1919, they got $20 million for intangibles and $5 million for real properties, the company secretary noting that 'the trade-mark was the basis of the business'.[56] During the battle between the Woodruff syndicate and the Parent Bottlers in the early 1920s, the latter claimed a share of the goodwill on the grounds that they had helped to fund its legal defence over the previous twenty years.

In 1934, The Company recapitalised its intangibles at $30 million, a 50 per cent gain in fifteen years; outlays on advertising during that time totalled twice those before 1919. The intangibles were not increased to full value, being listed at only $43 million in 1963. Challenged by PepsiCo, Atlanta had upped its value so much by 1967 that *Forbes* asked 'How can a formula and a trademark be worth $3 billion?'[57] The question soon became: how can Atlanta value them at only $3 billion? By 2000, the tag put on them by the stock market came close to $200 billion.

When Warren Buffett bought into Coca-Cola in 1988, he had calculated that its 'brand name was a sort of universal toll bridge'.[58] A Coke executive went further: 'We're not selling products; we're selling brands.'[59] Goizueta institutionalised this difference by dividing intangibles from physical assets and placing them in two corporations, The Coca-Cola Company and Coca-Cola Enterprises:

> At its core, The Coca-Cola Company really was just one thing: a trademark. The word Coke, the fancy script, the unique bottle, the red disc logo all emanated from the trademark. Coke's soft drinks themselves each had unique recipes. But their real value in the marketplace came when The Coca-Cola Company lent its name to the products.[60]

As recently as 1993, the publisher of *Beverage World* proposed that success still depended on 'focussing all your marketing efforts on one brand. Ideally all of the soft drink companies...would like to produce one brand...because the marketing of the brand becomes extraordinarily efficient'.[61]

The counter-argument is that brands should be extended beyond the product that established their value. In the late 1990s, Peter Drucker espoused a New Economy in which wealth was built on intangibles such as brand recognition. Gillette's advertising executive agreed:

> Of all the things that your company owns, brands are far and away the most important and the toughest. Founders die. Factories burn down. Machinery wears out. Inventories get depleted. Technology becomes obsolete...Brand loyalty is the only sound foundation on which business leaders can build enduring, profitable growth.[62]

Advocates of the New Economy criticised McDonald's for not extending the power of its name and logo in the 1990s 'beyond its basic formula of burgers and fries'. Instead of concentrating on what other kind of fast food McDonald's could sell to grow the business, its managers should have asked, 'What does our brand allow us to consider selling to our customers?'[63] The answer was toys and clothing.

The intangibility of brands does not make them easy to transfer to other lines. A soft-drink factory can add flavours to its range. It cannot manufacture breakfast cereals without an injection of funds for the required machinery. A comparable impediment faces a manager who wants to stick trusted brands and trademarks on products that have nothing to do with the original. Would you drink Caltex Cola or put Coke petrol in your Toyota?

While beverages branded with Coke or Coca-Cola are market leaders, their advantage has not secured dominance for The Coca-Cola Company over all other beverages. Of its eighteen brands in 1993, only eight carried either of the core logos. The Company dared not attach Coke or Coca-Cola to every try-out for fear of diminishing the worth of its trademark through association with too many flops. Instead, each brand now covers a line of drinks. In the case of Coca-Cola that means Classic, cherry, non-caffeine, New, Diet, or combinations thereof. Goizueta attempted a parallel strategy for citrus drinks, using one brand for a palate of flavours. 'Fruitopia will be the brand', he announced. "It's a lasting brand for an unlasting line of products.'[64] Economies of scale still come from standardising the public's preference for brands.

Fashion houses risk their credibility when they license their brand names to lines over which they have no control, or when they franchise manufacture to distant suppliers. The pursuit of lower labour costs can injure the brand's reputation, as happened to Nike.

The brand label that assured the consumer of Nike's quality became a liability when the shoe proved as durable as its reputation. Nike's high prices limited sales while they underwrote the status. The brand had to become a fashion statement, with an accelerating turnover of designs. The first Nike model had a promotional life of seven years. By 1989, the marketing cycle was down to ten months. The trademark that had secured repeat purchases through quality was enticing customers to swap that assurance for the pleasures of a new look. Small wonder that Nike advertisements said no more than 'Swoosh'.

CHAPTER 11   I'd Like to Buy the World

I have repeatedly shared with you my concern...that 'we are fresh out of Japans'.

Paul Austin, Coca-Cola President, 1973.[1]

Consumption is sunshine to capital. As corporations expand their output, they must produce 'a constantly widening sphere of circulation'.[2] The broadening of sales can be geographical or social, extending across national borders or into new social strata at home and abroad. This chapter attends to the territorial imperative, interweaving the thrust of the USA towards superpower status with Coca-Cola's emergence as a worldwide corporation.

An American century

United States capitalists achieved a continental market by purchase (Louisiana and Alaska) and annexation (Texas), through genocide of the indigenous peoples and by crushing Confederate independence. From the mid-1860s, with the South beaten back into the Union, produce from the mid-West could again move down the

Mississippi Valley, and Southern cotton could pay for imports by the rest of the country. US industrialists soon realised that they must 'look abroad...to provide a future market'.[3] Before the last massacre of Indians at Wounded Knee on the eve of 1891, US destiny had already manifested itself by kicking open doors into China and Japan, as it would soon do around the Caribbean (Cuba and Puerto Rico) and across the Pacific (Hawaii and the Philippines). From 1914, the Panama Canal linked these zones of intervention. US entrepreneurs did not confine themselves to the Americas or the Pacific. Exports of branded grains rose 550 per cent during the 1890s, when Quaker Oats attached its billboard to the cliffs at Dover. Chicago's Columbian Exposition in 1893 celebrated the US conquest of the continent; in 1904, the St Louis World Fair promoted its drive beyond the hemisphere.

Coca-Cola too had its eyes on new markets. Asa Candler thought his drink 'did right well in Honolulu in 1898', the year Congress approved the annexation of Hawaii. In 1900, he sent his sons to 'critically observe conditions etc in Europe' and the Orient. Then he summoned his family together 'to map our Great Conquest'.[4] He opened plants in Cuba and Canada, countries which US businessmen regarded as their dominions. During 1900, Asa also bought a controlling interest in a Georgia cotton mill. US exports to China had been halved by the Boxer Rebellion, so the mill 'did not cost what it is really worth', Candler noted; he expected that 'as soon as any Cotton mills prosper it will'. Returns from the US policy of slicing China up like a melon were slow, and his mill lost $5000 in 1902.[5]

Financiers facilitated US expansion. The House of Morgan operated in London and Paris as well as New York and Philadelphia. In 1919, the Guaranty Trust Company of New York linked the export of capital to the export of commodities in a program to sustain US industries that had expanded to supply the Great European War. 'The purchase of foreign securities and the development of an international finance market', it announced, would ensure that the 'investment of capital in other countries leads to the exportation, not of capital, but of products of American labour and capital'.[6] US purchases of foreign bonds gave its banks leverage over other nations' finances, a process known as 'dollar diplomacy'. The US Federal Reserve supervised Cuba's economy from Atlanta, sending convoys of cash to the island in 1926 and 1930 to avert runs on its banks.

To strengthen the competitive position of US firms abroad, Congress exempted 'certain business combinations engaged in foreign commerce from the provisions of the antitrust laws'.[7] Corporations moved in packs. In the 1920s, when General Motors began to sell vehicles offshore, its advertising agency, J. Walter Thompson, set up its own offices overseas, anxious to share in the opportunities and fearful lest a competitor intrude on its business with GM.

Because consumers in the USA had on average five times as much to spend as those in any other national market, the book value of direct investment overseas by US firms steadied at 7–8 per cent of Gross National Product until the 1960s. The growth of effective demand elsewhere then stimulated the global expansion of US capital until by 1998, two-thirds of the world's fifty largest corporations were headquartered in the USA.

Coca-Cola's overseas ventures chugged along until the mid-1920s, when Robert Woodruff overcame his fellow directors' resistance to the establishment of an International Division. In 1927, 11 426 gallons of syrup were exported for fountain sales, with more than half headed for the US territory of Hawaii. One attraction of exporting was that the price to new overseas bottlers was not fixed by a franchise contract, so that the full sale price returned to Atlanta without the 12.5 per cent deducted by a Parent Bottler. On the other side of the ledger, foreign governments could curb the repatriation of profits—even nationalise the operation—and exchange rates could fluctuate. In 1930, Woodruff set up the Coca-Cola Export Corporation, based in New York, to co-ordinate expansion. It mounted several ventures in alliance with the United Fruit Company, which, as Coca-Cola noted, 'practically owns' Central America.[8]

Although Coca-Cola boasted that fountain syrup went to forty-seven cities in thirty countries, its publicity preceded its presence and its profit-taking. From 1927 to 1933, the overseas operations lost money. Because The Company paid for Coca-Cola to appear in feature films, people outside North America had heard of Coke long before they tasted it. Much of Export's activity in the 1930s was showing the trademark.

In Germany, the Nazis attacked Coca-Cola as a Jewish capitalist plot to kill off local producers and pollute Aryan bodily fluids. To convince Berlin otherwise, Woodruff's lobbyists in New York invited the German Consul-General to assess 'the character of personnel and ownership of our Company'[9]—that is, to prove that Coke was kosher for Nazis. These negotiations had to be kept secret to avoid offending Jewish drinkers and sympathisers. Before the USA entered the war, Coca-Cola Export circumvented the Allied blockade of Germany by diverting concentrate through Rumania; communications had to be encrypted to avoid blacklisting by the British Empire.[10] The Nazis put Woodruff's Berlin representative in charge of Coca-Cola's properties across all the occupied territories, providing him with a uniform and a staff car. As a good German, he stored water in Coke bottles for air-raids, and invented Fanta when Coke concentrate could no longer be sneaked through.[11] Nonetheless, few Germans had tasted Coca-Cola before the US Army carried it to victory.

During World War Two, US corporations again lifted their sights. Late in 1940, Woodruff appointed the former chair of the Democratic Party, Jim Farley, as president of Coca-Cola Export. At Pepsi, Walter Mack employed a fellow liberal Republican, Wendell Wilkie, to negotiate with Washington over sugar quotas. Wilkie, an unsuccessful candidate in the 1940 presidential elections, had collaborated with Mack in shifting the Republican Party from isolation to intervention. Wilkie concluded his 1943 book, *One World*:

> In view of the astronomical figures our national debt will assume by the end of this war, and in a world reduced in size by industrial and transportation developments, even our present standard of living in America cannot be maintained unless the exchange of goods flows more freely over the whole world.[12]

Washington strategists equated prosperity with foreign trade. In 1946, an Assistant Secretary of State argued: 'We need markets—

big markets—around the world in which to buy and sell. We ask no special privileges in any of those markets.'[13] Officials assumed that the greater efficiency of US factories would give them the edge, aided by the General Agreement on Tariffs and Trade negotiated at Havana in 1947. Washington set up the International Monetary Fund in a way which pleased US financiers and upheld the USA as the world's creditor. The dollar guaranteed gold as the currency standard. These mechanisms would help US capital to impose terms of trade on rival nation-market-states, and would patrol their growth by limiting their ability to raise loans.

This strategy would work only if the rest of the world bought US produce. The Marshall Plan in 1947–48 had the long-term objective of keeping the Western European nations out of the Soviet bloc, where their markets would have been closed against US corporations. The Assistant Secretary of State for Economic Affairs, Will Clayton, argued: 'We would have to reorder and readjust our whole economy in this country if we lost the European market'. The creation of the Soviet bloc had deprived US firms of machinery sales to West European manufacturers, whose earnings relied on exchanging manufactured goods for agricultural products from the East. As a result, to acquire dollars, Germany's 'limited supplies of steel' were being 'used to manufacture cameras and toy trains for export to the United States rather than...desperately needed spare parts to increase the productivity of under-maintained European machines'.[14] Clayton called for a grant of $6–7 million worth of goods a year for three years. The US Treasury had to underpin Europe's revival so that US corporations could thrive.

The humanitarian extent of the Marshall Plan was clear when the US shipped $500 million worth of tobacco to the starving Europeans. Questioned on its nutritional value, the Secretary of Agriculture replied that 'when cigarettes are available as rewards for certain types of heavy labour...they are able to get production quite beyond what they are able to get by offering money'.[15] The inclusion also secured favourable votes by Senators from tobacco States.

The immediate aim of the Marshall Plan was to stem a flight of capital which was making US commodities even more unsaleable in Europe. The British government, for instance, was struggling with its balance-of-payments crisis, known as the dollar gap. Its response was to hold down consumption, cutting into the money that consumers had to buy US products. In addition, the squeeze on Britain's foreign currency threatened to reduce its military activity, which would advantage the Soviets or impose extra burdens on US taxpayers.[16]

With the British paying for US goods by the sale of rubber and tin from their Malayan colony, conflicts of interest appeared at every turn. Should the wealth of Southeast Asia be used to rebuild Japan, or Europe? As a concomitant to their Marshall Plan, US strategists agreed to put 'Japan back into...the old Co-Prosperity Sphere' to stop it from following China by going Red.[17] In 1949–50, Washington matched its North Atlantic Treaty Organisation with military intervention in Korea and a naval cordon across the Taiwan Strait, followed a year later by a security treaty with Japan.

Coke sales to Japanese locals were few in the 1950s because the country's trade deficit limited imports of concentrate. Coca-Cola's prospects also became tangled with the Japanese government's management of foreign exchange. Tokyo subsidised its shipbuilding exporters by granting them 'import quotas for raw sugar, which could be sold at a hefty profit' to soft-drink makers.[18] Opposition to Coca-Cola came from small and medium suppliers of soda pops, as well as from brewers with soft-drink subsidiaries. Success required more than patience. An early ally was Mitsubishi Heavy Industries, which had supplied Coke with bottling equipment during the occupation. Mitsubishi encouraged Kirin Beer, a fellow member of its conglomerate, to accept a Coke franchise before pressuring the government to allow Coca-Cola more room. This method of entering Japan replicated Atlanta's practice of franchising local bottlers. Japan would become the second-biggest overseas earner for Coca-Cola after Germany.

The Company had continued Candler's 'Great Conquest' by moving from Germany to Japan—but where to next? One possibility was to draw on the relationship with Mitsubishi, which already had a US mining partner in Brazil. Mining companies had been among the first corporations to operate in a number of continents— harbingers of the multinational enterprise. The idea of a US firm joining a Japanese one in a Brazilian venture twisted a new strand into triangular trading. By 1960, US companies were 'importing components, finished goods from overseas affiliates'.[19] In 1966, Coca-Cola president Paul Austin welcomed this practice as 'a technique for seeking money, goods, methods, and talents overseas'; he envisaged that 'some day Coca-Cola may be bottled in the United States by machinery manufactured in Brazil from a patent developed in Japan and based on a design originated in the United States'.[20]

Austin's vision ran far ahead of his practices, but summarised the strategy of US manufacturers abroad. Until 1958, IBM Europe produced parts for typewriters in the lowest-cost nations before assembling them in the country of sale; the next step was for each plant to make products 'for the whole of the European market'.[21] Ford began producing its world car in 1967 with a transmission plant at Bordeaux. By the late 1970s, car-makers had established complementary plants around the Asia-Pacific, gathering benefits from longer production runs before assembling the parts in each nation-market-state. To succeed, this corporate integration required the reshaping of tariff and other protective regimes into freer-trade zones. Trade was not to be set free. Rather, more of its control passed from governments to transnational corporations, which obtain 40 per cent of their supplies in-house.

In 1973, Paul Austin highlighted the significance of foreign sales to Coca-Cola. The Company's share price had been 45 times the earnings per share during the previous year. Austin hoped to lift the ratio to 47, but he feared that if 'we don't come up with additional sources of income we can kiss that 47 price/earnings ratio good bye'.[22] To secure profits from twenty countries, The Company had paid out $1.3 million in bribes before 1977, when it assured the Securities and Exchange Commission in Washington that 'the illegal or improper payments and practices have been terminated'.[23]

Other firms stepped up their foreign business to lift earnings. Gillette's overseas sales overtook those inside the USA in 1974. By 1996, Gillette was making 70 per cent of its sales and profits abroad. When asked what Gillette made in Brazil, its local general-manager replied: 'We make money'.[24] Proctor & Gamble's offshore sales of household cleansers rose from $1 billion in 1993 to $4.2 billion in 1997. The proportion of Wal-Mart sales outside the USA went from nothing to 14 per cent in the 1990s. GE doubled the fraction of its overseas sales to 30 per cent between 1993 and 1999.

The world fast-food market grew at twice the pace of the USA's. In 1988, McDonald's opened more sites abroad than at home; its number of foreign outlets then doubled in the seven years to 1995. Whereas 40 per cent of McDonald's earnings came from abroad in 1991, the portion was over 60 per cent by 1997–98. Between 1994 and 1998, sales in Brazil alone trebled to $900 million. McDonald's expects to have another 25 000 outlets by the year 2010, three-quarters of them overseas.

The 1997 exchange-rate crisis pushed the share of US corporate revenues gained overseas down from 30 to 21 per cent over the following year. Gillette shut fourteen plants and laid off 4700 staff, its sales remaining flat through 1999. Proctor & Gamble also suffered, losing a tenth of its world sales in the five years to 1999 and sacking one-eighth of its employees.

Coca-Cola was exposed because the portion of its profits from overseas had risen from 70 to 80 per cent in the 1990s. After the devaluation of the rouble in August 1998, Coke ran its plants in the Russian Federation at half capacity, sacking half its workforce when its retail turnover was halved between 1996 and 2000. Both Coke and PepsiCo were forced to write down assets.

Bottlers fared the worst. The contribution from Coca-Cola Enterprises to The Coca-Cola Company dropped 80 per cent, and the latter's net earnings fell for the first time since 1974. Indeed, The Company had to pump $1.8 billion into its global bottling network to ward off local competitors. After Brazil devalued in January 1999, cheaper second-tier brands began outselling Coke. Declines continued into 1999, when first-quarter earnings in Brazil, one of Coke's top markets, were down by 13 per cent, causing the share price of the local anchor bottler to suffer its first fall. In Indonesia, Coca-Cola sales slid by a fifth, a blow to the ambitions of 1991, when The Company's president had described the archipelago as soda-pop heaven because it was 'on the Equator with 180 million people, a median age of 18, and a Moslem ban on alcohol'.[25]

Coke's chairman, Doug Ivester, had been right to say that even 'in developing countries, many people can afford a Coca-Cola'.[26] One cause of his downfall was that his biggest exposures were in stagnant markets, while Coke's global bottling network was profitable 'only if it handles the high volume it was intended to accommodate'.[27] The tendency for capital investments to depress the rate of profit was compounded by the rising costs of marketing, which cut into absolute earnings. In 1999, a majority of Coke bottlers overseas did not earn their cost of capital.[28]

The prospect of the McDonaldisation of the world through the erasure of regional tastes encouraged belief in the actuality of globalisation. After 1997, the reversal of fortunes among the vanguard of globalising corporations perplexed their critics as much as their managers. The volatility was but one reason for scepticism about how much of the world economy had altered.

Globalisation: the hypothesis

Globalising has long been part of capitalism. From the seventeenth century, capital expanded on a triangle of trade between West Africa, North America and England:

> Without slavery, no cotton; without cotton, no modern industry. Slavery has given their value to the colonies; the colonies have created world trade; world trade is the necessary condition of large-scale industry.[29]

Around these times, the British Crown Corporations—the East India, Hudson's Bay and Muscovy Companies—along with the Dutch East India Company, had trading monopolies over vast tracts of the world. Although the term corporation has survived, the structure and dynamics remain mutable.

It is bootless to lump every kind of foreign business in every era under the same rubric, whether imperialism or globalisation. On the other hand, caution is necessary not to accept tarnished wares packaged in cellophane. The term 'globalisation' itself did not become widespread until 1987, when it was confined to finance, high-tech industries and communications. Today, 'globalisation' gives imperialism a public-relations gloss. The portrayal of monopolising capitals as the outcome of ineluctable forces of nature, rather than of contestable social practices, helps corporations to elude the hostility sparked by the word 'imperialism'.

Despite all the talk about globalisation, the question remains open: does it exist? And if the answer is yes, is globalisation other than classic imperialism in a PET bottle? To what extent has the formula been rejigged?

The case for the arrival of a new economy is slapdash and anecdotal. Its proponents cannot agree on any single model. Their historical ignorance accounts for most of the features they reckon as unique. Indeed, they extrapolate a horizonless future from the experience of a few years. It is too soon to tell whether we have registered the birth of new star or the coruscation from an imploding one.

Much of the popular belief in globalisation relies on the World Wide Web, but the Internet has yet to add much value beyond stock-market romps. Since 1995, the money available as venture capital, often squandered on Internet start-ups, has rocketed from almost nothing to $45 billion. Different aspects of selling become prominent according to the type of product. Financial trading is the ideal type of globalised commerce, far in advance of other sectors. The computer works best for services that the screen can transmit, such as pornography or money. We can order a pizza over the Net, but it still has to be cooked and delivered. To cable back a recipe or video of its being baked—a virtual meal—will not assuage real-time appetites.

In the political realm, globalisation is supposed to have disabled all nation-market-states. In fact, the imbalances between governments continue to shift without eliminating the sway that some have over others. The USA remains pre-eminent. China and India have enhanced their independence since the 1940s. Members of the European Union regulate corporations through the bureaucracy in Brussels as much as they did before joining together. No single pattern exists.

The statistical data to prove that globalisation represents more than a quantitative development of long-standing channels of trade and investment are not available. The surest generalisation, as Paul Hirst and Grahame Thompson have demonstrated, is that the richest third of the world is more interlocked than before the 1970s. The interchanges are concentrated between the USA, the European Union and Japan, which account for 84 per cent of foreign direct investment. In terms of relocating centres of production, no change since 1980 can compare with Japan's lifting itself between 1950 and 1970 from a third-world economy to become one pillar of the triad along with the USA and EU.[30]

Since the 1970s, the trajectory of monopolising capitals has acquired a new bias. Instead of external trade being embedded in the domestic economies, more domestic economies are being steered by their international connections. The foreign dimension is moving from periphery to pivot. The issue is one of dynamics and potential, not just percentages.

In 1915, Lenin sought to explain the Great War in his *Imperialism, the Highest Stage of Capitalism*, which adumbrated four elements: one, that 'the dominance of monopolies and finance capital has established itself'; two, that 'the export of capital has acquired pronounced importance'; thirdly, 'the division of the world among international trusts has begun'; and finally, 'the division of all territories of the globe among the great capitalist powers has been completed'.[31] In short, imperialism was Lenin's term for monopolising capitals; colonisation was a secondary aspect.

The first three of Lenin's conditions are truer than ever. Globalisation is a higher stage of imperialism. The extent of and limits to the changes that have brought about that elevation can be gauged by contrasting recent developments with the four elements set down by Lenin.

The dominance of finance capital: Finance capital now directs manufacturing via stock-market speculations as much as through the provision of investment funds. Around 1900, bankers took charge of production; since the 1980s, brokers have been stripping assets. In 1992, Alfred D. Chandler Jr complained that the restructuring of enterprises and of industries was now clearly affected by the desires of investment banks and other financial institutions to maintain the new and profitable business of buying and selling companies and the needs for pension and mutual fund managers to maintain the current value of their portfolios.[32]

The financial sector has spawned financial instruments which are traded for the fee, not as assets. Half of the Foreign Direct Investment in the 1990s went on mergers and acquisitions and so did not add to productive capacity.

Any substance behind the globalisation hypothesis derives from monetary deregulation, combined with an acceleration of financial transfers. The new economy relied on the rearrangement of debt in the US since 1995. The government runs a surplus while households have negative savings, a perversion of Keynesian demand management.

The export of capital now has four objectives: for stock-market speculation; to secure raw materials and labour; to produce and sell in a market overseas; and to produce overseas and sell back home or to third markets. The US economy has become a major importer of capital, which kept the New York stock exchange at record levels and paid for US imports in the 1990s. The boom and bubble of the New Economy there depended on its sucking in capital.

International trusts are far more extensive, though they can never take a final form because mergers—and company failures—persist. Oligopolies are still the norm for free markets, as shown in chapter 6.

The division of the globe among the great capitalist powers took a new form after struggles for national independence ended direct colonisation. Since the 1960s, cheap labour has drawn capital back to erstwhile colonies, some of which produce for metropolitan markets. The terms of trade have run against suppliers of raw materials. The overlords of even the most wretched of these societies are clients for armaments firms. In a new version of dollar diplomacy, the IMF supervises their economies, as was apparent during threatened loan defaults in the early 1980s, the 1995 Mexican collapse and the 1997–98 exchange-rate crisis.

In 1973, Harvard Professor of Marketing Theodore Levitt used The Coca-Cola Company as an exemplar of the global corporation because its products were sold throughout the world. In the 1990s, other firms looked to Coca-Cola because it had standardised its product quality across all its territories; the head of Gillette boasted that his company was one of the few to catch up with Coca-Cola. These two features were rudimentary compared with the multiplicity of processes now clustered around the globalisation hypothesis, the burden of which can be examined through reactions in corporate structures, production, marketing and tastes.

Globalisation: corporate structures

Corporations created to cope with a continental US market had to be remade to deal with worldwide markets after 1945. Domestic oligopolies provided the blueprint for global reach, the multi-divisional at home becoming the multinational abroad. Gillette reorganised itself in the 1980s to deal with its worldwide sales, splitting into two operational units, one for the 'mature' markets of Western Europe and North America, the second for the newer markets in the rest of the world. A similar 'two-world' structure was later adopted by Colgate–Palmolive.

Becoming dependent on overseas revenues, Coca-Cola also required corporate restructuring. As ever, the way ahead was not clear. The Company continued to expand overseas, as it had at home, by selling franchises to local bottlers. Atlanta enforced quality standards, but management and ownership were more diversified than in any corporation with so widespread a sales network. In 1980, the fact that Coca-Cola made the bulk of its profits outside the USA offended imperial pride and worried the domestic bottlers, who were concerned that 'the tail would start wagging the dog'.[33] Not until the mid-1980s did Atlanta proclaim the global market as its path to salvation. The realignment required a remaking of the firm. During the 1980s, Atlanta consolidated its operations overseas until, according to its chairman, Roberto Goizueta, reliance on a few anchor bottlers had

> eliminated some layers within the organisation and empowered the local executives to execute on a tactical basis against an overall strategy developed in Atlanta...Remember that years ago we had what we called zone offices around the world. Now we don't. The man who runs Spain reports directly to someone here in Atlanta... We have one less layer than we used to have.[34]

In 1996, The Company acknowledged at last that the USA did not provide the bulk of Coca-Cola's earnings by obliterating the domestic–international distinction in its corporate structures. The USA became merely one of its six territories. The home market, however, remained first among equals, because everyone had to report to Atlanta, an attitude summed up in Coke's simultaneous purchase of the song 'We Are the World'.[35]

Goizueta's removal of one rung of agents did not diminish control from the centre. In 2000, Doug Daft took charge of a corporate structure which his years in the field had taught him to hate. His early interviews as chairman were war stories of the stupidity of waiting on Atlanta for approval. As group president for Asia, he had been obliged to live in Atlanta, not where the business was. 'We had backups in Atlanta in case people failed, monitoring them, constantly checking on information', so that a local manager needed permission to 'shift advertising dollars among brands'. TV commercials for China were made in Atlanta, which also blocked the development of local websites. Reporters in Europe had to call Atlanta for press releases. Decisions for Russia would wait six months, by which time the network of bribe-takers would have changed. In Indonesia, Daft pushed Coke for three years with poor results: 'Then I launched Fanta and the business just trebled and quadrupled'.[36]

Daft applied his successes as organisational principles. His decision to cut 2000 jobs at the Atlanta head office was not down-sizing or a filleting of middle management. The rationale was that Coca-Coca was a global company operating through local businesses. The bottlers would now deal with representatives of The Coca-Cola Company on the spot. This new pattern was not borderless, because Coca-Cola Enterprises comprises the eleven anchor bottlers and The Company itself works through continental groups.

Daft's administrative overhaul was driven by financial facts as much as by regional taste buds. A case of Coke in Japan returns fifteen times more profit than one in Brazil. 'In reality then', a Wall Street analyst observed, 'Coke does not run a world-wide business, but rather a set of geographically diverse businesses'.[37] This complexity is one more indicator that the globalisation hypothesis is an imperfect guide to profit-taking.

Globalisation: production

The CEO of Nestlé, Helmut Maucher, explained in 1994 how production was shifting:

> Things were different when European products were being exported to developing countries or, later, when production facilities were opened in those countries. That increased the value added to products manufactured there—a trend that is continuing. Now, however, something completely different is taking shape: a greater separation between production and sales points, owing to the globalisation of markets and to liberalisation, which allows production sites to be set up far from where the products are consumed.[38]

The lowering of trade barriers inside Europe allowed Gillette to cut the number of its production facilities in Europe from four to two, while Coca-Cola Enterprises consolidated its depots and bottling plants in Europe and the UK.

Barriers persist inside freer trade areas, because some borders to business are too costly to dismantle. The domestic power voltage, for example, ranges from 100 in Japan to 230 in Europe. Customers will buy transformers for expensive items such as computers, but not for a light bulb. National power grids are not going to be reset to suit Philips or General Electric.

Until the 1930s, General Electric protected itself by licensing patents to competitors abroad and at home. When those rights expired, GE bought into foreign rivals. Up to the mid-1980s, the firm still held half the North American light-bulb market, which represented one-third of world sales. In 1983, the Dutch firm Philips attacked GE's home base with cheaper bulbs of higher quality, having bought a production facility inside the USA:

> In a competition with global players, matching and even beating their prices is not enough. You need access to their markets, for two reasons: first, to maximize your revenue opportunities; second, to weaken your competitors by attacking them in their home markets, just as Philips had hit GE.[39]

By 1989, GE was number two behind Philips in a $9 billion world market, but was selling very little outside the USA. GE then hit back by purchasing Tungsram, which had 7 per cent of the European market. During the later 1990s, GE moved production of all its lines out of the USA to cheap-labour areas. It then pushed its suppliers to do the same, mounting '"supplier migration" conferences to help them make the leap'.[40]

The current phase of monopolising capitals also differs from earlier patterns of world trade because flexible methods of production allow 'mass customisation' and the agglomeration of niches into a new kind of mass market. By the 1980s, computer-aided design and manufacture (CAD-CAM) had reduced the cost of retooling for shorter production runs. Customising has not gone as far in the car industry as it has for Dell computers, but most corporations can offer more variations without pricing themselves out of the market. The flexibility of production has reshaped the sales effort.

Globalisation: marketing

In 1983, Theodore Levitt distinguished old-style mass markets from emerging global ones. As well as chasing as many buyers as possible inside a single country, corporations had to realise that they could assemble markets of mass proportions by selling to the same stratum in every country. By combining niche markets in Uganda, Malaysia and Brazil, high-fashion corporations such as Vuitton, Rolex or Gucci could generate sales volumes comparable to those in Germany. Levitt wrote:

> Globalisation is the massification of segments...In almost all nations...are identical segments for Bach, Bauhaus, bicycles, pita bread, punk rock...What may start out as small, local segments... become gigantically global.

For Levitt, globalisation did not mean the end of segments. 'It means, instead, their expansion to world-wide proportions.'[41] His definition has come back as a reminder that global marketing is not built on a standardised product for the universal consumer.

Corporations were uncertain about adopting Levitt's advice. Before 1991, Gillette had 'made certain products in Malaysia, others in France, and tailored the products to those national markets'. Then its strategy changed to 'One blade fits all', treating 'all marketplaces as the same'. Gillette accepted that Egypt was not Malaysia and that different products would sell at different rates in each national market, but all markets were offered 'the same spectrum of products made to the same world standards under the same factory principles'.[42] Equalising quality and extending choice did not apply to advertising, where Gillette reduced its agencies from thirty-five to one, which stuck different languages over the same images.

Globalisation: tastes

Religious mores mean that McDonald's is not going to sell beef to Hindus, pork to Muslims, or flesh of any kind to Jains and some Buddhists. Even Christians in those parts of the world cling to the customary cuisines. In the Philippines, the market leader among fast-food chains is the indigenous Jollibee Foods, which seasons its chicken and beef to suit local tastebuds and sells a favourite noodle.

In the 1990s, according to Nestlé's Maucher:

Regional and national habits of consumption are not changing, particularly in the food branch. Therefore the proper balance must be found between such regional and global conditions...A dual strategy needs to be implemented in developing countries...we must meet the increasing demand for classic Nestlé products from a growing population with more purchasing power...On the other hand, Nestlé must produce products that employ local raw materials and correspond to local eating habits.[43]

Similarly, L'Oréal uses the French reputation for fashion leadership to market its cosmetics worldwide, but goes under the Maybelline label in Britain and the USA.

Against the persistence and parading of national preferences, Levitt recognised how malleable such differences could be outside their cultures of origin. Niche marketeers repackage synthetic ethnic flavourings in a mix called Mall-ticulturalism:

Without the generalised homogenisation of tastes and preferences there would be no distinction in ethnicity or specialisation. To have the latter requires the dominant presence of the former. The global growth of ethnic markets confirms the greater presence of global standardisation of segments. Everywhere there is Chinese food... country and western music, pizza and jazz. The global pervasiveness of ethnic forms represents the cosmopolitanisation of speciality segments.[44]

Nestlé's strategy of spicing its products to accord with the palate in each market has its counterpart in the use of those flavours as a marketing ploy elsewhere in the world.

Selling in non-European markets taught CEO Doug Daft that 'People don't buy drinks globally. You can't pander to similarities between people: you have to find the differences.'[45] Atlanta's quest for a worldwide strategy had slowed The Company's entry into the bottled water market: 'You can't apply a global standard of measurement to consumers because it reduces everything to the lowest common denominator'.[46]

In India, The Company sells four times as much of a local

concoction, Thums Up, as it does of the real thing.[47] The change of popular mood in the Russian Federation was dramatic. An initial passion for all things capitalist and foreign gave way to a resurgence of local preferences. By 1999, Coke's bottlers were marketing a favourite from the communist era, Kvas, a fizzy, sugary yeast drink. Its label was printed in Cyrillic script, with Coca-Cola in tiny letters.

Coca-colonisation

In the late 1940s, when Coca-Cola was taking less than one-fifth of its profits from abroad, its overseas operations were already under attack as the standard-bearer of US imperialism. The 1944 hit song *Rum and Coca-Cola* was about 'mother and daughter working for the Yankee dollar' as prostitutes. Epitomising the exploitation, the tune itself had been plagiarised from one written in Trinidad in 1906, with lyrics adapted from a calypso protest popular on the island after US forces arrived in 1942.[48]

The French coined 'Coca-colonisation' as a term of abuse for the expansion of US capital, commodities and cultures. Coca-colonisation applied to more than the worldwide marketing of a soft drink, because The Company's standardisation of product and marketing made it the prime target for those who feared that local preferences were being eroded by US Admass. Scholars too shy to mention imperialism, even in regard to culture, will use Coca-colonisation as a light-hearted admonition. Well before 1950, when *Time*'s cover story on Coca-Cola urged the world to 'Love that piaster, that lira, that tickey, and that American way of life', Coca-colonisation was a rallying cry and Coca-Cola a generic in anti-foreign rhetoric.[49] In India and the USSR, the term was used to attack Pepsi as well.

Proclamations of US exceptionalism deepened these resentments. When Bishop Warren Candler went to Cuba in the wake of the US military in 1898, he feared that the locals were so dirty that he would not be able to convert them to Methodism until they were made to 'think and feel like Americans'.[50] Any concern that such reformation might be intrusive or resented has been blunted by the marketeers' faith that the earth is populated by latent US Americans. US governments and corporations believe that they are supplying the rest of us with what we were born to want, be it plutocracy or Donald Duck. The president of McDonald's International announced in 1994: 'People are more the same than they are different. We don't think our food is seen as American. It's seen as McDonald's'.[51] A Coke executive was comforted to think that 'American culture broadly defined—music, film, fashion and food—has become world-wide'.[52] In 1998, Ivester responded to a 'Coca-Cola March': 'Doesn't it just make you want to get a flag and march and then go attack the world?'[53] These executives could not understand why their enthusiasms drove the Peasants Union in France to set alight to McDonald's.

Critiques of Coca-colonisation deserve support only when they illuminate how standardising benefits corporations such as Coke, Nestlé or McDonald's, which profit from channelling our prefer-ences. Otherwise, Coca-colonisation is but a snob's disdain for the grossness of Admass. The task is to analyse capital everywhere in order to identify the grounds from which to resist its destructive-ness. Coke's 1999 bid for the French firm Orangina deserved to be blocked because of its monopolising tendency, not because the bidder was from the USA. After all, forces impelling the com-modification of life are no less powerful in Europe, where media giants such as Italy's Silvio Berlusconi and France's Martin Bouygues have operated by the same rules as their Hollywood counterparts, several of which have had non-US owners: Matsushita at Universal, Sony at Columbia and Credit Lyonnais at MGM.

Many complaints by both radicals and conservatives against the United States sound like grouches against modernisation. Those prejudices have renovated nineteenth-century anti-Semitism, which pictured 'rich urbanised Jews as the advance agents of modernity'.[54] In the twentieth century, anti-Americanism became shorthand for the gaggle of objections to industrial urban existence, with its speed, conformity and waste. In a clash of cultures, despising Coke and McDonald's has taken over from hating Jews. Similarly, US alarms in the 1980s about a menace from Japan drew on an older resis-tance to modernity as the habitat of economic robots.

Throughout the 1990s, Coca-Cola's advertising strategists see-sawed between nostalgia and post-modernity. The rejection of New Coke in the USA was one instance of the conflict that Benjamin Barber summed up as *McWorld versus Jihad*, in which standardis-ation and modernising provoke extreme reactions, whether from Islam or Christianity. The trick for the marketing department is to marry change with continuity, as Bavaria's conservative politicians have done by campaigning for lasers and *Lederhosen*—that is, pros-perity from high technology allied to the comforts of commercialised tradition. The risks for Coca-Cola are acute: its appeal inside the USA rests on apple-pie associations, but overseas it is the marker of modernisation, making it both welcomed and loathed. A Coke and a Big Mac are cheap mass items in Detroit, but in Sierra Leone they buy the cachet that Krug and *Tour d'Argent* bestow in Paris.

Ole Southern Boys

Coca-Cola managers had trouble dealing with diversity at home. The Company carries the divided heritages of Southern racism and the New South's willingness to do business. While Atlanta was a city too busy to hate more than was absolutely necessary, its pre-occupation with profit did not prevent it from accommodating the headquarters of the Ku Klux Klan, which despised the foreign-born as much as it did coloured folk. In the 1950s, Atlanta's mayor warned businessmen pressing for an international airport that a black Brazilian executive would not be able to check into a whites-only hotel or use the executive bathroom at Coca-Cola.

Although Robert Woodruff often sided with the liberals in State and city politics, his firm was saturated with the attitudes that elected racial supremacists as governors and senators. As part of the civil rights movement in 1963, black church leaders in Atlanta imposed a selective boycott on Coca-Cola because it had only 200 Negro employees, all in menial positions. The shallowness of The Company's commitment to desegregation was exposed in an inter-nal document advising 'Negro employees not...to use the facilities without regard to tradition'.[55] These prejudices have remained irritants to trading with independent nations and with US minorities. US chauvinism has limited Coca-Cola's capacity to satisfy regional tastes and soothe cultural sensitivities.

At home, Coca-Cola has followed an integrated but unequal employment policy, so that few franchises or senior jobs are held by non-whites. A 1999 class action suit contended that, although African-Americans consumed a quarter of Coke's US volumes, The Company had 'failed to place the same importance on its African-American employees'.[56] The Company settled for $156 million late in 2000 and promised to transform its employment practices under the guidance of an outside panel. A potential for conflict exists between the economic imperatives of consolidating distribution and the survival of the Philadelphia Coca-Coca Bottling Company, the largest black-owned business in the USA.

Roberto Goizueta was the first immigrant executive at head office. A right-wing Cuban, he had graduated from Princeton and possessed the deference that masquerades as manners in the South. Yet when he was proposed as chief executive in 1980, a bottler from Alabama objected: 'This is an American company manufacturing an American product in an American way'.[57] The Peachtree Golf Club delayed admitting Goizueta to membership until Woodruff forced the issue. As a Latino, Roberto was not quite white. In the larger scheme of things, his preferment indicated that Coke was opening up to Hispanic Americans, at home and in the hemisphere; a quarter of Coke's earnings came from south of the border.

In 1972, Coca-Cola Export Corporation closed its office in New York. The move brought its managers to Atlanta, but did little to introduce a more cosmopolitan outlook, since many executives had never been out of the USA. The head of marketing could recite 'Have a Coke' in twenty languages, but that was as deep as his worldliness cut. The chairman from 1997 to 1999, Doug Ivester, had not travelled beyond North America until 1988. On a 1998 trip to China, he complained that he could not find a refrigerated Coke in Shanghai. A *Fortune* correspondent pointed out that the Chinese do not like their drinks cold; Ivester's annoyance showed 'his misunderstanding of Chinese tastes (and thus China's marketplace)'.[58]

Accepting that French intransigence was as solid as US arrogance, in 1988 Atlanta sent the head of its home-town bottler to Paris. He had never been there before and did not speak French. Through in-store displays, 500 extra sales staff, sexy ads and a vending machine at the base of the Eiffel Tower, he lifted volume by 22 per cent per year, pushing annual per capita consumption to forty-nine bottles, a quarter of the German rate.

The Company was more inclined to send US executives around the world than to bring the brightest and best to Atlanta. A Frenchman might preside over Coca-Cola in Japan, but The Company was slow to take a Frenchman or Japanese into the topmost ranks at home. By contrast, Pepsi's president is an Indian and a woman, Indra K. Nooyi. Similarly, Gillette moved its managers around the planet. By the mid-1990s, it was employing 400 expatriate managers from 43 countries. A Mexican was in charge of Turkey, reporting to a Spaniard in London.[59] Though money still speaks all languages, its mother tongue is English, which Gillette keeps as its *lingua franca*.

At Coca-Cola, the promotion of an Australian to the chairman's post early in 2000 was not a paradigm shift because Daft is another Anglo-Saxon. The revolution was that his experience had been outside the USA as controller of the Asia-Pacific, Africa and the Middle East. At dinner in Japan, he amazed a visiting Atlanta executive by choosing the sea urchin.

*

One of the few certainties about globalisation is that it is most often Americanisation. Its logic does not require the United States to be borderless, only everybody else. As the Washington-based Brookings Institution would have it, globalisation is 'the increasing economic linkage between the United States and other nations'.[60] One measure of this focus is that the US share of world equity markets grew from one-third in 1989 to one-half in 1999.[61] The US dollar is still the world currency. The USA remains the only superpower, its economic might matched by military clout and political networks.

PART FIVE # Out of Control

The less the workman is attracted by the nature of the work...the more close his attention is forced to be.

Karl Marx, *Capital*, 1867[1]

PART TWO   Out of Control

CHAPTER 12 **Look! No Hands!**

The labourer is himself a produced means of production, an item of capital equipment.

Harry G. Johnson, 1962[2]

The caption of a photograph of the workforce at Coca-Cola in the early 1890s identified its executives Asa Candler and the book-keeper Frank Robinson. Also present was a 'boy', that is to say, an African-American in his fifties. The racism of not giving his name indicated the subjugation of the freedman in the New South; the fact that he was the only manual labourer indicated the simplicity of Coke's manufacture. His job was to dump sugar into tanks of water, puddle it until it dissolved, then siphon the syrup into barrels ready to load onto wagons or freight cars. Elementary though this process was, without his labour there would have been no Coca-Cola—neither The Company nor the beverage.

At first Asa Candler and his staff used tools rather than machines, mixing the syrup, for example, with a hand-held paddle. Even after Candler installed a steam-powered stirring apparatus, the brewing of Coca-Cola remained rudimentary compared with other realms of manufacture, where machines were replacing the workers' motor and mental co-ordination. Because 'improvements of the machinery do not show their full effect until they are used in new, appropriately arranged factories',[3] The Company replaced the labour-intensive lifting of sugar bags with bulk loading from hopper cars, supplemented by a hydraulic lift. Technologies also reduced the labour per unit in franchised plants, where bottles were washed, sterilised, filled, labelled and capped on conveyor belts. The adoption of Crown tops after 1900 made it possible to mechanise the sealing. A semi-automatic washing machine could cleanse 3000 bottles per hour, and eventually automatic filling systems became available. Labour costs of retailing were further reduced when self-serve fountains and vending machines became available from the late 1930s.

Why work?

'A Negro is a Negro. He only becomes a *slave* in certain relations'.[4] Equally, only when human beings must sell their capacity to labour in order to live do they become enslaved to the wage system, as Adam Smith recognised:

> The produce of labour constitutes the natural recompense or wages of labour. In that original state of things, which precedes both the appropriation of land and the accumulation of stock, the whole produce of labour belongs to the labourer. He has neither land-lord nor master to share with him.[5]

Labourers under capitalism, however, must sell their labour power or starve. The coercion that underpins capitalism arises from the imbalance between the owners of productive resources and those who have nothing to sell but a capacity to work.

The outlawing of slavery removed the shackles but not the compulsion from relations between master and servant. By the 1830s, the British had developed 'a new system of slavery' known as indentured labour.[6] Gandhi went to South Africa to protect Indian labourers. Pacific Islanders worked the Australian cane fields. In the American South, share-cropping and chain gangs replaced slavery after 1865. Convicts built the reservoirs that fed Coca-Cola's plant in Atlanta. Convict labour kept down wages for other workers by depressing the labour market. Asa Candler rented prisoners for his cotton mill and paid their cook to spy on them. The supply of bonded workers gave him the best of both slavery and wage labour: he now had a compliant workforce without having to invest in purchasing them as an 'item of capital equipment' liable to depreciation through disease or death. Instead, he could operate on the principle: 'One dies, get another'.[7] Ownership of Coca-Cola or a cotton mill could not by itself make Candler a capitalist. For that, he needed others to work for him.

Without the wage labourer there is no capitalist, as the English coloniser Thomas Peel had discovered in 1829 when he arrived on the Swan River in Western Australia with

> means of subsistence and of production to the amount of £50 000. Mr Peel had the foresight to bring with him, besides, 3000 persons of the working class, men, women, and children. Once arrived at his destination, 'Mr Peel was left without a servant to make his bed or fetch him water from the river'. Unhappy Mr Peel who provided for everything except the export of English modes of production to Swan River![8]

Various methods have been employed to disembarrass the Mr Peels of this world by obliging workers to sell their labour power. Police have treated workers as criminals when they leave their employers. Goons still break strikes. Judges use anti-trust laws against trade unions rather than corporations.

Mr Peel's experience returned to educate Pepsi president Walter Mack in the late 1930s, after his firm had bought a sugar plantation in Cuba. A liberal Republican, Mack wanted to improve the conditions of his field labourers, who worked for four months and lived on debts to the company store for the rest of the year, then paid off their debts by working for another four months the following year. Mack hoped to break this cycle by supplying livestock and seed, and digging wells so that the families could become more self-sufficient. Once peons looked like becoming peasants, the Cuban Treasury discovered that Pepsi owed $9 million in taxes. If Pepsi withdrew its social program, the back taxes would be forgiven. If not, the penalties might well increase. Over lunch in Havana, an official explained how agrarian reform would ruin the economy:

> These men will never go out and cut cane for four months if they know that they can make a living another way. Cutting sugarcane is not pleasant... If the *colonas* become independent of the plantations' company stores, there will be no reason for them to break their back in *your* sugarcane fields.

Mack sold out to three Cuban senators. The encounter convinced him that had he been a Cuban he would have embraced Castro against 'the tyrants who ran the island as their own private company'.[9]

The last hour

To make labourers turn up for work is only the first task for the owners of capital and their allies in the state. Capitalists must also tighten their control over the labour process to increase the rate of return from the productive power they buy.

The simplest method for extracting more from each employee is to hold down the number of workers. At Coca-Cola, Howard Candler recalled that around 1900 a single staff member had supervised 'one or two Negroes who did all the work of receiving, manufacturing, drawing off and shipping'.[10] During the 1920s, although the volume of syrup increased, the number of hands at Coca-Cola in Atlanta would have declined had The Company not done its own cooperage. Because Coca-Cola used a relatively small portion of labour, it could make larger than average outlays on marketing. By 1945, the sales effort already absorbed five times as much as wages. Labour costs in 1963 reached almost 10 per cent of sales only because salaries for the marketing department were included.

Managers also slash workforces to make the remaining employees produce more. Delabourisation is used to sustain profit rates, with 'downsizing' its most recent alias. General Electric entered the 1990s with 170 000 fewer workers than it had had ten years earlier. Similarly, Gillette decimated its workforce and increased the value of its sales by 300 per cent between 1975 and 1990. Coca-Cola's 1991 workforce was down one-third from 1978, while net earnings had quadrupled.

Talk of the hollowing out of middle management is misleading. Indeed, as the number of workers declines, the amount of supervision increases to make sure that productivity grows. Between 1948 and 1982, the ratio of managerial positions to shop-floor employment in non-farm industries rose from 12 to 19 per cent, where it has remained. A survey revealed that in 1995 several conglomerates had more managers per 100 employees than in 1993. When a corporation sets out to become lean and mean against its rivals, parts of it must stay fat in order to be mean towards its workers.[11]

To sustain rates of profitability, capitalists seek not only to contain the total wages bill but also to reduce labour costs per unit through mechanisation. The ideal, as PepsiCo's president told a congressional committee in 1973, would be 'one big plant here in the United States where it was all computerised and run by robots and we did not have to do anything but ship it out'.[12] This Utopia for employers remains a wish. The increasing variety of soft drinks means that the wholesaler can no longer load a pallet with nothing more complicated than a forklift. Instead, Robotic Order Picking among brands reduces 'labor cost and worker compensation claims', and improves 'the ability to handle peak periods without adding more labor'.[13]

Wages

The price paid for labour is crucial to a firm's prospects. Wages are not driven down by any iron law, but are determined by the relative strengths of the contending classes. That balance tips as each side becomes better organised. Through unions and strikes, workers seek to increase their share of the values they produce. In consequence, as Adam Smith recognised:

Masters are always and every where in a sort of tacit, but constant and uniform combination, not to raise the wages of labour above their actual rate...We seldom, indeed, hear of this combination, because it is the usual, and one may say, the natural state of things which nobody ever hears of. Masters, too, sometimes enter into particular combinations to sink the wages of labour even below this rate.

To pay workers nothing at all would bring employers no lasting benefit, since the operatives would not be able to afford to eat and soon would not have the energy to toil. 'A man', Smith continued, 'must always live by his work, and his wages must at least be sufficient to maintain him'. On those grounds, Smith concluded that:

though in disputes with their workmen, masters must generally have the advantage, there is however a certain rate below which it seems impossible to reduce, for any considerable time, the ordinary wages even of the lowest species of labour.

In most situations, the labourer receives somewhat more than a survival ration, 'otherwise it would be impossible for him to bring up a family, and the race of such workmen could not last beyond the first generation'.[14]

After workers learned to read and to organise unions, Smith's disciples found it impolitic to acknowledge that the living of one class was achieved by the exploitation of another. In the 1820s, workers began organising to lift the quality of their existence above that of 'just another commodity'. Employers in turn set about liberalising trade to reduce the costs of reproducing the capacity to labour. The leaders of the Anti-Corn League in the 1840s praised themselves for extending the achievements of the Anti-Slavery Society by ensuring that the propertyless had a free right 'to exchange their labour for as much food as could be got for it'.[15] In practice, these free-traders sought to keep wages in Britain low by importing cheaper foods from slave economies.

As apologists for the slaveholders had predicted, industrial capitalism brought miseries at least as great as those of chattel slavery.

Around 1910, a quarter of the operatives in Georgia's cotton mills were children earning 10 to 50 cents a day, while their employers, including Asa Candler, drew dividends ranging from 60 to 95 per cent on his investment. Children as young as four or five began as unpaid helpers to their mothers and sisters. Candler resisted a ban on the employment of children under the age of twelve, reassuring the National Child Labor Committee that the 'most beautiful sight that we see is the child at labour; as early as he may get at labour the more beautiful, the more useful does his life get to be'.[16] Southern cotton millers persuaded the Supreme Court to declare a 1916 federal child labour law unconstitutional.

The Coca-Cola Company, like other companies in the New South, paid lower wages than the standard for factories elsewhere in the United States. Candler contained his wages bill by watching the pennies. He made clerks recompense him for their invoicing errors. He recalled one of his sons from the New York office in 1903 because the youth was not earning more than his weekly salary. At the same time, he was reluctant to buy a truck for deliveries around New York City because he looked upon the 'locomobile' as another 'fad', like the bicycle.[17] Asa's personality played its part in this niggardliness, but he also knew how the insouciance of countless Dr Pembertons had led to bankruptcy. Parsimony remained The Company policy. In the mid-1940s, Atlanta instructed its office staff to entertain judiciously and use airmail letters rather than telegrams: 'The practice of economy in your business transactions will benefit your employer'.[18]

Between 1935 and 1940, the number of Coca-Cola employees grew at nearly twice the national average for manufacturing, but The Company's payroll increased more slowly than for the rest of the industrial sector. The growth of the wages bill at Coke matched its rate of employment growth, whereas wages across the sector increased three times as fast as new jobs. The Coca-Cola Company circumvented the overtime provisions of the 1938 Fair Labor Standards Act by reclassifying its drivers as salesmen. By the 1940s, executives at Coca-Cola were so poorly paid that several defected to Pepsi, which doubled their salaries.

Coca-Cola's owners and chief executives have never stinted their own emoluments. Asa Candler took next to no salary because he retained most of the profits. Ernest Woodruff increased his own salary as president of the Trust Company of Georgia from $3600 in 1916 to $20 000 in 1919, yet opposed paying a 5 per cent bonus to the staff. His son, Robert, was also generous to himself. From 1928 to 1931, he took $100 000 a year as salary and another $60 000 in bonuses.

The labour costs of Coke's suppliers and distributors affect The Company's profits. Increased pay rates for transport, on farms or at fountains, must either be absorbed into the charge for syrup or added to the price. Conversely, PepsiCo was an unintended beneficiary when the firm that supplied its sweetener locked out its workers in 1994, broke their union and reduced wages, conditions and workforce numbers.[19] Pursuit of cost savings also creates conflict between sectors of the soft-drink industry, as when retailers try to reduce their labour costs by demanding more services from bottlers.[20]

The Coca-Cola Company has also gained from the low wages and poor conditions at McDonald's and other major customers under exclusive contracts. Cheap labour fuelled Ray Kroc's growth engine. As a percentage of sales, wages at McDonald's in the 1970s were the lowest in the fast-food industry, almost a quarter less than at Burger King or Pizza Hut. Kroc contained labour costs through strict management and right-wing politics. Standardisation of the meal was essential, he maintained, because the 'minute you get into customising...the labour triples'.[21] To lobby for a sub-minimum youth wage, he donated $225 000 to Richard Nixon's 1972 re-election campaign. Even without legislative backing, McDonald's policies helped to depress wages for under-skilled workers everywhere by undercutting industry standards for the working poor, that new reserve army of the employed.

Employees are nominally paid for all the hours they spend at work. The greater the difference between the length of the working day and the hours needed to cover the cost of their wages, the larger can be the profits. Consequently, unpaid work is widespread. Employer research in 1996 estimated that US businesses were saving at least $19 billion a year by illegally refusing to pay workers overtime. Because time-and-a-half does not apply to managers, firms advertise for 'assistant managers' who do the same work as the labourers. Another trick is to hire part-time supervisors for a 25–hour week and work them forty hours. A labour lawyer reported that the 'last hour or so of work—when the restaurants close, and the employees had to clean up—was often off the clock'.[22]

Unions

Unions surged in response to the monopolising of capitals in the final decades of the nineteenth century. In Atlanta, workers organised a secret society while their political arm campaigned for the city elections in 1884 and 1886. Later that year, unionists formed the American Federation of Labour. By then, for every US worker who knew of Coca-Cola, there were a million who had heard about socialism.

Adam Smith had foretold what would happen to workers who defended their wage levels:

> The masters...never cease to call aloud for the assistance of the civil magistrate, and the rigorous execution of those laws which have been enacted with so much severity against the combinations of servants, labourers, and journeymen.[23]

After strikers bested the US railroads early in 1885, the employing class became disturbed at the breakdown in the rule of their laws. A resurgence of union militancy in 1892 made most upholders of States Rights amenable to the *laissez-faire* argument that relations between capitalists and workers should be left to freedom of contract—supported, of course, by the military might of the executive arm. Between the 1885 railroad strike and the defeat of the Populists in the 1896 presidential campaign, US courts, legislatures and corporations found common cause against the tyranny of the majority. The Supreme Court struck down State laws setting minimum conditions and wages, turning freedom of contract into a freedom to conduct sweatshops. Despite some see-sawing, the weight of learned opinion in the USA went to the freedom-of-contract end of the scales of justice, provoking Justice Oliver Wendell Holmes in 1905 to accuse his brethren of misusing the Fourteenth Amendment to impose the most extreme forms of Social Darwinism on the American people.

Opposition to unionism has been an article of faith for The Coca-Cola Company and its bottlers. Asa Candler's presidential addresses to the Atlanta Chamber of Commerce in 1909 deplored the

> strikes, lockouts, and conflicts between labour and capital which often fill cities with disorder and municipal authorities with dismay...Hereby also socialism arises...With its inflammatory and immoral theories of property it stirs up dynamitic elements which may explode with a conflagration destructive of all social order and security.[24]

No sooner had Candler defeated a radical union candidate for Atlanta's mayoralty in August 1916 than he headed a law-and-order committee of 100 businessmen to break a strike against the Georgia Railway and Power Co. by calling out vigilantes to back the police. Georgia Power held the copyright for the cover illustration on the November 1916 issue of the journal of the Atlanta Chamber of Commerce, which depicted a taskmaster with a whip sitting on a millstone being turned by an ox and a man in chains.

Even in Robert Woodruff's most liberal years, he opposed the closed union shop and unemployment relief to strikers. The warm-hearted plant manager, Sanders Rowland, could not contain his annoyance when his workers organised: 'If a man wants to join a union, that's up to him. But I will not instigate it. In fact, I will fight it.'[25] Coca-Cola did not form a company union or use violence against its workers because the general repression in the South was sufficient to keep its people in line. In 1932, Atlanta courts used a statute left over from the days of slavery to sentence a black union organiser to twenty years on a chain gang for insurrection. While Coca-Cola was managing Brecon Loading Co. in 1944 as part of its contribution to the war effort, a guard pistol-whipped a 'darkie' who had fallen asleep on the graveyard shift. Fellow workers came to the victim's aid, but were met by a second armed guard. The manager reported that it 'was not necessary to shoot any of them, but I understand they are behaving very nicely now'.[26]

The sticking point for even the most generous employer remains the stipulations in agreements about the organisation of work—management prerogatives. After Coca-Cola transferred Sanders Rowland to Pittsburgh in the 1940s, he fumed because he could not run the plant as he had in the non-union towns of Connecticut or Rhode Island. Although 'trucks had a carrying capacity of two hundred cases of Coca-Cola, the union would allow only one hundred ninety-six cases to be loaded'. The union contract limited its members to only one dispatch each day, so that 'the routes were never on schedule' and stores waited days to be supplied.[27] In the 1980s, Jack Welch at General Electric railed against European labour policies that 'drastically limited companies' freedom to improve productivity by laying off employees or changing their work rules'.[28]

PepsiCo had put spies into the Teamsters Union in an FBI-style action against its transport workers. Had the beverage companies not been so anti-union, one might feel some sympathy for their problems in dealing with the Teamsters, then linked to the Mafia. Instead, management and Teamsters' bosses deserved each other; the drivers merited neither.

Bottlers were more outspokenly anti-union than Coca-Cola itself, but they banded together in the 1970s in pursuit of a better deal. They were incensed when Atlanta likened their combination to unionism, but the principle was the same. Individual workers, even more than bottlers, are at a disadvantage when negotiating with those who control their livelihood. As Samuel Griffith, who became the first Chief Justice of the Commonwealth of Australia, argued in 1889, if 'a measure of freedom of contract exists it has been obtained by combination on the part of labourers'. Without unions, negotiations remain unjust.[29]

In the late 1980s, Coca-Cola Enterprises sacked Atlanta drivers who were organising against poor pay and rising injury rates. More disputes flared in the mid-1990s. Enterprises lost $300 million in the four years to 1995 and faced higher prices for its cans. Managers saw that a return to profitability required new remuneration scales, which in turn required longer and harder work for no more money. An on-the-job fatality early in 1994 rekindled moves by drivers to join the Bakery, Confectionery and Tobacco Workers Union. The *Wall Street Journal* reported how Coca-Cola Enterprises 'struck back in force' to prevent the activists from gaining the majority vote needed to bring in the union:

> Company officials swarmed into the plants and held one-on-one meetings with workers...Managers rode in trucks with the delivery drivers, taking them to lunch and asking about their families. They showed the workers videos depicting a corrupt and self-serving union movement contrasted with a worker-friendly company.

The bottler beat the union when the vote was taken in August 1994. Next year, the Federal Justice Department charged two vice-presidents of Coca-Cola Enterprises, including its head of human resources, with bribing a driver $10 000 to disrupt union recruitment. The worker claimed to have a video of one pay-off, and to have taped telephone conversations during which a voice congratulated him on the union's rebuff: 'We couldn't have done this without your help. You need to be promoted.' He was. A jury acquitted the executives, but charges of violating union ballots remained. An attorney for the union complained that the case showed 'how outrageous companies have become in fighting off organising efforts'.[30]

In July 1999, South Carolina police committed a union activist to a mental hospital where he was given anti-psychotic drugs. The evidence of his madness was that he had asked for a union representative to address workers at a packing company. In the fast-food industry, fear of workers' organising prompted prohibitions on 'gossip' and edicts against 'any gathering of two or more employees' during meal breaks.[31]

Lawyers have replaced thugs in the front line against unionisation in the USA. In 1998, one attorney published a book called *Combating the Resurgence of Organised Labor: A Modern Guide to Union Prevention*, which told employers how to resist unionisation while staying just within the law. A company might, for instance, throw a party on the night before the vote, as long as its stated objective is to 'have fun'. Time is on the side of management. Lawyers challenge each stage of the recognition process, piling up court actions beyond the resources of the unions.[32]

Although by 1998 union membership in the USA had fallen to only 14 per cent of the workforce, 43 per cent of employees reported that they wanted union coverage. Unions win only half the elections held at corporations, but are voted in 85 per cent of the time by state-sector employees. The disparity, according to *Business Week*, resulted from the anti-union tactics pursued by the corporations. A third of the companies surveyed by a federal regulator had

> illegally fired union supporters during elections...half threatened to close facilities if the union won, and 91 per cent required workers to meet one-on-one with supervisors on the issue.
>
> If even half of the employees who say they want union representation had been allowed to vote for unions, organised labour would represent as much as 35 per cent of the American workforce today—the same share it held at the peak of its power in 1945.[33]

This 'secret war' to disorganise the US workforce was waged under the banner of globalised competitiveness.

When the boom in the late 1990s tilted bargaining power back towards employees, corporations became frantic to prevent unionisation. Management consultants warned that offers made necessary in boom years were harder to claw back in normal or depressed times if the workforce was unionised. The employees who could not organise voted with their feet. Firms had to increase rewards in order to maintain a workforce. After real wages had stagnated for fifteen years, they increased by 3.3 per cent in 1998 and 1999. At Coca-Cola, the rate of labour turnover rose from 6.7 to 12 per cent between 1996 and 1999. It was not until late in 2000 that The Company responded with increased benefits, flexible hours, permanent casual dress and a paid holiday on the anniversary of the first sale of a Coca-Cola on 8 May 1886.

Delivering the 1999 Adam Smith Award Address, the vice-chairman of the G7 Group of industrialised nations, Alan S. Blinder, recalled that corporations had become more aggressive during the 1980s when governments set out 'to break the back of the union movement'. Throughout the 1990s, they resorted to part-time, temporary and casual employees, which meant that labour was 'increasingly being treated as "just another commodity" to be bought and sold on a spot market'.[34] That condition had long been the norm for the most vulnerable workers.

The Florida fruit-pickers

The Coca-Cola Company's industrial relations have posed difficulties for its public relations. Atlanta's 1960 purchase of Minute Maid fruit groves in Florida from the United Fruit Company coincided with a television documentary exposing the miseries of the labourers who supplied juice for the brands that Coca-Cola was taking over. Yet an internal report revealed that Coke's labour cost was 'nearly 5c a case higher' than for other suppliers. Atlanta responded: 'With Minute Maid's volume, and its modern machinery, one would think that its labour costs would be lower'. Far from moving to improve conditions for field hands, the new owners reduced costs to match their competitors' price.[35]

Eight years elapsed before Coca-Cola president Paul Austin had his conscience pricked, not by human degradation but by distant union victories. In September 1969 he sent Woodruff a three-page memorandum identifying 'a serious threat...against our business' which could arise from its employing some 6000 itinerants in Florida:

> We collect them from pockets of poverty throughout the South... 90% black. We...work some of the children...The temporary workers...are housed in barrack-like structures. They are fed from field kitchens. There is no nutritionist in charge of their food. They have no indoor sanitary accommodations...They are paid minimum wages, and the minimum wage scale in agriculture is well below that of industry.

Austin proposed pre-emptive reforms and a public-relations campaign through sympathetic church leaders in the North.

The threat to profit rates was not from the prospect of strikes, which Minute Maid could have broken. The danger was that Coca-Cola's subsidiary would attract secondary boycotts like those the United Farm Workers had recently mounted, with backing from church groups, to defeat California's grape growers. 'In our own case it is infinitely worse', Austin warned. Were the union to widen its 'attack to include Coca-Cola and not just Minute Maid products, we could be in an extremely serious position'. If the boycott reached out to 'idealistically minded 20 year-olds, our heavy consumer group...we could be engulfed'.[36]

Austin warned that 'if we were the subject of a pictorial news report, we would come off badly'. A second television documentary in July 1970 bore out his fears. In the days before the NBC program went to air, Coca-Cola pressured the network to amend the script to include the stale news that Coca-Cola was promising improvements. Although the editors made this concession, Coca-Cola diverted $2 million in advertising from NBC during the first quarter of 1971, giving half of it to rival CBS, which had 'aired a long and "soft" feature on the new wondrous life of Coca-Cola's migrant workers'.[37] Atlanta's other response was to spend as much on a public-relations campaign as on bettering the lot of its pickers. Meanwhile, its hilltop jingle offered to teach the world to sing in harmony.

After a majority of the Minute Maid workers voted to join the United Farm Workers, The Coca-Cola Company guaranteed a weekly wage, holidays and medical benefits. But goodwill faded as media attention waned. In 1973 the Labor Department found Minute Maid guilty of undercounting when it paid by the box. At the same time, it cut wages by 18 per cent to match the levels elsewhere.[38] A ten-month dispute in 1975 saw a sit-in at Coke's Atlanta headquarters. The dangers of allowing unions to get a toehold became apparent when the United Farm Workers used its base in the Minute Maid groves to organise the rest of the Florida pickers.

Guatemala

Conditions in Florida were better than in Guatemala, where the United Fruit Company had bottled Coca-Cola since 1926. Atlanta knew United Fruit's reputation for calling in the Marines, and went out of its way to seal partnerships with the firm. United Fruit handed out Cokes to its plantation workers in exchange for their human rights.

In 1954, the CIA overthrew a Guatemalan administration which was attempting to redistribute some of the land held by United Fruit. For the next thirty years, the country was under military dictatorships. The Guatemalan regime suppressed the union at the Coca-Cola bottler as part of a wider campaign to disrupt the labour movement. In 1968, after Texan oil millionaires had acquired the Coca-Cola franchise for Guatemala City, a revival of unionism was brought to an end by the murder of an activist. When workers regrouped in 1975 they were sacked. They then occupied the factory. The bottler rented the Mobile Military Police to terrorise his erstwhile workforce. The murder of another union leader late in 1978 signalled a new round of attacks, co-ordinated by the bottler and the government.

Killings and kidnappings continued. By July 1980, four workers had been wounded, seven had been murdered and four had been 'disappeared'. Others went into exile. The murderers were commanded by officers trained at the US Army's School of the Americas—the School of Assassins—which moved from Panama to Fort Benning, south-west of Atlanta, in 1984. The School's manuals targeted 'union organising or recruiting' and those who hand around 'literature in favour of the interest of workers'. [39] In the 1980s Washington escalated its operations in Central America, arming the Contras in Nicaragua and intervening against the guerrillas in El Salvador. These moves strengthened the bargaining position of US companies in their labour relations across the region.

Graffitists altered Coca-Cola's Spanish slogan, 'The Sparkle of Life', to 'The Sparkle of Death'. One exile told a shareholders' meeting: 'In Guatemala, Coca-Cola is a name for murder'.[40] US church groups holding Coca-Cola shares pressured Atlanta to include a code of labour relations in its franchise contracts. The Company replied that it had no control over its affiliates. It had its own reasons to terminate the franchise in Guatemala City, where its sales were falling behind Pepsi's, but Atlanta did not want to be seen to intervene for fear of annoying US bottlers, who were already alarmed by negotiations to rewrite their agreements.

The International Union of Food and Allied Workers (IUF) initiated an international boycott on the grounds that the flow of profits back to Atlanta 'constitutes complicity'. In 1980, Coca-Cola and IUF executives agreed on a buy-out which would protect the workers. The Company advanced money to former salaried employees, who registered their company in Panama.

Less than four years later, the new bottler claimed bankruptcy, closed its doors and dismissed its employees, who again occupied the site. The unionists saw a chance to embarrass Coca-Cola, which was a principal sponsor of the Olympic Games in Los Angeles. They restarted international boycotts and sympathy strikes across Europe, causing another company retreat. The unionised workplace reopened in March 1985 under a different franchise-holder.

If human rights for the unionists were so poor despite attention from Geneva and Atlanta, what were conditions like for workers elsewhere in Guatemala, including those at the two non-unionised Coca-Cola sites, one of which Atlanta owned outright? In the 1990s, around 200 union activists were killed in Latin America each year.

Europe

Atlanta also had to deal with the International Union of Food Workers on its home turf in Europe. The Company's involvement in labour disputes deepened in the 1980s as Coca-Cola Enterprises (CCE) bought up bottlers, making it the boss over tens of thousands of employees around the world. Union-busting could no longer be blamed on cowboy franchise-holders backed by military dictators.

The consolidation of bottlers under the aegis of CCE added to the pressure on employees to knuckle under or lose their jobs. In the United Kingdom, CCE reduced the number of depots from fifty-two to sixteen and the number of plants from fourteen to seven, then to only two. With the completion of a £60 million plant in Yorkshire, management separated its manufacturing workers from those in delivery, breaking off talks with the IUF to secure sweet-heart arrangements with a tame-cat union, for which it agreed to collect membership dues. The workplace agreement proposed in 1987 gave management the right to 'object to any nomination' for the election of shop stewards. These practices spread across Europe in 1991. Coke's 'Code of Business Conduct' was termed 'a charter for slavery' by the IUF, because employees would have to sign away numerous rights, including their right to strike.

Driving down unit labour costs is a key to success in monopo-lising competition. Hence, PepsiCo circumvented the workplace consultation required by the European Union by locking out the IUF, bringing a majority of pro-company staff to the initial meet-ing of employees and keeping them 'in hotel rooms with no phone and a personnel manager as room mate'. The resultant agreement allowed the company to set the agenda for future negotiations.[41] *Business Week* described the agreement as breaking a 'cardinal rule of labour relations for multinational corporations', namely, 'to pre-vent unions from gaining enough power to negotiate on a multinational basis'.[42]

Pressure on wages from low-wage countries has meant job losses and real wage cuts in the metropolitan economies. If more unions acted globally, the reorganisation of capital would lose much of its appeal. How is it that transnational strikes sin against the gospel of free trade while corporate globalisation is a force of nature?

CHAPTER 13 **Time Conquers Space**

Of course, all the time would not usually be spent 'at' a job: sleep, food, even leisure are required for efficiency, and some time... would have to be spent on those activities...Slaves, for example, might be permitted time 'off' from work only in so far as that maximised their output ...

Gary S. Becker, *Economic Journal*, 1965[1]

When bad loans at Baring Brothers' bank rocked the British financial system late in 1890, the Bank of England imported gold bars worth £3 million from Paris to defend sterling. The shipments came by rail and sea, and took twenty-four hours to arrive. A hundred and five years later, a futures trader in Singapore bankrupted Barings by shifting millions of pounds around the planet in a matter of seconds.

To expand, capital must not only get more value out of the labour time it buys but also accelerate every aspect of the production–consumption cycle. The conquest of space by monopolising capitals has been called imperialism. Their simultaneous conquest of time has no name of its own, yet is at least as invasive.

The technologies that led to the collapse of Barings in 1995 had their beginnings in 1866, when the laying of a trans-Atlantic cable quickened business practices on both sides of the ocean. 'Transactions could be made with rapidity and they increased in volume. Capital was turned over rapidly and profit margins tended to be reduced to the bare minimum by sharp competition.'[2] Stockmarket ticker-tape machines followed in 1869, and telephones had linked New York to Boston and Chicago by 1886.

When every town ran on its own time, rail services were never on schedule. The railways and their customers lost revenue through missing freight and passengers. In 1883, the US railroads began to co-ordinate clock time along their routes, dividing the country into four zones. One of the boundaries ran through Georgia, delaying that State's adoption of standard time until its courts could agree at which hour of the day contracts expired. Although advocates of the New South welcomed the change as a 'standard on which Atlanta will progress into the future', the city's leading newspaper regretted 'the utter contempt into which the sun and moon have fallen'.[3] The time of day had become another item for sale. Universities and companies transmitted observatory signals to factories and jewellers for between $500 and $1000 a year.

Every cranny of everyday life has been transformed to make us go faster. Farmers might still rise with the sun, but the first factory hands had to internalise clock time to wake without an alarm. A pocket watch became a standard item of US male attire from the 1860s.

In 1861, a Baltimore canner, straining to meet demands from the Union army, found that by adding calcium chloride to water he could achieve higher temperatures and cut cooking time from six hours to thirty minutes, reducing the cost of fuel and wages. The zipper replaced buttons and hooks-and-eyes in the early 1890s as 'a saver of time...unequalled [in] this busy and progressive age'.[4] Packaged cigarettes—quicker to light than a pipe, faster to smoke than a cigar—saved the time needed to roll your own. By 1890, machines were producing 200 cigarettes a minute. During these years, the cinema affected the perception of time. The *Scientific American* recognised in 1915 that the motion picture was like a drug; it 'takes normal intervals of time and expands them one, two or a thousand fold, or compresses them by the same ratio'.[5]

Once 'King' Gillette patented his safety razor in 1901, a man could shave himself in less time than a barber took with a cut-throat. From the 1940s, electric razors eliminated the fuss of lathering; battery models allowed organisation men to shave while driving to work. In 1997, L'Oréal introduced Express Finish, a nail polish which dried in a minute. Today, almost all consumer durables include timers: washing machines, microwaves, automobiles, video recorders, computers and mobile phones.

This acceleration, with all its conveniences and discomfits, serves the need for capitalists to realise a return on their investments in ever briefer periods. The interval between the moment when they purchase raw materials and labour power and the moment when they get their investments back is divided into phases. During each of these stages, capital becomes dormant, losing more value the longer it takes to move through the cycle:

> As long as it [capital] remains in the production process it is not capable of circulating; and it is virtually devalued. As long as it remains in circulation, it is not capable of producing...not capable of engaging in the process as capital. As long as it cannot be brought to market, it is fixated as product. As long as it has to remain on the market, it is fixated as commodity. As long as it cannot be exchanged for conditions of production, it is fixated as money.[6]

The faster this cycle can be turned around, the more often a firm can expand its capital and begin the processes for accumulation again. 'First we sell them. Then we make them', was Benetton's start-up policy.[7]

To the extent that 'all economy ultimately reduces itself to the economy of time', the need to accelerate production and consumption rates is beyond the control of the individual capitalist.[8] Speed! Speed! More speed! Meeting those injunctions is obligatory if a firm is to stay in business. The impossible ideal for capital is *'Circulation without circulation time*—i.e. the transition of capital from one phase to the next at the speed of thought', a phrase Bill Gates has taken over from Karl Marx.[9]

Exhaustion

In the late nineteenth century, attention to clock time exacerbated an epidemic of nerves. These pressures stimulated the marketing of opiates and stimulants, faster food and instant drinks. Doctors blamed 'the necessity of punctuality' for an epidemic of neurasthenia or nervous exhaustion. *American Nervousness* (1884) popularised a condition which was said to afflict 'brain workers' because of pressures from the telegraph and the railroad to be on time.[10] Some commentators supposed the condition peculiar to the USA, where it was 'rooted in the cultural shocks of modernity'.[11] The leading authority described neurasthenics as being on the 'verge of bankruptcy'—a telling image given how the market was transmogrifying human relationships into a cash nexus.[12]

When Dr Pemberton promoted Coca-Cola as a 'Brain Tonic... Exhilarating, Invigorating'—he was borrowing from the literature on neurasthenia. The cocaine in his brew would vanquish lethargy.[13] Coca-Cola was but one of many quack cures that promised owners and managers relief from 'fatigue of brain, body and nerves'. Asa Candler continued to promote Coca-Cola as a tonic, reassuring the public that it had 'a very marked effect in refreshing and reviving the drooping spirits'. To persuade one soda-fountain operator to stock his nostrum, Candler identified potential customers as 'business and professional men' to whom coca and kola would bring relief from 'mental and physical exhaustion, headache, tired feeling, mental depression, etc.'[14] Although the active coca had been removed by 1904, the company went on promoting Coca-Cola as a stimulant. In 1909, billboards proclaimed that Coca-Cola 'Relieves Fatigue' while print advertisements appealed to businessmen identified as 'tired...thirsty...nerve-worn and brain-weary'.[15]

For manual labourers, Coca-Cola acted as an opiate, not by putting them to sleep, but by helping them to keep going. Coca-Cola as a beverage comes closest to being more than the metaphoric essence of capitalism when it helps workers to go faster for longer.

Both the substances in Coca-Cola's name had come to Dr Pemberton's attention as stimulants. He read a report by British colonialists about the use of the kola nut by native bearers, and he knew about the power of coca from the stevedores of New Orleans, who took cocaine to get through their seventy-hour shifts.

The Company later chased on-the-job sales, which it called 'the workers market—and what a whale of a market it is'.[16] The corporations that welcomed Coke's vending machines onto their factory floors included Frigidaire, National Cash Register, Anaconda Copper, Ford and International Harvester. The Director of Safety at US Steel's furnaces in Gary, Indiana, reported:

> Before 'Coke' was available to our employees, heat cramps and exhaustion were prevalent among our employees during the summer months, resulting in many lost man hours. 'Coke' has now reduced that problem to a minimum.[17]

A few employers feared that, if they let vending machines into workplaces, their employees would spend time away from their jobs and seek higher wages to pay for 'frivolous items'. A Coke sales manager countered: 'When they get refreshed they do better work—and Coca-Cola definitely refreshes. It has sugar in it, and sugar picks you up.'[18] The Coke rush relied on a dash of phosphoric acid, which speeds the breakdown of sucrose. The 1.25 cents profit that firms made on every bottle sold 'invariably appeals to an industrial organisation' because the earnings can be used to 'finance recreational facilities', giving the corporations a way to enhance employee goodwill at no cost to themselves.[19]

With the quickening of the war effort in 1941, Atlanta took advantage of the government's call for rest periods to enhance productivity. In presenting Woodruff with a booklet entitled 'Every Job Needs the Pause That Refreshes', the D'Arcy Advertising Agency announced: 'This busy world we live in needs its occasional pauses so it can go on being busy'.[20]

Coke's combination of a caffeine hit with a sugar buzz produces mild addiction. Withdrawal symptoms from three cans a day include 'headache, fatigue, stiffness, flu-like feelings, nausea'.[21] In 1951, one Coca-Cola stockholder asked a Company lawyer:

> Have you ever tried to dictate to a Stenographer before she has
> had her morning Coke? Haven't you noticed how restless office
> workers are until they get down about 10:00 o'clock each morning
> to get a coke, or a dope as I prefer to call it?[22]

Coke was mild compared with the amphetamines introduced to the
US workforce by the military. In 1970, '8 per cent of all prescriptions written were for amphetamines: ten billion pills'.[23]

To keep pace with the competition, Atlanta lifted the portions
of sugar and caffeine in the classic drink and put more sugar into
its fruit juices. Those ingredients provide a fix to keep going in the
era of fast capitalism, when we have less time to eat or shop. Coca-
Cola was among the first of the takeaways, a beverage to go, giving
a spurt of energy for faster work. The Coca-Cola Company promoted its brand of instant coffee as 'The Think Drink', and in the
early 1980s it declared Mellow Yellow 'the world's fastest soft drink'.
Because Coca-Cola can be taken on the run, it has some advantages over hot instant coffee as a stimulant. In the 1990s, US sales
of soft drink for immediate consumption grew faster than other
segments.[24]

Nowhere has the promise of more leisure from the tumble of
technologies been fulfilled. The leisure class is harried, modernity
is equated with speed, and the twentieth century has been branded
the fast century. Washing machines and vacuum cleaners made
housework less laborious, leaving housewives with more energy for
paid employment. Americans suffer from 'a time famine'; on average, they had nearly 40 per cent less leisure in 1989 than in 1973.[25]
One reason is that the productivity gains made by mechanisation
in manufacturing have not been matched in the service industries,
which are by definition more labour-intensive. In the last quarter
of the twentieth century, most advanced economies faced a paradox of high unemployment while those with jobs were working
longer, faster and harder.

The 'time famine' gave rise to energy drinks such as Gatorade
and Coca-Cola's Powerade, which were marketed to Tuppies—Tired
Urban Professionals too exhausted to sleep. Silicon Valley kept its
programmers alert on free supplies of JOLT, which promoted itself

as 'all the sugar and twice the caffeine'.[26] Coke's appeal has always had as much to do with imperatives at work as with any opportunities for leisure. In 1999, Coca-Cola's chairman promised that a Coke would leave 'you able to cope with any environment that isn't all that fun'.[27]

Faster foods

Faster foods appeared in domestic kitchens long before families grew impatient at takeaway counters. From the early 1880s, processed rolled oats could be cooked in twenty minutes, compared with the four hours needed for groats; porridge, with milk and a sweetener, became a one-course breakfast, replacing the ninety-minute spreads of rural America. By the early twentieth century, Dr Kellogg's corn flakes and other packaged cold fare had further speeded up the preparation in the morning.

As more wives and then mothers re-entered the paid workforce, the demand grew for breakfast foods that all but the most chauvinist male or dependent child could serve themselves. A bread-like substance had appeared in Japanese breakfasts during the early 1950s because it was faster to make toast than to boil rice; later, electric cookers obviated this violation of Shinto mores. Between 1945 and 1965, the percentage of US breakfast cereals eaten cold grew from under 40 to over 60 per cent. In the mid-1990s, cold cereals were overtaken by finger food such as pop-tarts, bagels or muffins, which 'are a lot easier to eat while you're driving a car'.[28] Kellogg's responded with Breakfast Mates, a single serve of cereal packaged with a spoon and a container of long-life milk.

Between late 1978 and 1993, the average time that housewives spent preparing meals in the USA fell from three-and-a-half hours to thirty minutes a day.[29] Frozen, canned, dehydrated and pre-cooked foods became the domestic servants of the 1950s. Home kitchens were redesigned to resemble an assembly line. After microwaves displaced ovens, a vice-president of Campbell's Soup reworded an old adage to 'You are what you heat'.[30] Along with faster foods came faster drinks. Instant coffee pushed tea aside. Instant teas flopped but tea-bags went from less than 3 per cent of the British market in 1968 to more than 12 per cent by 1971. In Australia, sales of tea-bags quadrupled between 1972 and 1975.

Takeaways

Takeaway food got a boost at the St Louis World Fair in 1904 with the creation of the hamburger as a meat patty inside a bread roll— a mobile meal. The Fair is also credited with introducing cones for ice creams, which allowed people to eat on the move. These innovations remained special treats; at Howard-Johnston outlets in the 1920s, most ice creams were still eaten with spoons from bowls served at tables. The drift to takeaways came with motorisation. Los Angeles led the way in 1932 with a drive-in restaurant where car-hops brought orders to the waiting automobiles.

Ray Kroc encountered the McDonald brothers in 1954, when they were operating eight machines which could mix five milk-shakes each. The brothers needed to prepare forty drinks at a time because long-distance buses called by their San Bernadino stand, which was at the terminus of transcontinental Route 66.[31] McDonald's had no seating till 1968; in the same year it installed its first drive-through windows. Twenty years later, McDonald's was making more than half its sales at drive-throughs, with some venues running a second bay. The percentage of fast food eaten off premises almost trebled in the 1980s. Family cars now come equipped with holders to facilitate driving while drinking out of cups with lids designed to prevent spillage.

McDonald's sites operate at only 70 per cent capacity from dawn to midnight because its fast foods are most sought after during the daylight hours, when they are consumed almost as a snack. Only 20 per cent of sales occur after 4 p.m. 'McDonald's is lunch. Pizza is dinner.'[32] Few regulars consider even a Big Mac to be a satisfying meal in the evenings, especially in countries where the outlets do not serve alcohol. McDonald's overcame down-time in the mornings with McMuffin and McEgg, but the drop-off of adult custom at night persists because all attempts at a dinner menu have flopped. McDonald's real-estate investments therefore remain under-utilised, and hence a drain on earnings.

Kroc adapted Henry Ford's production line to the preparation of food. The 15-cent burger was his T-model. Speed was 'The essence of Hamburger Science': a burger, shake and fries within fifty seconds. A high mark was scored in 1959 with thirty-six burgers in 110 seconds. McDonald's lifted the sugar content of its buns so they would toast faster. By 1990, one in three outlets had electric clam shells to cook burgers on both sides at once. Bottlenecks at the counter were later reduced by installing touch-screens to take orders. Test-marketing of salad in a cup prompted one industry analyst to ask whether the next move would be a Big Mac from a blender—'a frappamaco'.[33]

Fast food can never be fast enough. In the late 1930s, Harland Sanders used pressure cookers to reduce the preparation time for frying chickens from four hours to thirty minutes. He always hoped to invent cookers big enough to take twenty birds at once, instead of a maximum of four. As well as speeding up preparation and delivery time, fast-food chains tailor ingredients to fit the price. After Sanders sold Kentucky Fried Chicken, its new owners abandoned the gravy he had spent years developing because it was a time-consuming speciality. They also stopped ladling fat off by hand and put the birds on a rack to drain. Their chickens are now being bred to mature within seven weeks.

Speed of the line

In 1850 the founder of perceptual physiology, Hermann von Helmholtz, calculated the speed at which messages pass through the nervous system. Hitherto, these movements had been assumed to be too fast to calibrate. Helmholtz's measurements, aided by rapid-exposure photographs of human locomotion, opened the door to the regulation of movements at the work bench. In 1888, a union representative denounced the stopwatch as 'equivalent to a whip' since it 'fractured Time to suit the boss's agenda'.[34] The relentlessness of Henry Ford's production lines caused a rate of high labour turnover, which the payment of $5 a day could not stem. When Mitsubishi Electrical introduced time-and-motion studies in 1921, its managers set the standard time needed to perform tasks without any margin for retooling, delayed deliveries or personal needs.

Time-and-motion experts had to do more than make workers go faster. They also ensured that no essential step was omitted. The speed-up must not result in a product which was unsaleable or had to be sold below cost. Haste did not cause waste if work processes were closely managed. Standardisation meant that cutting costs did not necessarily mean cutting corners.

Imposition of a longer working week is the least efficient answer to capital's need to extract the maximum surplus from the labour power it buys from its workers. A firm needs its workers to be productive throughout all the hours for which they are being paid. Concentrated work for eight hours will reward the boss, whereas malingering for eighteen would be a waste. Union demands for a shorter working week without a reduction in pay made employers more determined to control the regime at work.

The first step was to ensure that workers were present for all the hours of their shift. The manufacturer of Bundy clocks trumpeted that they would 'save money, enforce discipline and add to the productive time' because employers could document when workers started and knocked off.[35] On an assembly line, any unauthorised absence became obvious.

Eliminating absenteeism is the passive side of managing productivity. McDonald's slogan 'You deserve a break' carries two suggestions. First, that parents are entitled to a rest from preparing family meals. Secondly, that the customer merits a respite from the rush of the day—a variant on 'The pause that refreshes'. McDonald's brisk turnaround of orders is paraded as a service to the public. That promise also extracts the maximum of labour power out of the workforce, because every customer becomes an overseer. In the early 1970s, staff were subjected to lie-detector tests: 'Did you ever steal a minute of McDonald's time?'[36] This approach internalised supervision by making teenage floor staff feel guilty. 'You deserve a break' never applied to them.

Economies of speed came 'from the ability to integrate and coordinate the flow of materials through the plant'.[37] When the productive process itself required labourers to wait between phases, the employer lost the wages he paid while the workers stood idle. From the mid-eighteenth century, Josiah Wedgwood reduced 'the excess of production time over the labour-time' by redesigning his pottery for a continuous flow of materials from barges through kilns and workshops, and back to barges. [38] From the 1890s, pulp and paper mills were located side by side to reduce the costs of storage and processing. Similarly, an integrated iron and steel works could produce girders without reheating the metal if all the stages were continuous and contiguous. Andrew Carnegie contained the costs of steel-making by 'forcing the largest quantity of material through the entire process in the shortest possible time'.[39]

Savings depended on cutting the time taken to finish the commodity. The advantages came in proportion to the speed of the line rather than the volume of production, irrespective of the time taken. In a depressed market, Carnegie could sell below his competitors and maintain absolute returns, even if his profit per item fell for a time. From 1907 Hershey had the fastest chocolate-making equipment available, but the firm lost its advantage when the expanded plant became a warren of tacked-on bits and pieces. In 1953, Hershey's main competitor, Forrest Mars, arranged his new machines into a continuous flow, reducing production time from 16 hours to 35 minutes.[40]

After Howard Candler took charge of the manufacture of Coca-Cola syrup in 1906, he battled to expedite the flow of ingredients to branch factories, making local managers remit a weekly docket of the raw materials on hand and in transit. Despite his systemisation, plants 'were frequently shut down for lack of supplies', [41] so that workers were paid for idle time. After 1904, Atlanta's output could not keep up with demand during the summer months because the city's high temperatures delayed the cooling of the syrup, even after the installation of a refrigeration plant. Necessity proved the mother of a different invention for Coca-Cola when the government rationed power supplies in 1917. Howard discovered that sugar would dissolve without heating; this realisation 'effected a real economy not only...in the cost of fuel, the operation and upkeep of a boiler, but also in the very considerable amount of time saved'. Workers no longer had to wait for the temperature to fall from 90 to 60 degrees Fahrenheit before dispatching the syrup; more production cycles could be completed each week.[42]

Eighty years later, retailers pressed bottlers to increase the frequency of their deliveries. During the 1990s, supplies went from one to three despatches a week. Now, stores push for 'just-in-time' arrivals to cut the working capital tied up in inventory. This cost saving for the retailer increases operating expenses for the wholesaler, who has to run more trucks and drivers. As more shops stay open around the clock, they cannot afford to be out of stock at 2 a.m. on a Sunday. Soon, daily deliveries will not be soon enough.[43]

Whose convenience?

If 'More light!' were Goethe's dying words, the fulfilment of his wish breathed life into dormant capital. With artificial lighting, manufacturers could extend the factory day by operating a second twelve-hour shift. A six-day week was inescapable for as long as employers found it easier to rely on the natural light of a sixth working day. Candles were too expensive and their luminosity too faint for large factories. Gas made the difference, then filament lamps took over from the 1870s. Fluorescent tubes, which came in during the 1930s, were closer to the wavelengths of sunlight and improved the quality of detailed work.

Artificial lighting also extended the time available for selling. The extra hours for shopping were prized because the 'closer the time taken for circulation approaches zero, the more can capital increase its productivity and expand its value'.[44] One of the creators of the chain store in the USA attributed its success almost entirely to 'a rapid turnover of merchandise'.[45] Street lighting extended shopping hours in winter just as air-conditioning would later do in summer.

When factory and office hours coincide more or less with shopping hours, the employer's need to keep workers at their benches comes into conflict with the workers' need to obtain the resources to replenish their capacity to labour: 'the time a labourer needs for the purchase of his means of subsistence is lost time' for the capitalist.[46] Hence, employers have pressed for flexible trading hours.

Convenience stores, 24-hour ATMs, daytime television commercials, telephonic banking and all-night eateries are convenient for employers who need their workers to slot their shopping into fractured work patterns.

Daylight saving also appealed to employers as a way to reduce costs and expand sales. In 1984 the lobbyist for one business coalition extolled the virtues of bringing clocks forward an hour from the beginning of April:

> You don't have to spend another advertising dollar. You don't have to wring anything out of the labor unions. You don't need additional plant or equipment. Here's a way to increase economic activity by doing nothing more than changing the time on your wrist.[47]

Idaho's congressional representatives switched their votes to favour daylight saving after McDonald's, the major buyer of the State's potato crop, pointed out that its outlets did more business in daylight than after dark.

With shoppers lacking the time to gather information about products, economists found 'a rationale for irrationality' in impulsive shopping. Increasingly, 'each buyer allocates her scarce time among alternative purchases'. Impulse buying in supermarkets during the 1950s rose from under 40 to over 50 per cent of items. This carefree approach extended to even more expensive products because 'people will prefer to make an occasional mistake, rather than spend a long time considering each decision'. Buyers also save time when they 'equate price with quality', seeking a brand name as a guarantee. [48]

In the 1950s, economists debated whether the squeeze on time would place a ceiling on consumption and hence cut short the postwar boom. They worried that the time needed to maintain appliances would limit the number of durables that a consumer would purchase. Such fears drew on inter-war experiences with the automobile and the wireless. In the age of affluence, those constraints were removed by new goods and services. Any lack of time to wash the family car would be solved by car-washes at garages. Other time-savers included motor mowers and dry cleaning. The quality of electrical goods improved and their complexity increased, so that the householder could not effect repairs, and seldom needed to. The pleasure of tinkering with the insides of a valve radio gave way to the menial task of adjusting a TV aerial. Replacement prices came down while repair costs increased, so that people tended to throw small appliances away rather than pay to have them fixed. Meanwhile, the definition of perishable changed. Fashion and marketing pressures shortened the life span of commodities. Motor cars appeared stale when their styling was overtaken by next year's model. The quickening of the product cycle caused marketing expenses to rise faster than Gross Domestic Product.

Spoils

Before money replaced the bartering of goods, their perishable nature had limited the accumulation of capital. Getting consumers to buy as soon as possible after production is another way to avoid losses from spoilage. Dorset dairy farmers prospered from the 1840s, once they could have their milk delivered fresh to London by rail. 'Use-values are perishable by nature. Hence, if they are not...sold within a certain period, they spoil and lose their usefulness' as well as their ability to be exchanged for money.[47] Unilever had to air-freight the blooms it cultivated in Zimbabwe to sell them to Europe while they were fresh. Additional storage costs could not be passed along if consignments were delayed:

> 'Too bad for you!' the Amsterdam flower broker would say. 'Right here alongside of you is another seller whose roses were cut only yesterday. Your stems are shop-worn and damaged by the ravages of time. Therefore you will have to sell cheaper than your competitor.'[50]

Producers have developed various means to avoid such liabilities: spoilt fruit goes into jams; preservatives are added to packaged foods; waxing and polishing give a gleam to tired stock; canning extends the saleable life of meats and vegetables; fruits are irradiated to prolong their shelf-life; marketing campaigns boost consumption in the peak season. Bio-engineering is intended to shorten the time required to produce a crop and to extend the period during which foods can be represented as fresh. Meanwhile, corporations remain reluctant to clarify use-by dates.

In the nineteenth century, syrups made from fresh fruit had to be used on the day of their manufacture, and all flavourings went off after a few weeks. Coca-Cola had the advantage of not going bad so quickly. Whenever its syrup did spoil, The Company lost heavily. To reduce this risk, Woodruff offered the same discount for small and larger units so that slower-selling outlets would not put customers off by serving a drink which was less than top quality. Druggists in the late 1930s were encouraged to buy no more than a fifteen-day supply. In 1943, The Company's post-war plan proposed that syrup be recalled thirty days after manufacture, that retailers take only seven days stock and that the large barrels be replaced with one-gallon glass containers.[51] The extra costs were more palatable than soured drinkers.

In the 1990s, the artificial sweetener used in Diet Coke, aspartame, lost its intensity over time. When this happened, The Company bore the expense of transporting and disposing of retailers' returned stock; it also had to absorb the costs of advancing money on raw materials and labour that would never realise any profit. The Company would have been richer had that batch never been brewed. The catch is that Coca-Cola must overproduce in order to be within arm's reach of everyone's desire and to block competitors out of shelf space.

Because Coca-Cola syrup did not need to be aged, its owners escaped the costs that faced whisky distillers, who had to tie up their capital for years before realising a return. If Asa Candler was conforming to what he saw as God's will by keeping 'my stuff continuously invested', heaven paid only part of his reward.[52] The Biblical meaning of 'speed' as good fortune applied in this world as well.

Instant managers

Whereas earlier capitalists would wait for the annual stocktaking to know their inventory, twentieth-century corporations began to require such information within days. In 1923, for example, General Motors responded to excess demand by stepping up its production, although its managers would not know until early March 1924 how many vehicles their dealers had sold the previous October. Suffering from having overestimated demand, GM began to gather sales numbers from dealers every ten days and then to shorten 'the reaction time when a forecast proved wrong'.[53]

The flow of information at The Coca-Cola Company moved in fits and starts. This disarray was typical of the stages through which most corporations have dragged themselves. In 1946, Woodruff was pleading for statistics of any kind. Well into the 1980s, executives in Atlanta waited two months for global results; a new chief financial officer trimmed the delay to less than a week.

The soft-drink business, as the chairman of the Pepsi Bottling Group should know, 'is absolutely a real-time business...if we are out of a product on Saturday and we do nothing about it, we'll be out of product on Monday'. Even getting end-of-week assessments is from 'way back when. In the bottling business, the periods don't roll; you either sell today or you don't.'[54] In 1999, Coca-Cola tested a vending machine which would automatically increase price with demand and transmit data on its inventory so that slots were never empty. Delivery trucks are directed by satellites, while production lines are a conflict zone between speed and quality control.

Corporate planning is now a continuous reassessment rather than a matter of taking aim at one- or three-year targets. Late in the 1970s, Standard Brands dumped its president, who wanted to hold monthly committee meetings at a time when decisions needed to be made hourly. Down at Bentonville, Arkansas, Sam Walton kept up with the stock and sales in more than a thousand stores by satellite. Computers 'cut 40 hours off weekly paperwork' for McDonald's store managers.[55] At J. C. Penny stores in the late 1990s, buyers had to wait for decisions by 1200 managers before ordering fashion goods. As a result, their stocks fell behind their competitors' until a 'centralised buying strategy' saved them four to five weeks.[56]

Managers suffer under the same pressures they must impose on their workforce. Although Sears CEO Ed Brennan dismissed *The One-Minute Manager* as 'pure, unadulterated bullshit', the book's title summed up the situation in which senior executives find themselves when their corporations grow and their bottom line depends on the velocity of turnover.[57] As managers move up the system they have less time to reflect. The one-minute manager is of a piece with the one-idea consultant, the one-notion text and the one-book executive. Brennan himself did not always have time to skim even the business press.

In the nineteenth century, Carnegie's generation could be confident that a new machine would not be bypassed before it had paid for itself; indeed, they expected to keep most equipment in use after it had been fully depreciated. That assumption was outdated by 1960. Management consultants were predicting that 95 per cent of the products that would be on sale a decade later did not yet exist. Nowadays, no technological lead is guaranteed for more than five years, and many will expire sooner. In 1965, Intel's co-founder, Gordon Moore, enunciated his law of integrated circuits: the number of their components would double every year. What seemed improbable then is now taken for granted. This rate of inventiveness challenges patent-holders and depreciates the values put on human skills along with the machines they operate.

Well before the Barings disaster in 1995, capitalists were pursuing economies of speed for their money as much as for their commodities. The management of exchange rates became decisive when corporations earned more of their profits offshore. Coca-Cola lost $13 million in currency movements during 1988, but gained $20 million a year later. By the 1990s, Gillette was drawing three-quarters of its profits from outside the USA and 'could scarcely exist without the world-shrinking impact of the jet aeroplane and the computer'. After its cash-management system became fully operational in 1993, Gillette could redeploy funds generated by its non-American businesses:

> Each night, cash that has accumulated in Gillette bank accounts around the world is 'swept' or transferred to Zurich…One goal is to avoid fees that banks charge for holding and moving cash. Another is to minimise taxes levied on bank accounts by ending the day with a zero balance.[58]

These arrangements saved Gillette $5 million in 1996.

Executives have joined the metaphysicians' quest for a fulcrum from which to lever their business in a world of dissolving certainties. Quantitative increases in the pace of financial and commodity trading add to the perplexities faced by strategists. In 1998, the retired chairman of a management firm reflected:

> We financial analysts were brought up looking at charts whose x axis represented time. You'd see trends. Time was a wave. In the New Economy, I'm beginning to think time is a quantum. What comes next bears no relationship to what came before. It used to be that information oozed out into the market. Now, it's dumped out all at once.[59]

Coca-Cola now has a Chief Knowledge Officer to speed the spread of ideas through its bottling networks. The Company's former chairman, Doug Ivester, was 'down on old-fashioned notions of time—namely, the time it takes to get a job done. He has played with all sorts of ways to avoid doing things sequentially, pushing instead for what he calls "viral growth".'[60] Instead of opening sales offices across China one at a time, Coca-Cola used each new unit to spawn several more. Ivester also referred to a sales territory as 'geography' to indicate that markets have to be treated as topographies marked by mountains and oceans. This resort to virology and geography spotlights the perplexities that led to Ivester's resignation.

Putting Coke within an 'arm's reach of desire' on a world scale has abridged the interval between wishing and satisfaction. Vending machines in the street appear to be battling for place, but they are also an assault on time. The more of them there are, the shorter is the period during which potential buyers can satisfy their thirst with some other firm's beverage. Marketing cannot wait to meet wants as they arise. In its drive for speed and scale, it refashions need.

PART SIX

Second Nature

Taking control over production of our own food supply, we became the first species in the 3.5-billion-year history of life to live outside the confines of the local ecosystem.

...in stepping away from local ecosystems and in substituting cultural devices for physiological and anatomical adaptations, we have unwittingly changed the rules of the evolutionary game.

Niles Eldredge, 1995[1]

CHAPTER 14

The Company Needs You

A Utopia where...turkeys fly around ready-roasted ...
Arthur Schopenhauer, 1851[2]

'Nobody needs it', a president of PepsiCo admitted. At The Coca-Cola Company, the president welcomed a Coke as 'a small pleasure on an average day'. The publisher of *Beverage World* concurred: 'Never before has a company created so much from so little...A coke and a smile, indeed.'[3] Yet the lengths to which people would go to obtain a Coke have become the stuff of legends. Nobel laureate William Faulkner portrayed a recently released lifer in the American South who, having saved just enough money to buy the gun he needs to exact vengeance, succumbs to his 38-year-old memory of Coca-Cola to buy a bottle. As he finishes it, he is horrified to hear 'his voice saying, "I'll have another one," even while he was telling himself *Stop it! Stop it!'*[4]

At issue is more than individual addiction, more even than the faith of the multitudes who growled in 1985 when Roberto Goizueta killed Classic Coke. The popularity of flavoured water indicates how corporations can influence demand. To say that nobody needs a cola is to overlook how very much The Coca-Cola Company needs us to need a Coke. As its Chief Financial Officer spelt out, 'beverages don't generate revenues. It's the art of selling somebody something and collecting money that generates revenues.'[5] The same truth held in 1898 when the National Biscuit Company needed people to choose its five-cent packages, so it changed 'You need a biscuit' into a brand name: 'Uneeda biscuit'. Many of our needs have been induced by capital, which thereby has sharpened the conflict between saving and spending, work and leisure.

True or false?

Needs cannot be categorised as true or false, biologically determined or socially conditioned. To convict marketeers of stimulating false wants, the prosecution must first identify true needs. One approach to distinguishing *true needs* from *false wants* has been to ground the former in biology. This method is as impoverished as Poor Tom in *King Lear*, who persisted, naked save for a blanket, by devouring toads or rats, and drinking stagnant water, in a life which was as nasty and brutish as it would have been short, had he not been rescued by Shakespeare in Act IV, scene vi. Physiological needs are neither few nor simple, and they do not fall outside the circle of social relations. To survive longer than a year, hunter-gatherers must provide themselves with tools and shelter. To thrive across generations, they require weapons and territories, language and song, affection and companionship, magic and ceremonies.

A compulsion to drink cannot explain the decoration on vessels or the rituals around a bar:

> Hunger is hunger, but the hunger gratified by cooked meat eaten with a knife and fork is a different hunger from that which bolts down raw meat with the aid of hand, nail and tooth. Production thus produces not only the object but also the manner of consumption.[6]

Biology is mute when faced with the explosion of needs in the last 200 years. Hence, to label the minimum that we require *true* and to disparage every need over and above the rawest necessities as *false* is to deny humanity our capacity to remake ourselves. Civilisation exists because we have spread our needs beyond those essential for existence.

Our remaking of human nature through the extension of needs has made us *homo sapiens sapiens*. Because 'historically developed social needs...become second nature',[7] they are now as much a part of our humanness as are any physiological drives we inherited from our forebears. Those original traits have been transformed through social practices, just as we are constantly remaking our second nature through the re-creation of needs and the means to their satisfaction.

In the process, capitalists have transformed 'what was previously superfluous into what is necessary'. At first, they hunted down new objects with which to satisfy existing needs:

> Hence exploration of all nature in order to discover new, useful qualities in things: universal exchange of the products of all alien climates and lands: new (artificial) preparation of natural objects, by which they are given new use values. The exploration of the earth in all directions, to discover new things of use as well as new useful qualities of the old.

The next stage was more ambitious because it operated on the consumers themselves, through cultivating 'all the qualities of the social human being'. The aim was to form a human type 'as rich as possible in needs' who 'can take gratification in a many-sided way'.[8]

Liquids are the essence of life, our bodies being 98 per cent water. We die of thirst long before we die of hunger. The need to drink is fixed in our physiology. How we meet that drive, however, varies with circumstance. Our natural thirst does not program a preference for any particular liquid. Physiology can never explain why billions have paid for a Coke when most of them can get water from a tap practically free. No one is born with a need for Coca-Cola. On the contrary, it is an acquired preference, as The Company acknowledged in its maxim 'Take five drinks and you'll like it'.[9]

In the USA of the 1880s, most people's incomes went on food, clothing and shelter, with next-to-no outlays on soda-pops. A century later, a firm launching a New Age beverage could assume that, while everyone in the USA 'may not have money for a new car, they've always got a couple of quarters for a soft-drink. It's fun, and it's a break.'[10] A purchase which had been exceptional when Pemberton invented Coca-Cola had become a norm throughout the First World.

Any object or service that anyone finds useful embodies a need, whether it springs 'from the stomach or from fancy'.[11] Uses are never confined to the physical, but include the psychological: 'In the factory, we make cosmetics; in the store, we sell hope', quipped the founder of Revlon cosmetics.[12] The chief of the agency directing the Pepsi Generation campaign mused: 'We don't buy the product. We buy the satisfaction the product will bring us.'[13] Celebrant of the triumph of materialism, James B. Twitchell, purchased a red Mazda 121 in order not to be mistaken for a yuppie, an action he acknowledged was 'nostalgic onanism'.[14] Intangible uses were not invented by marketeers. They merely attached a veneer of luxury or rarity to every product—their aura of glamour. The purchase itself, joked about as retail therapy, can satisfy a need. If buying a video game cheers up its buyer, then its usefulness has been achieved, whether it is played once or never. If it becomes an obsession, however, then SEGA suffers from losing a serial shopper, a prospect which carries our discussion back to the relation between the needs of the consumer and the needs of capital.

The inducements of capital

To accept that needs develop through the changing of social and cultural contexts is only a first step to understanding because the origin and purpose of needs differ in each economic system. Starting from the intimate relationship between production and consumption under capitalism, the Canadian political economist Michael Lebowitz replaced talk of false wants and socially produced needs with the idea of capital-induced needs. Because capital's need to expand requires a proliferation of needs in consumers, the yearnings elsewhere dismissed as false can be better analysed if they are seen as meeting the true needs of capital. Capital multiplies our needs, but in ways that further subjugate our lives to its need to expand. The result is that 'each new need becomes a new requirement to work'.[15] '*Deprivation* and *plenitude*' march hand-in-hand because these new needs place us 'in a new dependence', an enslavement exemplified by the tobacco industry.[16]

As an innovation of the 1860s, cigarettes were another commodity which consumers had to be taught to need. Their marketeers had to overcome three obstacles: first, men considered them an effeminate form of the cigar; secondly, respectable women were not supposed to use tobacco in any form in public; thirdly, consumers resisted machine-made products. Until a nicotine addiction had been acquired, the individual's demand was elastic in the extreme. Oscar Wilde judged a cigarette to be 'the perfect type of a perfect pleasure. It is exquisite, and it leaves one unsatisfied. What more can one want?' These properties also made the cigarette 'the perfect commodity'.[17]

Wilde had glimpsed how the needs of capital were met by the purchase itself as much as through any use we have for what we buy. The French semiotician Roland Barthes recognised that this element flourished through another of Oscar's trademarks, fashion: 'if clothing's producers and consumers had the same consciousness, clothing would be bought (and produced) only at the very slow rate of its dilapidation'. The model consumer, however, never wears a garment until it is worn out, a rule which does not only apply to *haute couture*. The economising that a particular capital requires for its own reproduction is the reverse of the behaviour that capitalists instil into their customers: 'Calculating, industrial society is obligated to form consumers who don't calculate'.[18] While the efficient factory turns its waste into commodities, its ideal customer will dispense with every item long before it has ceased to be usable.

A buyer's lack of interest in the use for which a commodity was designed has its parallel in the corporation's reason for producing it. The capitalist is not interested in

> a commodity for its own sake, nor for the sake of its use-value, or his personal consumption. The product in which the capitalist is

really interested is not the palpable product itself, but the excess value of the product over the value of the capital consumed by it.[19]

One true need of the capitalist is to expropriate as much as possible of the value added during production.

Work

The belief that needs must be either true or false haunts Coca-Cola's slogan 'It's the Real Thing©'. The attachment of the copyright mark signals that consumers are being invited to enter a reality that isn't Kansas, but is the kingdom of branded commodities. An historian of advertising, Stuart Ewen, perceived:

> Each time that the Coca-Cola Bottling Company informs us that their product is 'The Real Thing', implicit is the message that it isn't the real thing after all; and what is more, people do feel the need for the actual real thing.
>
> In a Coke ad, there is the understanding that the demand and struggle for something real will be diverted, defined as subversive or folly, and that 'The Real Thing©' will serve as an acceptable embodiment of the impulse for something more real, more gratifying. [20]

The 'actual real thing' that is missing is work that fulfils those who do it. That is the one need that capital can never satisfy for most workers. Indeed, capitalism cannot always provide work of any kind, or does so at low wages and under demoralising conditions. Instead, its marketing agents parade palliatives.

The falsehood within monopolising capitals is not their cornucopia of commodities but the claim that consumption is an answer to the alienation of work. Adapting a passage from the American social critic Christopher Lasch, we can say that:

> Consumption replicates the problems from which it is supposed to provide a refuge. It is the devastation of creative social labour, not

the retreat into shopping, that deserves to be criticised. The trouble with advertising is not so much that it deals with trivial or unreal issues but that it promises self-defeating solutions. Arising out of a pervasive dissatisfaction with the organisation of work, mass marketing advises workers to seek fulfilment in commercialised leisure, to avoid involvement with unions, or to invest for their retirement (as Puritans once did for heaven)—thereby compounding the conditions that created the loss of on-the-job satisfaction in the first place.[21]

In the 1950s, marketeers encouraged men to buy power-tool sets for do-it-yourself home repairs to fill the blank left by the routinisation of paid labour. Meanwhile, General Mills assuaged the guilt that its marketing had induced in housewives by removing the powdered egg from its Betty Crocker cake mixes to leave some space for creative baking.

Advertisers therefore avoid the workplace as a setting for their copy. By privileging the consumer, advertising masks how the growth of capital depends on human labour. In Pepsi's Live/Give campaigns from 1969, 'almost everyone depicted...is engaged in some sort of leisure-time play or consuming'.[22] A leading practitioner of the 1920s warned advertising agents against visiting the factory where the product was made: 'Don't watch people at work', she advised. 'Because, you see, when you know the truth about anything, the real, inner truth—it is very hard to write the surface fluff which sells it.'[23] Coca-Cola infringed this rule only when faced with wartime rationing, which its lawyers sought to circumvent by stressing that a Coke was not the 'poor man's luxury' but an 'essential'.[24] The Company's need for raw materials made its marketing march to a stricter tempo in 1942. A previous ad showing a disembodied hand holding a bottle 'was transformed into the powerful arm of the worker in overalls'.[25] Even then, workplace images remained unusual, and few ventured onto the factory floor, any more than marketeers dared to depict GIs dying.

Effective demand

Adam Smith knew that capital had its own definition of true needs, one which relied neither on morality, nor beauty nor biology. A 'very poor man', Smith wrote, 'may be said in some sense to have a demand for a coach and six; he might like to have it; but his demand is not an effectual demand, as the commodity can never be brought to market in order to satisfy it'.[26] The choices available under the rule of capital are limited by one's purchasing power. Capital will meet a need only when it is matched by the capacity to pay. Although beggars have preferences, and convicts trade their bread ration for tobacco or harder drugs, their effective demand can be close to zero. Social marginals attract capital only if they can make any of their preferences effective. For capital, a need is false only when its holder's pocket is empty. Coca-Cola chairman Doug Ivester seemed to forget this fact of business when he responded to the 1997 Asian meltdown by asserting that 'there's nothing about economic change that is going to change people's thirst'.[27] The level of thirst was not in question. His problem was the contraction of effective demand.

To analyse effective demand as a tug-of-war between supply and demand is to bypass the ways in which total demand is established through the contest between classes, and among strata within classes: 'absolutely nothing can be explained by the relation of supply to demand' without ascertaining the ratio of profit to wages.[28] That division is affected by the 'degree of comfort in which the class of free labourers has been formed'.[29] The more needs workers treat as socially necessary, the higher real wages they will strive to secure. Conversely, the more they have been accustomed to consider themselves as just another commodity with no say over 'where it should be offered for sale, to what purpose it should be used, at what price it should be allowed to change hands, and in what manner it should be consumed or destroyed', the less they will demand as their share.[30]

Two hundred years after Adam Smith distinguished effective demands from daydreams, the US economist Tibor Scitovsky used the vocabulary of free markets to criticise the inequality that flows from capital's control over demand:

> The market is like a voting machine in which dollars spent by consumers are counted as votes. The more a consumer spends, the greater his voting power. Therefore, consumer sovereignty in a free enterprise economy is a plutocracy, the rule of the rich, where each consumer's influence on what gets produced depends on how much he spends.[31]

The same distribution of purchasing power shapes the demand curve for particular products. For example, in the 1970s, the wealthiest 8 per cent of adult Brazilian males bought 66 per cent of Gillette's product, while the poorest 61 per cent took only 11.5 per cent.

Wealth and poverty are never absolutes but measure access to the goods and services needed to live in a particular time and place. Compared with the unemployed roving China, the homeless of Tokyo have high annual incomes, yet they are just as poor in relation to their surroundings. Capital's expansion of needs has intensified feelings of deprivation for those on or below the satisfaction line drawn by Admass. The more toys cost, the more miserable becomes the family who cannot afford them. Before the 1950s, children could go barefoot without shame; then came the thong; nowadays, some will nick Reeboks for their labels. Because needs 'are of a social nature, they are of a relative nature', which means the well-to-do will also feel deprived:

> A house may be large or small; as long as the surrounding houses are equally small it satisfies all social demands for a dwelling. But let a palace arise beside the little house, and it shrinks from a little house to a hut...and however high it may shoot up in the course of civilisation, if the neighbouring palace grows to an equal or even greater extent, the occupant of the relatively small house will feel more and more uncomfortable, dissatisfied and cramped within its four walls.[32]

Ethics and economics here intertwine, because covetousness nourishes the demand that helps capital to expand. The French novelist Honoré de Balzac observed in 1846 that no one 'knows how much obvious bad taste this retrospective envy accounts for'.[33]

Consumer sovereignty

Behind the claim that only a few needs are true lurks 'an ideal of autonomous individual rationality'. True needs are supposedly known without prompting, as in the rational consumer, that 'elegant fiction of conventional economics'.[34] The notion that the consumer is an autonomous individual is misleading for the same reason that Robinson Crusoe could not go shopping.

The adage that 'supply creates its own demand' acquired a new meaning once overproduction obliged corporations to stimulate custom. Coca-Cola president Paul Austin appreciated that market researchers had 'devised more sensitive methods...to anticipate future desires'.[35] The publisher of *Beverage World* observed: 'Coca-Cola didn't get where it is today by merely waiting for consumers in over 195 countries to ask for one of its products'.[36] The president of Coca-Cola Southern Africa saw its $300 million investment there as 'energising the market to increase demand'.[37] Robert Woodruff's promise to put Coca-Cola 'within arm's reach of desire' sounds as if capital would be serving the consumer. Roberto Goizueta turned that phrase around to expose Coca-Cola's need to keep customers within its grasp: 'To be successful, we've got to make it impossible for the consumer to escape The Coca-Cola Company'.[38] So whose desires are sovereign?

Management guru Peter Drucker was explicit about a firm's need to manipulate demand: 'Markets are not created by God, nature or economic forces, but by business men'. Therefore, the 'only one valid definition of business purpose [is] *to create a customer*'. From that premise, Drucker concluded that 'any business enterprise has two—and only these two—basic functions: marketing and innovation':

The want they satisfy may have been felt by the customer before he was offered the means to satisfy it. It may indeed, like the want of food in a famine, have dominated the customer's life and filled all his waking moments. But it was a theoretical want before: only when the action of business men makes it an effective demand is there a customer, a market. It may have been an unfelt want. There may have been no want at all until business action created it—by advertising, by salesmanship, or by inventing something new. In every case it is business action that creates the customer.

No sooner had Drucker placed producer sovereignty well above consumer sovereignty than he stumbled back into a version of the latter: 'It is the customer who determines what a business is. For it is the customer, and he alone, who through being willing to pay for a good or for a service, converts economic resources into wealth, things into goods.'[39] Drucker had lost track of Adam Smith's insight into the significance of the consumer's capacity to pay. In particular, Drucker reinterpreted the phrase 'effectual demand' to mean the corporation's fulfilment of a customer's wish. If this definition were right and wishing were enough to convert metal and leather into limousines, then capitalists have been wasting their fortunes on plant, equipment, raw materials and labour power.

In one respect, Drucker was right: corporations do prepare their marketing campaigns before manufacturing the commodity itself. In the Coca-Cola house journal, *Red Barrel*, an engineer reported in 1939 that a company would become concerned with 'how it can contrive to build a product of the proper design' only after market researchers had decided which item to make and at what price.[40] Thirty years later, John Sculley, who managed Pepsi and Apple, abandoned a career as an industrial designer when he 'discovered that marketers, not designers on the drafting boards, were calling the shots'.[41]

Advertising executives disparage their critics for having the effrontery to tell other people what they do not need. But how does an environmentalist's warning against pollution and waste differ from the marketing manager's insistence that we need more and more of everything? The answer is that the marketeer has the larger budget. The two English environmentalists sued by McDonald's for libel between 1990 and 1997 were unemployed and had to conduct their own defence against the $US20 million that McDonald's spent on legal representatives, not to mention the billion that it puts out each year on advertising. Despite that imbalance, the defendants gained support because their allegations were closer to people's experience of marketing than were McDonald's rebuttals. The advice of narks such as Ralph Nader is necessary only because of the effluent from corporations telling us to buy more brands.

The benefits to capital from planned obsolescence become obvious when contrasted with the practices of those who either cannot or will not dump items for as long as they can be put to some use. To cope with wartime food shortages, M. F. K. Fisher published her *How to Cook a Wolf* (1942) which proffered recipes for potato peelings and revelled in the glory of peasant cooking, with its reliance on scraps, offal, roots and leaves. The frugality of the conservationist who recycles a woollen jumper into tea cosies remains the norm for billions of people. Such inventiveness was the condition for the survival of our species throughout 100 000 years.

People of plenty

Gratification rubbed against the grain of Republican and Puritan America, where hard work and sparse living were the paths to blessings in this life and salvation in the next. Asa Candler in 1902 warned his son: 'Don't indulge S.E.L.F. He is a tyrant, never satisfied if indulged and usually wants most hurtful indulgence just in proportion to being indulged.'[42] Had Asa applied this precept to the marketing of Coca-Cola, his beverage would have slipped into oblivion along with his Botanic Blood Balm. His commitment to the work ethic suited the promotion of Coke as a tonic, but was in conflict with an enticement to pause.

Like other conservative moralists, Candler faced the dilemma that came with the expansion of wants: was worth tallied by possessions or by behaviour? Should a surplus go into leisure or on good works? Behind these scruples lurked the social question: could a democratic society advocate indulgence for the rich and frugality for the poor without endangering its division of ownership? In the language of the time, were property rights compatible with human rights? Abolitionists had asked that question of chattel slavery. Social reformers raised it about wage slavery. Asa confessed to his brother the bishop that when he heard a 'devout churchman talk both classes and talk warningly of the future unrest...I feel like calling for "Mercy on us"'. Bishop Warren Candler stood against such subversive currents, preaching that property rights paid for human rights.[43]

While conservatives were struggling for supremacy on the social question, the churches were losing control over the population's free time, which was being commercialised at Coney Island and Buffalo Bill's Wild West Show, by yellow journalism and eventually by motion pictures. The struggles that P. T. Barnum had waged against abstinence benefited the sale of all commodities. That erstwhile medicine man sanctified amusement as one of 'the Golden Rules for Money-Making', the subtitle he gave his autobiography, which sold a million copies. Entertainments were not just for fun but for profit, as Howard Candler appreciated in 1903 when he dealt with Barnum and Bailey's circus.[44] His father would have endorsed Barnum's aim of stimulating his readers 'to the exercise of that energy, industry, and courage in their callings, which will surely lead to happiness and prosperity'.[45]

Barnum's bluster became a national style as US Americans accepted that health might not be exclusively a matter of moderation. Alongside the prudential 'scarcity therapy', an exuberant 'abundance therapy' began to appear. Charging that the prudent man was only half alive, abundance therapists promised to reach untapped reservoirs of energy and open the way to a richer, fuller existence. Violent sports including boxing became popular well before the first issue of *Physical Culture* in 1899 declared that 'Weakness is a Crime'. The republic became an empire in its war against Spain, with Teddy Roosevelt as its bully president advocating a 'strenuous life'. In 1907, the author of *A New Basis for Civilisation* called on men to 'release virtues' instead of 'suppressing vice'.[46]

Coca-Cola's advertising harmonised with this transformation in values. Its early imagery relied on Southern belles posing in an atmosphere of 'sentimental, cavalier extravagance' to suggest that Coca-Cola was refreshing and wholesome, a construction of the Old South which could console both Yankees and Southerners suffering the stresses of industrial modernity. Had Candler attached his beverage solely to the lost cause of the Confederacy, it could never have seemed to be the essence of monopolising capitals. That transition was possible because, in 'Coke's ads, the indomitable hedonism of the Southern character was easily transposed into leisure; or in the modern context, consumption'.[47]

Indebtedness replaced thrift for both capitalists and workers as a result of the marketeers' 'relentless war against saving and in favour of consumption'.[48] Individual capitalists were caught in 'a Faustian conflict between the passion for accumulation, and the desire for enjoyment'.[49] J. Pierpont Morgan, for instance, left $50 million in an art collection against $68.3 million as investments to generate profit. He would have ruined himself had he converted the residue of his active capital into paintings. If he had bought those treasures in order to trade as an art dealer he would have remained a capitalist. By expanding his role as a collector, however, he was on the way to eliminating himself as a capitalist, leading his son to fear that his father's income would not cover his bills.

Such conspicuous consumption provoked the scorn of economics professor Thorstein Veblen in *The Theory of the Leisure Class* (1899). Veblen voiced the engineer's prejudice against spending on display, as a throwback to feudalism. He overlooked the fact that capital could never outgrow its need to absorb its oversupply. As capitalism developed into its monopolising stage, its need for debt made creditworthiness the measure of a citizen's reliability. As the president of Sears put it: 'The ability of the American consumer to purchase on credit is fundamental to the free enterprise system. Without that ability, the system we know will crumble'.[50]

Coke posters projected the American Dream. During the trough of the economic depression, its billboards depicted a happy land. When the dispossessed farmers of John Steinbeck's *The Grapes of Wrath* (1939) made their first stop in California at a gas station, they found its walls 'decorated with posters, bathing girls, blondes with big breasts and slender hips and waxen faces, in white bathing suits, and holding a bottle of Coca-Cola and smiling—see what you get with a Coca-Cola'.[51] Those posters also let women know what they had to buy in order to be happy.

Pepsi Girl print ads from the mid-1950s incorporated information about other commodities:

> Ads attract and hold feminine attention by being up to the minute in all such fashion detail. In our ads we always take great care in preparation with this point in mind, particularly those ads in colour. We even go down into background accessories.

Pepsi advertising in the post-war boom offered an 'escape from poverty'; its agency 'deliberately chose activities that were a step or two up for most of our public', such as antique car rallies. 'Americans have always been an upward mobile people. The public is not content to sit still.'[52]

The full blast of the consumer ethic came during the 1960s, when marketeers fashioned a generation who not only 'wanted it now', but also wanted it 'for now'.[53] The impact of the marketing revolution of the 1960s is clear if we compare the assumptions behind the campaigns that launched TAB in 1963 and Diet Coke twenty years later. Woodruff had resisted a diet drink in the 1950s because he believed releasing such a product would give credence to allegations that sugared beverages were bad for children's teeth. When TAB appeared in 1963, he ruled that it could not be marketed as a less injurious beverage than Coca-Cola. The advertising agency replied that the promotions 'will be all flavour and pleasure. Not a word about dieting in any one of them.'[54] In 1984, when The Company turned from TAB to Diet Coke, its marketing director was not worried about putting drinkers of sugared Coke offside, because research had convinced him that Coke's core consumers had

> a feeling of resignation...Things are the way they are, and things are the way they should be. There's a recognition of a lack of

personal control in the world...Gaining weight, getting a gut, are just facts of life.

Consumers of diet drinks, by contrast, took pleasure from knowing that they could 'delay gratification'.[55] To ensure that they did not defer the delight of self-control, The Coca-Cola Company spent $100 million promoting Diet Coke in its first year.

*

By applying the concept of capital-induced needs, we can begin to distinguish the civilising component in the extension of needs from the costs exacted by capital's compulsion to expand. Lebowitz's economic analysis supplies morality with the tools to inform resistance. Understanding how and why the effective demand for sweetened water has expanded provides a basis for perceiving what can be done to contain the damage that capital-induced needs exact from natural resources and human labour.

Although strictures against false wants are not enough to explain the effects of mass marketing, the ethical current that runs through the true-versus-false dichotomy should never be abandoned in an economy where marketeers package virtue as a choice between vanity and gluttony.

CHAPTER 15 I'll Never Go Thirsty Again

Coca-Cola can fill a package with liquid and put it in the consumer's hands much more cheaply than anybody else in the world...Whether it's filled with tea or New Age or Coca-Cola is really almost irrelevant.

Beverage World, 1993[1]

Whenever water flowed from a faucet bearing the letter 'C', Roberto Goizueta knew failure. 'Sometimes the competition is Pepsi', he used to reckon. 'Sometimes it is water, sometimes it is wine'.[2] He also considered soup a threat. Yet the competition for Coke has never been neat water, since much of what we drink has been flavoured in some way, with caffeine or cordial, or as a base for those dreaded soups.

In the mid-1960s, Coca-Cola's president recognised that 'companies dedicated to single products...found themselves diversifying, with the invention or acquisition of new lines'. Goizueta's ambition in 1991 was to erode the market share of 'juices, milk, coffee, tea, and beer'.[3] By 1994, The Company aspired 'to compete... "tap to tap"—between tap water on one side and tap beer on the other. Non-alcoholic, non-dairy beverages are all fair game for us'.[4] During 1999, Coca-Cola went one step further and bottled tap water. Its goal by then was to secure a larger 'stomach share' in a strategy which treated the human body as 'an undeveloped market: of the average 64 ounces of fluid drunk each day, less than two ounces was Coke'.[5] To lift that portion by one ounce would bring a bonanza—a 50 per cent increase in total volumes. The Coca-Cola Company retained its dominance only by offering much more than the eponymous drink. In 1999 Classic Coke was below 21 per cent of US soft-drink sales, while sixteen of its other lines accounted for 24 per cent. In addition, between 1994 and 2000, the share of the soft-drink market going to carbonated lines fell from 83 to 76 per cent. The trick now is to deliver the niche labels as profitably as the mass brands, and without hurting those bigger sellers.

Satisfying the immutable need for liquid allows for fashions in beverages. This commodification has extended into water itself. Pollution is being met by bottling water, to the detriment of the world's poor.

A drop to drink

Our immutable need for liquid places few limits on its source—from mare's milk to one's own urine. Preferences for the more popular beverages are neither fixed nor venerable, and continue to be shaped by politics and marketing. The following glimpses at tea, coffee, fruit juices and milk document the oscillation of tastes that helps marketeers steer demand among beverages.

Tea

The English were coffee drinkers until well into the nineteenth century, but then reductions in the tax on tea sparked a rise in its annual consumption from 2.3 pounds per head in 1850 to 5.7 pounds in the 1890s. The fall in price also encouraged the poor to alter their method of preparation, so that even when they drank the same volumes they used more spoonfuls in each pot and became less inclined to add hot water to spent leaves. Sales continued to rise, reaching ten pounds per head in 1961 before slipping by two pounds, the difference taken by instant coffee. British colonies such as Australia carried over the tea habit so completely that when an advance scout for The Coca-Cola Company reported on prospects in 1937 he identified tea as the enemy.

Coffee

North Americans turned to coffee in the 1760s when the British taxed tea imports. Settlers in the north-east preferred their brew white with sugar, while those in the west learnt to enjoy it black and bitter because sweeteners and milk were harder to come by. Consumption rose to ten pounds per head before World War One and doubled to twenty pounds by the end of the next war. From a 1962 peak of four cups a day for everyone over ten years of age, coffee drinking in the USA has declined to fewer than two cups, with the trend-setting twenty-somethings down to half as much. Colas had taken over. In 1994, the US Defense Department added caffeine to combat rations to keep GIs primed, because they were no longer drinking coffee. Since the 1980s, the Starbucks chain has drawn drinkers towards stronger brews, away from the tincture that masquerades as coffee in US diners.

Fruit juices

Because most fruit juice was squeezed in domestic kitchens, per capita consumption of brand-label varieties in the USA did not exceed a pound per month until the late 1930s. Volumes grew as canners extended from grape juice into grapefruit, tomato and the stone-fruit nectars as a way to market crops that could not be sold in season. The growth in disposable incomes had lifted sales 600 per cent by the mid-1950s. After Coca-Cola bought out Minute Maid in 1960, its sales effort turned orange juice from a breakfast health juice into another all-day soft drink. The Florida Citrus Commission went further, rescuing orange juice from its early-morning niche by denigrating soda-pops as 'sugary junk... goo, fizzy or phoney colours', allegations which enraged Atlanta.

Milk

Milk held its place as autocrat of the US breakfast table. In 1967, annual consumption was 35 gallons per head against 26 of soft drinks. In 1982, children and teenagers were still drinking more milk-based drinks than juices, coffee, tea or soft drinks, 'with over 50 per cent of mealtime beverages being milk'.[6] That statistic did not reveal how much milk had been pre-sugared and flavoured. While teenage males were still drinking twice as much milk as pop in 1978, the ratio had been reversed by 1998. During the 1990s, total volumes were flat, suggesting that milk drinking was set to decline even further. Low-fat milk with added nutrients is already more popular than natural milk.

Coca-Cola was slow to move into dairy lines, though it tried to displace milk from menus. McDonald's deal of a burger, fries and a shake is set against the offer of a free burger with every Coke purchase. Not every Coca-Cola salesman has gone as far as the one who poured Coke over his corn flakes every morning.

*

How we drink also changes with circumstance, whether slurping our scalding tea from a saucer, setting half-a-dozen wine glasses on a banquet table, or slugging whisky from the jug. We use individual tea bags when we are in a rush, but a pot of tea for family meals. The manner of drinking affected Coca-Cola, because sharing a receptacle spread contagion when glasses had not been thoroughly washed. After authorities traced an outbreak of typhoid among New York children to a shared tin mug, a German baroness promoted the disposable paper cup under the brand name Lily-Tulip.

Straws offered another prophylactic, but Robert Woodruff resisted their use for Coca-Cola because their waxed surfaces altered its taste. He insisted that people should swig Coke from the bottle, and chastised President Eisenhower for being photographed sipping it through a straw. When Coca-Cola arrived in Australia, milk-bar proprietors fumed that The Company's 'insistence on the public drinking out of the bottle was turning the shops into pigsties... The proper way to drink' they huffed, 'is out of a glass or goblet', for which they charged a penny.[7]

The case of Japan

Japan offers a case study of how far marketeers can change preferences and of how national cultures can change, even subvert, global business strategies. An expert in matching Western products with Japanese preferences, Japanese-Australian George Fields, has distinguished six stages between the transitory and the intransigent in a culture. At the top of his pyramid are the songs or movies that come and go within a year. Towards the middle are changes to habits and customs that need a new generation to find acceptance, as when the Japanese adapt US fast foods to their own traditions, using rice patties in place of buns for Big Macs. Even longer spans, up to 300 years, are required to transform primary values, such as the purity that is central to Shinto and makes the Japanese value rice for its whiteness more than its cheapness, and cleanse themselves before entering the bath. Slower still are transformations in the grammar of a language.[8]

National preferences impinge on every aspect of marketing, from the package to the product. Pocari Sweat could succeed as a brand name for an athletic reviver only in the land of Japlish. Is a soft drink with as much dietary fibre as half a cabbage, a fermented milk drink, or a jellied energy drink likely to win many takers elsewhere?

Not only do the Japanese drink green tea, but the teas that Europeans call black, because of the colour of their leaves, the Japanese know as red because of the colour of their brew. Today, the 'intricate and ancient ritual of the Japanese tea ceremony' is rare. Instead, most Japanese have a new liturgy to make green tea: 'Insert coins, make selection and pop the top'.[9] One of the biggest canned tea successes has been Coca-Cola's Sokenbicha, which has gained half the market. Sales of canned Oolong grew to thirteen million hectolitres in 1992 against thirty million for carbonated drinks. These canned teas suited Japanese palates, which are still being taught to like the very sweet.

The first coffee shop in Japan opened in 1889 and adapted the German habit of long sittings. Prices are now around four or five dollars for a cup served in the finest china. A cheap stand-up chain, Doutor, began in 1980 at $1.50 a cup. From 1986, coffee overtook green tea, making Japan the world's fourth-largest coffee market. The Coca-Cola Company took a large share after 1975 by selling its Georgia brand of hot and cold cans through vending machines. Two-thirds of Coke revenues in Japan now come from coffee and tea.

During the bubble economy of the 1980s, the Japanese adopted the practice of paying for table water, initially as a mixer for Johnny Walker Black Label. Total sales trebled in the five years to 1991. Although importing water affronted Shinto assumptions about the purity of all things Japanese, its high price was a marketing plus for diners, who kept the foreign bottle on the table to 'be seen drinking it'. In 1993, the more superstitious and hypochondriacal were attracted to water drawn from the base of their mystical moun-tain, Fuji-san.[10] By 1998, bottled water was the fastest-growing segment of the beverage market. The taste for soft drinks meta-morphosed into a liking for barely sweetened 'near water'. Japanese firms won younger drinkers over with fruit and vegetable flavours for a population accustomed to taking vitamins and medicines in liquid form. The leading brand was 'Eau+', containing ten fruits, herbs, and as much vitamin C as 50 lemons, but it lost market share after it was found to have 'a laxative side effect'.[11]

These shifts and predilections are evidence of the fracturing of the mass market by a multiplicity of short-term preferences. Japanese soft-drink firms test the level of demand by releasing up to 1000 products a year, 900 of which are dumped within the first month. Even Coca-Cola tried out thirty new drinks there in less than three years. This method is no more wasteful or less scientific than the $10 billion turned over in 1997 by market researchers around the world.

The stomach share for any beverage is far from fixed. The same adaptability applies to water itself.

Commodification

'Just like the body with which it maintains such a privileged relationship, water has known different ages', observed its French historian, Jean-Pierre Goubert. Goubert specified three overlapping phases, starting from the 'cosmological...when the cult of the sacred magical fountains was celebrated' and water was treated as one of the four primary forces with fire, air and earth. Some ancients supposed water to be the basis of all things. From this age of ritual emerged the 'religious' period under Christianity, with its baptismal rites and prudish reluctance to bathe.[12] After the 1780s, water became the domain of scientists, who produced a few drops by igniting hydrogen in oxygen and then used electricity to separate those elements again, showing that water was not itself an element. These experiments went to the heart of chemistry, for 'it was a "drop of water" which extinguished phlogiston' as the explanation for weight changes during combustion.[13] A century later, water played a comparable role in the transformation of the life sciences when Pasteur devised a technique for its purification, which became secularised into the cult of hygiene. Germs dispersed miasmas as surely as oxygen had absorbed phlogiston.

The ideologies prevalent in the first two of these eras were embedded in the practices of magic and religion. The rationalist attitude, by contrast, considered water as neutral, leaving space for commerce to work its own witchcraft. Christ had turned water into wine for the pleasure of his hosts. Corporations turned the intake of all fluids into a commodity for profit. For two centuries, the means to satisfaction have been modified by the thirst of capital.

The movement of soda water from treatment to treat exemplified this process. In 1789, reports that soda waters could prevent scurvy encouraged Jacob Schweppe to form a company which continues to market soft drinks under one of the world's oldest brand names, though it is now tied to The Coca-Cola Company. In New York, Benjamin Silliman manufactured soda water from 1807, also as part of a health program, in a society with sufficient indolent and overfed members to make the provision of mineral waters a profitable concern. His advertisements brought this novelty to the attention of people who could not afford to visit the springs at Saratoga, creating, he noted, 'a demand where none before had existed'.[14] A competitor was unscrupulous enough to serve ladies, to trade on the Sabbath, to ice the water and to mix it with wine. A fancy refreshment could be marketed more readily than a pallid medicine. Silliman failed. The huckster prospered. Soda water was deleted from the 1831 edition of the US pharmacopoeia. The term soon came to mean any carbonated water, whether or not it had a soda content.

Chilled water attracted more customers in summer and absorbed more gas, so from the late 1850s engineers developed cooling devices; where these were not available, druggists shaved ice into the glass. Small self-contained cooling units for steamboats and country drugstores came on the market in the early 1850s. By the time Coca-Cola appeared in 1886, these units cost as little as $40. At the 1893 Exposition in Chicago, the concession for the sale of mineral waters fetched $150000. The successful bidder contracted to pipe natural spring water at 38 degrees Fahrenheit across a hundred miles to supply more than a hundred outlets inside the fairgrounds, where twenty domestic and thirteen British mineral-water firms exhibited their products.

Fountains for dispensing carbonated waters had operated in US drugstores before 1820. Shortly afterwards, machines could dispense a variety of flavours from a single tap by using the soda water to flush out the syrup between serves. Dozens of fruit flavourings came on the market, including peach, pear, pineapple and plum— to mention only those beginning with the letter 'p'. The cocktail 'Don't Care' was a concoction of pineapple, strawberry, vanilla and port wine. By the end of the nineteenth century, syrups were distinguished as much by their colourings—red, white, black or brown—as by any natural flavour. In the 1870s, soda-fountain attendants added sweet cream or ice cream to make creaming sodas.

Ginger ale, an Irish creation, gained popularity because it kept well. Lemon's Superior Sparkling Ginger Ale was the first soft drink patented in the USA. In 1892, it sold three million bottles, a volume Coca-Cola would not attain for more than another decade. From being the most favoured drink in 1890, ginger ale is now only a mixer, holding one per cent of US soft-drink sales.

Blue gold

The industrialisation of the water supply coincided with the corporatisation of soft drinks. Although water is a gift of nature, its delivery commands a fee, earning it the title 'blue gold', alongside oil as black gold. Water carriers plied their trade for millennia before businesses and municipalities in the nineteenth century diverted the relationship between suppliers and consumers. The mass supply and marketing of water was another strand in the great transformation as the market economy moved from atomised to monopolising agents. The volume of water used for all purposes rose. For example, the average daily per capita use in Manchester went from 35 to 84 gallons between 1913 and 1974.

The twentieth century has been described as 'the age of dams'.[15] Hydro-electric reservoirs became the biggest projects on every continent, from the Dneiper in the Soviet Union to the Tennessee Valley Authority to the Aswan across the Nile and Australia's Snowy Mountains Scheme. Brazil's Amazon dam and Three Gorges in China are under way to supply hydro-electricity to industry and cities, displacing millions of peasants and salinating the soils. Not all the effects are material. The dream factories of Hollywood, with an annual rainfall of some five inches, could not exist without the Hoover Dam, dedicated in 1935.

Most of the dam construction was state funded, even where private companies did the reticulation. That pattern is changing; in the name of competition, some Western governments are arranging for a variety of firms to supply water to individual consumers. The vendors will be no longer families of water carriers but global conglomerates. The French-based Vivendi is linked to the first US-based global water company, Azurix; Vivendi has huge investments in the communications giants CANAL, Universal Studios and Seagram. Another major player is the US Bechtel Corporation, which controls International Waters Ltd of London. Bechtel is known as 'the corporation that engineered the world' because of its construction work in the petroleum industry, and its access to governments. Two of its executives, George Shultz and Caspar Weinberger, served in Reagan cabinets as Secretaries of State and Defense respectively.

Purity

Coca-Cola managers have always had to deal with water as an industrial input, while druggists needed water to fill their soda fountains. In both cases, the water had to be free of impurities that would spoil the flavourings or mar the taste. Those dangers were rife in Atlanta, where one resident praised the water as 'excellent for drowning puppies, killing crabgrass, and dyeing white goods buff-brown'.[16]

Atlanta's problems were repeated in cities across the nation, where tap water was not safe to drink until well into the twentieth century. Before then, water quality was acceptable if the number of cases of typhoid did not exceed 20–25 a year for every 100 000 people. Action to improve the drinking water gained support in the 1870s with the establishment of the Association for Health in Cities. Although Massachusetts built a purification plant in 1883, its experiment remained rare.

The year before Dr Pemberton first brewed Coca-Cola, a crisis in the cleanliness and availability of Atlanta's water led to calls to sell off its municipal supply. The move was opposed by 500 businessmen, who advocated that the city install meters and filtration instead. By 1893, a storage capable of supplying 20 million gallons a day had been built, but there were no means of delivering it or removing its red clay discoloration. To combat the continuing shortage, the city issued $200 000 worth of bonds in 1901, and by 1905 Atlanta had clean water, though storage capacity had again fallen behind demand. The health crisis returned between 1906 and 1910, when Atlanta had the second-highest death rate from typhoid of any US city.

Asa Candler had to purify this water before he could mix it with his sugar and flavourings. The risk of impure water going into Coca-Cola was not confined to Atlanta. Bottlers across the USA complained of guck. Some tried to sterilise the syrup, but that killed its flavour. Bottles were cleaned with caustic soda, itself a blight if not rinsed resolutely.

After Candler followed the US military into Cuba, Havana's water not only had to be boiled to make Coca-Cola germ-free but also had to pass through precipitation tanks to remove lime, an operation funded out of public works. The Company faced comparable problems in the late 1930s when it moved to southern Europe, where one city had not analysed its water quality since 1892. Coca-Cola Export installed its own active carbon filter and chlorination plants. A sales conference late in 1941 set out the principles on which worldwide manufacture would be conducted:

> We want sparkling clean and colourless water for 'Coca-Cola', to prevent the formation of unsightly precipitates in the finished product, and because 'Coca-Cola' made with such water retains carbonation better...We require a water for 'Coca-Cola' free from disease-producing organisms, because 'Coca-Cola' should be a pure wholesome product. People now drink it and should always be able to drink it with confidence.

Instances were given of people choosing Coca-Cola because they would not drink the public water supply.[17]

Coca-Cola maintained its reputation for quality until 1999, when Mad Coke Disease spread across Europe. Substandard carbon dioxide and contamination from a wood preservative caused Coke's biggest ever recall. 'It may make you feel sick', Atlanta insisted, 'but it is not harmful'. The Company kept arguing that the complaints were 'psychosomatic', because the amounts of contaminant detected were too small to have caused nausea.[18] The explanation of self-delusion seemed more likely because Coca-Cola had marketed an image of purity. Elsewhere, globalisation and job cuts have contributed to Coke's quality-control problems. In February 2000, Minute Maid in Florida had to recall product after selling a plant to a Brazilian partner who replaced long-time staff with ill-trained temporary labour.

Perrier held a quarter of the US market for sparkling table waters until 1990, when a batch containing infinitesimal amounts of cancer-linked benzene forced the recall of 280 million bottles. The threat to Perrier was that rival brands would take over its slots in stores and restaurants during its absence. To regain market leadership, Perrier mounted a $25 million relaunch. That expenditure was as essential in its getting back on top as previous marketing had been in putting it there.

Sales of bottled tap water have flourished because of environmental alarms over fertilisers and fallout from Chernobyl, and concerns about chlorine or fluorides. Fear of poison from the tap flared in the USA in 1993. Boston, New York and Washington issued warnings to boil city water, while in Milwaukee sixty-nine people died from cryptosporidium. Four million Sydney residents boiled their water for several months during 1998. Meanwhile, Coors Brewery marketed the purity of its ECO water by donating $4 million to environmental causes in the USA.

Eau+

Among the miracles of mass marketing, none is more marvellous than the sale of bottled water in countries where tap water is both pure and inoffensive to the nose or palate. Perrier commercials acknowledged: 'C'est fou'. In 1998, *Beverage World* wondered how much longer US children would believe that drinking water had once upon a time come out of a tap rather than a plastic container from the store.

In the second half of the nineteenth century, tap water was served as a matter of course at most US meal tables, although Southerners preferred iced tea. With the spread of affluence, the custom has shifted towards bottled water. In 1966, The Company took its first steps to sell water per se as a product when it bought firms in Belgium and New England. Atlanta had already let four other suppliers fall to competitors, and strategists with its New Enterprises Division feared that Coca-Cola might be too late in stepping sideways to match a social phenomenon, associated with the maturing of our culture, which will cause consumers to attribute an increased aesthetic value to purified packaged waters from a known source.

At the same time it can be expected that the future quality of the public water supplies in the US will continue to deteriorate, thereby generating for bottled water an increasing physical quality advantage. Thus there are in existence two separate trends, each of which will tend to make the purified drinking water business have a future brighter than its past.[19]

This memo confirmed J. K. Galbraith's 1958 warning that public squalor would be the price paid for private affluence.

The French have the reputation of mixing waters with their *vin ordinaire*, yet Perrier did not begin business until 1948, and only in the late 1970s did the firm turn its fizz into a fashion statement. The volume of bottled waters sold in France doubled during the 1980s. The English had drunk bottled water only when abroad. Queen Elizabeth II takes Malvern spa water on tour to calm the royal tummy and maintain the royal schedule. The hot summer of 1989 helped to double sales of bottled waters among her subjects, and the prospect of a profit promptly divined forty natural springs across Britain.

When Pepsi launched H2OH! as its reply to Perrier in 1989, 600 local brands and 75 imports already had US sales of $2 billion and were growing at 10–15 per cent each year. In the 1990s, US sales of bottled waters increased 150 per cent, reaching fourteen gallons per head per annum. The cultural kink in the demand for bottled waters is clear from the distribution of their sales. Pacific coast States account for half the sales, with twice the rate of the remaining US population.

The bottling of tap water put the entire beverage industry into reverse, for it now had to make water taste like water. All cola sales fell 5 per cent during the decade to 1993, while New Age beverages went from nothing to 12 per cent. The niche was not yet mainline, but the non-colas were attracting the kind of free media time and space that would have kept Coke hot. During 1999, bottled water sales grew 10 per cent against only 3.4 per cent for soft drinks. Bottlers had altered 'the way that people got their water, drank their water, expected their water'.[20]

Poor folk

While water was being air-freighted around the planet for the rich, in the 1990s the proportion of the world's population with access to safe drinking water sank from 80 per cent to two-thirds. Against the $600 billion needed to meet this lack, Coca-Cola investments appear small, yet their effects can be considerable. In countries such as Mexico, branded beverages protect the well-to-do and tourists and so weaken the political pressure to make water safe for those who cannot afford a bottle or can every time they are thirsty. Only half of Mexican households have piped water, and in some States a quarter of the population has no easy access to safe drinking water. Yet Mexico is Coke's second-largest market, with one eight-ounce serve sold for every person every day of the year.

The gulf between village custom and corporate profit became conspicuous on the equatorial island group of Yap. The arrival of Coca-Cola slashed sales of home-grown coconuts until the mid-1970s, when activists began to promote the local product. During that fight back, consumption of imported soft drinks fell by three-quarters. The Yapese had earlier demonstrated their capacity to create low-cost reticulation to deliver potable water closer to each household. A Coke vending machine costs many times more than the $30 that it costs Community Aid Abroad to provide two aluminium well liners for a village in Papua New Guinea to help fortify a well and provide hygienic water.

In April 2000 in Bolivia, where only a third of rural dwellers have water connections, the military shot dead six peasants protesting against a 35 per cent increase in the price of water supplied by the Bechtel Corporation. After the demonstrations, the Bolivian president, a born-again military dictator, declared a state of siege. Bechtel needed the higher earnings to fund its new dam, which will supply water at six times the cost from alternative sources. This scheme is part of an IMF–World Bank program of making more water available by pushing up its price so that corporations will take over its supply from public utilities. Investors who bought into water supply in advanced industrial nation-market-states in the 1980s are being subsidised by the World Bank and IMF to take charge of the Third World systems, with a rate of return assured by the state's enforcement of prices. Consumers who cannot pay have their supply cut off, pushing them back to polluted sources.

The Bolivian demonstrations coincided with a conference of the World Water Council, a gathering of government experts, corporate executives and financiers in the Hague. In its statement of aims, the council described water as a human need, not a human right. That distinction provides the basis for its three-pronged strategy of 'commodification, privatisation and oligopolistic integration between the sectors worldwide—drinking [tap] water, bottled water, water treatment and purification, and soft drinks'.[21]

In 1968, Atlanta had publicised its test-marketing of a non-carbonated protein-base soybean drink named SACI in Brazil. The move was a ploy to divert a US Senate committee away from charges that soft drinks increased malnutrition.[22] Little was heard of SACI once that inquiry ended. Nonetheless, Coca-Cola promotes itself in Latin America as fostering maternal instincts. Meanwhile, the United Nations reported in 1989 that 'well-off children, who could afford to drink Coke, often suffered from vitamin deficiencies'.[23]

Nestlé's promotion of its powdered baby food, Nestrogen, as a substitute for breast milk endangered infant health because the powder had to be mixed with water which was often impure and induced diarrhoea. Twelve million infants and children die of diarrhoea every year. In India, the rate of mortality is fourteen times higher for infants fed with formula than for those raised on their mothers' milk. In its marketing of Nestrogen, Nestlé had adopted the tactic, pioneered by Coca-Cola, of giving away samples. Under pressure, Nestlé changed tack in the Philippines and instead gave gifts to health volunteers who sold Nestrogen in their districts. Nestlé's drive into emerging economies had the same motive as McDonald's, Coca-Cola's and Hollywood's: to profit from the higher rate of growth in effective demand in Asia before the 1997 crisis.

Infant health became a concern only after public relations were damaged.

In 1997, Coca-Cola announced a plan to spend $361 million in South Africa between 1997 and 2002 to 'buy coolers and other equipment to improve support systems' in towns only recently connected to electricity.[24] Justifying the push into some of the poorest parts of the world, its chairman argued that The Company did 'a great service because it encourages people to take in more liquids... Fluid replenishment is a key to health, and when you have a population that has appropriate fluid intake, what you find is that they have a lot less kidney problems'.[25] Such talk smacks of the quackery that marked Cola-Cola's origins.

CHAPTER 16 **Bitter Sweet**

As if increase of appetite had grown
By what it fed on
Hamlet, Act I, Scene ii, 144–45

A thousand years ago, sweetness was prized in Europe and supplied by bees. During the sixteenth century, sugar became a passion
among the rich, with Giam Bologna sculpting confections to cele-
brate the Florentine nobility. In the eighteenth century, sugar
remained too expensive to be called a necessity. Yet by the time
Coca-Cola went on sale in 1886, sugars were supplying almost a
fifth of the calories in English and North American diets. Sidney
Mintz has asked, 'What turned an exotic, foreign and costly substance into the daily fare of even the poorest and humblest people?'[1]
The answer introduces another precondition for Coca-Cola's success: no sweetened tooth, no Coca-Cola. Because sweetness had
already become second nature, soda pop needed only three decades
to achieve a popularity which had taken sugar three centuries.

Although our pleasure from sweetness rests in our physiology,

Homo sapiens evolved without sugar in the form of sucrose. Food is oxidised to blood sugars but they are not sucrose, any more than we need the latter to produce the former. How far our liking for sugar is gratified and how we satisfy that longing depends on social and economic factors. Addiction to the sweet is a product of the last 200 years, just as the sweet things we consume are now corporate inventions. Americans guzzle fructose-heavy Classic Cokes, while Orientals decline to sweeten their tea. Per capita consumption of sugar in Japan is only a third of that in the USA.

Slavery

Slaves and sugar were among the first fruits of European civilisation abroad. Contrary to the Hollywood image of slavery as blacks working the cotton fields, Africans and cotton came second. After Europeans failed to profit from enslaving the Indians, they shipped in other whites as convicts or indentured labourers. The English traffic in Africans did not become significant until the 1660s, when a triangular trade opened between sugar planters in the West Indies, New England distillers and English slavers. Enforcement of a British tax on foreign sugar and molasses in 1764 sparked the American revolution as much as did the duty on tea. The second US president chided his countrymen not to 'blush to confess that molasses was an essential ingredient in American independence'.[2]

Britain's outlawing of the slave trade in 1807, and of slavery itself in 1833, did not diminish British enthusiasm for the profits from slave labour. Although British capitalists could no longer buy and sell human flesh, it was no crime for them to advance money to those who did, or for British merchants to import the produce of slaves. The British consumed slave-grown sugar until the 1880s, keeping wage costs down at home.

Planting a sweet tooth

For sugar to move from rarity to necessity, merchandisers had to learn how to profit from the masses as well as from the classes, making novelty the norm. Sugar made coffee, chocolate and tea more palatable. A Britisher's yearly consumption of sugar stayed below twenty pounds per head until the lifting of import duties in 1845. Intake reached eighty pounds by 1900, mostly because jam was two-thirds sugar. Made from the poorest crops and bulked out with vegetables, jam replaced butter in working-class kitchens, a three-pound jar costing less than sixpence. In the 1880s, Lyles marketed Golden Syrup as a poor man's honey, with a bee on its label. Among British labourers, a jar of weak tea with milk and sugar 'made many a cold supper seem like a hot meal'.[3] Wives and children filled up on sugars; any meat went to the men, because their energies brought in the wages so that all might dunk a crust. In the 1930s, *per capita* sugar consumption reached 100 pounds, more than five times as much as a century earlier, and an index of impoverishment during that great depression.

The Pilgrim Fathers imported slaves to Massachusetts in 1620 but did not bring a passion for sweetness, since sugar was still a rarity in England. North America's experience differed from Britain's because the factory system came later, urbanisation was less intense, and immigration established a diversity of cuisine. Settlers imported bees and learnt from the Indians how to tap maple trees for syrup. Molasses became an essential in the diet of slaves and poor whites. Average annual sugar consumption was only 5 pounds per head around the time of Independence, doubling by 1820 and again before the 1860s. During the Civil War, the canning of a very sweet condensed milk 'educated the palates of thousands of Union soldiers'.[4] Per capita consumption of refined sugars reached 40 pounds in the later 1870s, then climbed towards 70 pounds at the turn of the century. In 1918, the government made 25-pound lots of sugar available to home bottlers in a campaign that reversed the squeeze that commerce had put on domestic food processing. World war stalled but could not halt the industrialisation of how workers replenished their capacity to labour. During the 1920s, sugar consumption jumped to 100 pounds per head, some of it to feed liquor stills during Prohibition. Between the wars, cigarette manufacturers promoted nicotine in place of sugar with the slogan 'Reach for a Lucky instead of a sweet'. Candy firms promoted their sugar hits to workers to counter the '4 o'clock slump'.

Throughout the twentieth century, sweeteners have supplied 15–20 per cent of US calories from a varying range of processed foods. Sales of condensed milk peaked in 1950. Consumption of ice cream increased from a single quart per head per annum in 1900 to nine quarts by 1950. It edged up to fourteen quarts by 1980, then bulged to twenty-three in 1987. In the late 1960s, average annual sugar consumption exceeded 100 pounds per person for the first time in thirty years as food conglomerates sweetened every comestible from tomato juice to peanut butter. The makers of breakfast cereals transformed 'a basic grain...into a confection'.[5] A 1970 US Senate report on the nutritional value of corn flakes and rice bubbles showed that rats fed on the cereal packets got more nutrients than those eating the contents. Investigators accused the manufacturers of replacing food values with sugar in order to addict pre-teen children, who still sprinkled sugar on top of sweetened cereals.[6]

Coca-Cola's Minute Maid and Hi-C encouraged the Citrus Growers Co-operative to add sugar in order to appeal to children. Packaged juice became sweeter, more intensely coloured and more aromatic than any orange on a tree, so that some youngsters now find a fresh orange as tart as a lemon. In the 1990s, Coke introduced Surge, which is so laden with sugar that the attendant behind the soda fountain in Atlanta's World of Coca-Cola told my tour group he rationed his children to one a day. Despite the use of artificial sweeteners, US sugar intake passed 150 pounds per head in the late 1990s, with a third coming from 'liquid candy', as nutritionists call soda pops.[7]

Against this indoctrination of the palate, contrary attitudes towards sweetness have persisted. A sweet tooth increases dental caries and fatal diseases. Sugar began as a medicine and is still used to help the bitterness go down. 'Syrup' was part of the brand name for Coca-Cola when it was a nerve tonic. Sweetness is a pleasure and hence an occasion for sin, and was once linked to self-abuse as a cause of debilitation. Although sugar is one of the first items to be cut when people try to lose weight, honey and raw sugar are welcomed as natural while artificial sweeteners and white sugar are feared as carcinogens, or a cause of sterility. 'Pure, white and deadly', one nutritionist declared in the 1970s.[8] Sugar is criticised as 'empty calories' because it provides no vitamins or minerals, as Coca-Cola's attorneys acknowledged in 1941 when they warned against advertisements that confused energy with nutrition.[9] Nonetheless, a scientific witness in the McLibel case could declare that 'Coca-Cola has a good source of energy', which he equated with nutrients.[10]

Today's belief that brown sugar is healthier than white has reversed an older prejudice. Refiners in the 1890s, keen to banish brown sugar and secure the higher profits from white, warned housewives that brown sugar contained 'a formidably organised, exceedingly lively and decidedly ugly little animal', which did 'not occur in refined sugar of any quality'.[11] Consumption of white sugar doubled between 1880 and 1915. Various manufacturers promoted whiteness as a mark of superiority, often advertising its purity by denigrating Negroes whose forebears had been shipped to the Americas to raise cane.

The sugar trust

Between the plantation and the palate, between the eighteenth-century slave to sugar production and the twentieth-century captive to its consumption, came the oligopolies.

Sugar was the largest cost among Coca-Cola's ingredients, so the establishment of a trust among refiners in 1887 towered over Dr Pemberton's tiny business. While total production of sugar had almost doubled in the previous twenty years, the number of firms and refineries had been halved to twenty. A similar contraction occurred in the United Kingdom, where the number of refineries fell from 120 in 1800 to 26 in 1882 and 16 by 1900.

Branches of the Havemeyer family owned more than half of the refining capacity in the United States. Whether or not all poor families are alike, this rich one pursued wealth after its own fashion. Divided by temper and marriages, the Havemeyers hesitated to reunite even for the sake of profit, debating their creation of a trust for three years. After a renewed bout of competition squashed processors' margins, William Havemeyer summoned a banker, who took the family down the path opened by Standard Oil. To control capacity and output for a stable return on investment, the sugar trust bought out competitors until it controlled 80 per cent of national capacity. During its first year, it halved the number of refineries to ten. To maintain prices, it ran its plants at only 80 per cent capacity. In 1889, refiners outside the trust increased their production, hoping for higher profits from the trust's reorganisation of the industry. The trust again cut its output; by 1891, it controlled only half of the sugar used in the USA. Market forces appeared to have been vindicated. Then one of the Havemeyers bought out his major competitors and sold their firms on to the trust. Monopolisers were still learning their trade while coping with technical and political innovations.

By 1893 the American Sugar Refining Company, to give the trust its new title, held 95 per cent of the nation's production. Then the independents returned, flush with cash from the sale of their businesses to Havemeyer. They faced no barrier to re-entry because the trust had not tied up raw materials or industrial customers. Furthermore, technological changes had reduced the start-up cost of a new refinery to $500 000.

All oligopolies were sufficiently alike for the 1895 prosecution of the Sugar Trust to determine how ownership of any industry could be concentrated and yet stay within the law. The US Supreme Court ruled that, although price-fixing or market-sharing cartels were illegal, such actions by a holding company, or trust, were beyond the power of the federal authorities. Thereafter, 'oligopoly became the accepted form for organising the US economy'.[12]

The trust also came under attack from Arbuckle Bros, one of the country's largest coffee wholesalers, which began to retail sugar after it realised that its machine for packaging coffee could handle sugar as well. Arbuckle then set up its own refinery and undercut the trust. In retaliation, the Havemeyers bought up the third-largest US coffee wholesaler. With both sides losing money, the combatants combined their businesses in 1901.

The outbreak of the Spanish–American War in 1898 disrupted supplies of raw sugar from Cuba and the Philippines, lifting prices by 25 per cent. War meant monopolising as usual for William Havemeyer, who merged three members of the trust into the

National Sugar Refining Company. The trust never had the capital or managerial resources to absorb growers, wholesale grocers and manufacturers, but it could use its purchasing power to depress the prices it paid for raw sugar. Mill owners were so anxious to sell to the trust that they lowered their prices in the hope of larger volumes. This variant of monopolising, known as monopsony, occurs when a single buyer dominates a host of small sellers. To buttress its dominance over suppliers, the trust later bought beet farms in the USA and cane plantations in Cuba. At the other end of the refining stream, corporate customers tied their purchases to the trust in exchange for discounts that would hobble entrants into their fields.

Asa Candler did not purchase sugar plantations, mills or refineries. At first, he bought all his sugar from the Revere company in Boston, then from Arbuckle and only later from Havemeyer's American. The quality of the sugars in Coke declined. Candler initially had insisted on Confectioners 'A', a soft sugar with 7 per cent water, which tended to sour. Then American in New Orleans designed a variant especially for Coca-Cola, but in the end The Company resorted to standard granulated. Continuity of supply was as much a concern as quality, so Asa built his own warehouse in Baltimore. Demand for syrup grew to a hundred barrels a week in the summer of 1908, and he feared that he would 'not have enough sugar to keep up with orders'. Branch plants had to send Atlanta weekly reports of inventories on hand and in transit, yet the works were 'frequently shut down for lack of supplies'.[13]

The Great War

Such interruptions became a way of life after the USA went to war in April 1917. Washington had begun to marshal raw materials three years earlier. After appeals to patriotism failed to curb the consumption of sugar, the Food Administration announced rationing in August 1917, but then took months to establish the regulations. The authorities allocated soft-drink makers 80 per cent of their previous year's sugar, leaving enforcement 'largely to the conscience of the manufacturer'.[14] Coca-Cola promised to comply with advertisements headed 'Making a Soldier of Sugar'. Once rationing was decided on, it could be enforced readily because refining was oligopolised, with the Havemeyers and four others now handling three-quarters of the market.

At first, Coca-Cola secured the same amount of sugar as in 1916. Then, in the autumn of 1917, the Food Administration halved the quantity of sugar allotted to soft drinks for November and December, emptying Coca-Cola's warehouses in ten days. The order went out from Atlanta: 'Instruct every wagon man to sell as LITTLE Coca-Cola as possible—not as MUCH, as heretofore'.[15] By the end of 1918, The Company was using the lowest grades from Louisiana, supplemented by corn syrup, glucose and invert sugar, none of which altered the taste.

When supplies were available, their price seemed exorbitant. Deprived of beet sugar from Europe, the Allies had quadrupled their purchases of Cuban raw, lifting its price from 6 to 7.5 cents per pound; then the USA set a limit of 9 cents. When the Cubans called for a higher return on their 1918 crop, Washington blocked wheat sales until Havana capitulated. To meet the production boom, Cuba imported 217 000 labourers from around the Caribbean.

By 1916, Coca-Cola sales had reached 16 million gallons. The following year, sugar shortages caused the first reverse, down to 12 million, followed by a further slide to 10 million in 1918. Victory brought its rewards in 1919 with a near-doubling of Coca-Cola volume to 19 million gallons, or 2.5 billion serves, which meant thirty glasses for each US adult and child. In many industries, demand exceeded the capacity to adjust to peace. As the country's largest consumer of sugar, Coca-Cola contributed to inflation by doubling its output as soon as controls were lifted in November 1919. Anticipating deregulation, suppliers had withheld sales in October. All Coca-Cola plants except Los Angeles had to suspend operations.

'Dance of the Millions'

The Woodruff syndicate's inclusion of a sugar refiner among its Coca-Cola directors proved providential, because panic buying and stockpiling began once Washington declined to purchase the 1920 Cuban crop. The new owners faced disaster as the price of sugar performed its 'Dance of the Millions', peaking late in May 1920 at 28 cents per pound, five times its pre-war level. Even at those prices supplies were limited, because producers were hoarding in anticipation of even greater profits. A gallon of syrup was costing Atlanta more to make than the Parent Bottlers had contracted to pay. Because the franchises provided no way to pass on additional costs, an increase in the price for any ingredient reduced Company profits.

Coca-Cola's profits came from syrup, half of which was sugar. Its price had not been a concern in 1899, when Asa Candler had contracted to supply the Parent Bottlers at a set rate. For the next twenty years, relations between the Candlers, the Parent Bottlers and the hundreds of Actual Bottlers had been more amicable than a cash nexus normally allows. Deals were done on handshakes. Contracts were statements of intent, not scads of sub-clauses.

The Parent Bottlers had co-operated with Atlanta in 1917 by accepting a 5-cent rise in the syrup price, which they could carry since they got 12.5 per cent for almost no outlay or effort. This give-and-take broke down with the arrival of Ernest Woodruff and his New York bankers in July 1919. They asked the Parent Bottlers to make them 'a temporary loan' by paying for syrup in advance, as Coca-Cola was having to do to secure supplies: 'otherwise it's going to be necessary for us to go into the money market and borrow heavily at high rates of interest'.[16] Woodruff next tried to sell direct to the Actual Bottlers. If he could eradicate the middle-man by taking over the unearned income of the Parent Bottlers, he could increase his returns by forcing up the price of syrup to Actual Bottlers. Soda fountains were already paying more, pushing the price of a Coke at the drugstore up from five to eight cents.

Fearful that the escalation would continue, The Company contracted for six months supply of sugar. The rocket stalled mid-year. Sugar slumped to 10 cents, leaving Coca-Cola to pay twice that rate on its forward contracts while its lawyers prayed that a ship bearing the most expensive sugar would sink, and tried to 'defer deliveries...bought for January' until July 1921.[17]

Woodruff Sr now demanded $1.80 for a gallon of syrup, twice the pre-war rate. In January 1920, the Parent Bottlers refused to negotiate without a written list of sugar prices, alleging that 'the average cost for the year 1920 would...not be more than fourteen cents a pound', not the 27.5 cents claimed by The Company. [18] Coca-Cola was copying the Havemeyers, who kept their price of refined sugar at twice that for raw until they could clear stocks produced at the higher rate. 'Refiners lost money for eight weeks and "soaked" the consumer for more than fourteen'.[19]

Hesitant though bottlers were to renegotiate the fixed price for syrup, they were anxious lest their supplier dissolve into bankruptcy. In October 1921, they signed new contracts that allowed for variations in the cost of syrup according to the price of sugar but continued the fixed rate for all other ingredients. In exchange, Atlanta accepted that the bottlers' franchises were perpetual. Woodruff senior had had enough trouble getting them to agree to vary the sugar price without risking that gain by quibbling.

If the Woodruff syndicate had hoped to make a stock-market killing on Coca-Cola, they had not calculated on inflation followed by a slump. Danger signals had flashed from October 1919 that profits would not be enough even to maintain the share price. No dividends were paid for the June or October quarters of 1920 because The Company needed 'to reserve the present cash resources' in light of 'the uncertainties of the general financial situation'.[20] The syndicate had spent $25 million to purchase The Company and so lacked the reserves that the Candlers might have employed. To stay solvent, Woodruff Sr needed to borrow $5 million at once, and $22 million in the medium term.

Woodruff also tried to preserve the share price by making inventories look like earnings. The vehicles for this manipulation were the Atkins refinery and the Guaranty Trust Co., both of which had directors on the new Coca-Cola board. The sugar man was to obtain sureties from the money men; the lolly-water men would then get their sugar free, so that they could loan it back to the sugar men. The actual sugar would stay with the lolly-water men throughout, and their numbers men would call it income, not surplus stock.[21]

It is debatable whether Asa Candler would have been more

adroit. His caution deserted him after the death of his wife in 1919; he went courting women half his age, starting with one who was 'a Catholic, a divorcee, a Creole, and a suffragette—all cardinal sins in the South, especially among Methodists'.[22] A breach-of-promise hearing, however, was less threatening than the bankruptcy proceedings into which Coca-Cola's auditor feared The Company was headed as its stock price fell from $40 to $18.

That Pepsi faced the same problems and made worse mistakes was small consolation. As sugar prices rose, Pepsi's founder-president held out against stockpiling in the belief that what had shot up must soon plummet. Day after day he waited for his faith in gravity to be vindicated. At last his nerve broke and he too plunged into the market. Almost at once, the price did what he had too long anticipated. With only two of its bottlers remaining, Pepsi followed Coca-Cola to Wall Street but found no investors. Its broker bought up the bankrupt company. Atlanta missed a chance to close down a rival because the cash-strapped Woodruff was not sure whether he was in the beverage business for keeps.

The shortages of materials feared in early 1920 never eventuated because the Europeans were too impoverished to return to their pre-war levels of consumption. In 1921–22, the world economy tumbled into a depression as sharp as in 1929-32, but less protracted. Coca-Cola sales for both 1921 and 1922 slipped back below 16 million gallons. The economic consequences of the war did not end for Coca-Cola with that slump. In 1923, France's occupation of the Rhineland and hyperinflation in Germany pushed the price of Cuban raw sugar to its second-highest levels ever, before it declined by two-thirds during the later 1920s.

To cope with dislocations after the Great War, the USA renewed tariff protection for sugar growers, which kept up prices to industrial users. The Havemeyers continued to manage supplies. No new refineries opened after 1926, and four were closed in the 1930s. Although anti-trust prosecutions overturned the 1895 judgement, the oligopoly survived. The big refiners wrote the sugar legislation that allocated them the largest quotas.

Even though Atlanta could pass higher sugar prices on to its bottlers, it feared that tariffs would one day push up the cost of syrup and bust the five-cent price to the consumer. Coca-Cola joined Westinghouse Electric to oppose the 1921 Sugar Bill. The alliance showed how close the lolly-water kings had come to the centres of US capitalism.

Cuba

US interests had long attempted to absorb Cuba, by purchase or by force. Anxious to add another slave territory to the Union, Georgians had initiated several invasions of the Spanish colony before 1855. After the American Civil War, Cuban slave-owners expected to take Louisiana's place as a supplier of sugar to the USA. Slavery in Cuba was then being supplemented by indentured labour, with planters importing 125 000 Chinese to work the fields.

Even upholders of the USA as the champion of national independence concede that US imperialism did exist between 22 April 1898 and 19 April 1901. That three-year lapse from rectitude began with a move against the Spanish in Cuba, and ended with the conquest of the Philippines. The US actions in Cuba alone suggest a vaster destiny and a wider design. After the US military withdrew from Cuba in 1902, they left a constitution that obliged the Cubans to lease bases to the US navy and to allow the USA to intervene in their domestic affairs to preserve order and maintain the island's independence from everybody else. US troops returned three times before Washington abrogated those provisions in 1934. By that stage, the USA was taking four-fifths of Cuba's exports, 84 per cent of which was raw sugar; in exchange, Cuba imported food and machinery.

The histories of Cuba and Coca-Cola criss-crossed as the USA subverted the island's quest for freedom. As a colonel in the Third Georgia Volunteer Infantry, Asa Candler's younger brother, John, prepared US forces for the 1898 invasion. One of the troops who went on that rough ride returned to franchise the bottling rights. By August 1900, Asa Candler was wholesaling his syrup in Havana, while his brother Warren, the bishop, set out to redeem the Cubans from Popery, opening the Asa Candler College in Havana in 1913.

A second Coca-Cola bottling plant went to Santiago to supply the US naval base.

Annexation of Spain's Caribbean and Pacific colonies gave US manufacturers and merchants control over the world's largest cane-sugar producing area.[23] Cuba would occupy an anomalous position in the US market. Unlike Puerto Rico, Hawaii and the Philippines, it was not a direct dependency. In 1915, when the British were seeking ways to replace German beet sugar, a syndicate was formed in New York to buy mills in the Caribbean. Among its directors was Eugene Stetson, vice-president at Guaranty Trust Co. of New York and the Cuba Cane Sugar Corporation. Stetson's position—and his Southern origins—made him the ideal points-man for Ernest Woodruff's buy-out of the Candlers. The Guaranty Trust, however, invested so heavily in Cuban sugar at the end of the war that it had to be rescued by the Morgan group in May 1921. The National City Bank, which acted as Cuba's central bank, ended up owning a fifth of the island's sugar mills.

Between 1904 and 1925, Cuban sugar production soared from one million tons to five million. Two-thirds of the increase came from newly cultivated areas held by US planters whose investments went from $200 million to $1000 million, securing a fifth of the island's landmass and half the mills. Eventually, Wall Street owned 70 per cent of Cuba's sugar output.[24] The outsiders established large-scale production with a continuous flow from fields through mills and into the ports. Local growers could only compete by expanding, thereby adding to excess supplies.

Although the US authorities no longer regarded Cuba as a territory for conquest, food and beverage corporations argued that Washington had to make the island's planters 'insure a fair sugar supply at fair prices'.[25] When the price slipped to 2 cents a pound in 1927, Cubans cut production by a fifth, only to find that the rest of the world went on expanding its output. After Havana lifted its self-imposed restrictions, the price fell below 2 cents. The Cubans then set a minimum sales price at 2 cents a pound, and soon had a stockpile of 3.4 million tons. Robert Woodruff more than doubled the value of Coca-Cola's sugar inventory to $9.1 million between 1928 and 1929 in the expectation that prices would rise.[26] The

Company also agreed to buy the sugar from a refinery which the chocolate maker Hershey had just opened on Cuba.

The island had supplied half of US demand until 1929, but the new US tariff slashed sales from 4.1 million tons to 1.6 million by 1933. With the world average price below 1 cent a pound, the hourly wage for agricultural labourers fell from one dollar to twenty-five cents, provoking strikes and then revolution in 1933. The new Roosevelt administration avoided sending in the Marines because Cuban soldiers, led by a Sergeant Batista, put their patriotism at the disposal of US investors, whose shares were then worth only five cents in the dollar. During 1934, the US crafted a new Sugar Act and offered a quota to the Cuban growers. By 1940, US pro-tectionism had so depleted Cuba's earnings that social disturbances again posed a security risk, which Washington avoided by buying the island's sugar crop for the duration of World War Two.

World War Two

In anticipation of war, Coca-Cola built up a two-year supply of sugar. The US government, however, banned stockpiles and acquired half The Company's store of 100 million pounds at cost. Rationing began in 1942, holding industrial users to 80 per cent of their 1940 volumes. Coca-Cola had two compensations. First, its size meant that a 20 per cent cut would not hurt it as much as the smaller brands. Secondly, it had its sales to eleven million troops who con-sumed twice as much Coke per head as civilians, but whose sugar was excluded from the rationed allotment.[27] Per capita civilian intake of sugar fell from 103 pounds in 1941 to 73 pounds in 1945. Households were allowed an extra 10 pounds for home canning, less than half the allotment in 1917, another sign of how far food had been industrialised.

Pepsi meanwhile began buying sugar in Mexico and shipping the barrels across the border until Atlanta prompted the govern-ment to deprive its rival of these 'unwarranted advantages'.[28] In a tit-for-tat war around Washington, Pepsi secured the dismissal of the man in charge of sugar rationing, who had resigned as a vice-president at Coca-Cola to take on that job. Despite difficulties with

the Havana regime in the 1930s, Pepsi bought a 77 000-acre plantation on Cuba in 1944. As a hedge against any repeat of the 1920
price spiral it also had its own mill capable of producing 200 000
tons—more than it needed.

By the late 1950s, Coca-Cola was keeping two months inventory in case of strikes, and was buying from six refiners to avoid
being screwed by the three largest ones, who still controlled 60 per
cent of output. In 1963, The Company decided to 'take an active
part in efforts...to secure certain changes to the Sugar Act...a
most difficult undertaking with delicate implications'.[29] Securing a
tariff cut was complicated because the two senators from Georgia
had to please Coca-Cola in Atlanta and sugar-growers on the coast.
The Company now found common ground with the American Sugar
Refining Company, which hoped that lower prices from a tariff cut
would increase demand and boost its earnings.

Castro

Cuba remained the most likely source for more and cheaper raw
sugar, just as US tariffs remained a source of disagreements between
Washington and its client government in Havana. The US sugar
tariff proved as much a diplomatic as a domestic issue because of
its effects on US relations with Cuba: 'if Cuba lowered its costs,
America would raise its tariffs'.[30] Cuba also remained the hub of
Coca-Cola distribution throughout the Caribbean, with a new syrup
plant opening there in 1957.

After touring Cuba in July 1956, President Eisenhower passed
on to his friend Bob Woodruff the cigars that dictator Batista had
presented to him, claiming they were 'a little strong even for a vet-
eran like me'.[31] The next year, Woodruff learnt more about Cuba's
'political differences' when a resident advised him not to come down
bird-shooting because 'civilians carrying guns have been very unpop-
ular'.[32]

US dominance of Cuban sugar had kept the island's economy
stagnant, leaving the USA open 'to the serious charge—one not
without its own illustrious counterpart in American colonial history
—that a metropolitan country is denying to its raw-material

supplying areas a kind of industrial processing entirely appropriate to their resources'.[33] Instead of initiating a take-off from agriculture to industry, Cuban sugar rarely got further than milling. Refineries could not expand because of the US limits on imports. Ethanol plants had operated only for as long as the US military required fuel during World War Two. Earnings from sugar exports were used to buy US manufactures, which stymied import substitution. This blocking of alternative investments encouraged local planters into conspicuous consumption on residences, gambling and grand tours. Cuba's impoverishment resulted from the overdevelopment of its cane-growing, which produced what Che Guevara identified as distorted development—not underdevelopment.

High on the priorities of Castro's forces when they entered Havana on New Year's Day 1959 was an end to US dominance of the island's economy through the sugar quota. The new regime announced the break-up of the big estates, mostly US-owned, with compensation to be paid in government bonds at the value set for taxation under Batista. A promise of land reform did not alarm Washington; most of its own sons-of-bitches had grabbed at power behind similar rhetoric. The difference became apparent when Castro set a June 1960 deadline for his program. Washington and Havana spent the second half of 1959 trying not to rupture relations, with Castro offering more sugar at a price lower than that from US growers, and the State Department pursuing higher compensation than figured in the fraudulent bookkeeping of US corporations. Well-informed about its oldest dominion, Coca-Cola had already been preparing to move its operations out of Castro's reach and into the Bahamas.

Breaking point came in February 1960, when the Soviet bloc ordered 1.5 million tons of sugar. Washington suspended Cuba's quota. Castro retaliated by expropriating all US properties. The USA initiated a program of harassment, notably the CIA invasion at the Bay of Pigs, assassination plots and a continuing trade embargo. The effects spread through the Caribbean when the Kennedys granted a slice of Cuba's quota to the Dominican Republic and authorised the assassination of its dictator, Rafael Trujillo, who was now deemed a blot on Washington's discovery of democracy.

In Havana, on the Fourth of July, 1952, the 22-year-old Roberto Goizueta had joined Coca-Cola as a chemical engineer. His family had come from Spain in the late nineteenth century to grow fibre for the bags used to export raw sugar. By 1960, Goizueta was introducing Sprite around the Caribbean. This task gave him the cover he needed to travel and prepare for relocation. He memorised company records before making his final flight to Miami. Three weeks later, on 25 October 1960, Castro, himself a Coke fan, nationalised Coca-Cola.

Revolution in Cuba had two consequences for Coca-Cola. Its loss of an investment and of sales was less important than the disruption of the world's sugar trade. Throughout the 1950s, raw cane sugar prices in the USA had remained steady at around 6 cents per pound; access to the Cuban surplus had helped the USA to hold down the world price. 'Excess capacity in Cuba could be called on to meet any sudden increase in American requirements...When controls had to be tightened...contraction could be placed more easily on her shoulders.'[34] This ratchet was now lost. Although prices never performed another 'Dance of the Millions', for a few days in July 1960 they pirouetted towards those levels, only to slump once the US government lifted limits on imports and restrictions on domestic beet production. These measures secured supplies for industrial users, but did nothing to stabilise their costs.

After the 1962 Cuban missile crisis, sugar prices rose past 13 cents per pound. 'Supplies were so critical' that the destruction of 77 000 tons in a warehouse fire in Australia 'caused a violent reaction on the market'.[35] Only intervention by the US Department of Agriculture brought the world price down to 8.5 cents.

Sugar prices remained volatile into the 1980s. The first oil crisis in 1973, combined with the failure of Soviet and Cuban crops, quadrupled the cost of raw sugar to 30 cents. Coke sales fell for the first time in fifty years—not surprising when a six-pack of Cokes in New York City cost more than a six-pack of beer.[36] World prices slipped, rocketed back towards 30 cents during the second oil shock in 1980, then again plunged to 8 cents by 1982.

In 1977, Coke president Paul Austin went to Cuba and met Castro, whether to discuss the purchase of sugar for Coca-Cola's non-US operations or to reopen a plant is not clear. On his return, Austin briefed his buddy President Carter, who was then contemplating a new start in hemispheric relations. Austin also delivered a box of cigars from Castro to Woodruff. This gesture of goodwill fell far short of the $27.5 million compensation that Atlanta is still demanding for the nationalisation of its Cuban venture.

Higher prices were not the disaster for Atlanta that they had been in 1920 because the Actual Bottlers now bore that part of the burden. Yet uncertainty over sugar prices and supplies continued to complicate planning in Atlanta. A roller-coaster of costs can be as troublesome as consistently high prices, because investments are predicated on some predictability of earnings. The Company responded by seeking alternative ways to satisfy capital-induced cravings for sweetness.

CHAPTER 17 **Sweet Reason**

Any worthwhile change in the conduct of a business must first
and last have the element of lessening cost.

Cooper Proctor, 1886[1]

Coca-Cola's need for a sweetener has never bound it to cane sugar.
Wars and tariffs encouraged experiments with beet and saccharin
long before artificial sweeteners became permanent in 1963.
Sometimes the changes have been made to secure supplies, but the
lasting ones confirm Cooper Proctor's insight. In the 1970s every
one-cent increase in the cost of a pound of sugar reduced Coca-
Cola's operating profits by $20 million. By 1985, corn-based
sweeteners were saving Coca-Cola and PepsiCo $100 million a year.

Corn syrups

Extracting sweeteners from grains is as ancient as brewing with
them, but large-scale applications became possible in the 1930s after
hybrid corn multiplied the yield. The change ruined those farmers
who had been accustomed to holding back a portion of their crop

for next year's seed but could not afford the new types. Manufacturers had begun to graft seeds, fertilisers and herbicides into the great chain of profit.

Twenty years of research went into the production of High Fructose Corn Syrup (HFCS-55) in 1978. By 1982, US beverage makers had reduced their use of sucrose by a third, while their consumption of HFCS-55 had more than doubled. With artificial sweeteners making further inroads, sucrose now supplies only 5 per cent of the sweeteners used by the soft-drink industry in the USA.

The instability of sugar prices had encouraged the swap. Atlanta and the larger bottlers could cushion themselves against these swings, but many franchise-holders postponed re-equipment and trimmed their promotions, reducing outlays to keep up dividends to stockholders. Their choices endangered medium to long-term earnings at a time when the Pepsi challenge called for brassier promotions, new delivery vehicles and the most up-to-date machinery. When sugar prices skyrocketed in 1963, Atlanta helped its bottlers by splitting the 40-cent price difference between a gallon of TAB and a gallon of Coke. Consumers did not benefit; Atlanta had no intention of letting TAB compete against Coca-Cola on price.[2]

The sliding scale for sugar agreed to by The Company and the bottlers in 1921 had not covered other ingredients. As a result, in the general inflation of the 1970s Atlanta again faced the prospect of selling syrup at a loss. The Company now sought to amend its contracts so that it could set its syrup price to cover variations in all its inputs. Many bottlers agreed, but a few large ones refused. The tussle continued for more than a decade. During that time, Coca-Cola found a financial sweetener for franchisees who signed up, namely, the lower-priced HFCS-55. In 1987, hold-out bottlers won a legal battle to receive the cheaper syrup without surrendering their contract rights. Atlanta struck back by offering them sucrose-based syrup, but at the much higher price for sugar. Since few plants had the facilities to run two lines of syrup, the recalcitrant bottlers would also pay additional production and transport charges. Their lawyer accused Atlanta of 'spite' and of 'bad faith to coerce the bottlers into a waiver of their rights'.[3]

The Company itself had had to weigh the benefits from the

lower price of corn syrup against the capital costs of abandoning sugar. Because sweeteners were added to the concentrate at the plants, replacing sucrose involved mechanical adjustments in hundreds of locations. Chemistry added to the caution, because sweeteners cannot be substituted for each other without adjustments to the remaining ingredients. Fructose accentuates fruit flavours, making Coca-Cola taste sweeter than an equal volume of sucrose. Balance also depends on temperature: fructose is sweeter at lower temperatures and so 'most advantageous...in very cold liquids', which is the way a Coke is supposed to be served.[4] PepsiCo feared losing its challenge if it altered its formula to corn: 'We have based our whole marketing program on taste, and we're not going to switch', was the line late in 1982, though that soon changed.[5]

Political considerations also intervened at home and abroad. After being at the mercy of domestic sugar growers for fifty years, Coca-Cola saw an escape from the higher costs imposed by the sugar tariff. HFCS-55 came on the market at around 10–13 cents per pound when wholesale sugar was at 15.6 cents and rising. During the decade from 1986 to 1996, the price gap ranged between 2.5 and 10 cents per pound. Of course, corn syrup was cheaper only because the price of sugar in the USA was kept high to subsidise the local industry. If cane sugar had been sold there at the world price, neither beet nor HCFS-55 would have many takers. The US sugar program provides 'a golden umbrella' for corn millers.[6]

Because Coca-Cola exports concentrate rather than syrup, sugar-growing economies such as Brazil or Australia continued to use sucrose, which suited Atlanta because its profit margin on concentrate overseas was greater than on syrup in the USA.[7] Notwithstanding this shared interest, Coke's switch to corn syrup in the 1980s injured non-US sugar growers by depressing world demand, which softened prices. The share of world production being stockpiled climbed from 25 to 45 per cent. Although the soft-drink industry had been the world's largest single user of sucrose, producers had not trembled when Coca-Cola spoke—until they lost a million tons of sales to fructose. During the 1990s, Brazil took up the role that Cuba had had before 1960 in capping the world price for sugar. Indeed, the explosion of the Brazilian output from

7.5 to 18.8 million tons threatens to bankrupt several higher-cost producers such as those in Australia.[8]

The New Coke misadventure also came out of the move away from cane and beet sugars. Goizueta decided that since Coca-Cola had substituted fructose for sucrose without a backlash, he could sweeten the Coke formula to win the young from Pepsi. Cheaper corn syrups made a sweeter New Coke more attractive than it would have been had Goizueta had to pay 25 cents for sucrose instead of 17 cents for fructose.

Monopolising operated for HFCS-55 as it had for sugar. Fourteen refiners were charged with price-fixing during the 1970s, when one of the Havemeyer successors still controlled a quarter of the sugar market. Corn syrup is in the hands of agribusinesses such as Archer-Daniels-Midland (ADM), which in 1996–97 pleaded guilty to price-fixing. A simultaneous suit alleged that ADM had manipulated the world price of corn syrup through an alliance with Japan's Ajinomoto. Under those arrangements, 'return on net assets for the industry averaged well over 30 per cent'.[9]

Despite the oligopoly power of the HFCS firms, overproduction dragged prices to a twenty-year low in 1997. They had failed to foresee the threat from artificials which were taken up as a cost-cutting measure for all soft drinks, not just diets. In 1998, the $100 million launch of Pepsi One, with just one calorie, did not mention weight control. A spokesman for an artificial sweetener firm in Atlanta welcomed this approach as an indication that the 'word "diet" is most likely going to be a thing of the past'.[10]

Artificials

A German scientist discovered the sweetness of saccharin in 1879 by spilling some onto his hands shortly before eating bread. This characteristic was not commercialised because of opposition from beet growers. In 1901, a clerk with a Missouri importer of saccharin to the USA for medical applications began to manufacture it on his own account under his wife's maiden name, Monsanto. The food police denounced the substitute but it won endorsement from that burly fitness fanatic, President Theodore Roosevelt. World pro-

duction shot up during both world wars, attracting more manufacturers and spawning other synthetics such as cyclamate, which
was marketed from 1949.

A substitute can disrupt market dominance as radically as any
outbreak of competition among existing oligopolists. From the early
1950s, the US sugar industry noted that although artificials 'might
never command a really damaging share of the market...in terms
of human prejudice [they] might be damaging indeed'.[11] Trouble
came on both fronts. During the 1960s, consumption of artificials
expanded by 300 per cent; it went on to average 20 per cent growth
throughout the 1970s. Tariff protection for US sugar producers had
made their industry lopsided; Big Sugar had no research program
to produce artificials of its own. Not until the late 1970s would
Britain's Tate & Lyle 'develop new chemical entities from sugar'
and market its no-calorie sweetener.[12]

Growers and refiners hoped to beat off the artificials by bad-
mouthing them. To that end, the sugar combines funded the research
into the health effects of cyclamates that they had resisted into
sugar. Industry fronts such as the Sugar Research Foundation publicised findings that bladder cancers appeared in rats fed cyclamates
in amounts equivalent to eleven pounds of sugar a day for two
years. Those results coincided with Nixon's $2 billion war on cancer
and triggered a ban under a 1938 law prohibiting the use of any
additive in any way linked to cancer.

Varieties of Coca-Cola were anathema to Woodruff's gospel of
standardising taste. In the 1940s, when bottlers faced wartime shortages of sugar, they were prepared to substitute saccharin, but
Woodruff confessed himself 'very leery' about tampering with the
formula. He agreed to include beet sugar only 'as a matter of life
and death'.[13] Not until 1963, when diet drinks were taking 3 per
cent of US soft-drink sales, did The Company provide a low-cal
variant, TAB. The Company mixed cyclamate with saccharin to
soften a tang that reminded drinkers of kerosene. Behind the objections to tampering with brand loyalty was a fear that soft drinks
would not become addictive without a high sugar content.
Nutritionists have since shown that sweetness from whatever source
stimulates the desire for more sweets. Replacing sugar with an

artificial is less effective in weight loss than cutting back on all sweeteners.

The 1969 prohibition on cyclamate was a respite for the sugar industry. The demand for calorie-free sweeteners had been established in a population already rolling towards obesity. Saccharin was still available for TAB, which the Atlanta-based Calorie Control Council, another Company front, defended the public's right to choose. The election of the deregulating Reagan in 1980 tamed Congressional staffers and Food and Drug Administrators, but Atlanta worried that a civil action could be taken against the Food and Drug Administration for not enforcing that old anti-cancer law against saccharin. The lobbyist for Coca-Cola got its friends at Twentieth Century Fox to ask Hollywood's Congressman Waxman, the ranking Democrat on the health sub-committee, to look into the matter.[14] In 1997, executives of another artificial brand, Sweet 'n' Low, pleaded guilty to more than a decade of illegal donations to buy influence in favour of saccharin.[15]

The popularity of low-calorie products made Atlanta rethink its strategies, especially since half the diet drinkers were new to soft drinks. Its Fresca sold on its taste, not for its healthiness. The Company was preparing to give TAB a makeover before president Paul Austin killed the project in 1980. His successor was Roberto Goizueta, a chemical engineer, who had been involved with the development of the new diet version. Six months into the job, Goizueta decided on release for early 1983, allocating $250 million for laboratory and market research. More marvellous still, he authorised the use of Coke in its name.

Diet Coke appealed to Goizueta because saccharin was even cheaper than HFCS-55, and not subject to price fluctuations. The less bulky artificials also cost less to transport and store than sucrose or fructose. When Goizueta restarted the Diet Coke project in 1981, raw sugar had gone close to its all-time record price. Synthetics would help him achieve his goal of a 20 per cent return on capital. With diet and sugared lines selling at the same price, the profit margin from Diet Coke was larger. Equalising their retail prices absorbed some of the stellar costs for sugar. Indeed, Coca-Cola would have profited more had everyone switched to its saccharin version. Diet Coke soon became the nation's top-selling no-cal beverage; by 1985 it was the third-best-selling soft drink after Coca-Cola and Pepsi. *Advertising Age* proclaiming it the brand of the decade, a distinction it should share with NutraSweet.

NutraSweet

NutraSweet began in 1965 when another chemist stumbled onto sweetness by licking his 'finger to pick up a piece of paper' smeared with aspartame.[16] Despite his bad laboratory practice, he informed his supervisor at G. D. Searle & Co., which patented its use as a sweetener. In 1969, the year the Food and Drug Administration banned cyclamates, Searle applied to the FDA for approval of aspartame. The FDA sanctioned certain dry uses of aspartame in 1974, only to withdraw permission because of doubts about the scientific reports presented by Searle. So frustrated did Searle executives become that they wrote off $21 million of stock before approval to include aspartame in food was restored in October 1981. The better news was that, because of the prolonged regulatory procedure, Congress agreed to extend the use patent by six years to the end of 1992. Searle had the green light to proceed into a cul-de-sac of dry uses, which had annual sales worth a mere $110 million. The objective was to speed up FDA permission for aspartame's entry to the $25 billion beverage market. That decision came in 1983.

At once, Searle expanded its plant in Augusta, Georgia, to be within putting distance of The Coca-Cola Company, which would take around half of the output. Diet Coke had been launched when saccharin was the only licensed synthetic. As soon as aspartame gained approval, Coke blended it into its diet lines, switching to 100 per cent aspartame before the end of 1984. Aspartame cost more than saccharin and had a shorter shelf-life, but it also lacked the bitter, metallic aftertaste, which drew in more first-time drinkers. The prohibition on cyclamates was keeping industrial users of other artificial sweeteners nervous about their viability. A move from saccharin to aspartame needed funds for reformulation and marketing; for instance, the change from an aspartame–saccharin blend to 100 per cent aspartame had cost PepsiCo $60 million. Such investments would be wasted if aspartame were withdrawn within a year or two. The soft-drink industry therefore encouraged the FDA to grant aspartame a once-and-forever clearance.

With cyclamates banned and saccharin requiring a health warning, Searle's aspartame dominated the artificial sweetener market in the USA—but only till the end of its use patent in 1992. To make the most of this power, Searle engaged in monopoly pricing. Facing no competitor, it could boost supply without endangering its returns. Its problem in 1983–84 was keeping up with demand.

In the early 1970s, lacking the technology to make one of the two amino acids essential for aspartame, Searle had turned to Ajinomoto, the world leader in the field. By 1984, Searle also needed Ajinomoto's production capacity, so they formed an alliance in which both sides squabbled like hostile monopolisers rather than long-haul partners. Despite supply shortages, Searle engaged in retail advertising, making industrial users suspect that its executives were 'trying to get demand, and price, as high as possible'.[17] 'Their game', according to Roger Enrico at PepsiCo, was 'to make immense profits before the clock runs out...without this patent, they couldn't sell their way out of a paper bag'.[18]

By the early 1980s, annual sales of $700 million had made G. D. Searle & Co. a takeover target. Goizueta passed it up when Coca-Cola bought Columbia Pictures. The Monsanto Chemical Company saw Searle as a route into pharmaceuticals. It was less sure about NutraSweet, but it bought the lot for $2.8 billion in 1985, declining Ajinomoto's offer for the sweetener division.

To establish aspartame with the public while its patent held, Searle had followed the methods of oligopoly marketing, coining the brand name NutraSweet and imposing its logo on every product that contained aspartame, so that its industrial customers would underwrite its corporate identity. Searle also went after the far smaller household market. It took two competitors to the US Supreme Court, without success, to prevent them from colouring their packets in a shade of blue close to NutraSweet's. Searle gave away ten million aspartame-sweetened gum-balls, making NutraSweet the first food additive to promote itself to shoppers as a branded ingredient. By the close of the 1980s, NutraSweet held

70 per cent of the artificial sweetener market in the USA, where 70 per cent of shoppers could 'name NutraSweet unprompted as a sweetener'.[19] Shortly before its patent expired, Searle tied up its two major customers, The Coca-Cola Company and PepsiCo, with long-term exclusive supply contracts.

Searle used equally aggressive selling to 'obliterate competition' around the world.[20] A fifth of NutraSweet custom was overseas, giving it 70 per cent of the world market by the close of 1988. The alliance with Ajinomoto had secured a monopoly over Japan. Without patent protection in Europe, however, NutraSweet had to compete on price; it sold at $27 a pound, a third of the rate in its home territory. This differential led to anti-dumping penalties in the European Community and Canada.

By 1996, NutraSweet–Ajinomoto produced three-quarters of the world's aspartame, which in turn made up almost 70 per cent of all sales of artificials. Monopoly pricing was impeded by a 20 per cent oversupply and the presence of a European rival. Competitors meanwhile were developing superior products with longer shelf-lives and more stability at the temperatures needed for baking. Approval of a new sweetener for use in US diet beverages doubled the stockpile, threatening the smaller producers. In this situation, Coca-Cola could either spread its orders around several suppliers or negotiate a keener price from Searle, an option open to neither small firms nor domestic consumers.

NutraSweet suspected that its best customers might become its worst competitors. Its dealings with Coca-Cola operated 'in a tight range of anger, dislike, mistrust and bad feeling'.[21] In 1988, Coca-Cola announced it had developed an artificial which was 1900 times sweeter than sugar. Atlanta did not proceed to production because of the difficulties in gaining FDA approval, the costs of marketing, and the problems of yet again rebalancing the formula. Publicising the new sweetener's existence, however, was a negotiating ploy against NutraSweet.

Blended sweeteners soon edged NutraSweet aside. A division of Hoechst, the German chemical giant, patented a combination of aspartame and acesulfame-K, which took 'the European soft drink market by storm'. By 1997, it was used in 90 per cent of diet beverages in Britain and 70 per cent in Canada. US approval followed. The new mixture provided Coca-Cola with two cost savings. First, the blend delivered 40 per cent more sweetness than 'the properties of the individual sweeteners' would have predicted. With the prices of aspartame and acesulfame about the same, Atlanta saved on ingredients. Secondly, the blend had twice the shelf-life of aspartame and so reduced the loss from drinks returned by retailers.[22]

Searle's ambitions crumbled during the 1990s. Marketing failed to reinvent its sweetener. By 1994, Coke had downsized the NutraSweet logo on its products. A Coca-Cola vice-president sneered that NutraSweet 'used to be magic in a bottle. Now it's boring'. He blamed a slowdown of Diet Coke sales on poor marketing by NutraSweet.[23] In fact, diets had peaked at 30 per cent of soft drinks in 1991; from then on, their market share was challenged by bottled waters, juices and New Age lines.

The battle of the artificials was won by Splenda, an intensifier based on sugar. Where aspartame lost half of its sweetness in six months, Splenda retained 99 per cent of its original power. Technologists had alchemised the natural into the perfect artificial. Just as marketeers were blurring the distinction between regular and diet lines, they clamoured for products that blended farming with pharmacy.[24]

G. D. Searle had set himself up in 1888 as an inventor–druggist, a younger version of Atlanta's Dr Pemberton. That their legacies coalesced a century later when a 1980s synthetic was mixed into an 1880s soda pop—an artificial sweetener with the Real Thing—was one more marker in the integration of agriculture and industry.

CHAPTER 18 **Juggernaut**

Nor can certain harmful effects of deforestation, or of some methods of farming, or of the smoke and noise of factories, be confined to the owner of the property in question or to those who are willing to submit to the damage for an agreed compensation. In such instances we must find some substitute for the regulation of the price mechanism.

Friedrich-August von Hayek, 1944[1]

The Monsanto Chemical Company had begun supplying Coca-Cola with caffeine extracts and synthetics in the early twentieth century when those earnings kept the newcomer going. By 1941, Monsanto was Coke's largest single source of caffeine. Their relationship broke down after 1946 when Monsanto's synthetics became more expensive than the natural extract, causing Coke to find another provider.[2] Monsanto meanwhile was expanding into plastics, styrenes, fertilisers and pesticides. To the war against the Vietnamese, it delivered Agent Orange.

During the late 1990s, Monsanto refocused its operations three times, a sign of the turmoil in the life-science sector. In 1996, it moved to integrate agricultural biotechnology and pharmaceuticals with food ingredients.[3] Almost at once, it bought up seed companies such as Asgrow soybeans, and the biotech firms Agracetus and Calgene. In 1998, Monsanto disposed of several ventures to consolidate its place in the agribusiness chain. It put its foods division, including NutraSweet, up for sale at some $2 billion to reduce the debt it had accumulated during its $8 billion plunge into buying seed companies. The Monsanto board wanted to hold on to Searle's drug unit because it believed that 'science-based nutritional business is at the intersection of agriculture and pharmaceuticals'.[4] In March 2000, Monsanto had to sell off Searle as well in a $30 billion deal with Pharmacia & Upjohn. What remained of Monsanto as an agribusiness was scheduled for sale. Monsanto's break-up is one of the consequences of the public's revulsion at the genetically modified organisms that the corporation anticipated would make its next fortune.

What Jeremy Rifkin calls 'pharming'—the combination of pharmacy and farming[5]—had appealed to Searle's management even before Monsanto took it over in 1985. Searle had a vision of marketing foods invented in laboratories and grown in factories. It aimed to produce its own branded lines of food and drink as well as selling ingredients such as its fake fat, called Simplesse, to its competitors, Kraft and Unilever. Not surprisingly, they came up with their own versions.[6] Searle also hoped to replace sweeteners derived from living plants with factory brews. In 1991, it targeted Sweetener 2000 at sugar, the substitute being 10 000 times sweeter and able to be produced for less than half a cent per kilogram.[7] Searle's larger ambition was to market 'an increasing volume of food and fiber... grown indoors in tissue culture in giant bacteria baths, at a fraction of the price of growing staples on the land'.[8]

This trend to replace farm produce appeared at its crudest in General Foods' instant *cafe au lait*, where the *lait* was not powdered milk but a compound of vegetable oil, casein, solids, sweeteners, flavours, colouring, glycerides and dipotassium phosphate. More advanced science had to be applied to reduce the labour intensity of pollinating, harvesting and curing vanilla beans: 'gene-splicing technologies allow[ed] researchers to produce commercial volumes of vanilla in laboratory vats...eliminating the bean, the plant, the soil, the cultivation, the harvest, and the farmer'.[9]

This determination to replace the fruits of nature with concoctions from the test tube has touched many products. Du Pont is planning to 'make many of its chemicals in plants rather than cook them in a vat of petroleum', [10] returning the definition of 'plant' from industry to botany. Monsanto sold off a comparable venture because production costs were $4 a pound compared with 40 cents from petrochemicals, though technologists expected to get the differential down to a competitive level within five years. On that assumption, Dow Chemical and Cargill built a $300 million plant in Nebraska for a conversion process called *NatureWorks*. Instead of asking 'Is that flower plastic?', we will soon be asking 'Was that plastic a flower?'

Despite Monsanto's hunger for the foods and fabrics of the future, its cash cow remained a 1971 herbicide, Roundup, sales of which had increased by 20 per cent each year. Aware that Roundup was nearing the limit of its capacity to increase crop yields, and that its patent expired in 2000, Monsanto started to bio-engineer soybean crops to be Roundup resistant. Farmers could then kill weeds but leave soybeans safe from predators other than Monsanto, which charged $20 a bag for the genetically modified (GM) seed, plus a $5 technology fee. The marketing of a seed resistant to Roundup would extend the effective life of Monsanto's patent. In addition, Roundup-resistant crops make it possible to use higher doses of Roundup to kill weeds; in turn, the surviving weeds will propagate strains ever more resistant to Roundup and thus be in need of heavier applications. Monsanto developed equivalent resistances in corn, cotton and canola. Roundup Ready canola escaped in Canada in 1997 to cross-bred with weeds, which became herbicide resistant.

Monsanto brandishes 'Food, Health, Hope' as its motto for the industrialisation of life. While some foods are promoted for their health benefits—with cereal packets promising protection against cancers and heart disease—most are spiced with artificials or laced with residues from fertilisers, pesticides and herbicides. The mix perplexes consumers, who welcome some additives but fear others.

Low-fat milk enriched with calcium is deemed desirable—providing the cow has not been treated with a Monsanto hormone to increase yield.

In 1998, Monsanto spent £1 million in the British press to sell the merits of genetic engineering, but succeeded only in awakening the public to its dangers. The hole in the public relations was that Monsanto opposed the labelling of GM products, although its advertisements promised 'as much substance as possible'.[11] Reporting the genetic modification of foods has been even rarer in the USA, so consumers there have not been able to make an informed choice. The US Food and Drug Administration ruled in 1992 that no labelling was required 'as long as a GM food is no more toxic or allergenic or any less "substantially equivalent" than its standard counterpart'.[12] The National Soft Drink Association is against labelling because of its members' reliance on corn syrup. To regain the initiative in the debate, Monsanto joined Aventis, Du Pont and Novartis in a $50 million campaign to market the benefits of GM food. Monsanto, meanwhile, operates a 'scientific research team' to place GM supporters on food safety committees at the United Nations and World Health Organisation.[13]

Genetic modifications may prove benign, but the catalogue of approved products that have turned toxic gives reason to pause. In the 1970s, women trusted the brand name 'Rely' tampons until several died, compelling Proctor & Gamble to pay out millions in compensation. In 1999, American Home Products (AHP) offered nearly $5 billion to the tens of thousands who suffered heart disease and often fatal lung conditions from two diet drugs. AHP had opposed having prominent warnings on their packaging because that 'could have cut sales by as much as 50 per cent'.[14] This 'buyer beware' approach is at one with the tobacco industry's concealing the results of its own research on the harm from smoking.

Less waste, more speed

To accuse Monsanto of bio-engineering food for profit is to say no more than that Monsanto is a capitalist corporation. The point is to identify how biotechnics can augment capital. The answer is through the management of time. The more rapidly an investment can be turned over, the more value can be accumulated. Natural selection moves too slowly to satisfy capital's need for food crops that will mature earlier and weigh more. Economies from speed led one firm to insert 'a mammalian growth hormone into fertilised eggs producing faster growing and heavier fish'.[15]

Monsanto's Law declares that genetic know-how 'doubles every twelve to twenty-four months'. A key to this acceleration is the integration of chemistry with microbiology. Chemists can already synthesise 'almost anything given the resources'.[16] Corporations look forward to reducing the costs of synthesis by copying the mechanisms of evolution to breed catalytic enzymes.

A second imperative for the control of time arises from the perishable nature of foods. Although capitalists would prefer to reduce the time taken to get their money back, they must also extend the period during which they can realise on their investments. Calgene doctored its Flavr Savr Tomato to delay softening and thus extend its shelf-life. Genetic manipulation will also make more products cheaper to process and sell. Breeding crops to standardised shapes and sizes has reduced costs of transport and packaging. Russet Burbank potatoes were bred for McDonald's to simplify the production of its fries. The modification of crops to suit mass processing results in the dominance of a single variety, the factory type eliminating the table ones.

Corporations also need to eliminate losses that occur before harvesting. Every seed that does not germinate diminishes capital's own capacity to grow. Seedlings that wither are a blight on revenue. If pharming reaps a heavier and more durable crop in a shorter time, then the rate of profit should be less prone to decline.

Some aspects of nature move too quickly for maximum profit-taking. By selling a seed that can generate its own seeds, Monsanto relinquishes control of the expansion of that capital. To protect its treasure, Monsanto offered nearly $2 billion in May 1998 for the firm that had developed the 'Terminator' seed in collaboration with the US Department of Agriculture. The Terminator would germinate for only one season, compelling the farmer to buy new stock each year. Sterile seeds bring no benefit to the grower but secure a profit stream to its patent-holder.

In 1999, however, Monsanto shelved its Terminator project because it was fuelling the public's fear of genetically modified foods.[17] Wisdom dictated one step at a time. The first necessity was to get GM seed over its public-relations hurdles; then would be the moment to return to the Terminator, which was several years from commercial application anyway. Moreover, there was no pressing need for such a seed where contracts forbade the grower to hold back grain for next year's planting, as was the case with Monsanto's soybean. Should the Terminator return, it will prevent the adaptation of crops to their local environments. One suggested solution is that the Terminator gene be fitted to GM seeds so that they cannot infect other plants.

More alarming is the patenting by Novartis of a gene that can switch off the immune systems of plants. The commercialisation of this procedure would mean that farmers using the disabled seed could turn its protection back on only by applying chemicals supplied by Novartis.

Cultivating nature

In the 1940s, Monsanto's owner, Edgar Queeny, seeking spiritual values in the wild, called himself a 'naturalist', which meant that he set aside game reserves on his properties so that he and his friend Bob Woodruff would have plenty of creatures to kill.[18] These days, agribusinesses hasten the death of all nature while marketing their inventions as natural. On that premise, one Monsanto chemist declared that a ban on saccharin 'would be a crime against nature'.[19] To hasten FDA approval of NutraSweet and Simplesse, Searle & Co. argued that because the constituents of these artificials occurred in nature, their recombination must also be natural and hence benign. In line with this economically correct thinking, Searle's term for synthetic sweeteners is no longer 'artificials' but 'intensifiers'. That new usage captures their cost-saving qualities and deflects consumer doubts about artificial foods.

Anthropologists connect culture with the behaviours that human beings create or acquire, such as an appetite for sugared cola. They reserve 'nature' for the capacities that we inherit, such as the conversion of food into blood sugars. That divide can prove misleading. Human nature couples the learned with the innate so inextricably that the proper study of humankind is their mix.

Confusions about what is culture and what is nature are extending past what we do and consume, and into who we are. US courts allow patents over all living things except human beings. We remain exempt because the Thirteenth Amendment forbids slavery. When we recall how judges converted the Fourteenth Amendment from a bastion for the freedman into a defence of corporations, can we be confident that this anti-slavery protection will survive? Several US States have already made it possible to libel branded foods. In addition, the bar against slavery through science is being circumvented by the patenting of single genes. The human genome project celebrates the view that life is molecular, leaving no place for individuality, consciousness, personality, soul, or whatever holistic term appeals. Splicing the commercial to the molecular, biotech firms are redefining humanness by commodifying life.

Malthus or Liebig?

Monsanto has affected surprise that its intentions with Roundup Ready and Terminator seeds have been misunderstood. Its research scientists thought the corporation was 'helping the environment, not harming it'.[20] This defence sounded plausible after 200 years of scares about famine from overpopulation.

In 1798, the Reverend Thomas Malthus published his essay on population, regurgitating the view that human numbers rose geometrically while food resources increased arithmetically. A doubling of the population in each generation, he argued, would force people into lands with lower productivity. Diminishing yields would bring mass starvation. His prescription was that governments should not alleviate poverty because such efforts only encouraged the poor to breed.

In particular, Malthus opposed the 1795 extension of the Poor Laws, which made the municipal rate into a redistributive tax and drove up its cost to the landed proprietors. Social movements to excise the causes of poverty were criminal. Malthus did not suppose that poverty was a curse of nature. He knew that it was the outcome of struggles over access to productive resources. He therefore wanted to end the Poor Laws in order to release the well-off from their obligations to those they were driving off the common lands. He defended the Corn Laws, which restricted the import of grains, and he championed the landlords who benefited from them, blaming the rise in prices of grain on the expense of Poor Law relief. Furthermore, he regarded all measures to limit population as vicious, calling population growth 'necessary' because it kept down wages.[21]

Malthus ridiculed the prospect of average agricultural output increasing to keep pace with population growth, which would require it to grow eightfold in 200 years. When he wrote, most of the five million non-indigenous inhabitants of the USA were involved in agriculture. They could feed themselves and supply one-third as many again. By 1950, only 12 per cent of the US workforce were on the land, but they could feed seventeen times their own numbers. In other words, food production had gone up approximately twice as much as Malthus had alleged was impossible, and in only three-quarters of the time. Since then, butter mountains and wine lakes in Europe, with farmers paid not to produce, testify that production has run far in excess of effective demand.[22]

Malthus also defended one root of impoverishment, namely, the enclosure of common agricultural lands. One-fifth of the cultivated land in England went into private hands between 1760 and 1815. If the poor were farming marginal lands, they had been driven there by the Enclosure Acts and anti-poaching laws, not by rising numbers. As an anonymous rhymester would put it in 1821:

> The fault is great in man or woman
> Who steals a goose from off a common;
> But what can plead that man's excuse
> Who steals a common from a goose?

This expropriation was also creating the 'free' labourers necessary for capitalist production, whether on the land or in factories.

Even as Malthus condemned social reform as contributing to overpopulation, the agricultural revolutions of crop rotation, deep ploughing and fertilisers were challenging the inevitability of famine. In 1840, Justus von Liebig published his *Chemistry in Its Application to Agriculture and Physiology*. The book became available in English and French within a year, making Liebig as significant as Darwin would be twenty years later. Liebig's key proposal was that minerals had to be restored to soils. The chemist who had introduced artificial soda water to the United States in the 1800s, Professor Benjamin Silliman, looked on Liebig as a genius, and by 1847 he had convinced Yale University to establish chairs in both Agricultural and Practical Chemistry.

Liebig protested against the despoliation of the earth by capitalist farmers who 'robbed' nature by felling native forests and cropping virgin fields. To repair the soils, Liebig trained industrial chemists to manufacture nutrients to replenish the land. His own artificial fertiliser company failed, but a century later his ideas on superphosphates were still inspiring farmers as far afield as Australia.[23]

On the centenary of Malthus's essay on population in 1898, the president of the Royal Society identified the artificial combination of nitrogen and hydrogen into ammonia as the single discovery most essential to prevent starvation. Supplies of fertilisers were limited, and the cost of synthesis exorbitant. The search was on for a catalyst to lower the pressures and temperatures at which this combination could be achieved. Germany funded thousands of experiments to give it the ammonia it would need for its farms and high explosives if supplies of nitrates from Chile were endangered by the British navy. Success came in 1913 to Fritz Haber, who earned 'one pfennig for every kilogram of ammonia' sold by BASF.[24] When war broke out a year later, Haber supervised the release of poison gas and won the Nobel Prize for Chemistry in 1918. In 1919, British capitalists took over the industrial application of synthetic ammonia as part of the spoils of victory.

Liebig's difficulties in balancing the rewards from commerce

322   The Essence of Capitalism

with his commitments to conservation foreshadowed a choice which would face all scientists. For £5000 down and £1000 a year, Liebig lent his name to the raising of funds on the London Stock Exchange for a company to manufacture his beef extract, although he had already made its formula available to all comers to benefit the needy. After patenting another discovery, he acknowledged: 'People will gossip about me for a couple of weeks and then everyone will say to themselves that they would have done exactly the same in my position'.[25] Academics have done so ever since. Harvard biology professor Richard Lewontin observed in 1993: 'No prominent molecular biologist of my acquaintance is without a financial stake in the biotechnology business'.[26]

Bad faith leads scientists who have signed such Faustian bargains to view criticism of their research as a flight from reason by feminists, post-modernists, eco-terrorists and neo-Marxists. What that assortment of critics objects to is not science but its subservience to the war machine and the bottom line. Since the emergence of Big Science early in the twentieth century, most researchers have been employed on projects tied to state terrorism or corporate plunder. In the early 1990s, the Princeton Dental Resource Center advised dentists that a chocolate a day was as good as an apple a day. The Center later paid a $25 000 fine for having concealed its funding by the Mars candy corporation.[27] A nastier instance occurred when lawyers for women suing Proctor & Gamble over its Rely tampons 'found it nearly impossible to enlist a doctor to serve as an expert witness, because P&G quickly offered hefty research grants' to anyone working on that topic.[28]

Cutbacks to tax-funded science are reducing the scope for disinterested inquiry as universities chase corporate sponsorship and their findings become trade secrets. The US Food and Drug Administration's budget has been stagnant in real dollars at a time when the FDA is confronted by 'an explosion of new and challenging products'.[29] In Australia, the body that evaluates therapeutic drugs depends on pharmaceutical companies for funding.

Overconsumption

At the beginning of the twenty-first century, one ground for pessimism is the diminishing return from what remains of nature. Threats also come from the technologies that have held off global famine. Monsanto is supplying the replenishment Liebig called for, but in ways which will require even greater repairs to the earth, or may prove irreparable.

In the 1850s, Liebig denounced Great Britain for depriving 'all countries of the conditions of their fertility...Like a vampire it hangs on the breast of Europe, and even the world, sucking its lifeblood without any real necessity or permanent gain for itself'. The final part of that denunciation cannot be directed at Monsanto, because its behaviour is a real necessity if capital is to secure its essential and life-giving expansion.

While the rise in agricultural productivity has been stupendous, its distribution remains unjust. When supply exceeds effective demand, a fall in prices can depress the entire economy. This prospect caused Malthus to redirect his attention from overpopulation to under-consumption, a revision which eludes many of his devotees. By 1820, Malthus was worried that the 'increase in the quantity of the funds for the maintenance of labour [runs] faster than the increase of population'. His solution was to pray to god for an increase in the birth rate of parsons, soldiers, aristocrats and their retainers, who consumed without producing, and whom Marx honoured as 'gluttonous drones'.[30] Malthus, however, exalted 'the passion for expenditure' as the way to absorb the surplus, recognising that the excess must not be returned to its wage-labouring creators because they then would not feel compelled to work:

> It is the want of necessaries which mainly stimulates the labouring classes to produce luxuries; and where this stimulus is removed or greatly weakened, so that the necessaries of life could be obtained with very little labour, instead of more time being devoted to the product of conveniences, there is every reason to think that less time would be so devoted.[31]

Malthus understood the class struggle better than many of his current disciples comprehend the connections between poverty, power, population and property.

Malthus doubted that supply would create its own demand, because he assumed that desires could not be expanded quickly enough to absorb the surplus supplies. Reflecting on the means to quicken appetites, he had devoted the final chapter of his *Essay* to 'Excitements of the wants of the body'. Mass marketing was sixty or more years in the future when he published his *Principles* in 1820.

The dominance of Admass now means that the prospects for our species would not necessarily improve if our numbers fell by half. Throughout his 1998 paean to 'the triumph of American materialism', James B. Twitchell was never tempted to count the cost in natural resources of expanding consumption. The threat to survival does not come from billions of the poor so much as from millions of the rich. With only 5 per cent of the world's people, US residents use more than a third of the global resources consumed each year, although even there people still go to bed hungry. Freedom from want is further away than ever for most of the world's population. Freedom from wanting is equally remote for the rest of us, because capital must multiply our needs if it is to survive.

Contraception brings advantages for individuals, but these benefits cannot be extrapolated to the human race or to planet Earth. Rising standards of living may reduce birth rates, but they often increase consumption. In the First World, growth in consumption has turned geometric, while population has become arithmetical. The population of Japan is stagnant, but consumption continues to rise, with fads for luxuries such as cigarette lighters fitted with battery-driven sweepers for spilt ash. A population explosion of automobiles in China is more destructive than a doubling in the numbers of Chinese children on bicycles. Caps on consumption are more pertinent to sustaining our ecology than any controls over population.

Biologists might argue that increasing the numbers of one's own species is the meaning of life, but the element of truth in that version does not account for the capitalist imperative behind the drive for consumption goods. The threat to survival is not from a self-ish gene but from an Adtopia which identifies self-worth with commodities.

To speak of moving into natural capitalism is to misunderstand both. The mechanisms of nature cannot supply capital with a model for its survival because evolution is not efficient in the way that capital requires. The wonder that is the natural world is antithetical to engineering and standardisation: why are there so many ways of being a fish or a bird? Biological adaptation is far from neat and perfect, but relies on rough fits to get by with one contraption after another.[32]

By contrast, capital is wasteful of nature and labour but niggardly with itself. Du Pont is planning a zero-waste policy. Between 1988 and 1998, it produced only three-quarters of a pound of goods from each pound of its raw material. For Lycra, by contrast, the yield was above 90 per cent.[33] The prospects for this strategy depend on the ability to lower production costs. If the scrap is not easily returned to the productive processes, then transforming it into commodities may cost more in labour power, energy and depreciation than is gained by recycling. The win-win promises of natural capitalism may be blocked by diminishing rates of return from inputs. Recycling is a poor substitute for reducing production and consumption—the one contribution that capital can never afford. The risks of recycling are clear from the spread of Mad Cow Disease, which resulted from feeding cattle with animal by-products.

The limits to slowth

The grand narrative of capital's expansion is now far more inimical to sustainable development than it was at the start of the modern era, when Niccolo Machiavelli and Leonardo da Vinci collaborated on schemes to deflect the force of nature. In 1513, Machiavelli compared fortune with

> an impetuous river that, when turbulent, inundates the plains, casts down trees and buildings, removes earth from this side and places it on the other;...and yet...when it is quiet, men can make provision

against it by dykes and banks...So it is with fortune, which shows
her power where no measures have been taken to resist her, and
directs her fury where she knows that no dykes or barriers have
been made to hold her.[34]

After 500 years of capital's redirecting nature, the question has
become how to blunt the force of the market, whether it is manifest in Admass, biotechnologies, globalisation or monopolising. What
Karl Polanyi called 'the juggernaut, improvement' will be most
destructive 'where no measures are taken to resist'.

The term 'juggernaut' came into English from India, where it is
customary for the devotees of Vishnu in the city of Puri to pull a
huge cart through the sand. In a piece of colonial propaganda,
Anglo-Saxon schoolchildren were taught that Hindu fanatics threw
themselves under its wheels. The word has since come to mean an
unstoppable force, which seems appropriate to the expansion of
capital. Indeed, the parallels appear exact when we consider how
capital is moved forward by labour power and how marketing leads
frenzied consumers to hurl themselves under the wheels of debt.
In Sanskrit, however, 'Juggernaut' means 'the Preserver of the
World'. The danger in moving Vishnu's shrine is not that the cart
is unstoppable, but that it cannot be deflected from its path. Our
task now is to deflect 'the juggernaut, improvement' away from
being the destroyer of the world.

Polanyi reflected on the approach that should have been adopted
when the market began to dominate society in the nineteenth
century:

> The rate of change is often of no less importance than the direc-
> tion of the change itself: but while the latter frequently does not
> depend upon our volition, it is the rate at which we allow change
> to take place which well may depend upon us.[35]

After the failure of so many plans to command the juggernaut into
reverse, Polanyi's modest proposal has renewed appeal.

Our ability to limit the speed of capital's accumulation was shown
by the derailing of the Multilateral Agreement on Investment (MAI)

in 1998. Under the MAI, The Coca-Cola Company and the vendor of fresh coconuts at a village stall on Yap would have been treated as equals before the law. The superior force available to an oligopoly would have been deemed irrelevant to the freedom of the market. Similarly, the MAI would have prevented Indian authorities from restraining Monsanto's power in its dealings with a farmers' co-operative. Alarm among citizens' groups has put the MAI on hold, though its sponsors cannot afford to abandon their goal. Faced with popular resistance, GM foods are being labelled where they are not outlawed, and the Terminator gene has been delayed. Protesters have put the World Trade Organisation on the defensive.

Capital can be slowed for a time, but it will not survive if it stops growing. Indeed, its expansion depends on the economies of speed. When capital cannot expand, it implodes, as happened in the USA throughout the 1930s, until it was rescued by perpetual war for eternal peace. Were capital to falter across the globe, that slowdown would not abate environmental devastation or narrow the gulf between rich and poor. Rather, a world recession would provoke more robbing of the earth to get capital going again, while the most impoverished would have to eat the future.

*

The Essence of Capitalism has outlined the dynamics driving the juggernaut to which humankind is bound. To understand why capital must behave as it does is the precondition for reshaping the relations between nature and human creativity, and for reducing the inequalities within our species. Futurologists claim that just as chemistry dominated the nineteenth century and physics the twentieth, so will biology rule in the twenty-first. This litany misses the point that the greatest need for the greatest number is not another technological breakthrough. The real thing will be the permanent gains to be had from transforming the social relations between the beneficence of nature and the inventiveness of labour.

AFTERWORD # Killing Time

Capitalism is being tossed by another of the destructive blasts from its gales of creation. Shortly after the Australian edition of this book appeared in May 2001, stock markets slumped while corporate collapses rendered accounting transparent. The mentality behind the ENRON and WorldCom frauds had been set out in Chapter 4, where, reflecting upon the Asian financial meltdown of 1997, I had asked "was the time bomb in Bangkok or on Manhattan?" If an independent researcher in Australia could know that the sky was about to fall, why didn't the analysts on Wall Street? At one level, they did. Whatever I knew about corporate malfeasance had come from the business press, which had been reporting scams throughout the 1990s.

In the two years since publication, I have garnered enough materials to compose a book of equal length. This "Afterword," however, will touch on those chapter topics only in the course of criticizing my treatment of globalization, particularly my failure to tie its development to the control of labor-times.[1] I was right to argue that capitalism, imperialism and globalization are three of a kind. I failed to track the mechanisms by which Imperialism, as monopolizing capitals, might have moved on to a newer phase of globalization. My revised starting point is to follow the turnover of capitals through their transformations as money, commodities and production.[2]

These circuits have spread out geographically at varying rates across the past 600 years. Money-capital went first, though it was tied to commodity-capital through trade. The export of production-capital is recent, and remains the least pronounced.[3] Each circuit is now aided by its own global organisation: commodity-capital through the WTO; money-capital through the IMF and World Bank; and production-capital in multinational corporations. The rules of those global organizations have to be enforced by nation-market-states, both inside their domains and against each other.

No more than an outline of this project for comprehending globalization can be given here. The account will begin by sketching five phases of the spread of capitals around the globe. The second part deals with the control of labor-times. Then follow three sections, one each for money-capital, commodity-capital and production-capital. A concluding segment circles back to the opening chapter as a reminder of why the state is not our friend.

Globalizing capitals

The expansion of capitals has proceeded through five phases, which we can call Globalization Mark I–V. These shifting patterns will be sketched around changes to the labor-process, principally the spread of wage-labor. Mark I centered on Merchant's capital with its plunder of new worlds, while much labor was forced despite craftsmen operating outside the guilds.[4] Mark II was the Mercantilist era when free, that is, dispossessed laborers encountered the discipline of clock-time, while particularization added a new division of labor, and machinery challenged manu-facture.[5] Mark III was the free-trade interlude in the nineteenth century when slavery in the Americas and serfdom in Russia were being displaced by either free or indentured labor, with a further re-division of labor between nation-market-states. Mark IV was Lenin's Imperialism when the labor process accommodated both a waning aristocracy of labor and the beginnings of Fordism.[6]

Mark V began with the world car in the later 1970s. After the 1940s, tariffs had secured monopoly profits for US auto-makers. When those corporations faced competition from Japan, and then retooling costs to deal with oil-price rises, the oligopolies negotiated new protective arrangements. Worldwide production led on to financial deregulation to facilitate the transfer of investment funds and the reflux of profits. Despite the later association of Globalization V with intangibles such as banking and infotainment, its seedbed was in meeting the needs of the exemplar of rust-bucket industries.

New things happen. Social formations are not fixed by god, nature or the market. For instance, Globalization Mark IV was marked by a rise in tariffs whereas today's free-trading globalizers have unraveled much of that form of protectionism. So, it is possible that Globalization Mark V is a qualitatively different expression of capitalism, just as monopolizing capitals had been. Imperialism need not be the last stage just because Lenin called it the Highest. Indeed, today's globalization may yet prove to be a distinct plateau within capitalism and not just another phase within Imperialism. The answer will require a reworking of concepts with which to comprehend further experience. Whatever the truth about Globalization Mark V proves to be, it is carrying forward the plundering of natural resources, expropriation of the surplus produced by labor, and a monopolizing competitiveness.

Indeed, oligopolization keeps becoming ever more extensive and intensive. Mergers among oligopolies have been a feature of recent years because, more than ever, businesses must either consolidate or disappear. According to the *Harvard Business Review*, managers need to perfect their acquisition skills because "merger competence is paramount."[7] Information Technology is not neutral when Microsoft can build code that "will tilt the playing field in their direction."[8] Similarly, the collapse of the dot.coms did not signal the disappearance of that field for monopolizing. On the contrary, such contractions trigger fresh bouts of concentration.[9] Coca-Cola's consolidation of its Latin American bottlers late in 2002 came in reaction to a similar consolidation by the Pepsi Bottling Group, supplying another instance of how competition contributes to monopolizing.[10]

The substance of each phase of globalization has to be distinguished from its mechanisms, such as on-line banking. The Internet is no more globalization than the telegraph was Imperialism. In that first round of monopolizing competition, the railroads and electricity speeded up the circuits for all three forms of capital. Railroads allowed the movement of larger volumes of commodities at a faster rate over longer distances. Financing their construction contributed to the concentration of banking. Building the rolling stock and the tracks encouraged consolidation in the iron and coal industries.[11] Electricity delivered an equal variety of influences. Transmission lines allowed production at a distance from the generation of power. Electric light completed the erasure of distinctions between day work and night work. Similar patterns could be traced for the internal combustion engine and petrochemicals. All three became highly oligopolized and provided an unprecedented expansion of values.[12] The scarcity of comparable new productive forces, telecommunications no longer excepted, is one reason for skepticism about the distinctiveness of the recent globalization. The "good-will" spewed out as a book- keeping entry by AOL is a long way from the wealth generated at General-Motors, AEG or ICI.

Labor-times

The animal spirits that stalk the expansion of capital rarely disrupt the calculation of labor-time. The1990s exuberance will mean, as *Business Week* spelt out,

> ...far more pain for workers... To get [corporate] earnings up— without accounting tricks—executives are going to have make deep cuts in payrolls and productive capacity... The road to higher profits will be a painful one. To meet their profit targets, companies will cut costs again and again, shuttering factories and offices and shedding unprofitable lines of business.

Business Week estimated that "in order to boost operating profits by 12% during the next year, companies in the S&P 500 may have to cut some 900,000 jobs, or 4% of their workforce."[13]

The background to this latest assault is the spurt in real wages during the final phase of the 1990s boom. Earlier increases in profits had followed the driving down of labor costs throughout the 1980s. Most of those savings had come by slashing labor levels in the advanced economies, glamorized as flexibility. Some firms started up in locations with few, if any, inhibitions about the ill-treatment of labor. This need to trim labor costs is normal. Hence, post-war affluence is better understood as a "trough in unemployment" than as the norm to which we are bound to return.[14]

Although our perceptions of time are affected by the micro-management of the working day, subjective responses cannot alter the nature of cosmological time.[15] Nor can time be produced, have value added to it, or sold. At most, a firm can manufacture devices to tell the time of day, or sell signals of its finest measurement. Hence, to lament the commodification of time is a nonsense.[16] Commodification is the province of labor-times.

Our focus, therefore, will be on how firms structure the time of their employees. Pulsing through capitalism is commodification, though labor itself cannot be bought. All that can be bought is a worker's capacity to add value. Having hired that labor-power, bosses still have to apply it to raw materials or semi-finished goods. In short, the firm has to keep its workers at it. The managers can seek more value by demanding longer hours for no more pay, or by enforcing a faster output within the existing working-day, notably by mechanization.

Workers, meanwhile, organize to reduce hours, improve conditions and safety, as well as to lift real wages. The conflict between this range of demands and the profit-taking of their employers is therefore multi-layered. Driving down wages is only part of how corporations extract the maximum surplus from the labor-power they buy. Managers seek to set all the rules to suit their production schedules. Hence, they may trade higher wages for stricter time controls. That outlay is recouped when the firm shifts the costs of downtime to its workers, for example, through casualization. The race is not a sprint to the bottom where the prize is the lowest wage, but a marathon for reducing all the costs of production per unit, crucially by the control of labor-time.

Of course, firms prefer both time controls and wage cuts. Chrysler's plan for a new factory at Windsor, Ontario, will slash its capital outlays and trim labor. Suppliers will be required to invest 60 percent of the construction costs and transfer their lower wages into the auto maker. The Canadian Auto-workers Union accepted the deal after the loss of 15,000 jobs since 1999.[17]

Labor-time takes three forms: concrete, universal and abstract. The first is the interval that a worker takes to complete a task, and so varies with each operator. The task of the overseer is to drive all concrete labor-times towards the most efficient existing time, known as universal labor-time. A related duty for managers is to speed up that universal labor-time in order to beat the times achieved at competitors. That is why capitalism became a perpetual acceleration machine.

Concrete labor-times are always a host of actions with no abstract or conceptual equivalent. Universal labor-times are a smaller multitude of actual lengths of time. Their universal aspect is the pressure on all factories, service-providers or offices to keep up with the larger volumes and keener prices from competitors while workers are making claims that would install higher unit-costs. The universal is a mobile standard that capitalists are compelled to pursue if their firms are to survive. For a long time, its achievement could be recognized only after profits had been reported. That index was rough-and-ready because book-keeping remained rudimentary. Moreover, the realization of any part of the surplus depended on the employer's ability to sell his workers' output. Fordism and Taylorism moved beyond this *post hoc* measure of the success at matching the workers' universal labor times with the best time at the competition.

Abstract labor-time is on a different level of analysis than this historical sketch of the quest after universal labor-times. Universal and abstract labor times are connected, but need to be distinguished as practices and concepts. Abstract labor-time is a universal equivalent in the way that money, by acting "as reification of labor-time," provides a measure for the exchange of all other commodities: "The particular labor of an isolated individual can become socially effective only if it is expressed as its direct opposite, i.e., abstract universal labor."[18]

Over the centuries, the driving of concrete labor-times into ever accelerating universal labor-times has spread geographically. The process began with the severing of serfs and peasants from their productive resources so that they were forced to sell their capacity to work in order to exist. Gathered together in factories, these hands were driven to work at the same pace as each other. That rate became universal around that factory's locale, and then across entire industries in a national market. Within Globalization Mark V, the hope is to install, for every product or service, universal labor-times that will, indeed, cover the universe.

An alternative way of understanding the import of this compulsion is to ask why excessive hours are a prime problem for so many workers. In the mid-1950s, the panic was that automation would re-instate mass unemployment. By the 1970s, the concern was that there would be a social crisis as people failed to cope with an excess of leisure. One commentator proposed in 1974, that "if everyone did a short stint of factory work each year, it would be possible for everyone to be free from such work for most of the year."[19] The reverse has happened. The reason is that no firm or national economy could survive against its monopolizing competitors if it gave up so large a share of the value that its workers add to capitals.

The irrationality of capitalism is manifested in the contradiction between its sociotechnical capacity to grant much reduced hours and the socioeconomic impossibility of its doing so. The expansion of capitals has provided enough for everyone to live well, yet that abundance can not be absorbed because the proletarianization of the populace precludes the effective demand to consume the surplus.

The closest Lenin came to discussing labor-time in his *Imperialism* was the aristocracy of labor.[20] Such a privileged sector of workers is possible only if there is an aristocracy of capital, that is, a stratum of firms which can achieve higher-than-average rates of profit, perhaps through monopolizing. That advantage need not depend on colonized societies. Unequal exchanges can happen between sectors or firms within a nation-market-state such as the United States, as well as between the United Sates and Mexico. Globalisation Mark V overthrew the *ancient regime* of tradesmen. The screen jockeys—those masters of the new economy—have not been ennobled because their careers have been as brief as they are inglorious.

Money-capital

Apologists for capitalism cannot make up their minds whether corporate crimes are the result of a few bad apples or should be sheeted home to all of human nature, genetically determined. In practice, greed is stimulated by the expansion of capital far more than the other way around. If avarice were all there was to the multiplying of values, it would never appear. Either, the surplus would be hoarded, or it would be squandered on consumption that did not extend its reproduction.

Warren Buffett is portrayed as the good capitalist whose personal style is modest and who invests for long-term growth, not speculative plunder. These attributes are compared favorably with the excesses of Dennis Kozlowski at Tyco, and with the havoc that George Soros wrecks on entire economies by betting against their exchange-rates. From the standpoint of the expansion of capital, Buffett's behavior is more exploitative than any speculator's. The surplus that he reinvests, rather than lavishes on himself, extracts ever more value from workers at the firms into which he has put his clients' money. The morality of capitalism is to be judged by its logic, not its folklorists.

Since the 15th century, the trade in futures (Merchant's capital) has quickened accumulation by reducing the number and length of interruptions. Futures trading has also allowed more space for swindles. In the 1970s, derivatives spun out of futures-trading, continuing its contribution to a reduction in turnover times. That necessity for speed does not make theft necessary. Rather, mechanisms for acceleration have multiplied the opportunities for capitalists to rob each other, which is a less expensive undertaking than making their workers go harder and faster. As Marx observed: "All nations with a capitalist mode of production are therefore seized periodically by a feverish attempt to make money without the intervention of the process of production."[21]

Much of the recent stock-market losses have ended up with financiers, not producers or providers. This transfer extended one of the reasons for the 1990s boom. The productive capacity of corporate mines, farms and factories has exceeded the demand from those who can afford to buy. One result is fewer opportunities to invest in the expansion of capital. The paucity of profitable stocks in the old economy drove the stampede into telecommunications, the base for the high-tech start-ups. Their consequent excess capacity and collapse has left fund managers with even fewer places to invest.[22] One response is to do nothing for fear of making another mistake and thus attract a pink slip. The alternative is to take even bigger risks than before, if only to collect a broker's fee.

This displacement of making profits from production by the arranging of financial deals had required the invention of discount brokerage, indexed funds, cash-management accounts, junk bonds and spreadsheets. These new instruments marshaled the retirement savings of employees, a lot of which have been lost in the current stock-market crash. After the 1960s, the fiscal crisis of the state saw governments and employers encourage workers to contribute to superannuation schemes. Swathes of these funds were then invested in their employers' businesses. Workers were advancing money as well as labor to their bosses.[23] For instance, at The Coca-Cola Company, four- fifths of the 401(k) retirement assets of employees had been invested in company stock, the value of which slumped by 30 percent in the three years to late 2001. The CEO who presided over that slide exited with $17m. on top of his stock options which had already siphoned value out of his employees' assets. The depletion of retirement provisions represents a transfer from the workers' earnings on top of the expropriation of surplus value at the point of production. The German middle-class was bankrupted in 1923 by inflation that stripped the purchasing power from their bank deposits and government bonds. Today, working people are in danger of a similar fate, but by a deflation of their savings held in stocks.

Commodity-capital

Cheap labor, of itself, cannot guarantee profits. They must be realized through the three circuits of capital, that is, from money going into production and onto commodities. Only by getting products to market, selling them at a price above the cost of their production and distribution, and then getting as large a share as possible of those earnings back to the firm's bank account is it possible for capitalists to show a profit. Starvation wages are little help if the commodities are too shoddy to sell, the warehouse is burnt down during a strike, or the value of the local currency see-saws. Inadequate transport and communications disrupt the realization of the surplus. Mobile phones leapt over the poor landline system in Thailand, but it is still hard to get a crate from a Bangkok factory to its airport.

For a 1997 survey, managers ranked, on a scale of five down to one, thirteen criteria for deciding whether to invest in a foreign market. The size of that market and the need to exclude rivals were towards the top of the list. Quality of labor came fifth, whereas labor costs were down in ninth position.[24] These results confirm what every MBA course preaches and what Marx argued about the expansion of capital: lowering the wages bill will not of itself maintain the rate of profit, or attract foreign direct investment. Although wage-rates are secondary, weak protections for labor do ease the exiting of capital. Sweatshops do not face the redundancy payments that firms in the EU economies incur when they close. Nike's suppliers can walk away without lay-off costs.

In their case, a 1995 breakdown of the costs of producing and delivering a pair of Nike shoes to a retailer showed that production-labor accounted for $2.75 out of $29.00 before profit. Materials cost the contractor $9, rent and equipment was $3 and government duties were $3. Sales, distribution and administration expenses at Nike itself were $5.[25] Even a management consultant should grasp that the wages bill deserves to be towards the end of the items to be cut back to get profits up for the supplier, or for Nike. Wage-rates are significant but insufficient as the explanation for any of the five phases of capital's expansion.

Production-capital

Despite all the talk about the mobility of capital as the key to globalization, the movement of production equipment from one site to another remains an almost prohibitive option. Money-capital can go at near the speed of light through a fiber-optic cable, and commodity-capital close to the speed of sound in a cargo jet. Meanwhile, production-capital shifts at walking pace. A feature of Globalization Mark V is that equipment moves at all. Yet, very few firms transfer existing plant and machines from one nation-market-state to another. Mostly, they start up in green fields. The idea that production capital can slip across borders like a backpacker is believable only if you have never run anything bigger than a photocopier.

Nike does not move any productive capital between countries. The bulk of the costs of relocating has been carried by its suppliers, who must recoup it from their workforce. Nike appears "weightless" by externalizing the burden of relocation, as The Coca-Cola Company did at first through franchising. Even contracting to a new supply house is never easy, as Nike found when it tried to work with state enterprises in mainland China. It is cheaper for Nike to switch its orders around between producers once they are up and running. Even then, delays and disruptions will arise, incurring costs for Nike as well as for its contractors.

The worth of Nike's suppliers remains sunk in their investments in plant and machinery. To abandon those facilities before they have passed their use-by-dates would be to risk bankruptcy. Once machinery is installed in Bangkok, the costs of moving it lock, stock and barrel to Hanoi could have the same result. A supplier, however, could follow Nike's example and hire the machines as well as renting a factory. The costs of moving would then be passed down the line to the machine-makers. Either way, the expense has to be borne, though it can be reduced by designing equipment and buildings which can be assembled with a minimum of delay, turnover-times being of the essence.

Access to production-capital, that is, resources for the wherewithal to live, is at the root of capitalism. The want of productive property is why the vast majority must offer to sell their labor-power. That condition is also the basis for deciding whether the poor have got poorer, or more numerous, during Globalization Mark V. A long-run study indicates that inequalities within countries widened from the 1820s until the Second World War, since when the spread has been between countries.[26] A study of incomes alone for only the past thirty years concluded that "global inequality increased slightly during the 1970s, declined during the 1980s and went back up during the 1990s" while "within-country inequality has increased monotonically."[27] Changing levels of poverty or inequality cannot be discerned from comparative earnings.[28]

The communal or familial proprietorship of productive resources in land or at sea is more significant than income. Their loss is absolute, not relative.[29] Erstwhile land-owners are thus reduced to potential wage-laborers—installing a reserve army of the under-employed. In addition, separation from the capacity to grow or gather one's own food leaves the landless more dependent on store goods, which are more expensive and often less nutritious. The costs of reproducing labor-power thereby increase, while health deteriorates. The loss of productive resources also disrupts family-based welfare whereby the aged can be sustained by their children. Without traditional resources, the family becomes subject to the vagaries of the labor-market rather than the weather.

A current instance of this appropriation of natural resource is found in the Indian village of Plachimada where Hindustan Coca-Cola Beverages Ltd operates on a 16-hectare site once used for irrigated crops. The factory draws underground water to make a million bottles of Coke beverages every day, for which the company paid nothing. This extraction has reduced the supply available for village agriculture. The remaining water is less drinkable because of concentrations of natural contaminants and the seepage of chemicals from the factory.[30]

The arms trade is pivotal in the impoverishment drive. Dictatorships sell natural resources at or below the costs of production to generate revenues to purchase weapons to maintain their dominance. This massive trade in weapons of destruction enriches arms manufacturers. The Pentagon approves because the guns suppress resistance to exploitation, a defence of property rights denigrated as terrorism. The masters who drove self-sufficient producers to sell their labor-power by depriving them of their productive property have been succeeded by authorities who confine the natural right to property to the right of capitals to expand values by realizing the surplus extracted from the current wage-laborers.

The state

To distill the essence of capitalism, this book opened by defining the nation-market-state as attempting "for capital what its managers cannot achieve through corporations." That epigram continues to be written in blood. The slaughter of indigenous peoples is carried out by the police and the army, not by executives from the corporations that will take over their forests or other resources.

For instance, in Bolivia, no civilian judge was game to try the US-trained army captain, Robinson Iriarte de la Fuente, accused of murdering a 17-year old, Victor Hugo Daza, who had been protesting against the control by the Vivendi Corporation of his community's water. It was left to a military tribunal to acquit their fellow officer.[31] Colombian lawyers have filed suit in Miami, alleging that Coca-Cola and its affiliates have been complicit in the murder of union activists by the paramilitary. Those charges include the shooting of one organizer in June 2001. The assaults in Colombia follow decades of repression under the aegis of the US security state, through Operation Condor, which coordinated assassinations across the sub-continent.[32]

The campaigns against Saddam Hussein show that not even the oil giants can go it alone but need the punch of the Pentagon. Similarly, the coups and plots against the Chavez government in Venezuela also needed backing from US state-terrorists to keep democracy safe for oil. Washington's subverting of Venezuela is connected to US ambitions for Iraq. Chavez had rebuilt OPEC, keeping oil prices up around the $25 a barrel mark. Under the robber barons who had ruled in Caracas before Chavez's election in 1998, the state-owned Venezuelan oil industry had been as obliging as Saudi Arabia in keeping the US supplied. The counter-revolutionaries in Venezuela also show that government ownership is no guarantee of serving of the people. The decisive factor is class control of the state.

The slaying of Carlo Giuliani during the Genoa G-8 protests in July 2001 grew out of plans by the Special Operations Group (ROS) in the Carabinieri to disrupt the anti-globalization movement. The provocations at Genoa could not scare off 50,000 delegates from the Social Forum in Florence in November 2002. The half-million who joined the anti-war demonstration there proved that a mass movement can frustrate state conspirators. After police and media provocations failed at Florence, the Italian state resorted to laws from the fascist era to arrest twenty activists. The charges included "conspiracy to commit crimes against the economic order." The round-up sought to disorganize the movement by deflecting energies from extra-parliamentary offensives to a court-room defense. That attack stumbled on an alliance of No-Global activists with unionists protesting the closure of FIAT factories.

These assaults on campaigners against corporate clout remind us that our opponents have the armed power of the state as their backstop. As a result, No-Global activists have had to lift our sights beyond the mocking of brand logos to the countering of military logistics.

At the political heart of this book is the conviction that the effectiveness of our political efforts will be proportional to our comprehension of why capitals perform within limited but adjustable channels. Documenting conditions in a Nike supplier in Thailand can fuel anger for protests. Those details will not of themselves explain why capitalism has always behaved in comparable ways, and why Globalization V continues to do so. Failure to shift its course promises catastrophe.

At the start of the *Communist Manifesto*, Marx and Engels recalled that, historically, the alternative to the revolutionary reconstruction of society has been "the mutual ruin of the contending classes." Wars, the immiserization of labor and environmental degradation are corralling us towards that disaster, while generating ever more opposition to the prospect. As we continue to defend our species against annihilation, our class against exploit- ation and our planet against polluters, the warning that Engels penned in 1876 is at once an exhortation to struggle and a caveat about all success:

> Let us not, however, flatter ourselves overmuch on account of our human victories over nature. For each such victory, nature takes its revenge on us. Each victory, it is true, in the first place brings about the results we expected, but in the second and third places it has quite different, unforeseen effects which only too often cancel the first…Thus, at every step we are reminded that we by no means rule over nature like a conqueror over a foreign people, like someone standing outside nature—but that we, with flesh, blood and brain, belong to nature, and exist in its midst, and that all our mastery of it consists in the fact that we have the advantage over all other creatures of being able to learn its laws and apply them correctly.[33]

Humphrey McQueen
Canberra, February 2003

Acknowledgements

In the late 1980s, when I began to think about basing a survey of the era of monopolising capitals on Coca-Cola, I feared that I would have to detail the story of both the beverage and the company before I could use its experiences to distill the essence of capitalism. Works by Pat Watters, E. J. Kahn Jr, Tom Oliver and J. C. Louis and Harvey Yazijian had convinced me that Coca-Cola was a suitable vehicle for conceptual treatment. Then, Mark Pendergrast in 1993 and Frederick Allen in 1994 provided historical surveys of Coca-Cola, which reduced my need to compile a narrative before proceeding to thematic analysis. David Griesing's 1998 biography of Roberto Goizueta similarly saved me from documenting later developments. Of course, none of these writers will agree with all my views, any more than they agreed with each other on every detail.

Caroline Lurie welcomed the book at Hodder Headline and secured a $A25 000 commissioning grant from the Australia Council. That sum allowed me to leave a message on my answering machine in March 1998 asking people to call back in July 1999. Without the money to buy those fifteen months, this book would still be scattered through a filing cabinet. The grant also paid for a six-week research trip to the United States in late 1998. Months of rewriting were funded from savings.

Andrew Franklin at Profile Books accepted the proposal after it had been turned down more often than a bedspread. Jenny Darling and Associates managed the contract in Australia and Bruce Hunter in London.

The Robert W. Woodruff Research Library for Advanced Studies at Emory University in Atlanta is the ideal place for scholarship, open around the clock 363 days of the year, with a staff who are as expert as they helpful. The Special Collections, guided by Dr Linda M. Matthews, are six floors closer to heaven than any writer deserves.

The Coca-Cola Company declined access to its archives.

In 1991, when I forayed into Coca-Cola and monopolising capitals, the National Library of Australia provided almost every book or periodical I needed. Its subsequent decline means that the conditions for scholarship are no longer available. The institution has perfected the great lie of the 1990s: 'It's on the web'. The portion of staff who know what research involves is minimal. The worst of it is that the directorate deludes itself that it can match world's best practice by diverting millions from materials to technical toys that they cannot get to work. For almost thirty years, when asked why I lived in Canberra rather than a big city, I have answered: 'Because the National Library is here.' That remains my response, but no longer because of the Library's excellence; it is simply that conditions elsewhere in Australia are worse.

Bill Tully and Rod Stroud at the National Library of Australia and Walter Struve at the State Library of Victoria provided the expertise and enthusiasm that were once normal.

No one could have done more to make this book possible than Judy McQueen, who maintained a flow of clippings, catalogues and books, compiled a flight schedule inside the USA, and scouted out affordable accommodation in Atlanta—the signs of our abiding affection.

Ruth Blair, Tim Bonyhady, Michael Dunn, Heather Radi and John Walker read all or sections of the manuscripts to its advantage.

Jenny Lee once more came to the rescue as editor. Their remarks confirmed Theodor Adorno's principle that 'No improvement is too small or trivial to be worthwhile. Of a hundred alterations each may seem trifling or pedantic by itself; together they can raise the text to a new level'. Ruth encouraged me to make my reach exceed my grasp.

Also lending a hand, or an ear, have been Peter Applegarth, Kathy Bail, Suzy Baldwin, Marcus Beresford, Marshall Berman, Paul Booth, Trevor Cobbold, Rob Darby, Steve Davis, Jim Davidson, Luke Deer, Peter Elder, Lynette French, Rowe Freney, the late Joan Gold, Bet and Rodney Hall, Wayne Harrison, Nick Jose, Paul Kuske, Peter Lyssiotis, Mark McAuliffe, Chris McConville, Stephen McDonald, Ben McGuire, David Mepham, Paule and Bertell Ollman, David Peasley, Nicholas Pounder, Graham Rowlands, Sharon de Smet, Giuseppe Stramandinoli, Max and Jenny Suich, Katherine West, Alexander Wightman and Howard White.

Peter Curtis has had to put up with my mind often being else-where. Dedicating the product of these distractions to him is small compensation for his supplying the excitements and assurances that keep me going.

Notes

To footnote the source of every skerrick of information or trigger for an idea in *The Essence of Capitalism* would have required a volume as long as this one. My compromise has been to footnote direct quotations. On contentious points, I have footnoted indirect quotations, usually to primary sources. A mention in the footnotes is often a sign that the book or article has informed surrounding passages.

Throughout the footnotes, MS1 refers to the Candler family papers; MS10 to the Woodruff collection; MS741 to Mark Pendergrast's generous deposit of documents he had photocopied for his project. These materials are available in the Special Collections, Robert W. Woodruff Research Library, Emory University, Atlanta, Georgia.

Abbreviations

AFR	*Australian Financial Review*
MS	manuscript
NYT	*New York Times*
P&G	Proctor and Gamble
RWW	Robert Winslow Woodruff
SOC	Standard Oil Company
SMH	*Sydney Morning Herald*
WSJ	*Wall Street Journal*
ff	folios following

References

Introduction   *The Origins of Our Future*

1 A. K. Cairncross, 'Economic Schizophrenia', *Scottish Journal of Political Economy*, 5 (1), February 1958, p. 17.
2 J. B. Priestley, *Journey Down a Rainbow*, Heinemann-Cresset, London, 1955, p. 51.
3 Spalding to RWW, MS10/259/11.
4 *New York Review of Books*, 14 January 1999, p. 40.
5 Karl Marx, *Capital*, vol. 1, Foreign Languages Publishing House, Moscow, 1958, pp. 152–3.
6 *Management Today*, March 1993, p. 56.
7 Karl Polanyi, *The Great Transformation*, Beacon, Boston, 1957 edition, p. 57.
8 *Beverage World*, July 1999, p. 62.
9 Quoted Harvey C. Livesay, *Andrew Carnegie*, Little, Brown, London, 1975, p. 46.

Chapter 1   *The Nation-Market-State*

1 Adam Smith, *The Wealth of Nations*, vol. 1, Clarendon Press, Oxford, 1976, p. 613.
2 Joan Robinson, *Collected Economic Papers*, vol. 4, Blackwell, Oxford, 1973, pp. 5–6.
3 L. J. Louis and Harvey Yazijian, *The Cola Wars*, Everest, New York, 1980, pp. 223–7.
4 Quoted Richard H. Gamble, *A History of the Federal Reserve Bank of Atlanta, 1914–1989*, The Bank, Atlanta, 1989, p. 37.
5 Vannevar Bush quoted Michael Riordan and Lillian Hodeson, *Crystal Fire*, Norton, New York, 1997, p. 115; Address to AAAS, 24 January 1999, www.aaas.org/meetings/Scope/gore99.htm, p. 6; quoted *Multinational Monitor*, 19 (11), November 1998, p. 14.
6 Adam Smith, *Lectures on Jurisprudence*, The Clarendon Press, Oxford, 1978, p. 208.
7 Quoted Arnold M. Paul, *Conservative Crisis and the Rule of Law*, Cornell University Press, Ithaca, 1960, p. 45.
8 John J. Riley, *A History of the American Soft Drink Industry*, American Association of Carbonated Beverages, Washington, D.C., 1958, p. 147.
9 M. A. Adelman, 'The Anti-Merger Act, 1950–60', *American Economic Review*, 51 (2), May 1961, p. 236.
10 7 May 1923, MS10/12/11.
11 Quoted Charles L. Mee Jr, *The Marshall Plan*, Touchstone, New York, 1984, p. 79.
12 *NYT*, 24 January 1953, p. 8.
13 MS10/12/11; Marion Smith to J. R. Nutt, 22 December 1930, MS10/283/3.
14 C-C Bottling Co., Rome, Ga, 30 March 1965, MS10/50/16.
15 RWW to Robert B. Troutman, 12 February 1934, MS10/277.
16 Thomas J. Heston, *Sweet Subsidy*, Garland Publishing, New York, 1987, pp. 204–5.

17 John Wood, Innovations Lecture, 29 April 1998.

18 Gordon C. McKibben, *Cutting Edge: Gillette's Journey to Global Leadership*, Harvard Business School Press, Boston, 1998, p. 113.

19 *American Foreign Policy Current Documents 1986*, Department of State, Washington, 1987, p. 43.

20 Karl Marx to Frederick Engels, 25 September 1857, *Selected Correspondence*, Foreign Languages Publishing House, Moscow, 1953, p. 118.

21 Gareth Morgan, *Images of Organization*, Sage, Newbury Park, Ca., 1986, pp. 23–4.

22 *Forbes*, 5 October 1998, pp. 156–8.

23 Charles P. Kindleberger, *The World in Depression*, Allen Lane, London, 1973, p. 272.

24 Deborah Shapley, *Promise and Power*, Little, Brown, Boston, 1993, pp. 45–6.

25 Noel M. Tichy and Stratford Sherman, *Control Your Destiny or Someone Else Will*, Currency, New York, 1993, p. 37.

26 Gregory Hooks, 'The United States of America: the Second World War and the Retreat from New Deal Era Corporatism', Wyn Grant *et al.* (eds), *Organizing Business for War*, Berg, Providence, RI, 1991, p. 101.

27 Alfred P. Sloan Jr, *My Years with General Motors*, Anchor, New York, 1972, pp. 266 & 240–41.

28 Quoted Paul A. Baran & Paul M. Sweezy, *Monopoly Capital*, Penguin, Harmondsworth, 1965, p. 210.

29 Nigel Harris, *Of Bread and Guns, The World Economy in Crisis*, Penguin, Harmondsworth, 1983, p. 223.

30 Quoted Steven A. Sass, *The Pragmatic Imagination*, University of Pennsylvania Press, Philadelphia, 1982, p. 20.

31 David W. Ewing, *Inside the Harvard Business School*, Times Books, New York, 1990, p. 275.

32 Peter Cohen, *The Gospel According to the Harvard Business School*, Doubleday, New York, 1973, p. 8.

33 *Barrons*, 24 March 1997, p. 38.

34 *WSJ*, 14 December 1995, A1.

35 Russ Johnston, *Marion Harper*, Crain, Chicago, 1982, p. 114.

36 Roger Enrico, *The Other Guy Blinked*, Bantam, New York, 1986, pp. 34 & 263.

37 John Sculley, *Odyssey*, Fontana, Glasgow, 1989, p. 23.

38 Bryan Burrough and John Helyar, *Barbarians at the Gate*, Harper Perennial, New York, 1991, pp. 277 & 253.

39 *Beverage World*, September 2000, p. 8.

40 T. J. Jackson Lears, *Fables of Abundance*, Basic Books, New York, 1994, pp. 248–9; MS10/39/4.

41 Quoted Frederick Allen, *Secret Formula*, Harper, New York, 1994, p. 251.

42 *Vital Speeches of the Day*, 15 January 1946, p. 210.

43 29 June 1943, MS741, Eisenhower file.

44 Insert in Stephen Bayley, *Coke: Designing a World Brand*, Conran Foundation, 1986, unpaginated.

45 *Advertiser*, 23 August 1944, p. 5.

46 Riley, pp. 142–3. 150 & 157.

47 Hughes Spalding to RWW, 17 October 1945, MS10/260/6; MS10/97/5.

48 Della Wager Wells, *The First Hundred Years*, Atlanta, King & Spalding, 1985, pp. 156–7; Hughes Spalding to RWW, 27 February 1939, MS10/259/6.

49 RWW to C-C bottler in Rome, Ga., 4 March 1950, MS10/190/16.

50 Asa to Warren Candler, 5 August 1907, MS1/1/6.

51 *Barron's*, 1 August 1921, p. 11.

52 Carl Thompson to RWW, 9 November 1938, MS10/272.

53 Ed Forio to RWW, 12 March 1951, MS10.

54 Quoted Wells, p. 158.

55 *Atlanta Constitution*, 23 September 1969, MS10/277.

56 Ralph Hayes to RWW, April 1934, MS10/54/3; MS 10/274/2; *NYT*, 22 June 1977, 2, p. 4.

57 Quoted Charles Lewis, *The Buying of Congress*, Avon, New York, 1998, p. 232.

58 RWW to Hoover, 1 July 1957, and Hoover to RWW, 2 August 1963, MS10/134/3.

59 Morton Downey to RWW, 20 January 1950, and J. F. Curtis to RWW, 4 April 1950, MS10/51/12.

60 Edgar Queeny to RWW, 19 February 1945, MS10/230/18.

61 Memo to RWW, 19 July 1945, MS10/5/4.

62 Quoted Ron Chernow, *Titan*, Random House, New York, 1998, p. 266.

63 Thomas C. Reeves, *The Life and Times of Joe McCarthy*, Stein & Day, New York, 1982, pp. 118–22.

64 *Asian WSJ*, 16 August 1989, p. 6.

65 Lewis, p. 236.

66 Walter Mack, *No Time Lost*, Atheneum, New York, 1982, p. 155.

67 Lewis, p. 234.

68 Quoted Paul Roberts, 'The Sweet Hereafter', *Harper's Magazine*, November 1999, p. 66.

69 Clifford Roberts to RWW, 27 August 1951, MS741/4; MS10, King and Spalding Files, Box 1; MS10/265 and 10/259/9.

70 Dan Morgan, *Merchants of Grain*, Viking, New York, 1979, p. 285n.

71 *Harper's Magazine*, November 1999, p. 66.

72 Laurence H. Shoup, 'Jimmy Carter and the Trilateralists: Presidential Roots', in Holly Sklar (ed.), *Trilateralism*, South End Press, Boston, 1980, p. 203.

73 Alfred D. Chandler, *The Visible Hand*, The Belknap Press of Harvard University Press, Cambridge, Mass., 1977, p. 1.

Chapter 2 *A Law Unto Themselves*

1 *Vital Speeches of Today*, 35 (19), 15 July 1959, p. 602.

2 Alfred D. Chandler Jr, *The Visible Hand*, The Belknap Press of Harvard University Press, Cambridge, Mass., 1977, p. 1.

3 Karl Polanyi, *The Great Transformation*, Beacon, Boston, 1957, pp. 119.

4 Alfred D. Chandler, *Scale and Scope*, The Belknap Press of Harvard University Press, Cambridge, Mass., 1990, p. 593; Barry Supple, '*Scale and Scope*: Alfred Chandler and the dynamics of industrial capitalism', *Economic History Review*, 43 (3), August 1991, p. 509.

5 *Business Week*, 28 October 2000.

6 Joseph A. Schumpeter, *Capitalism, Socialism and Democracy*, George Allen & Unwin, London, 1947 edition, p. 84.

7 Johannes Hirschmeier and Yui Tsunehiko, *The Development of Japanese Business, 1600–1973*, London, Allen & Unwin, 1975, pp. 111 & 187.

8 Edward Q. Keasbey, 'New Jersey and the Great Corporations', *Harvard Law Review*, 13 (3), November 1899, p. 209.

9 George J. Stigler, 'Monopoly and Oligopoly by Merger', *American Economic Review*, 40 (2), May 1950, p. 28.

10 Howard Jay Graham, 'An Innocent Abroad: the Constitutional Corporate "Person"', *UCLA Law Review*, 2 (2), February 1955, p. 167.

11 Howard Jay Graham, '"Builded Better Than They Knew" Part I: The Framers, The Railroads and the Fourteenth Amendment', *University of Pittsburgh Law Review*, 17 (4), Summer 1956, p. 540.

12 Quoted Graham, 1956, p. 539.

13 Quoted Arnold M. Paul, *Conservative Crisis and the Rule of Law, 1887–1895*, Cornell University Press, Ithaca, 1960, p. 56.

14 Charles Nadler, *Georgia Corporation Law*, Harrison, Atlanta, 1950, p. 30.

15 Mary A. de Credico, *Patriotism for Profit*, University of North Carolina Press, Chapel Hill, NC, 1990, pp. 16 & 18.

16 Della Wager Wells, *The First Hundred Years*, King & Spalding, Atlanta, 1985, p. 31.

17 Alex M. Hitz, 'Georgia's Early Laws of Incorporation', *Georgia Bar Journal*, 11 (2), November 1948, p. 171; quoted Nadler, p. 33.

18 Charles H. Candler, *Asa Griggs Candler*, Emory University Press, Emory University, 1950, p. 107.

19 Charles W. McCurdy, 'American Law and the Marketing Structure of the Large Corporation, 1875–1890', *Journal of Economic History*, 38 (3), September 1978, p. 633.

20 McCurdy, pp. 641–3.

21 Harold G. Vatter, *The Drive to Industrial Maturity*, Greenwood Press, Westport, 1975, p. 78.

22 Ron Chernow, *The House of Morgan*, Atlantic Monthly Press, New York, 1990, p. 68.

23 Quoted Alan Nevins, *John D. Rockefeller*, vol. 1, Scribners, New York, 1940, p. 622.

24 Quoted Harold F. Williamson and Arnold R. Daum, *The American Petroleum Industry*, vol. 1, Northwestern University Press, Evanston, 1959, p. 368.

25 Richard Tennant, *The American Cigarette Industry*, Yale University Press, New Haven, 1950, p. 9.

26 Kenneth Lepartito, 'What Have Lawyers Done for American Business? The Case of Baker & Botts of Houston', *Business History Review*, 64 (3), Autumn 1990, p. 495.

27 Alfred D. Chandler, 'Managerial Enterprise and Competitive Capabilities', *Business History*, 34(1), January 1992, p. 35.

Chapter 3   *Hands-On*

1 *Journal of Economic Literature*, March 1988, p. 65.

2 Alfred D. Chandler, *The Visible Hand*, The Belknap Press of Harvard University Press, Cambridge, Mass., 1977, p. 1.

3 R. B. Du Boff and Edward S. Herman, 'Alfred Chandler's New Business History: A Review', *Politics and Society*, 10 (1), March 1980, p. 96.

4 Alfred P. Sloan Jr, *My Years with General Motors*, Doubleday Anchor, New York, 1972, pp. xii–xiii.

5 *Fortune*, 22 June 1998, p. 34.

6 *Fortune*, 10 January 2000, p. 48.

7 Harold C. Livesay, 'Entrepreneurial Persistence Through the Bureaucratic Age', *Business History Review*, 51 (4), Winter 1977, p. 420.

8 Robert B. Troutman to IRS, 3 October 1947, MS10, King and Spalding file 3.

9 George J. Stigler, '*Palgrave's Dictionary of Economics*', *Journal of Economic Literature*, 26 (4), December 1988, p. 1729.

10 Sloan, p. 478.

11 *Forbes*, 18 May 1998, p. 215; *Business Week*, 17 April 2000, 100ff; *Forbes*, 18 September 2000, pp. 50–68.

12 *Business Week*, 16 August 1993, p. 38.

13 Thomas Oliver, *The Real Coke, The Real Story*, Pan, London, 1987, p. 35.

14 *WSJ*, 9 March 1998, A1.

15 Quoted Chandler, p. 8.

16 Karl Marx, *Capital*, vol. 1, Foreign Languages Publishing House, Moscow, 1958, pp. 162 and 403.

17 Quoted Allan Nevins, *John D. Rockefeller*, vol. 1, Scribners, New York, 1940, p. 622.

18 Donald R. Katz, *The Big Store*, Viking, New York, 1987, pp. 527 & 258.

19 Ralph Hayes to RWW, 13 December 1937, MS10/124.

20 Quoted Nancy Millman, *Emperors of Adland*, Warner Books, New York, 1988, p. 15.

21 Katz, p. 100.

22 Chandler, p. 8.

23 Ralph McGill interview with Kahn, MS741/25.

24 Roger Enrico, *The Other Guy Blinked*, Bantam, New York, 1986, p. 4.

25 Quoted Vincent P. Carosso, 'The Morgan Houses: The Seniors, Their Partners, and Their Aides', in Joseph R. Frese and Jacob Judd (eds), *American Industrialization, Economic Expansion, and the Law*, Sleepy Hollow Press, Tarrytown, 1981, p. 9.

26 Stevan A. Sass, *The Pragmatic Imagination*, University of Pennsylvania Press, Philadelphia, 1982, pp. 4–5.

27 Quoted Sass, p. 22.

28 David W. Ewing, *Inside the Harvard Business School*, Times Books, New York, 1990, pp. 24 & 268.

29 John G. B. Hutchins, 'Education for Business Administration', *Administrative Science Quarterly*, 5 (2), September 1960, p. 280.

30 John Sculley, *Odyssey. Pepsi to Apple*, Fontana, Glasgow, 1988, p. 32.

31 *Forbes*, 28 July 1997, p. 94.

32 F. W. Taylor, *The Principles of Scientific Management*, Harper & Brothers, New York, 1913, pp. 6–7.

33 David Landes, *The Unbound Prometheus*, Cambridge University Press, Cambridge, 1969, p. 322.

34 Quoted Nevins, p. 615.

35 Quoted Alfred D. Chandler, *Strategy and Structure*, Doubleday, New York, 1966 edition, p. 49.

36 Giorgio Pellicelli, 'Management 1920–1970', in Carlo M. Cipolla (ed.), *The Fontana Economic History of Europe. The Twentieth Century* vol. 1, Fontana, London, 1976, p. 190.

37 Quoted Ron Chernow, *The House of Morgan*, Atlantic Monthly Press, 1990, p. 110.

38 Paul R. Lawrence, *et al.*, *Behind the Factory Walls*, Harvard Business School Press, Boston, 1990, pp. 272.

39 *Business Week*, 2 January 1960, p. 59.

40 Noel M. Tichy and Stratford Sherman, *Control Your Destiny or Someone Else Will*, Doubleday, New York, 1993, pp. 6 & 38.

41 James M. Buchanan, *Post-Socialist Political Economy*, Edward Elgar, Cheltenham, 1997, p. 130.

42 Quoted Katz, p. 106.

43 Swasy, pp. 24 & 33.

44 Buchanan, p. 131.

45 Adolf A. Berle and Gardiner C. Means, *The Modern Corporation and Private Property*, Macmillan, New York, 1933, pp. 119, 124–5 and 354.

46 Tichy and Sherman, p. 40.

47 Bryan Burrough and John Helyar, *Barbarians at the Gate*, Harper, New York, 1991, p. 71.

48 Katz, p. 82.

49 Sam Walton with John Huey, *Sam Walton*, Doubleday, New York, 1992, p. 50, see also pp. 53, 84 & 86.

50 Burrough and Heylar, p. 33.

51 Peter Lewin, 'The Firm, Money, and Economic Calculation: Considering the Institutional Nexus of Market Production', *Journal of Economics and Sociology*, 57 (4), October 1998, p. 501.

Chapter 4   Cash Flows

1 Kurt H. Wolff (ed.), *The Sociology of Georg Simmel*, The Free Press, Glencoe, 1964, p. 414.

2 Asa to Warren Candler, 16 June 1908, MS1/1/7.

3 Asa to Warren Candler, 13 January 1913, MS1/1/8.

4 C. H. Candler, *Asa Griggs Candler*, Emory University Press, Emory University, 1950, p. 93.

5 R. W. Bowling to RWW, 16 July 1951, MS10.

6 Karl Polanyi, *The Great Transformation*, Beacon, Boston, 1957, p. 24.

7 Benjamin J. Klebaner, *Commercial Banking in the United States*, Dryden Press, Hinsdale, 1974, p. 91.

8 Milton Friedman and Anna J. Swartz, *Monetary Trends in the United States and the United Kingdom*, University of Chicago Press, Chicago, 1982, pp. 3 & 140–41.

9 Candler, p. 87.

10 Sanders Rowland, *Papa Coke*, Bright Mountain Books, Asheville, NC, 1986, pp. 18 and 88.

11 Alfred D. Chandler Jr, *The Visible Hand*, The Belknap Press of Harvard University Press, Cambridge, Mass., 1977, pp. 1 and 9.

12 Harold C. Livesay, *Andrew Carnegie*, Little, Brown, Boston, 1975, p. 77.

13 Quoted Paul B. Trescott, *Financing American Enterprise*, Harper & Row, New York, 1963, p. 72.

14 Andre Millard, *Edison and the Business of Innovation*, Johns Hopkins University Press, Baltimore, 1990, pp. 194–97.

15 George J. Stigler, 'Monopoly and Oligopoly by Merger', *American Economic Review*, 40 (2), May 1950, p. 30.

16 Quoted Ron Chernow, *The House of Morgan*, Atlantic Monthly Press, New York, 1990, pp. 93 and 152.

17 Harold S. Goodman, *King Cotton and his Retainers*, University of Kentucky Press, Lexington, 1968, p. 346.

18 Quoted Harry Kuniansky, *A Business History of Atlantic Steel Company*, Arno Press, New York, 1976, p. 66.

19 Harold M. Martin, *Three Strong Pillars*, Trust Company of Georgia, Atlanta, 1974, p. 45.

20 Martin, p. 33.

21 *Fortune*, September 1945, p. 142; Kahn interviews, p. 37, MS741/25; *Barron's*, 24 February 1930, p. 10.

22 A. A. Acklin to RWW, 19 April 1935, MS10/5/4.

23 John A. Sibley to U.S. Congressional Committee, 8 February 1956, MS10, King and Spalding files, Box 2; see also MS10/230/5.

24 *Fortune*, 31 May 1993, pp. 52 & 54; David Greising, *I'd Like the World to Buy a Coke*, Wiley, New York, 1998, chapter 4.

25 Gary J. Previts and Barbara D. Merino, *A History of Accounting in the United States*, Wiley, New York, 1979, p. 85.

26 Quoted Richard H. Gamble, *A History of the Federal Reserve Bank of Atlanta*, The Bank, Atlanta, 1989, p. 16.

27 Quoted Livesay, 1975, p. 112.

28 Harold C. Livesay, 'Entrepreneurial Persistence Through the Bureaucratic Age', *Business History Review*, 51 (4), Winter 1977, p. 432.

29 Lawrence R. Gustin, *Billy Durant*, Eerdmans, Grand Rapids, 1973, p. 135; cf Karl Marx, *Capital*, vol. 3, Progress Publishers, Moscow, 1959, pp. 74–6.

30 Robert F. Wesser, 'New York State Regulation of the Insurance Industry', in Joseph R. Frese and Jacob Judd (eds), *American Industrialisation, Economic Expansion, and the Law*, Sleepy Hollow Press, Tarrytown, 1981, p. 226.

31 Livesay, 1977, p. 432.

32 Quoted Richard P. Brief, 'The Origin and Evolution of Nineteenth-Century Asset Accounting', *Business History Review*, 40 (1), Spring 1966, pp. 7–8n.

33 Asa to Howard Candler, 31 July 1899, MS1/1/3.

34 Asa to Howard Candler, 12 January 1901, MS1/1/5.

35 Karl Marx, *Capital*, vol. 3, Progress Publishers, Moscow, 1959, p. 58.

36 C. H. Candler to Hunter in Chattanooga, 15 December 1919, Exhibit 26, p. 937, MS741/4.

37 C. H. Candler to King and Spalding, 13 March 1920, MS10, King and Spalding files, Box 2.

38 Richard S. Tedlow, *New and Improved*, Harvard Business School Press, Boston, 1996, p. 202.

39 *Fortune*, December 1938, p. 110.

40 *Australasian Grocer*, April 1937, p. 963; *Australasian Confectioner and Soda-Fountain Journal*, 24 May 1939, pp. 28–30.

41 26 July 1946, MS10/5/4; MS10/55/6.

42 Barry Supple, 'Scale and Scope: Alfred Chandler and the Dynamics of Industrial Capitalism', *Economic History Review*, 44 (3), August 1991, p. 501.

43 *Fortune*, 31 May 1993, p. 54.

44 Paul Carroll, *Big Blues*, Weidenfeld & Nicolson, London, 1994, p. 63.

45 *Barron's*, 24 March 1997, p. 42.

46 Quoted David W. Ewing, *Inside the Harvard Business School*, Times Books, New York, 1990, p. 161; H. Thomas Johnson and Robert S. Kaplan, *Relevance Lost*, Harvard Business School Press, Boston, 1987, p. 205.

47 *Fortune*, October 1931, pp. 46–51; *Business Week*, 12 October 1998, p. 44.

48 *Barron's*, 8 July 1974, pp. 3, 14–15 & 25; *Fortune*, November and December 1960, pp. 151ff. and 144ff.

49 Carroll, p. 59.

50 Ewing, p. 170; *Business Week*, 25 September 2000, pp. 156–72.

51 *Business Week*, 25 September 2000, pp. 156 & 166

52 *Economist*, 11 April 1998, p. 15.

53 *Business Week*, 12 October 1998, p. 46; *Fortune*, 20 March 2000, p. 90.

54 *Economist*, 20 March 1999, p. 63.

55 *Business Week*, 13 June 1994, p. 22. Cf *AFR*, 15 November 1996, Weekend 1 & 4; *Washington Post*, 7 December 1997; *SMH*, 20 July 1996, p. 60.

56 *Fortune*, 26 October 1998, p. 104.

57 *Barron's*, 24 March 1997, MW4; *WSJ*, 11 November 1998, B2; *Business Week*, 26 April 1999, pp. 96–7; *Fortune*, 26 April 1999, p. 470.

58 *Forbes*, 18 May 1998, p. 216.

59 *Fortune*, 6 July 1998, p. 207.

60 *NYT*, 14 August 1998, C5.

61 *International Herald Tribune*, 5 August 1998, p. 11.

62 *NYT*, 5 May 1999, C9.

63 *Economist*, 15 January 2000, p. 23.

64 *Accounting & Business*, November/December 1999, pp. 22–4.

65 *Fortune*, 26 April 1999, pp. 206–8.

66 *Fortune*, 20 March 2000, pp. 90ff.

67 *Fortune*, 26 April 1999, p. 206; *Forbes*, 9 March 1998, p. 129.

68 Roger Lowenstein, *Buffett*, Orion, London, 1996, pp. 38–9, 132, 154, 165 and 329.

69 Quoted Sandra S. Vance and Roy V. Scott, *Wal-Mart*, Twayne, New York, 1994, p. 98.

Chapter 5   *A Capital Idea*

1 Karl Marx, *Capital*, vol. 1, Foreign Languages Publishing House, Moscow, 1958, p. 628.

2 Harrison Jones to H. Hirsch, 31 January 1935, MS741/4; *Beverage World*, October 1999, p. 56.
3 Samuel C. Dobbs, court transcript, p. 2269, MS741/4.
4 Paul H. Rubin, 'The Theory of the Firm and the Structure in the Franchise Contract', *Journal of Law and Economics*, 21 (2), April 1978, pp. 225–6.
5 Sam Walton with John Huey, *Sam Walton*, Doubleday, New York, 1992, p. 53.
6 Asa to Howard Candler, 5 August 1899, MS1/1/3; 7 March 1895, MS1/1/1.
7 Asa to Howard Candler, 14 August 1899, MS1/1/3.
8 Asa to Howard Candler, 14 August 1899, 30 March 1899, MS1/1/2.
9 Asa to Howard Candler, 30 May 1899, MS1/1/2.
10 Asa to Howard Candler, 1 February 1902, MS1/1/6.
11 Harvey A. Levenstein, *Revolution at the Table*, OUP, New York, 1988, p. 32.
12 Harold Hirsch to the Florida bottler, 11 September 1916, MS741/4.
13 Sanders Rowland, *Papa Coke*, Bright Mountain Books, Asheville, NC, 1986, p. 28; quoted Frederick Allen, *Secret Formula*, Harper, New York, 1994, p. 67.
14 Pope F. Brock to RWW, 21 September 1959, MS10/51/2.
15 Walter Mack, *No Time Lost*, Atheneum, New York, 1982, p. 132.
16 John J. Riley, *A History of the American Soft Drink Industry*, American Bottlers of Carbonated Beverages, Washington, DC, 1958, p. 133, 88, 108–10, 137 and 102.
17 Naomi R. Lamoreaux, *The Great Merger Movement in American Business*, Cambridge University Press, Cambridge, 1985, p. 30.
18 *Beverage World*, Fall 1993, p. 96.
19 *WSJ*, 26 April 1966, p. 16; *Fortune*, March 1970, pp. 116ff.
20 Rubin, p. 223.
21 Rubin, p. 229.
22 *Chicago Tribune*, 22 May 1997: 3, 1.
23 *Business Week*, 9 March 1998, p. 72, 10 April 2000, pp. 166 & 170.
24 Samuel C. Dobbs, court transcript, p. 2269, MS741/4.
25 Charles Elliott, '*Mr Anonymous*', Cherokee, Atlanta, 1982, p. 22.
26 Quoted Mark Pendergrast, *For God, Country and Coca-Cola*, Scribners, New York, 1993, p. 132.
27 Memo to RWW, 5 August 1943, MS10/5/4.
28 The Coca-Cola Co. to Philadelphia Bottling Co., 6 December 1945, MS10/5/4.
29 Statement, 27 March 1963, MS10/267/6.
30 F. Brooks Walker to DeSalles Harrison, 15 May 1963, MS10/264/6.
31 Quoted Thomas Oliver, *The Real Coke, The Real Story*, Pan, London, 1987, p. 32.
32 *NYT*, 14 August 1998, C5.
33 Memo to RWW, 8 October 1977, MS10/56/2.
34 David Hackett Fischer, *The Great Wave*, OUP, New York, 1996, p. 210.
35 *Beverage World*, August 2000, p. 32; October 2000, p. 35.
36 *NYT*, 14 August 1998, C5.
37 *Beverage World*, August 1999, p. 41.
38 *Beverage World*, Fall 1993, p. 10.
39 Quoted *Business Week*, 20 December 1999, p. 46.
40 David Greising, *I'd Like the World to Buy a Coke*, Wiley, New York, 1998, pp. 169 & 180.

41 *Australian*, 9 September 1998, p. 41; *AFR*, 30 March 1998, p. 18.
42 *AFR*, 7–8 February 1998, p. 21.
43 *Australian*, 9 September 1998, p. 41.
44 *AFR*, 16 December 2000, pp. 1 & 35; 7 February 2001, pp. 1 & 22; *Bulletin*, 29 August 2000, pp. 54–5.

Chapter 6 *In Rockefeller We Trust*

1 Karl Marx, *Capital*, vol. 1, Foreign Languages Publishing House, Moscow, 1958, p. 763.
2 Adam Smith, *The Wealth of Nations*, vol. 1, Clarendon Press, Oxford, 1976, chapter 10, part 2.
3 Karl Marx, *Capital*, vol. 3, Progress Publishers, Moscow, 1959, p. 439.
4 Richard C. Edwards, 'Corporate Stability', *Journal of Economic History*, 35 (1), March 1973, pp. 442–3.
5 Joseph Schumpeter, *Capitalism, Socialism and Democracy*, George Allen & Unwin, London, 1947 edition, pp. 84 & 88.
6 Robert L. Heilbroner, *The Worldly Philosophers*, Touchstone, New York, 1972, p. 70.
7 Charles P. Kindleberger, *American Business Abroad*, Yale University Press, New Haven, 1969, p. 20.
8 Alfred D. Chandler Jr, *Strategy and Structure*, Doubleday Anchor, New York, 1962, p. 29.
9 H. Thomas Johnson, 'Management Accounting in an Early Integrated Industrial: E. I. du Pont de Nemours Powder Company, 1903–1912', *Business History Review*, 49 (2), Summer 1975, p. 202.
10 George J. Stigler and Robert A. Sherwin, 'The Extent of the Market', *Journal of Law and Economics*, 28 (3), October 1985, p. 55.
11 Massimo G. Colombo (ed.), *The Changing Boundaries of the Firm*, Routledge, London, 1998.
12 Maurice Dobb, *Theories of Value and Distribution*, Cambridge University Press, London, 1973, pp. 212–13.
13 Paul Baran and Paul Sweezy, *Monopoly Capital*, Penguin, Harmondsworth, 1965, pp. 17–18 & 20.
14 Michael A. Lebowitz, 'The Theoretical Status of *Monopoly Capital*', Stephen Resnich and Richard Wolff (eds), *Rethinking Marxism*, Automedia, New York, 1985, p. 200.
15 US v Aluminium Co. 148F [2d] 424, quoted George J. Stigler, 'Monopoly and Oligopoly by Merger', *American Economic Review*, 40 (2), May 1950, p. 32.
16 Louis Galambos, 'What Have CEOs Been Doing?', *Journal of Economic History*, 48 (2), June 1988, pp. 250–51.
17 Alfred D. Chandler Jr., *The Visible Hand*, The Belknap Press of Harvard University Press, Cambridge, Mass., 1977, p. 6.
18 Edward C. Bursk, 'Selling the Idea of Free Enterprise', *American Business Review*, 26 (3), May 1948, p. 378.
19 Richard S. Tedlow, *New and Improved*, Harvard Business School Press, Boston, 1996, p. 215.
20 Russell Adams, *King Gillette*, Little, Brown, Boston, 1978, p. 24.

21 Quoted Mitchell Okun, *Fair Play in the Market Place*, Northern Illinois University Press, Dekalb, 1986, p. 105.

22 Stigler, p. 32.

23 Tedlow, p. 223.

24 Daniel Yergin, *The Prize*, Simon & Schuster, New York, 1991, p. 226.

25 Prentiss L. Coonley to RWW, 17 November 1942, MS10/50/2.

26 Tedlow, p. 225.

27 Quoted Richard Thomas DeLamarter, *Big Blue: IBM's Use and Abuse of Power*, Pan, London, 1988, p. 24.

28 Quoted DeLamarter, pp. 67, 212.

29 *Time*, 29 December 1997–2 January 1998, p. 26.

30 Harold G. Vatter, *The Drive to Industrial Maturity: The U.S. Economy*, Greenwood, Westport, 1975, p. 79.

31 *Fortune*, July 1945, pp. 132ff.

32 Alfred D. Chandler, 'Managerial Enterprise and Competitive Capabilities', *Business History*, 34 (1), January 1992, p. 23.

33 Quoted DeLamarter, p. 62; see also pp. 244, 377–8.

34 DeLamarter, p. 9.

35 *Fortune*, June 1970, p. 85; see also June 1964, pp. 112ff ; September 1966, pp. 118ff, and October 1966, pp. 138ff.

36 Paul Carroll, *Big Blues*, Weidenfeld & Nicolson, London, 1994, p. 64.

37 *Forbes*, 10 March 1997, p. 124.

38 *Business Week*, 15 July 1996, p. 63.

39 Bill Gates, *The Road Ahead*, Viking, New York, 1995, chapters 11 and 8.

40 *Business Week*, 14 October 1991, pp. 41 & 44.

41 *Fortune*, 11 January 1999, p. 34.

42 *Fortune*, 11 January 1999, pp. 32–4.

43 Naomi R. Lamoreaux, *The Great Merger Movement in American Business*, Cambridge University Press, Cambridge, 1985, p. 46.

44 Charles Hoffman, *The Depression of the Nineties*, Greenwood, Westport, 1970, p. 147.

45 Karl Marx, *Capital*, vol. 1, p. 627–28.

46 Thomas R. Naven and Marian V. Sears, 'The Rise of a Market for Industrial Securities, 1887–1902', *Business History Review*, 29 (2), June 1955, p. 106.

47 Quoted Bryan Burrough & John Helyar, *Barbarians at the Gate*, Harper, New York, 1991, p. 165.

48 Alfred D. Chandler, *Scale and Scope*, The Belknap Press of Harvard University Press, Cambridge, Mass., 1990, p. 625.

49 *Business Week*, 13 September 1999, pp. 72–4.

Chapter 7   What Challenge?

1 Quoted John Sculley, *Odyssey*, Fontana, 1989, p. 25; quoted David Greising, *I'd Like the World to Buy a Coke*, Wiley, New York, 1998, p. 225; *Beverage World*, Fall 1993, p. 60.

2 Antoine Augstin Cournot, *Recherche sur les Principes Mathematiques de la Theorie des Richesses*, Hachette, Paris, 1838, p. 61; G. Brennan, J. Buchanan and D. Lees, 'On Monopoly Price', *Kyklos*, 36 (4), 1983, p. 543.

3 *Beverage World*, August 2000, pp. 24–30.
4 Robert D. Willig, 'Contestable Markets', *Palgrave's Dictionary of Economics*, vol. 1, Macmillan, London, 1987, pp. 618–22.
5 *Advertising Age*, 10 July 1989, p. 42; *Beverage World*, June 1998, p. 36; November 1999, p. 16.
6 Alecia Swasy, *Soap Opera*, Touchstone, New York, 1994, p. 99.
7 A. H. Staton memo, 1939, MS10/51/4.
8 Swasy, p. 96.
9 *Beverage World*, Fall 1993, p. 12.
10 Alfred P. Sloan Jr, *My Years with General Motors*, Doubleday, New York, 1972, p. 207; chapters 13 & 15.
11 Richard Thomas DeLamarter, *Big Blue. IBM's Use and Abuse of Power*, Pan, London, 1986, p. 19.
12 Paul Carroll, *Big Blues*, Weidenfeld & Nicolson, London, 1994, pp. 124 & 217.
13 DeLamarter, p. 118.
14 Quoted DeLamarter, p. 52.
15 Stanley C. Hollander and Richard Germain, *Was There a Pepsi Generation before Pepsi Discovered It?*, NTC Business Books, Lincolnwood, Ill., 1992, p. 9.
16 *Beverage World*, June 1998, p. 34, February 1999, p. 60.
17 Albert H. Staton, Brief on Company Policies, 1939, MS10/51/4.
18 *NYT*, 22 October 2000, p. 24.
19 Quoted Paul Baran and Paul A. Sweezy, *Monopoly Capital*, Penguin, Harmondsworth, 1968, p. 68n.
20 *Fortune*, April and May 1961, pp. 132ff & 161ff.
21 Stanley Adams, *Roche versus Adams*, Fontana, Glasgow, 1985, chapters 2 & 3.
22 *Chemistry and Industry*, 20 September 1999, p. 688.
23 *Fortune*, 5 October 1981, p. 180.
24 Sculley, p. 83.
25 Prices Surveillance Authority, *Report on Instant Coffee*, The Authority, Canberra, 1992, pp. 104–7.
26 *Business Week*, 23 October 2000, pp. 118–24.
27 Karl Marx, *Capital*, vol. 3, Progress Publishers, Moscow, 1959, p. 38.
28 *WSJ*, 6 January 1999, C16; *NYT*, 6 August 2000, Bu 11.
29 *WSJ*, 8 May 1998, C1.
30 *Beverage World*, Fall 1993, p. 60.
31 Quoted *Forbes*, 2 March 1992, p. 91.
32 *WSJ*, 6 January 1999, C16.
33 *Beverage World*, June 1998, p. 34.
34 *NYT*, 6 August 2000, Bu 1.
35 *Forbes*, 18 November 1996, p. 186.
36 Quoted *Beverage World*, September 1999, p. 8.
37 *Beverage World*, November 1999, p. 12.
38 *Beverage World*, May 2000, p. 38.
39 *Advertising Age*, 24 July 1989, S1.
40 *Advertising Age*, 27 April 1987, S21.
41 *Beverage World*, March 2000, p. 70.
42 *NYT*, 22 November 1999, C2; *Beverage World*, October 1999, pp. 50–1, January 2000, pp. 30 & 34.

43 *Beverage World*, May 2000, p. 36.
44 *Fortune*, December 1938, p. 115.
45 MS10, King and Spalding files, Box 2.
46 *Fortune*, December 1938, p. 115.
47 Sculley, pp. 44–5.
48 *NYT*, 18 December 1998, C3.
49 *WSJ*, 27 May 1997, B11.
50 *NYT*, 18 December 1998, C3.
51 *Nikkei Weekly*, 19 July 1999, p. 7.
52 *Business Week*, 10 April 2000, pp. 172–84.
53 *Fortune*, July 1931, p. 65.
54 1998 Annual Report.
55 *Advertising and Selling*, October 1941.
56 RWW memo, MS10/76/16.
57 Coca-Cola to Charles Duncan, 26 November 1963, MS10/76/15.
58 *Advertising Age*, 29 September 1988, p. 54.
59 David Ogilvy, *Confessions of an Advertising Man*, Atheneum, New York, 1964, p. 155.
60 *Nikkei Weekly*, 22 March 1999, p. 8.

Chapter 8   *The Force of the Market*

1 Karl Marx, *A Contribution to the Critique of Political Economy*, Progress Publishers, Moscow, 1970, p. 196.
2 *Vital Speeches of Today*, 35 (17), 15 June 1959, p. 536.
3 David W. Ewing, *Inside the Harvard Business School*, Times Books, New York, 1990, p. 124.
4 Alfred D. Chandler, *The Visible Hand*, The Belknap Press of Harvard University Press, Cambridge, Mass., 1977, p. 1.
5 Chandler, *The Visible Hand*, p. 11.
6 Adam Smith, *The Wealth of Nations*, Penguin, Harmondsworth, 1970, p. 164.
7 Stanley Adams, *Roche Versus Adams*, Fontana, Glasgow, 1985, p. 15.
8 Karl Marx, *Capital*, vol. 3, Progress Publishers, Moscow, 1959, p. 213.
9 Michael A. Lebowitz, 'Marx's Falling Rate of Profit: A Dialectical View', *Canadian Journal of Economics*, 9 (2), May 1976, p. 232.
10 Marx, p. 237.
11 D. H. Aldcroft, *Versailles to Wall Street*, Allen Lane, London, 1977, p. 280.
12 *Life*, 21 February 1955, cover; Thomas Hine, *The Total Package*, Little, Brown, Boston, 1995, p. 153.
13 Karal Ann Marling, *As Seen on TV*, Harvard University Press, Cambridge, Mass, 1994, pp. 144–5.
14 *Advertising Age*, 31 July 1995, pp. 24–5.
15 Adrian Forty, *Objects of Desire*, Thames & Hudson, London, 1986, pp. 30–1.
16 Quoted James B. Twitchell, *Adcult USA*, Columbia University Press, 1996, p. 28.
17 Robert Fitzgerald, *Rowntree and the Marketing Revolution*, Cambridge University Press, New York, 1995, pp. 139–45.
18 *Coca-Cola Bottler*, May 1909, p. 5.
19 *Fortune*, July 1931, p. 106.

20 Quoted Pat Watters, *Coca-Cola*, Doubleday, New York, 1978, p. 71.

21 Quoted Lawrence Dietz, *Soda Pop*, Simon & Schuster, New York, 1973, pp. 126–8.

22 *Coca-Cola Bottler*, 21 (1), April 1929, p. 81.

23 Quoted Salme Harju Steinberg, *Reformer in the Marketplace*, Louisiana State University Press, Baton Rouge, 1979, p. 19.

24 *B&T Weekly*, 23 September 1994, p. 5.

25 *Advertising Age*, 7 January 1980, p. 4.

26 Roger Enrico, *The Other Guy Blinked*, Bantam, New York, 1986, p. 81.

27 Quoted *Advertising Age*, 27 April 1987, S21.

28 Sergio Zyman, *The End of Marketing As We Know It*, Harper, New York, 1999, pp. xiv–xv & 35–37; *Business Week*, 7 June 1999, p. 59.

29 Edward Bernays, *Propaganda*, Horace Liveright, New York, 1928, p. 50.

30 George J. Stigler, 'Perfect Competition, Historically Contemplated', *Journal of Political Economy*, 65 (1), February 1957, pp. 14–15.

31 *American Economic Review*, 40 (2), 1950, p. 64.

32 *Asian WSJ*, 20 January 1997, p. 6.

33 E. H. Chamberlin, *The Theory of Monopolistic Competition*, Harvard University Press, Cambridge, Mass., 1935, pp. 119–20.

34 Paul Falk, 'The Benetton-Toscani Effect: Testing the Limits of Conventional Advertising', in Mica Nava *et al.* (eds), *Buy This Book*, Routledge, London, 1997, p. 68.

35 Prices Surveillance Authority, *Report on Instant Coffee*, The Authority, Canberra, 1992, p. 90.

36 Karl Marx–Frederick Engels, *Collected Works*, vol. 1, Lawrence and Wishart, London, 1975, p. 175.

37 *WSJ*, 30 April 1997, A1.

38 Quoted James T. Hamilton, *Channelling Violence*, Princeton University Press, Princeton, NJ, 1998, p. 195.

39 MS10/67/1.

40 Ed Forio to RWW, 15 April 1952, MS10/67/1.

41 24 October 1951, MS10/67/1.

42 RWW to Deane W. Malott, 23 December 1952; George F. Rogalsky, 18 November 1950; Kansas to RWW, 6 June 1951, MS10/67/1.

43 7 December 1950, MS10/67/1.

44 20 & 26 October 1950, 26 November 1952, MS10/67/1; Frederick Allen, *Secret Formula*, Harper, New York, 1994, p. 301.

45 MS10/67/1.

46 Forio to RWW, 27 March 1964, MS10/100/5.

47 12 June 1951, MS10/67/1.

48 *Asian WSJ*, 3 January 1990, p. 7.

49 Quoted *Fortune*, July 1931, p. 67.

50 *NYT*, 10 March 1998, D4.

51 *Multinational Monitor*, 20 (1&2), January/February 1999, p. 20.

52 *NYT*, 19 April 2000, A19.

53 *WSJ*, 26 March 1998, B1.

54 *NYT*, 21 May 1999, D9.

55 Enrico, p. 86.

56 Thomas Frank, *The Conquest of Cool*, University of Chicago Press, Chicago, 1997, p. 234.
57 Frank, p. 121.
58 Hine, p. 12.
59 *Business Week*, 15 February 1999, p. 86; *Asian WSJ*, 2 September 1999, p. 1.
60 *Fortune*, 24 July 2000, pp. 144–68.
61 *Advertising Age*, 23 March 1987, p. 38.

Chapter 9   Adtopia

1 Raymond Williams, *Communications*, Penguin, Harmondsworth, 1968, p. 25; Michael Schudson, *Discovering the News*, Basic Books, New York, 1978, pp. 93 & 206.
2 Ernest Dichter, *The Strategy of Desire*, Broadman, London, 1960, p. 186.
3 Quoted David Cohen, *J. B. Watson*, Routledge & Kegan Paul, London, 1979, p. 181.
4 Herbert Marshall McLuhan, *The Mechanical Bride*, Vanguard, New York, 1951, p. 120.
5 Sigmund Freud, *Complete Works*, vol. 7, Hogarth Press, London, 1953, p. 191.
6 Theodor Adorno, 'Sociology and Psychology', *New Left Review*, 46, November–December 1967, p. 68.
7 Adrian Forty, *Objects of Desire*, Thames & Hudson, London, 1986, p. 132.
8 Richard Simon, 'Advertising as Literature: The Utopian Fiction of the Modern Marketplace', *Texas Studies in Language and Literature*, 22 (2), Summer 1980, pp.162–4.
9 Michael Schudson, *Advertising. The Uneasy Persuasion*, Basic Books, New York, 1984, pp. 210–18.
10 Raymond Williams, 'The Magic System', *New Left Review*, July–August 1960, p. 27.
11 Quoted Steven Naifeh and Gregory White Smith, *Jackson Pollock*, Pimlico, London, 1992, p. 763.
12 Quoted Jan Cohn, *Creating America*, University of Pittsburgh Press, Pittsburgh, 1989, p. 94.
13 *Fortune*, April 1930, p. 4.
14 Quoted *Fortune*, June 1930, p. 117.
15 Quoted V. G. Venturini, *Mal Practice*, Non Mallare, Sydney, 1980, p. 226.
16 Industries Assistance Commission (IAC), *Draft Report on Soaps and Detergents*, AGPS, Canberra, 1976, p. 40.
17 IAC, p. 42.
18 David J. Ravenscraft and F. M. Scherer, *Mergers, Sell-offs, and Economic Efficiency*, Brookings Institution, Washington, D. C., 1987, p. 239.
19 Paul A. Baran and Paul M. Sweezy, *Monopoly Capital*, Penguin, Harmondsworth, 1968, p. 120.
20 *Editor and Publisher*, 26 March 1960, p. 86.
21 Quoted J. A. P. Treasure, *The History of British Advertising Agencies, 1875–1939*, Scottish Academic Press, Edinburgh, 1977, p. 19.
22 Karl Marx, *Capital*, vol. 1, Foreign Languages Publishing House, Moscow, 1958, pp. 165–6.

23 Fiorella LaGuardia quoted Howard Zinn, 'History as Private Enterprise', K. H. Wolff and B. Moore (eds), *The Critical Spirit*, Beacon, Boston, 1967, p. 181.

24 *Advertising Age*, 23 February 1987, p. 58.

25 *Forbes*, 2 March 1992, p. 91.

26 Quoted Russ Johnston, *Marion Harper*, Crain, Chicago, 1982, p. 176.

27 Quoted *Chicago Tribune*, 16 February 1992, Section 5, p. 6.

28 *Fortune*, July 1931, p. 107; *Barron's*, 25 January 1932, pp. 12–13. Wrigleys was spending even more of its income on advertisements.

29 E. H. Chamberlin, *The Theory of Monopolistic Competition*, Harvard University Press, Cambridge, Mass., 1935, p. 117.

30 Joseph A. Wyant, 'The Coca-Cola Industry', Harvard University, Honours Thesis, 1940, p. 90, MS10/53/13.

31 Quoted *AFR*, 7–8 February 1998, p. 21; *Barron's*, 14 December 1998, MW6.

32 *WSJ*, 8 February 1999, A8.

33 *Fortune*, 25 May 1998, p. 50.

34 Roger Enrico, *The Other Guy Blinked*, Bantam, New York, 1986, p. 26.

35 Enrico, p. 81.

36 John Sculley, *Odyssey*, Fontana, Glasgow, 1989, p. 54.

37 Enrico, p. 16.

38 Enrico, p. 12.

39 *Multinational Monitor*, 20 (1&2), January–February 1999, pp. 18–19.

40 William Meyers, *The Image Makers*, Macmillan, London, 1984, p. 35.

41 James B. Twitchell, *Adcult USA*, Columbia University Press, New York, 1996, p. 132.

42 Paul Falk, 'The Benetton-Toscani Effect: Testing the Limits of Conventional Advertising', in Mica Nava *et al.* (eds), *Buy This Book*, Routledge, London, 1997, p. 70.

43 *NYT*, 24 January 1982, F8.

44 Archie Lee to RWW, 25 August 1931, MS10/186/1.

45 Quoted Mark Crispin Miller, 'Hollywood: The Ad', *Atlantic Monthly*, April 1990, p. 48; cf Ben Elton, *This Other Eden*, Pocket Books, London, 1993, pp. 358–59.

46 Bill Gates, *The Road Ahead*, Viking, New York, 1995, p. 165.

47 *WSJ*, 12 January 1999, B17.

48 *Business Week*, 3 May 1999, p. 151; 19 July 1999, p. 42.

49 Enrico, p. 98.

50 *NYT Magazine*, 18 October 1998.

51 *Fortune*, 22 June 1998, p. 130.

52 *WSJ*, 4 September 1996, B1.

53 *Advertising Age*, 15 October 1990, p. 52.

54 *NYT*, 6 March 1996, D7.

55 *NYT*, 21 July 1996, F9.

Chapter 10 *Drinking the Label*

1 William Gaddis, *A Frolic of His Own*, Poseidon Press, New York, 1994, p. 579.

2 MS1/1/1.

3 Quoted Peter Novick, *That Noble Dream*, Cambridge University Press, Cambridge, 1988, p. 51n.

4 Denys Forrest, *Tea for the British*, Chatto & Windus, London, 1983, pp. 164 & 171.

5 Quoted Matthew Josephson, *Edison*, Eyre & Spottiswoode, London, 1961, p. 355.

6 Quoted Mira Wilkins, 'The Neglected Intangible Asset: The Influence of the Trade Mark on the Rise of the Modern Corporation', *Business History*, 34 (1), January 1992, p. 74.

7 254 U.S. 146 (1920).

8 *Australasian Confectioner and Soda Fountain Journal*, 24 July 1939, p. 22; *Australian Cordial-Maker*, September 1939, p. 7.

9 Lord Chancellor, Privy Council, 19 December 1940.

10 Asa to Howard Candler, 27 July 1908, MS1/1/7.

11 254 U.S. 146 (1920).

12 Harold Hirsch to Coca-Cola Export Corporation, 5 March 1936, MS10/5/12.

13 Ralph Hayes to RWW, 21 April 1941, MS10/124; MS10/5/4.

14 Asa to Warren Candler, 2 June 1888, MS1/1/1.

15 Asa to Howard Candler, 26 June 1899, MS1/1/3.

16 John A. Sibley to RWW, 27 August 1941, MS10/39/4.

17 Memo, 15 September 1980, MS 10.

18 B. H. Oehlert to RWW, 13 June 1961, MS10/180.

19 Quoted Robert E. LeBlanc, *Trademarks and Unfair Competition*, Lerner Law Book Co., Washington, 1967, p. 361.

20 Sanders Rowland, *Papa Coke*, Bright Mountain Books, Asheville, NC, 1986, p. 91.

21 P. Wursch and N. Daget, 'Sweeteners in Product Development', in John Dobbing (ed.), *Sweetness*, Springer–Verlag, London, 1987, p. 244.

22 John Sculley, *Odyssey*, Fontana, London, 1987, p. 82.

23 Quoted Helen Shirley Thomas, *Felix Frankfurter*, Johns Hopkins University Press, Baltimore, 1960, p. 91.

24 Veazey Rainwater Sr to RWW, 30 July 1941, and RWW to Rainwater, 2 August 1941, MS10/230/4.

25 Bernd H. Schmitt and Y. Pan, 'Managing Corporate and Brand Identities in the Asia-Pacific Region', *California Management Review*, 36 (4), Summer 1994, p. 38; *Focus Japan*, 21 (5), May 1994, p. 7.

26 Quoted Bernard Asbell, *The Pill*, Random House, New York, 1995, p. 169.

27 Monte Thomas to RWW, 8 May 1961, MS10.

28 Quoted Thomas Oliver, *The Real Coke, The Real Story*, Pan, London, 1987, pp. 41–3.

29 Thomas Hine, *The Total Package*, Little, Brown, Boston, 1995, p. 214.

30 Gerald Carson, *The Old Country Store*, OUP, New York, 1954, p. 102.

31 Per Mollerup, *Marks of Excellence*, Phaidon, London, 1997, pp. 11, 24 and 122.

32 Christopher Wadlow, *The Law of Passing Off*, Sweet & Maxwell, London, 1995, p. 457.

33 *Editor and Publisher*, 26 March 1960, p. 86.

34 *Australian*, 4 April 1996, p. 28.

35 *Advertising Age*, 20 August 1987, p. 4.

36 Stan Luxemberg, *Roadside Empires*, Penguin, Harmondsworth, 1986, p. 279.

37 M. M. Manring, *Slave in a Box*, University Press of Virginia, Charlottesville, 1998, p. 1.

38 Karal Ann Marling, *As Seen on TV*, Harvard University Press, Cambridge, Mass., 1994, pp. 206–8.

39 Jeanne Frances I. Illo, 'Fair Skin and Sexy Body: Imprints of Colonialism and Capitalism on the Filipina', *Australian Feminist Studies*, 11 (24), 1996, p. 222.

40 Quoted Stephen Bayley, *Coke: Designing a World Brand*, Conran Foundation, London, 1986, p. 46.

41 John J. Riley, *A History of the American Soft Drink Industry Bottled Beverages*, American Bottlers of Carbonated Beverages, New York, 1958, pp. 104 & 236.

42 *Fortune*, May 1961, p. 128.

43 Quoted Pat Watters, *Coca-Cola*, Doubleday, New York, 1978, p. 209.

44 *Atlanta Constitution*, 8 November 1998, R5.

45 Naomi R. Lamoreaux, *The Great Merger Movement in American Business, 1895–1904*, Cambridge University Press, Cambridge, 1985, pp. 16–19.

46 John Wood, Innovations Lecture, 29 April 1998, www.abc.net.au/news/

47 *Advertising Age*, 6 April 1987, p. 38.

48 Quoted Roger Lowenstein, *Buffett*, Orion, London, 1996, p. 234.

49 Max Sutherland, *Advertising and the Mind of the Consumer*, Allen & Unwin, St Leonards, 1993, pp. 16–17.

50 Armand Mattelart, *Advertising International*, Routledge, London, 1991, p. 205.

51 Coca-Cola Co. to Charles Duncan, 26 November 1963, MS10/76/15.

52 Robert Friedel, *Zipper*, Norton, New York, 1994, pp. 57 and 134.

53 Michael O'Malley, *Keeping Watch*, Smithsonian Institution Press, Washington, 1990, p. 146.

54 Quoted Arthur F. Marquette, *Brands, Trademarks and Good Will: The Story of the Quaker Oats Company*, McGraw-Hill, New York, 1967, p. 265.

55 C. H. Candler, *Asa Griggs Candler*, Emory University Press, Emory University, 1950, p. 90.

56 Samuel Dobbs, 27 April 1920, p. 2227 of transcript, see also pp. 2239–41, MS741/4.

57 *Forbes*, 1 August 1967, p. 26.

58 Lowenstein, p. 327.

59 *Advertising Age*, 6 April 1987, p. 38.

60 Quoted David Greising, *I'd Like the World to Buy a Coke*, Wiley, New York, 1998, p. 226.

61 *Beverage World*, Fall 1993, p. 82.

62 *New Yorker*, 15 June 1998, p. 48.

63 Quoted *Business Week*, 9 March 1998, pp. 71–2.

64 Quoted Greising, p. 234.

Chapter 11 I'd Like to Buy the World

1 Paul Austin to RWW, 4 May 1973, MS10/39/1.

2 Karl Marx, *Grundrisse*, Penguin, Harmondsworth, 1973, p. 407.

3 Quoted Patrick J. Heardon, *Independence and Empire*, North Illinois University Press, Dekalb, 1982, p. 65.
4 Asa to Howard Candler, 7 and 17 April, 20 July 1900, MS1/1/4.
5 Asa to Howard Candler, 27 February 1901, MS1/1/5; 5 October 1902, MS1/1/6.
6 The Guaranty Trust Co. of New York, *America's Opportunity in Foreign Investment*, New York, 1919, p. 10.
7 Bernard I. Kaufman, 'Oil and Antitrust: The Oil Cartel Case and the Cold War', *Business History Review*, 51 (1), Spring 1977, p. 35.
8 Hughes Spalding to William Hobbs, President Coca-Cola Export, MS10/259/10.
9 4 September 1936, MS10/5/5; 23 June 1938, MS10/124.
10 16 February 1940, MS10/5/12.
11 Charles Newton Elliott, *'Mr Anonymous'*, Cherokee, Atlanta, 1982, p. 163.
12 Wendell Wilkie, *One World*, Halstead Press, Sydney, 1943, p. 157.
13 Quoted Gabriel Kolko, *The Politics of War*, Random House, New York, 1969, p. 13.
14 Charles P. Kindleberger, *Marshall Plan days*, Allen & Unwin, Boston, 1987, p. 11.
15 *Hearings before the Committee on Foreign Relations, United States Senate*, 13 January 1948, p. 343, for which I am indebted to Bruce Kent.
16 Quoted Charles L. Mee Jr, *The Marshall Plan*, Touchstone, New York, 1984, pp. 97, 171, 183 & 239.
17 Quoted Michael Schaller, *The American Occupation of Japan*, OUP, New York, 1985, p. 179.
18 Philip Armstrong *et al.*, *Capitalism Since World War II*, Fontana, London, 1984, p. 207.
19 *Business Week*, 2 January 1960, p. 66.
20 *Journal of Marketing*, 31 (1), January 1966, p. 3.
21 Jacques Maisonrouge, *Inside IBM*, Fontana, London, 1989, p. 103.
22 Paul Austin to RWW, 17 April 1973, MS10/39/1.
23 The Coca-Cola Company to the SEC, 3 August 1977, MS10/56/2; *WSJ*, 11 August 1977, p. 3.
24 Gordon C. McKibben, *Cutting Edge: Gillette's Journey to Global Leadership*. Havard Business School Press, Boston, 1998, p. 326.
25 *NYT*, 21 November 1991, D1.
26 *NYT*, 2 March 1999, C9; *WSJ*, 8 February 1999, p. 1.
27 *NYT*, 5 May 1999, C9.
28 *Beverage World*, January 2000, p. 34.
29 Karl Marx to Annenkov, 28 December 1846, Marx–Engels, *Selected Correspondence*, Foreign Languages Publishing House, Moscow, 1953, p. 47.
30 Paul Hirst and Grahame Thompson, *Globalisation in Question*, Polity, Cambridge, 1999 edition, pp. 66–71 & 105.
31 V.I. Lenin, 'Imperialism the Highest State of Capitalism', *Selected Works*, vol. 1, Foreign Languages Publishing House, Moscow, 1946, p. 709.
32 Alfred D. Chandler Jr, 'Organisational Capability and Competitive Advantage', *Business History*, 34 (1), January 1992, p. 29.
33 Quoted Mark Pendergrast, *For God, Country and Coca-Cola*, Scribners, New York, 1993, p. 308.
34 *Beverage World*, Fall 1993, p. 9.

35 *NYT*, 13 January 1996, B1.

36 *NYT*, 6 February 2000, Bu5.

37 Quoted *Beverage World*, October 2000, p. 54.

38 Helmut Maucher, *Leadership in Action*, McGraw-Hill, New York, 1994, p. 140.

39 Noel M. Tichy and Stratford Sherman, *Control Your Destiny or Someone Else Will*, Doubleday, New York, 1993, p. 179.

40 *Business Week*, 6 December 1999, p. 74.

41 Theodore Levitt, *The Marketing Imagination*, Free Press, New York, 1986, pp. xvi and 31.

42 McGibben, pp. 111, 114, 238 and 322–3; *NYT*, 3 January 1994, C3.

43 Maucher, pp. 140–1.

44 Levitt, pp. 30–1.

45 *Economist*, 12 February 2000, p. 92.

46 *NYT*, 6 February 2000, Bu 5.

47 John Micklethwait and Adrian Wooldridge, *Future Perfect*, Heinemann, London, 2000, p. 105.

48 Louis Nizer, *My Life in Court*, Doubleday, New York, 1961, chapter 3.

49 *Time*, 15 May 1950, pp. 28–32.

50 Quoted J. C. Louis and Harvey Yazijian, *Cola Wars*, Everest, New York, 1980, p. 29.

51 *Fortune*, 17 October 1994, p. 106.

52 Quoted Benjamin R. Barber, *Jihad vs McWorld*, Random House, New York, 1997, p. 62.

53 *NYT*, 1 November 1998, p. 1.

54 J. P. Stern, *The Politics of Cultural Despair*, University of California Press, Berkeley, 1961, p. 64.

55 Office Report, Greater Atlanta Council on Human Relations, August 1963, Paschall MS3/11, Woodruff Library; I am indebted to Kevin Kruse for this reference.

56 *NYT*, 23 April 1999, C3.

57 Quoted David Griesing, *I'd Like the World to Buy a Coke*, Wiley, New York, 1998, p. 58.

58 *Fortune*, 7 June 1998, p. 21.

59 McKibben, pp. 318–19.

60 Gary Burtless *et al.* (eds), *Globaphobia*, Brookings Institution, Washington, 1998, p. 4.

61 *Australian*, 20 September 1990, p. 18; *AFR*, 1 June 1998, p. 17.

Chapter 12   Look! No Hands!

1 Karl Marx, *Capital*, vol. 1, Foreign Languages Publishing House, Moscow, 1958, p. 178.

2 Harry G. Johnson, *Money, Trade and Economic Growth*, Allen & Unwin, London, 1962, p. 177.

3 Karl Marx, *Capital*, vol. 3, Progress Publishers, Moscow, 1959, p. 100.

4 Marx–Engels, *Collected Works*, vol. 9, Lawrence & Wishart, London, 1977, p. 211.

5 Adam Smith, *The Wealth of Nations*, vol. 1, The Clarendon Press, Oxford, 1976, pp. 82–3.

6 Hugh Tinker, *A New System of Slavery*, Oxford University Press, London, 1974.

7 Matthew J. Mancini, *One Dies, Get Another: Convict Leasing in the American South, 1866–1928*, University of South Carolina Press, Columbia, 1996.

8 Karl Marx, *Capital*, vol. 1, Foreign Languages Publishing House, Moscow, 1958, p. 766.

9 Walter Mack, *No Time Lost*, Atheneum, New York, 1982, pp. 144–8.

10 C. Howard Candler, Draft History, 1928, Candler MS1.

11 David M. Gordon, *Fat and Mean. The Corporate Squeeze on Working Americans*, Free Press, New York, 1996, pp. 47–58.

12 Quoted in J. C. Louis & Harvey Z. Yazijian, *The Cola Wars*, Everest, New York, 1980, p. 200.

13 *Beverage World*, October 2000, p. 120.

14 Smith, pp. 84–5.

15 Quoted in Eric Williams, *Capitalism and Slavery*, Capricorn Books, New York, 1966, p. 137.

16 Quoted C. Vann Woodward, *Origins of the New South*, Louisiana University Press, Baton Rouge, 1951, p. 418.

17 Asa to Howard Candler, MS1/1/4.

18 Memo from The Coca-Cola Company, 30 July 1946, MS10/5/4.

19 *Multinational Monitor*, 17 (1 & 2), January–February 1996, pp. 39–40.

20 *Beverage World*, May 2000, p. 34.

21 Quoted Max Boas and Steve Chain, *Big Mac*, Mentor, New York, 1976, p. 43.

22 *NYT*, 24 January 1999, 4: 15.

23 Smith, p. 85.

24 MS1/2/9.

25 RWW to W. C. Teagle, 14 September 1934, MS 10/267/3; Sanders Rowland, *Papa Coke*, Bright Mountain Books, Asheville, NC, 1986, p. 133.

26 Brecon Loading Co. to Acklin, 15 August 1944, MS10/39/1.

27 Rowland, pp. 133–4.

28 Noel M. Tichy and Stratford Sherman, *Control Your Destiny or Someone Else Will*, Doubleday, New York, 1993, p. 186.

29 S. W. Griffith, 'The Distribution of Wealth', *Centennial Magazine*, 1 (12), July 1889, pp. 833–42.

30 *WSJ*, 6 October 1995, A1 & A6; 12 March 1997, A6; 16 December 1997, B12.

31 *NYT Magazine*, 5 March 2000, p. 88.

32 Quoted *New York Review of Books*, 18 February 1999, p. 47.

33 *Business Week*, 19 July 1999, p. 43.

34 *Business Economics*, January 2000, p. 20.

35 B. H. Oehlert to Hodgson, 19 July and 18 August 1961, MS10/215/1.

36 Austin to RWW, 19 September 1969, MS10.

37 Reuven Frank, *Out of Thin Air*, Simon & Schuster, New York, 1991, pp. 320–1; *NYT*, 25 July 1970, p. 23.

38 MS10/196/11.

39 Jack Nelson-Pallmeyer, *School of Assassins*, Orbis, Maryknoll, NY, 1997; www.soaw.org.

40 Quoted Miguel Angel Reyes and Mike Gatehouse, *Soft Drink, Hard Labour*,

Latin American Bureau, London, 1987, p. 14. *Nation* (25 August–1 September 1979) reported his saying '...is referred to as crime'.

41 Kim Moody, *Workers in a Lean World*, Verso, London, 1997, p. 246.
42 *Business Week*, 24 November 1980, p.133.

Chapter 13   Time Conquers Space

1 Gary S. Becker, 'A Theory of the Allocation of Time', *Economic Journal*, 75 (3), September 1965, p. 498.
2 Lee Benson, *Merchants, Farmers, and Railroads*, Harvard University Press, Cambridge, Mass., 1955, p. 37.
3 Michael O'Malley, *Keeping Watch*, Smithsonian, Washington, 1990, pp. 127 & 135; Ian R. Bartky, 'The Adoption of Standard Time', *Technology and Society*, 30 (1), January 1989, pp. 54–5.
4 Quoted Robert Friedel, *Zipper*, Norton, New York, 1994, pp. 34–7.
5 *Scientific American*, 15 May 1915, pp. 454–5
6 Karl Marx, *Grundrisse*, Penguin, Harmondsworth, 1973, p. 621.
7 Jonathon Mantle, *Benetton: The Family, the Business and the Brand*, Little, Brown, London, 1999, p. 56.
8 Marx, *Grundrisse*, p. 173.
9 Marx, *Grundrisse*, p. 630–1.
10 Quoted Glenn Porter and Harold C. Livesay, *Merchants and Manufacturers*, Johns Hopkins University Press, Baltimore, 1971, p. 199.
11 Anson Rabinbach, *The Human Motor*, Basic Books, NY, 1990, p. 20.
12 Quoted F. G. Gosling, *Before Freud*, University of Illinois Press, Urbana, 1987, p. 9.
13 Quoted Germaine Reed, 'When "Coca" was It', *Georgia Historical Quarterly*, 69 (3), 1985, pp. 373–8.
14 Asa Candler to Green, early 1890, MS1/1/1.
15 *Coca-Cola Bottler*, 1 (1), April 1909, back cover; Pat Watters, *Coca-Cola*, Doubleday, Garden City, NY, 1978, pp. 95–97.
16 Archie Lee to RWW, 24 July 1941, MS10/39/4.
17 A. G. Whisman, 12 August 1955, MS10/277.
18 Sanders Rowland, *Papa Coke*, Bright Mountain Books, Asheville, NC, 1986, pp. 105–6.
19 Ralph Hayes to Studebaker Corp., 5 November 1941, MS10/39/4.
20 Archie Lee to RWW, 18 April 1941, MS 10/39/4.
21 *Journal of Pharmacology and Experimental Therapeutics*, 255 (3), 1990, p. 1123.
22 Isaac S. Peebles Jr to Hughes Spalding, 10 April 1951, MS 10/260/2.
23 Hillel Schwartz, *Never Satisfied*, Anchor Books, New York, 1990, p. 197.
24 *Beverage World*, February 2000, p. 66.
25 *Time*, 24 April 1989, pp. 64–6; *Fortune*, March 1970, pp. 86ff; *Le Monde Diplomatique*, November 1999, p. 5.
26 *Advertising Age*, 16 March 1987, p. 6.
27 *New York Times*, 7 December 1999, C2.
28 *Business Week*, 12 October 1998, p. 75.
29 Thomas Hine, *The Total Package*, Little, Brown, Boston, 1995, p. 20.
30 *Advertising Age*, 13 November 1989, S2.

31 Max Boas and Steve Chain, *Big Mac*, Mentor, New York, 1976, pp. 10–11. The Hell's Angels motorcycle gang also originated there.

32 *Business Week*, 10 April 2000, p. 170; cf. *Fortune*, 26 February 1990, pp. 53–5.

33 *Chicago Tribune*, 12 March 1999, C4.

34 Quoted O'Malley, p. 170.

35 Quoted O'Malley, p. 161.

36 Boas and Chain, pp. 21 & 93.

37 Alfred D. Chandler, *The Visible Hand*, The Belknap Press of Harvard University Press, Cambridge, Mass., 1977, p. 281.

38 Karl Marx, *Capital*, vol. 2, Foreign Languages Publishing House, Moscow, 1957, p. 124.

39 Harold C. Livesay, 'Entrepreneurial Persistence through the Bureaucratic Age', *Business Review History*, 51 (4), Winter 1977, p. 413.

40 Joel Glenn Brenner, *The Chocolate Wars*, HarperCollins, London, 1999, pp. 118 & 175.

41 C. Howard Candler, Draft History, 1928, p. 44, MS1.

42 Candler, pp. 40 & 66–7.

43 *Beverage World*, May 2000, pp. 34–5.

44 Marx, *Capital*, vol. 2, p. 125.

45 Quoted Richard S. Tedlow, *New and Improved*, Harvard Business School Press, Boston, 1996, p. 247.

46 Marx, *Capital*, vol. 2, p. 149.

47 *Fortune*, 12 November 1984, p. 150.

48 Staffan Burenstam Linder, *The Harried Leisure Class*, Columbia University Press, New York, 1970, p. 243.

49 Marx, *Capital*, vol. 2, p. 127.

50 Marx, *Capital*, vol. 2, p. 145. (Wording adapted slightly to suit the context.)

51 RWW MS 10/226/12.

52 Asa to Warren Candler, 16 June 1908, MS1/1/7.

53 Alfred P. Sloan Jr, *My Years with General Motors*, Anchor, New York, 1972, pp. 147–55.

54 *Beverage World*, August 1999, p. 44.

55 Robert L. Emerson, *The New Economics of Fast Food*, Van Nostrand Reinhold, New York, 1990, p. 98.

56 *Business Week*, 23 March 1998, p. 86.

57 Donald R. Katz, *The Big Store,* Penguin, London, 1988, p. 527.

58 Gordon McKibben, *Cutting Edge: Gillette's Journey to Global Leadership*, Harvard Business School Press, Boston, 1998, p. 313.

59 *Fortune*, 6 July 1998, p. 208.

60 *Fortune*, 25 May 1998, p. 46.

Chapter 14   The Company Needs You

1 Niles Eldredge, *Dominion*, Henry Holt, New York, 1995, pp. xiv & 139.

2 Arthur Schopenhauer, *Essays and Aphorisms*, Penguin, Harmondsworth, 1970, p. 43.

3 Quoted Stephen Bayley, *Coke: Designing a World Brand*, Victoria and Albert Museum, 1986, p. 7; quoted David Greising, *I'd Like the World to Buy a Coke*,

Wiley, New York, 1998, p. 211; Gerald E. Keller, *Beverage World*, Fall 1993, p. 6.

4 William Faulkner, *The Mansion*, Chatto & Windus, London, 1961, p. 244.

5 *Beverage World*, Fall 1993, p. 58.

6 Karl Marx, *Grundrisse*, Penguin, Harmondsworth, 1973, p. 92.

7 Karl Marx, *Capital*, vol. 3, Progress Publishers, Moscow, 1959, p. 837.

8 Marx, *Grundrisse*, pp. 407 & 409–10.

9 *Fortune*, July 1931, p. 111.

10 Daniel Horowitz, *The Morality of Spending*, Johns Hopkins University Press, Baltimore, 1985, pp. 15–20; *Advertising Age*, 5 November 1990, p. 4.

11 Karl Marx, *Capital*, vol. 1, Foreign Languages Publishing House, Moscow, 1958, p. 41.

12 Quoted Andrew Tobias, *Fire and Ice*, William Morrow, New York, 1976, p. 107.

13 'CBS Reports', 26 April 1973, quoted James W. Tankard Jr, 'The Effects of Advertising on Language', *Journal of Popular Culture*, 9 (2), Fall 1975, p. 329.

14 James B. Twitchell, *Lead Us Into Temptation*, Columbia University Press, New York, 1999, pp. 277 and 282.

15 Michael A. Lebowitz, 'Capital and the Production of Needs', *Science and Society*, 41 (4), Winter 1977–78, p. 442.

16 Karl Marx, *Capital*, vol. 1, Penguin, Harmondsworth, 1976 edition, p. 1062; Karl Marx–Frederick Engels, *Collected Works*, 3, Lawrence & Wishart, London, 1975, p. 306.

17 Oscar Wilde, *The Picture of Dorian Gray*, OUP, Oxford, 1981, p. 79; Regenia Gagnier, 'On the Insatiability of Human Wants: Economic and Aesthetic Man', *Victorian Studies*, 36 (2), Winter 1993, p. 126.

18 Roland Barthes, *The Fashion System*, University of California Press, Berkeley, 1985, p. xi.

19 Marx, *Capital*, vol. 3, p. 41.

20 Stuart Ewen, *Captains of Consciousness*, McGraw-Hill, New York, 1976, p. 189.

21 Christopher Lasch, *The Culture of Narcissism*, Warner Books, New York, 1979, pp. 64–5.

22 Thomas Frank, *The Conquest of Cool*, University of Chicago Press, Chicago, 1997, p. 180.

23 Quoted Ewen, p. 80.

24 Legal Department to RWW, 24 September 1941, MS10/39/4.

25 V. Dennis Wrynn, *Coke Goes To War*, Pictorial Histories Publishing, Missoula, Ma., 1996, p. 36.

26 Adam Smith, *The Wealth of Nations*, Penguin, Harmondsworth, 1970, p. 159.

27 *Business Week*, 3 May 1999, p. 148.

28 Marx, *Capital*, vol. 3, pp. 181–2. The pattern of consumption is further shaped by how industrialists, financiers, landowners and bureaucrats divvy up the surpluses produced by their employees.

29 Marx, *Capital*, vol. 1, 1958 edition, p. 171.

30 Karl Polanyi, *The Great Transformation*, Beacon, Boston, 1957, p. 176.

31 Tibor Scitovsky, *The Joyless Economy*, OUP, New York, 1992, pp. 8–9.

32 Karl Marx/Frederick Engels, *Collected Works*, vol. 9, Lawrence & Wishart, London, 1977, p. 216.

33 Honoré de Balzac, *Cousin Bette*, Penguin, Harmondsworth, 1965, p. 122.

34 William Leiss's review of Stuart Ewen, *Telos*, 29, Fall 1976, p. 208.
35 *Journal of Marketing*, 30 (1), January 1966, p. 2.
36 Gerald E. Keller, *Beverage World*, Fall 1993, p. 6.
37 *Sydney Morning Herald*, 5 April 1997, p. 26.
38 Quoted Greising, p. 233.
39 Peter F. Drucker, *The Practice of Management*, Pan, London, 1968, pp. 52–3.
40 Reprinted *The Storekeeper* (Syd.), 27 April 1939, p. 18.
41 John Sculley, *Odyssey*, Fontana, London, 1988, p. 28.
42 Asa to Howard Candler, 22 March 1902, MS1/1/6.
43 Asa to Warren Candler, 4 February 1909 and 10 October 1911, MS1/1/7.
44 C. H. Candler, 12 and 24 March 1903, MS1/1/6.
45 P. T. Barnum, *Struggles and Triumphs*, Penguin, Harmondsworth, 1981, pp. 33 & 47.
46 Quoted Horowitz, p. 33; T. J. Jackson Lears, *Fables of Abundance*, Basic Books, New York, 1994, pp. 12 & 23.
47 J. C. Louis & Harvey Yazimian, *The Cola Wars*, Everest, New York, 1980, pp. 19 & 96.
48 Paul Baran and Paul Sweezy, *Monopoly Capital*, Penguin, Harmondsworth, 1968, p. 132.
49 Marx, *Capital*, vol. 1, 1958 edition, p. 594.
50 Quoted Donald R. Katz, *The Big Store*, Penguin, New York, 1988, p. 174.
51 John Steinbeck, *The Grapes of Wrath*, Bantam, New York, 1972 edition, p. 166.
52 *Editor and Publisher*, 26 March 1960, p. 86.
53 Thomas Frank, *The Conquest of Cool*, University of Chicago Press, Chicago, 1997, pp. 86 & 122.
54 *New Yorker*, 14 March 1964, p. 34.
55 Sergio Zyman to M. Beindorf, 15 October 1984, MS741/12/21.

Chapter 15   I'll Never Go Thirsty Again

1 *Beverage World*, Fall 1993, p. 82.
2 *AFR*, 15 March 1988, p. 42.
3 *NYT*, 21 November 1991, D1.
4 *Beverage World*, April 1994, p. 31.
5 *Forbes*, 18 November 1996, pp. 184–5; *Economist*, 25 October 1997, p. 113.
6 John Dobbing (ed.), *Sweetness*, Springer-Verlag, London, 1987, p. 269.
7 *Australasian Confectioner and Soda-Fountain Journal*, 23 December 1938, p. 12.
8 George Fields, *From Bonsai to Levis*, Mentor, New York, 1983, pp. 234–7.
9 *Nikkei Weekly*, 11 September 1992, p. 3.
10 *Focus Japan*, 17 (2), February 1990, p. 8; 19 (9), August 1992, p. 4.
11 *Nikkei Weekly*, 22 March 1999, p. 8.
12 Jean-Pierre Goubert, *The Conquest of Water*, Princeton University Press, Princeton NJ, 1989, pp. 27–9.
13 Bernadette Bensuade-Vincent and Isabelle Stengers, *A History of Chemistry*, Harvard University Press, Cambridge, Mass., 1996, p. 86.
14 Quoted Chandos Michael Brown, *Benjamin Silliman*, Princeton University Press, Princeton, NJ, 1989, pp. 206–57 passim.
15 *Time*, April–May 2000, p. 67.

16 Quoted John Ellis and Stuart Galeshoff, 'Atlanta's Water Supply 1865–1918', *Maryland Historical Quarterly*, 8 (1), 1977, p. 9.

17 Coca-Cola Export Conference Report, 16 December 1941, MS10/5/12.

18 *NYT*, 30 June 1999, C1 and 6; *Beverage World*, July 1999, p. 79.

19 Memo, 10 March and 21 May 1971, Woodruff collection MS10/34/8.

20 *Beverage World*, December 1999, p. 30.

21 *Guardian Weekly*, 27 April 2000, p. 12; *Le Monde Diplomatique*, March 2000, p. 16.

22 Woodruff collection MS10/191/8.

23 *Asian WSJ*, 3 January 1990, p. 7.

24 *SMH*, 5 February 1997, p. 26.

25 *NYT*, 26 May 1998, D1.

Chapter 16   Bitter Sweet

1 Sidney W. Mintz, *Sweetness and Power*, Penguin, Harmondsworth, 1985, p. 6.

2 Quoted Eric Williams, *Capitalism and Slavery*, Capricorn Books, New York, 1966, p. 120.

3 John Burnett, *Plenty and Want*, Nelson, London, 1966, pp. 37–8.

4 Thomas Horst, *At Home Abroad*, Bellinger, Cambridge, Mass., 1974, pp. 14–15.

5 *Fortune*, December 1967, pp. 131 & 184; Beatrice Hunter, *Consumer Beware!*, Simon & Schuster, New York, 1971, p. 304.

6 Douglas Boucher (ed.), *Paradox of Plenty*, Food First Books, Oakland, Ca., 1999, p. 192. Cf *Fortune*, December 1967, pp. 131ff.

7 *NYT*, 24 November 1998, F7.

8 John Yudkin, *Pure, White and Deadly*, Davis-Poynter, London, 1972.

9 Legal Department to RWW, 28 August 1941, MS10/39/4.

10 Quoted John Vidal, *McLibel*, Macmillan, London, 1997, p. 115.

11 Quoted Waverley Root and Richard de Rochemont, *Eating in America*, Morrow, New York, 1976, p. 232.

12 George J. Stigler, 'Monopoly and Oligopoly by Merger', *American Economic Review*, 40 (2), June 1950, p. 32.

13 Asa to Howard Candler, 25 August 1908, MS1/1/7; C. H. Candler, Draft History of Coca-Cola, 1928 typescript, pp. 44–5.

14 W. C. Mullendore, *History of the United States Food Administration, 1917–1919*, Stanford University Press, Stanford, 1941, p. 111.

15 The Coca-Cola Company to Western Co. (Milwaukee), 31 October 1917, MS10.

16 Howard Candler to George Hunter, 3 December 1919, Transcripts, p. 934, MS741/4.

17 Howard to Asa Candler, 31 January 1921, MS1/1/11.

18 Rainwater affidavit, p. 2588, MS741/4.

19 Thomas J. Heston, *Sweet Subsidy*, Garland, New York, 1987, p. 58.

20 *NYT*, 26 October 1920, p. 24.

21 Harold Hirsh to lawyers for Atkins & Co., 27 December 1920, MS 741/4.

22 Elizabeth Candler Graham, *The Real Ones*, Bookman, Melbourne, 1992, p. 117.

23 C. B. Kuhlmann, 'The Processing of Agricultural Products after 1860', in Harold Williamson (ed.), *The Growth of the American Economy*, Prentice Hall, New York, 1944, p. 455.

24 Heston, p. 80.
25 *Barron's*, 8 August 1921, p. 9.
26 *Fortune*, July 1931, pp. 21ff; *Barron's*, 25 January 1932, p. 13.
27 Sanders Rowland, *Papa Coke*, Bright Mountain Books, Asheville, NC, 1986, pp. 123–4.
28 V. P. Timoshenko and B. C. Swerling, *The World's Sugar*, University of California Press, Stanford, 1957, p. 183.
29 Paul Austin to Coca-Cola Executive, 16 April 1963, MS10/265/12.
30 Heston, p. 81.
31 Eisenhower to RWW, 24 July 1956, MS 741, Eisenhower box.
32 R. M. Thomas to RWW, 7 July 1957, MS10/272.
33 Timoshenko and Swerling, p. 163.
34 Timoshenko and Swerling, p. 161.
35 Heston, p. 363.
36 J. C. Louis and Harvey Yazijian, *The Cola Wars*, Everest, New York, 1980, p. 364.

Chapter 17   Sweet Reason

1 Cooper Proctor 1886 diary, quoted *Advertising Age*, 20 August 1987, p. 164.
2 F. B. Eisenberg to Paul Austin, 4 March 1963, MS10/267/6.
3 Emmet J. Bondurant to Charles L. Wallace, 9 April 1987, MS741/4.
4 P. Wursch and N. Daget, 'Sweeteners in Product Development', John Dobbing (ed.), *Sweetness*, Springer-Verlag, London, 1987, pp. 252–3.
5 *WSJ*, 9 November 1982, p. 37.
6 D. C. Witt, 'The US Ethanol Industry and its Relationship to the Sweetener Market', *F. O. Licht's World Sugar and Sweetener Yearbook, 1996–97*, F. O. Licht, Ratzeburg, 1997, D57.
7 Typescript Doug Ivester interview with Mark Pendergrast, 21 May 1991, p. 3, MS741/32.
8 Albert Viton, 'The World Sugar and Sweetener Economy in 2010', in *F. O. Licht's Sugar and Sweetener Yearbook, 1999–2000*, F. O. Licht, Ratzeburg, 2000, D14–17.
9 *Beverage World*, April 1999, p. 72.
10 *Beverage World*, April 1999, p. 79.
11 Quoted John Yudkin, *Pure, White and Deadly*, Davis-Poynter, London, 1972, p. 154.
12 Gary A. Miller, 'Sucralose', in Lyn O'Brien Nabors and Robert C. Gelardi (eds), *Alternative Sweeteners*, Dekker, New York, 1991, p. 173.
13 Quoted Frederick Allen, *Secret Formula*, Harper, New York, 1994, p. 253.
14 Earl T. Leonard to Roberto Goizueta, 9 March 1981, MS10/246.
15 *NYT*, 26 November 1997, B6.
16 Quoted O'Brien Nabors and Gelardi, p. 39.
17 Joseph E. McCann, *Sweet Success*, Business One Irwin, Homewood, Ill., 1990, p. 78.
18 Roger Enrico, *The Other Guy Blinked*, Bantam, New York, 1986, pp. 73–4.
19 H. J. Roberts, *Aspartame (NutraSweet)*, Charles Press, Philadelphia, 1990, p. 20; McCann, pp. 57–8.

20 *NYT*, 19 November 1989, III:4.

21 *WSJ*, 31 July 1991, A12.

22 *F. O. Licht's World Sugar and Sweetener Yearbook, 1997–98*, F. O. Licht, Ratzeburg, 1997, D6–7.

23 *WSJ*, 12 January 1996, B5.

24 Jeremy Rifkin, *The Bio-Tech Century*, Putnam Penguin, New York, 1998, p. 20.

Chapter 18   Juggernaut

1 F. A. von Hayek, *The Road to Serfdom*, Dymock's, Sydney, 1945, pp. 52–3.

2 Edgar Queeny to RWW, 11 March 1955, MS10/242; MS10/1/62; MS10/5/4; MS10/230/17.

3 *Chicago Tribune*, 2 February 1997, 5:4.

4 *WSJ*, 2 July 1999, A3.

5 Jeremy Rifkin, *The Bio-Tech Century*, Putnam Penguin, New York, 1998, p. 20.

6 *WSJ*, 31 July 1991, A1 & 12, and 14 August 1991, B1.

7 *WSJ*, 29 March 1991, B1.

8 Rifkin, p. 2.

9 Rifkin, p. 18.

10 *Fortune*, 26 April 1999, p. 154.

11 Monsanto spokesperson, *Chemistry and Industry*, 20 July 1998, p. 584.

12 *Economist*, 19 June 1999, p. 24.

13 *Guardian Weekly*, 28 September 2000, p. 9.

14 *Asian WSJ*, 11 October 1999, p. 7.

15 Rifkin, p. 22; cf Karl Marx, *Capital*, vol. 2, Foreign Languages Publishing House, 1957, p. 244.

16 *Chemistry and Industry*, 4 October 1999, p. 745.

17 *WSJ*, 28 June 1999, B5.

18 *Forbes*, 15 May 1949, p. 20.

19 Quoted *New England Journal of Medicine*, 302 (10), 6 March 1980, p. 573.

20 *Financial Times*, 11 November 1999, p. 21.

21 Thomas Malthus, *An Essay on Population*, Penguin, Harmondsworth, 1970, pp. 177, 187–89, 196, 245–47 and 270.

22 Malthus, p. 240; *Fortune*, February 1940, pp. 70–71.

23 H. F. White and C. Stanton Hicks, *Life from the Soil*, Longmans, Melbourne, 1953, pp. 208–37.

24 Bernadette Bensaude-Vincent and Isabelle Stengers, *A History of Chemistry*, Harvard University Press, Cambridge, Mass., 1996, p. 179.

25 William H. Brock, *Justus von Liebig*, Cambridge University Press, Cambridge, 1997, p. 132.

26 R. C. Lewontin, *The Doctrine of DNA*, Penguin, Harmondsworth, 1993, p. 74.

27 Joel Glenn Brenner, *The Chocolate Wars*, HarperCollins, London, 1999, p. 254.

28 Alecia Swasy, *Soap Opera*, Touchstone, New York, 1994, p. 142.

29 *Business Week*, 11 October 1999, p. 68.

30 Karl Marx, *Theories of Surplus Value*, Part 3, Progress Publishers, Moscow, 1971, p. 52.

31 Thomas Malthus, *Principles of Political Economy*, William Pickering, London, 1836, pp. 320, 326, 334 & 408ff.

32 Stephen Jay Gould, *The Panda's Thumb*, Penguin, Harmondsworth, 1980, pp. 19–25.
33 *Economist*, 2 October 1999, pp. 101–02.
34 Niccolo Machiavelli, *The Prince and The Discourses*, Modern Library, New York, 1940, p. 91.
35 Karl Polanyi, *The Great Transformation*, Beacon, Boston, 1957, pp. 36–7.

Afterword   Killing Time

1 Ellen Meiskins Wood, "Global capital, national states," Mark Rupert and Hazel Smith (eds), *Historical Materialism and Globalization*, Routledge, London, 2002, pp. 30-34.
2 Karl Marx, *Capital*, II, Foreign Languages Publishing House, Moscow, 1957, pp. 23-120; Robert Went, *The enigma of globalization: a journey to a new stage of capitalism*, Routledge, London, 2002, pp. 65-71.
3 C. Palloix, "The Internationalization of Capital and the Circuit of Social Capital," Hugo Radice (ed.), *International firms and modern imperialism: selected readings*, Penguin, Harmondsworth, 1975, pp. 63-88.
4 Robert Brenner, "The Origins of Capitalist Development: A Critique of Neo-Smithian Marxism," *New Left Review*, 104, July-August 1977, pp. 49-53.
5 Rob Beamish, *Marx, Method and the Division of Labor*, University of Illinois Press, Urbana, 1992, chapter four.
6 For an extended treatment see my "Making capitals tick," *Overland*, 169, Autumn 2003.
7 *Harvard Business Review*, December 2002, pp. 20-21.
8 *NYT*, 1 July 2001, WK 3.
9 *Forbes*, 11 November 2002, pp. 45-48.
10 *WSJ*, 24 December 2002, A3 & A5.
11 V. I. Lenin, *Imperialism, the Highest Stage of Capitalism*, Foreign Languages Press, Peking, 1975, pp. 116-18.
12 N. Bukharin, *Imperialism and the World Economy*, Merlin, London, 1972, pp. 28-29 & 56.
13 *Business Week*, 4 November 2002, pp. 107 & 110.
14 Walter Korpi, "The Great Trough in Unemployment: A Long-Term View of Unemployment, Inflation, Strikes and the Profit/Wage ratio," *Politics and Society*, 30 (3), September 2002, pp. 365-426.
15 Andri W. Stahel, "Time Contradictions of Capitalism," *Capitalism, Nature, Socialism*, 10 (1), March 1999, pp. 101-32.
16 E. P. Thompson provided a much-quoted but misguided instance in his "Time, work-discipline and Industrial Capitalism," *Past and Present*, 38, December 1967, p. 91.
17 *Forbes*, 23 December 2002, pp. 20-21.
18 Karl Marx, *A Contribution to a Critique of Political Economy*, Progress Publishers, Moscow, 1970, pp. 67 & 70.
19 Donald D. Weiss, "Marx vs. Smith on the Division of Labor," *Monthly Review*, 28 (3), July-August 1976, p. 110.
20 Lenin, *op. cit.*, pp. 9-10, 127-32; cf Bukharin, *op. cit.*, pp. 23-27; Eric Hobsbawm, *Workers*, Pantheon, New York, 1984, pp. 214-72.

21 Marx, *Capital, op. cit.*, p. 56.
22 Robert Brenner, "Towards the precipice," *London Review of Books*, 7 February 2003.
23 Robin Blackburn, "The Enron Debacle and the Pension Crisis," *New Left Review*, 14 (2nd Series), March/April 2002, pp. 26-51.
24 Summarised by David Kucera, "Core Labor Standards and foreign direct investment," *International Labor Review*, 141 (1-2), 2002, p. 35.
25 Jeff Atkinson and Tim Connor, *Sweating for Nike: labor conditions in the sports shoe industry*, Community Aid Abroad, Fitzroy, 1996, pp. 7-8.
26 Francois Bourguigon and Christian Morrisson, "Inequality Among World Citizens: 1820-1992," *American Economic Review*, 92 (4), September 2002, pp. 727-44.
27 Xavier Sala-i-Martin, "The Myth of Exploding income Inequality in Europe and the World," Henryk Kierzkowski (ed.), *Europe and globalization*, Palgrave, Basingstoke, 2002, pp. 11-31.
28 James K. Galbraith and Maureen Berner (eds), *Inequality and industrial change: a global view*, Cambridge University Press, Cambridge, 2002.
29 Paul Cammack, "Attacking the Global Poor," *New Left Review*, 13, (2nd Series), January/February 2002, pp. 125-35.
30 See corpwatchindia.org and cokewatch.org; for the corporate take-over of the world's water see Maude Barlow and Tony Clarke, *Blue Gold* (New Press, New York, 2002); *U. S. News and World Report*, 12 August 2002, pp. 23-30.
31 William Finegan, "Leasing the Rain," *New Yorker*, 8 April 2002, pp. 50 & 52; Galbraith and Berner, *op. cit.*, chapter ten.
32 *Nation* (NY), 3 September 2001; *Le Monde Diplomatique*, August 2001, pp. 12-13.
33 F. Engels, *Dialectics of Nature*, Progress Publishers, Moscow, 1964, pp. 182-3.

Further Reading

Where a work has contributed to my understanding but not yielded a quotation, I have listed it below according to the most relevant chapter.

Introduction   The Origins of Our Future

Maurice Dobb, *Political Economy and Capitalism*, Routledge & Kegan Paul, London, 1940.

Ben Fine and Laurence Harris, *Rereading Capital*, Macmillan, London, 1979.

David Harvey, *The Limits to Capital*, University of Chicago Press, Chicago, 1982.

Makoto Itoh, *The Basic Theory of Capitalism. The Forms and Substance of the Capitalist Economy*, Macmillan, London, 1988.

Steve Keen, 'The Misinterpretation of Marx's Theory of Value', *Journal of the History of Economic Thought*, 15 (3), Fall 1993, pp. 282–300.

David S. Landes, 'What Do Bosses Really Do?', *Journal of Economic History*, 46 (3), September 1986, pp. 585–624.

Stephen Marglin, 'What Do Bosses Do?', *Review of Radical Political Economics*, 6, Summer 1974, pp. 60–112.

Pierro Sraffa, 'The Laws of Returns under Competitive Conditions', *Economic Journal*, 36 (144), December 1926, pp. 535–50.

Keith Tribe, *Land, Labour and Economic Discourse*, Routledge & Kegan Paul, London, 1978.

Chapter 1   The Nation-Market-State

Kai Bird, *The Chairman. John J. McCloy*, Simon & Schuster, New York, 1992.

Scott M. Cutlip, *The Unseen Power: Public Relations, A History*, Erlbaum Associates, Hillsdale, NJ, 1994.

Barton C. and Sally L. Hacker, 'Military Institutions and the Labor Process: Non-economic Sources of Technological Change, Women's Subordination, and the Organization of Work', *Technology and Culture*, 28 (4), October 1987, pp. 743–75.

Jeffrey Haydu, 'Two Logics of Class Formation? Collective Identities among Proprietary Employers, 1880–1900', *Politics and Society*, 27 (4), December 1999, pp. 507–27.

Eric Helleiner, *States and the Re-emergence of Global Finances*, Cornell University Press, Ithaca, 1994.

Harold P. Henderson, *The Politics of Change in Georgia: a Political Biography of Ellis Arnall*, University of Georgia Press, Atlanta, 1991.

Gabriel Kolko, *Railroads and Regulation*, Princeton University Press, Princeton, NJ, 1965.

David C. Korten, *When Corporations Rule the World*, Earthscan, London, 1995.

Harold B. Martin, *William Barry Hartsfield, Mayor of Atlanta*, University of Georgia Press, Athens, 1978.

William H. McNeill, *Keeping Together in Time: Dance and Drill in Human History*, Harvard University Press, Cambridge, Mass., 1995, and review by John Keegan in *Times Literary Supplement*, 12 July 1996, pp. 3–4.

John Staube and Sheldon Rampton, *Toxic Sludge is Good for You: Lies, Damn Lies and the Public Relations Industry*, Common Courage Press, Monroe, 1995.

A. Viton, 'US Sugar's Change of Course', *F. O. Licht's World Sugar and Sweetener Year Book, 1996–97*, F. O. Licht, Ratzeburg, 1996, D45–51.

James Weinstein, *The Corporate Ideal in the Liberal State*, Beacon Press, Boston, 1968.

Linda Weiss, *The Myth of the Powerless State*, Polity, Cambridge, 1998.

Chapter 2   *A Law Unto Themselves*

Ron Chernow, *Titan. The Life of John D. Rockefeller, Sr*, Random House, New York, 1998.

Richard Allan Gerber, 'The Reinterpretation of the Due Process Clause of the Fourteenth Amendment in the Age of Industrialization', in Joseph R. Frese and Jacob Judd (eds), *American Industrialization, Economic Expansion and the Law*, Sleepy Hollow Press, Tarrytown, 1981, pp. 143–209.

Howard Jay Graham, 'The "Conspiracy Theory" of the Fourteenth Amendment', *Yale Law Journal*, 47 (3), January 1938, pp. 371–403, and 48 (2), December 1938, pp. 171–94.

Christopher Grandy, 'New Jersey Corporate Chartermongering, 1875–1929', *Journal of Economic Literature*, 49 (3), September 1989, pp. 677–92.

Oscar and Mary F. Handlin, 'Origins of the American Business Corporation', *Journal of Economic History*, 5 (1), May 1945, pp. 1–23.

M. S. Heath, *Constructive Liberalism: The Role of the State in Economic Development in Georgia to 1860*, Harvard University Press, Cambridge, 1954, chapter 12.

Herbert Hovenkamp, 'The Corporation in Classical Political Economy', *Georgetown Law Review*, 76 (5), June 1988, pp. 1594–1689.

Morton Keller, *Affairs of State*, The Belknap Press of Harvard University Press, Cambridge, Mass, 1977.

Helen Shirley Thomas, *Felix Frankfurter*, Johns Hopkins University Press, Baltimore, 1960, chapter 7.

Chapter 3   Hands-On

Susan Ariel Aaronson, 'Serving America's Business? Graduate Business Schools and American Business, 1945–60', *Business History*, 34 (1), January 1992, pp. 160–82.

Colloquium on Scale and Scope, *Business History Review*, 64 (4), Winter 1990, pp. 690–758.

Economy and Society, Special Issue on Shareholder Value and the Political Economy of Late Capitalism, 29 (1), February 2000.

Alexander J. Field, 'Modern Business Enterprise as a Capital-Saving Innovation', *Journal of Economic History*, 47 (2), June 1987, pp. 473–85.

John M. Jordan, '"Society Improved the Way You Can Ignore a Dynamo": Charles P. Steinmetz and the Politics of Efficiency', *Technology and Culture*, 30 (1), January 1989, pp. 57–82.

Karel Williams, *et al.*, 'The Myth of the Line: Ford's Production of the Model-T at Highland Park, 1909–16', *Business History*, 35 (3), July 1993, pp. 66–87.

Chapter 4   Cash Flows

Jacqueline P. Bull, 'The General Merchant in the Economic History of the New South', *Journal of Southern History*, 18 (1), February 1952, pp. 37–59.

Abraham J. Briloff, '*Unaccountable Accounting* Revisited', *Critical Perspectives on Accounting*, 4 (4), December 1993, pp. 301–33.

Patricia C. Cohen, *A Calculating People. The Spread of Numeracy in Early America*, University of Chicago Press, Chicago, 1982.

Alan Friedman, *Agnelli and the Network of Italian Power*, Mandarin, London, 1989, chapter 6.

David R. Johnson, *Illegal Tender*, Smithsonian, Washington, 1995.

Dudley S. Johnson, 'The Southern Express Company: A Georgia Corporation', *Georgia Historical Quarterly*, 56 (2), Summer 1972, pp. 224–42.

Lewis Mandell, *The Credit Card Industry*, Twayne, Boston, 1990.

Linda Simpson, 'The Annual Report: An Exercise in Ignorance?', *Accounting Forum*, 24 (3), September 2000, pp. 231–47.

Paul Studenski & Herman E. Krooss, *Financial History of the United States*, Random House, New York, 1963.

Frank J. Swetz, *Capitalism and Arithmetic*, Open Court, La Salle, Ill., 1987.

Chapter 5   A Capital Idea

Warren J. Belasco, 'Towards a Culinary Common Denominator: The Rise of Howard-Johnson's, 1935–1940', *Journal of American Culture*, 2 (3), 1979, pp. 503–18.

Richard E. Caves and William F. Murphy II, 'Franchising: Firm, Markets, and Intangible Assets', *Journal of Southern Economics*, 42 (4), April 1976, pp. 572–86.

Mike Cheatham, 'They're Thirsty on Main Street and All Over: Georgia's Coca-Cola Bottlers as Entrepreneurs and Civic Leaders', *Georgia Historical Quarterly*, 80 (1), Spring 1996, pp. 117–35.

Stanley C. Hollander, 'Nineteenth Century Anti-drummer Legislation in the United States', *Business History Review*, 38 (4), Winter 1964, pp. 479–500.

Andrew B. Jack, 'The Channels of Distribution for an Innovation: the Sewing Machine Industry in America, 1860–1865', *Explorations in Entrepreneurial History*, 9, 1957, pp. 131–41.

John A. Jackle and Keith A. Sculle, *Fast Food. Roadside Restaurants in the Automobile Age*, Johns Hopkins University Press, Baltimore, 1999.

Benjamin Klein and Lester F. Saft, 'The Law and Economics of Franchise Tying Contracts', *Journal of Law and Economics*, 28 (2), May 1985, pp. 345–61.

Naomi R. Lamoreaux and Kenneth L. Sokoloff, 'The Geography of Invention in the American Glass Industry, 1870–1925', *Journal of Economic History*, 60 (3), September 2000, pp. 700–29.

John F. Love, *McDonald's Behind the Arches*, Bantam, New York, 1986.

Stan Luxenberg, *Roadside Empires*, Viking, New York, 1985.

Jonathon Mantle, *Benetton: The Family, the Business and the Brand*, Little, Brown, London, 1999.

Robert E. Martin, 'Franchising and Risk Management', *American Economic Review*, 78 (5), December 1988, pp. 954–68.

Jeffrey P. Osleeb and Robert G. Cromley, 'The Location of Plants of the Uniform Delivered Price Manufacturer: A Case Study of Coca-Cola', *Economic Geographer*, 54 (1), January 1978, pp. 40–52.

Glenn Porter and Harold C. Livesay, *Merchants and Manufacturers*, Johns Hopkins University Press, Baltimore, 1971.

Timothy B. Spears, *100 Years on the Road*, Yale University Press, New Haven, 1994.

Susan Strasser, '"The Smile that Pays": The Culture of Travelling Salesmen, 1880–1920', in James Gilbert (ed.), *The Mythmaking Frame of Mind*, Wadsworth, Belmont, 1993, pp. 155–77.

R. David Thomas, *Dave's Way*, Berkley, New York, 1991.

Chapter 6   In Rockefeller We Trust

Joe S. Bain, 'Industrial Concentration and Government Anti-Trust Policy', in Harold F. Williamson (ed.), *The Growth of the American Economy*, Prentice-Hall, New York, 1944, pp. 708–29.

George Bittlingmayer, 'Did Antitrust Policy Cause the Great Merger Wave?', *Journal of Law and Economics*, 28 (1), April 1985, pp. 77–118.

Malcolm R. Burns, 'Outside Intervention in Monopolistic Price Warfare: The Case of the "Plug War" and the Union Tobacco Company', *Business History Review*, 56 (1), Spring 1982, pp. 33–53.

Howard Cox, *The Global Cigarette. Origins and Evolution of British American Tobacco, 1880–1945*, Oxford University Press, Oxford, 2000.

Carl Eis, 'The 1919–1930 Merger Movement in American Industry', *Journal of Law and Economics*, 12 (2), October 1969, pp. 267–96.

Kenneth G. Elzinga, 'Predatory Pricing: The Case of the Gunpowder Trust', *Journal of Law and Economics*, 13 (1), April 1970, pp. 223–40.

Robert F. Himmelberg, 'Business, Antitrust Policy, and the Industrial Board of the Department of Commerce, 1919', *Business History Review*, 52 (1), Spring 1968, pp. 1–23.

Andrew Hopkins, 'Anti-trust and the Bourgeoisie: 1906 and 1965', in E. L. Wheelwright and Ken Buckley (eds), *Essays in the Political Economy of Australian Capitalism*, vol. 2, ANZ Publishing, Sydney, 1978, pp. 87–109.

Anthony Patrick O'Brien, 'Factory Size, Economies of Scale, and the Great Merger Wave of 1898–1902', *Journal of Economic History*, 48 (3), September 1988, pp. 639–49.

P. L. Payne, 'The Emergence of the Large-scale Company in Great Britain, 1870–1914', *Economic History Review*, 20 (3), December 1967, pp. 519–47.

Joseph A. Pratt, 'The Petroleum Industry in Transition: Anti-trust and the Decline of Monopoly Control in Oil', *Journal of Economic History*, 40 (4), December 1980, pp. 815–37.

Leo Sleuwaegen, 'Cross-border Mergers and EC Competition Policy', *World Economy*, 21 (8), November 1998, pp. 1077–94.

Bob Stoddard, *Pepsi-Cola. 100 years*, General Publishing Group, Los Angeles, 1997.

George Rogers Taylor and Irene D. Neu, *The American Railroad Network, 1861–1890*, Harvard University Press, Cambridge, Mass., 1956.

Richard Tennant, *The American Cigarette Industry*, Yale University Press, New Haven, 1950.

V. G. Venturini, *Mal Practice*, Non Mallare, Sydney, 1980.

Oliver E. Williamson and Sidney G. Wingter (eds), *The Nature of the Firm*, OUP, New York, 1991.

Chapter 7   What Challenge?

Harold Saltzman, Roy Levy and John Hike, *Transformation and Continuity. The US Carbonated Soft Drink Bottling Industry and Antitrust Policy Since 1980*, Federal Trade Commission, Washington, 1999.

Chapter 8   The Force of the Market

'Standards in Industry', Special Issue, *Annals of the American Academy of Political and Social Science*, 137, May 1928.

Marcus Alexis, 'The Changing Consumer Market: 1935–1959', *Journal of Marketing*, 26 (1), January 1962, pp. 42–5.

Sue Bowden and Avner Offer, 'Household Appliances and the Use of Time: The United States and Britain since the 1920s', *Economic History Review*, 47 (4), November 1994, pp. 725–48.

Henry A. Giroux, *Stealing Innocence: Youth, Corporate Power, and the Politics of Culture*, St Martin's Press, New York, 2000.

Thomas R. H. Havens, *Architects of Affluence. The Tsutsumi Family and the Seibu-Saison Enterprises in Twentieth-Century Japan*, Council on East Asian Studies, Harvard University, Cambridge, Mass., 1994.

Ray W. Johnson and Russell W. Lynch, *The Sales Strategy of John H. Patterson, Founder of the National Cash Register Company*, Dartnell, New York, 1932.

Richard B. Kielbowicz, 'Postal Subsidies for the Press and the Business of Mass Culture, 1880–1920', *Business History Review*, 64 (3), Autumn 1990, pp. 451–88.

Alex Molnar, *Giving Kids the Business: The Commercialization of America's Schools*, Westview Press, Boulder, 1996.

Avner Offer, 'The American Automobile Frenzy of the 1950s', in Kristine Bruland and Patrick O'Brien (eds), *From Family Firms to Corporate Capitalism*, Clarendon Press, Oxford, 1998, pp. 315–53.

Grace Palladino, *Teenagers*, Basic Books, New York, 1996.

George J. Stigler, 'The Economics of Information', *Journal of Political Economy*, 69 (3), June 1961, pp. 213–25.

Susan Strasser, *Satisfaction Guaranteed. The Making of the American Mass Market*, Pantheon, New York, 1989.

Mariko Tatsuki, 'The Rise of the Mass Market and Modern Retailers in Japan', *Business History*, 37 (2), April 1995, pp. 70–88.

Larry Tye, *The Father of Spin: Edward I. Bernays and the Birth of Public Relations*, Crown Publishers, New York, 1998.

Chapter 9   Adtopia

Advertising Age (New York), Special Issue on 'Twentieth Century Advertising and the Economy of Abundance', 30 April 1980, and Special Issue on 'The Power of Advertising', 9 November 1988.

James R. Beniger, *The Control Revolution*, Harvard University Press, Cambridge, Mass., 1986.

Edward L. Bernays, *Biography of an Idea*, Simon & Schuster, New York, 1965.

Sue Best, 'Foundations of Femininity: Berlei Corsets and the (Un)making of the Modern Body', *Continuum*, 5 (1), 1991, pp. 191–214.

Merle Curti, 'The Changing Concept of "Human Nature" in the Literature of American Advertising', *Business Review History*, 41 (4), Winter 1967, pp. 335–57.

Denise E. DeLorme & Leonard N. Reid, 'Moviegoers' Experiences and Interpretations of Brands in Films Revisited', *Journal of Advertising*, 28 (2), Summer 1999, pp. 71–90.

Frank W. Fox, *Madison Avenue Goes to War*, Brigham Young University Press, Provo, Utah, 1975.

Stephen Fox, *The Mirror Makers*, Heinemann, London, 1990.

Morris B. Holbrook and Mark W. Grayson, 'The Semiology of Cinematic Consumption: Symbolic Consumer Behaviour in *Out of Africa*', *Journal of Consumer Research*, 13 (3), December 1986, pp. 374–82.

William Leiss, *The Limits to Satisfaction*, University of Toronto Press, Toronto, 1976.

Christine Lindey, *Art in the Cold War From Vladivostok to Kalamazoo, 1945–1962*, Herbert, London, 1990.

Edmund C. Lynch, 'Walter Dill Scott: Pioneer Industrial Psychologist', *Business History Review*, 42 (2), Summer 1968, pp. 149–170.

Roland Marchand, *Advertising the American Dream*, University of California Press, Berkeley, 1985.

Martin Mayer, *Madison Avenue, USA*, Bodley Head, London, 1958.

Douglas T. Miller, 'Popular Religion of the 1950s: Norman Vincent Peale and Billy Graham', *Journal of Popular Culture*, 9 (1), Summer 1975, pp. 66–76.

Vance Packard, *The Hidden Persuaders*, Penguin, Harmondsworth, 1957.

Daniel Pope, *The Making of Modern Advertising*, Basic Books, New York, 1983.

Robert Pritchard, *Marketing Success Stories*, Milner Books, Burra Creek, 1997, pp. 57–64.

Charles Rutheiser, *Imagineering Atlanta*, Verso, London, 1996, chapter 5.

Quentin J. Schultze, '"An Honourable Place": The Quest for Professional Advertising Education, 1900–1917', *Business History Review*, 56 (1), Spring 1982, pp. 16–32.

Terry Smith, *Making the Modern*, University of Chicago Press, Chicago, 1993.

Dallas W. Smythe, 'Communications: Blindspot of Western Marxism', *Canadian Journal of Political and Social Theory*, 1 (3), Fall 1977, pp. 1–28.

Warren Sussman, '"Personality" and the Making of Twentieth-century Culture', in *Culture as History: The Transformation of American Society in the Twentieth Century*, Pantheon, New York, 1984, pp. 271–85.

Raymond Williams, *Problems in Materialism and Culture*, Verso, London, 1980, pp. 170–85.

Judith Williamson, *Decoding Advertisements*, Marion Boyars, London, 1978.

Jennifer A. Wicke, *Advertising Fictions. Literature, Advertisement, and Social Reading*, Columbia University Press, New York, 1988.

Peter Wollen, *Raiding the Icebox*, Verso, London, 1993.

Chapter 10   Drinking the Label

The Coca-Cola Call, journal of Coca-Cola Collectors.

James K. Boudreau, 'Protecting the Trademark "Coca-Cola" in the Courts', *Georgia State Bar Journal*, 28 (1), August 1991, pp. 42–9.

Naomi Kline, *No Logo. Taking Aim at the Brand Bullies*, Picador, New York, 2000.

W. L. Putnam, 'Unfair Competition by the Deceptive Use of One's Own Name', *Harvard Law Review*, 12 (4), November 1898, pp. 243–61.

Ronald Hambleton, *The Branding of America*, Yankee Books, Maine, 1987.

Hal Morgan, *Symbols of America*, Viking, New York, 1987.

Ian Skoggard, 'Transnational Commodity Flows and the Global Phenomenon of the Brand', in Anne Brydon and Sandra Niessen (eds), *Consuming Fashion: Adorning the Transnational Body*, Berg, Oxford, 1998, pp. 57–70.

Elizabeth Weston, 'A Drug by any Other Name. Brand Power in the Pharmaceutical Industry', *New Doctor*, 71, Spring 1999, pp. 2–11.

Chapter 11   I'd Like to Buy the World

Mark Alfino, John S. Caputo and Robin Wynword (eds), *McDonaldization Revisited: Critical Essays on Consumer Culture*, Praeger, Westport, 1998.

Lawrence Birkin, 'Lenin's Revolution in Time, Space and Economics and its Implications: An Analysis of Imperialism', *History of Political Economy*, 23 (4), Winter 1991, pp. 613–23.

Robert Brenner, 'The Economics of Global Turbulence', *New Left Review*, 229, May–June 1998.

Robert Brenner, 'The Boom and the Bubble', *New Left Review*, Second Series, 6, November–December 2000, pp. 5–44.

Noam Chomsky, *World Orders, Old and New*, Pluto, London, 1994.

Pascal Galinier, *CocaPepsi. Le Conflit d'un Siecle entre deux World Companies*, Editions Assouline, Paris, 1999.

Kenneth Jackson, 'Atlanta: The Imperial City', in *The Ku Klux Klan in the City, 1913–1930*, OUP, New York, 1967, chapter 3.

Tom Kemp, *Theories of Imperialism*, Dobson, London, 1967.

Richard F. Kuisel, *Seducing the French*, University of California Press, Berkeley, 1993, pp. 52–69.

John A. Lent (ed.), *Asian Popular Culture*, Westview, Boulder, 1995.

Nicholas Levis (ed.), 'Global Circus', Special Issue, *International Journal of Political Economy*, 26 (3), Fall 1996.

Christopher Lloyd, 'Globalisation: Beyond the Ultra-Modernist Narrative to a Critical Realist Perspective on Geopolitics in the Cyber Age', *International Journal of Urban and Regional Research*, 24 (2), June 2000, pp. 258–73.

Humphrey McQueen, 'Repressive Pluralism', in D. Y. H. Wu, H. McQueen & Y. Yamamoto (eds), *Emerging Pluralism in Asia and the Pacific*, Hong Kong Institute of Asia-Pacific Studies, Hong Kong, 1997, pp. 3–27.

Tennant McWilliams, 'New South "Functionals" Look Outward: The Brunswick Seven and the Cuban Crisis, 1897', *Georgia Historical Quarterly*, 63 (4), 1979, pp. 469–75.

Mark Mason, *American Multinationals and Japan*, Harvard University Press, Cambridge, Mass., 1992, chapter 4.

Leonard S. Reich, 'Lighting the Path to Profit: GE's Control of the Electric Lamp Industry, 1892–1941', *Business History Review*, 66 (2), Summer 1992, pp. 305–34.

George Ritzer, *The McDonaldization of Society: An Investigation into the Changing Character of Contemporary Social Life*, Pine Forge Press, Thousand Oaks, Calif., 1993.

Emily S. Rosenberg, *Financial Missionaries to the World. The Politics and Culture of Dollar Diplomacy, 1900–1930*, Harvard University Press, Cambridge, Mass., 1999.

Reinhold Wagnleitner, *Coca-Colonization and the Cold War*, University of North Carolina Press, Chapel Hill, 1994.

James L. Watson, (ed.), *Golden Arches East*, Stanford University Press, Stanford, 1997.

Ralph Willett, *The Americanization of Germany 1945–1949*, Routledge, London, 1989.

Chapter 12 *Look! No Hands!*

Harry Braverman, *Labor and Monopoly Capital*, Monthly Review Press, New York, 1974.

Maurice Dobb, *Wages*, Cambridge University Press, Cambridge, 1959 edition.

Henry J. Frundt, *Refreshing Pauses. Coca-Cola and Human Rights in Guatemala*, Praeger, New York, 1987.

Georgia Historical Quarterly, 81 (2), Summer 1997, Special Issue on Labor in
Georgia.

Alton Du Mar Jones, 'The Child Labor Reform Movement in Georgia', *Georgia
Historical Quarterly*, 69 (4), December 1965, pp. 396–417.

Michael McClintock, *The American Connection. Volume 2: State Terror and Popular
Resistance in Guatemala*, Zed, London, 1985.

Daniel Nelson, 'Scientific Management, Systematic Management, and Labor,
1880–1915', *Business History Review*, 68 (4), Winter 1974, pp. 479–500.

Brian Pollitt, 'The Cuban Sugar Economy in the 1930s', in Bill Albert and Adrian
Groves (eds), *The World Sugar Economy in War and Depression, 1914–40*,
Routledge, London, 1988, p. 102.

Ronald B. Taylor, *Chavez and the Farm Workers*, Beacon Press, Boston, 1975.

Chapter 13   Time Conquers Space

Raymond Arsenault, 'The End of the Long Hot Summer', *Journal of Southern
History*, 50 (4), December 1984, pp. 597–628.

Martha Banta, *Taylored Lives*, University of Chicago Press, Chicago, 1993.

Stephen Braun, *BUZZ. The Science and Lore of Alcohol and Caffeine*, OUP, Oxford,
1996.

David T. Courtwright, 'The Hidden Epidemic: Opiate Addiction and Cocaine Use
in the South, 1860–1920', *Journal of Southern History*, 69 (1), February 1963,
pp. 57–72.

Rick Fantasia, 'Fast Food in France', *Theory and Society*, 24 (2), April 1995, pp.
201–43.

John A. Jackle and Keith A. Sculle, *Fast Food. Roadside Restaurants in the Automobile
Age*, Johns Hopkins University Press, Baltimore, 1999.

Ray Kroc, *Grinding it Out*, Berkley, New York, 1977.

David Landes, *Revolution in Time. Clocks and the Making of the Modern World*,
Harvard University Press, Cambridge, Mass., 1983.

John F. Love, *McDonald's: Behind the Arches*, Bantam, New York, 1986.

Paul E. Lovejoy, *Caravans of Kola*, Ahmadu Bello University Press, Zaria, 1980.

Janet Oppenheim, *'Shattered Nerves'. Doctors, Patients, and Depression in Victorian
England*, OUP, New York, 1991.

John Ed Pearce, *The Colonel*, Doubleday, New York, 1982.

Daniel M. G. Raff, 'Wage Determination Theory and the Five-Dollar Day at Ford',
Journal of Economic History, 47 (2), June 1988, pp. 387–99.

Satoshi Sasaki, 'Scientific Management in Japan in the 1920s and 1930s', *Business
History*, 34 (2), April 1992, pp. 12–27.

Joseph F. Spillane, *Cocaine: From Medical Marvel to Modern Menace in the United
States 1884–1920*, Johns Hopkins University Press, Baltimore, 1999.

R. David Thomas, *Dave's Way*, Berkley, New York, 1991.

E. P. Thompson, 'Time, Work-Discipline, and Industrial Capitalism', *Past and
Present*, 38, December 1967, pp. 56–97.

Karel Williams *et al.*, 'The Myth of the Line: Ford's Production of the Model-T at
Highland Park, 1909–1916', *Business History*, 35 (3), July 1993, pp. 66–87.

Chapter 14   The Company Needs You

Ben Fine and Ellen Leopold, *The World of Consumption*, Routledge, London, 1993.

Peter Gardella, *Innocent Ecstasy. How Christianity Gave America an Ethic of Sexual Pleasure*, OUP, New York, 1985.

Herb Gintis, 'Consumer Behaviour and the Concept of Sovereignty', *American Economic Review*, 62 (2), May 1972, pp. 267–78.

W. F. Haug, *Critique of Commodity Aesthetics. Appearance, Sexuality and Advertising in Capitalist Society*, Polity, Cambridge, 1986.

Agnes Heller, *The Theory of Need in Marx*, Allison & Busby, London, 1976.

Hillel Schwartz, *Never Satisfied. A Cultural History of Diets, Fantasies and Fat*, Anchor Books, New York, 1990.

Michael Shirley, 'The "Conscientious Conservatism" of Asa Griggs Candler', *Georgia Historical Quarterly*, 67 (3), 1983, pp. 356–65.

Chapter 15   I'll Never Go Thirsty Again

Maude Barlow, *Blue Gold. Commodification of the World's Water Supply*, International Forum on Globalisation, San Francisco, 1999.

F. Clairmonte and S. Laing, *Merchants of Drink*, Third World Network, Penang, 1988.

Economic Affairs, 18 (2), June 1998, Special Issue on 'The "Crisis" in Water'.

Denys Forrest, *Tea for the British*, Chatto & Windus, London, 1973.

Denys Forrest, *The World Tea Trade*, Woodhead-Faulkner, Cambridge, 1985.

Peter H. Gleick, *The World's Water, 1998–1999*, Island Press, Washington, DC, 1998.

John Hassan, *A History of Water in Modern England and Wales*, Manchester University Press, Manchester, 1998.

Rosalind L. Hunter-Anderson, *Indigenous Fresh Water Management Technology of the Yap Islands, Micronesia*, University of Guam, Guam, 1986.

Laton McCartney, *Friends in High Places. The Bechtel Corporation*, Simon & Schuster, New York, 1989.

Milward Martin, *Twelve Full Ounces*, Holt, Rinehart & Winston, New York, 1962.

Roy Porter, *The Medical History of Waters and Spas*, Wellcome Institute, London, 1990.

Mark Pendergrast, *Uncommon Grounds. The History of Coffee*, Basic Books, New York, 1999.

M. Brian Riley *et al.*, 'A Reversal of Tides: Drinking Water Quality in Oaxaca de Juarez, Mexico', in John M. Donahue and Barbara Ross Johnston (eds), *Water, Culture, and Power*, Island Press, Washington, DC, 1998, pp. 237–61.

Todd L. Savitt and James Harvey Young, *Disease and Distinctiveness in the American South*, University of Tennessee Press, Knoxville, 1988.

Prakash S. Sethi, *Multinational Corporations and the Impact of Public Advocacy on Corporate Strategy: Nestlé and the Infant Formula Controversy*, Kluwer Academic, Boston, 1994.

Christopher Sheil, *Water's Fall. Running the Risks with Economic Rationalism*, Pluto Press, Sydney, 2000.

Douglas A. Simmons, *Schweppes. The First 200 Years*, London, Springwood Books, 1983.

S. D. Smith, 'Accounting for Taste: British Coffee Consumption in Historical Perspective', *Journal of Interdisciplinary History*, 27 (2), Autumn 1996, pp. 183–214.

Allerd Stikker, 'Water Today and Tomorrow. Prospects for Overcoming Scarcity', *Futures*, 30 (1), February 1998, pp. 43–62.

Chapter 16   Bitter Sweet

Ralph A. Austen and Woodruff D. Smith, 'Private Tooth Decay as Public Economic Virtue: The Slave-Sugar Triangle, Consumerism and Europe's Industrialisation', in Joseph E. Inkori and Stanley L. Engerman (eds), *The Atlantic Slave Trade*, Duke University Press, Durham, 1992, pp. 183–203.

Robin Blackburn, *The Overthrow of Colonial Slavery*, Verso, London, 1988.

Robin Blackburn, *The Making of New World Slavery*, Verso, London, 1997.

Adrienne Moore Bond, *Eugene W. Stetson*, Mercer University Press, Macon, 1983.

Heinrich Brunner, *Cuban Sugar Policy from 1963 to 1970*, University of Pittsburgh Press, Pittsburgh, 1977.

Philippe Chalmin, *The Making of a Sugar Giant: Tate and Lyle*, Harwood, New York, 1990.

Alan Dye, *Cuban Sugar in the Age of Mass Production*, Stanford University Press, Stanford, 1998.

Alfred S. Eichner, *The Emergence of Oligopoly*, Johns Hopkins University Press, Baltimore, 1969.

Sidney M. Greenfield, 'Plantations, Sugar Cane and Slavery', *Historical Reflections*, 6 (1), Summer 1979, pp. 85–119.

Charles W. McCurdy, 'The *Knight* Sugar Decision of 1895 and the Modernization of American Corporate Law, 1869–1903', *Business History Review*, 53 (3), Autumn 1979, pp. 304–42.

Hugh Thomas, *Cuba*, Eyre & Spottiswoode, London, 1971.

Alec Wilkinson, *Big Sugar. Seasons in the Cane Fields of Florida*, Knopf, New York, 1989.

Richard Zerbe, 'Monopoly, the Emergence of Oligopoly and the Case of Sugar Refining', *Journal of Law and Economics*, 13 (2), October 1970, pp. 501–15.

Chapter 17   Sweet Reason

James B. Lieber, *Rats in the Grain. The Dirty Tricks of the 'Supermarket to the World', Archer Daniels Midland*, Four Walls Eight Windows, New York, 1999.

Chapter 18   Juggernaut

Jean-Pierre Berlan, 'The Commodification of Life', *Monthly Review*, December 1989, pp. 24–30.

Paul Burkett, *Marx and Nature*, St Martin's Press, New York, 1999.

Gerald Colby, *Du Pont: Behind the Nylon Curtain*, Prentice-Hall, Englewood Cliffs, NJ, 1974.

Nicols Fax, *Spoiled. The Dangerous Truth About a Food Chain Gone Haywire*, Basic Books, New York, 1997.

John Bellamy Forster, 'The Communist Manifesto and the Environment', in Leo Panitch & Colin Leys (eds), *Socialist Register, 1998*, Merlin, London, 1998, pp. 169–89.

Paul Hawken, Amory Lovins and I. Hunter Lovins, *Natural Capitalism: Creating the Next Industrial Revolution*, Little, Brown & Co., Boston, 1999.

Marc Lappe and Britt Bailey, *Against the Grain. The Genetic Transformation of Global Agriculture*, Earthscan, London, 1999.

Dan Morgan, *Merchants of Grain*, Viking, New York, 1979.

Delia Paul (ed.), *The Troubled Helix*, Australian Conservation Foundation, Melbourne, 1992–94, volumes 1–4.

Eric B. Ross, *The Malthus Factor*, Zed Books, London, 1998.

Margaret M. Rossiter, *The Emergence of Agricultural Science. Justus Liebig and the Americans, 1840–1880*, Yale University Press, New Haven, 1975.

Safety Assessment of Genetically Engineered Fruits and Vegetables, CRC Press, Boca Raton, 1992.

James C. Scott, *Weapons of the Weak: Everyday Forms of Peasant Resistance*, Yale University Press, New Haven, 1985.

F. M. L. Thompson, 'The Second Agricultural Revolution, 1815–1880', *Economic History Review*, Second Series, 21 (1), April 1968, pp. 62–77.

Index

Also Published by Black Rose Books

TRIUMPH OF THE MARKET
Essays on Economics, Politics, and the Media
Edward S. Herman

The unifying theme of the essays in this volume is the increasing national and global power and reach of the market and its growing impact on all aspects of human life.

> *Penetrating and brilliant analysis of the linkages between U.S. and global economics, politics, and media ever published in one volume.*
> —Robert W. McChesney, University of Wisconsin

> *A disturbingly blunt warning about the clear and present dangers to democracy, economic rationality, global economic stability, and international peace.* —Samori Marksman, WBAI-FM, Pacifica Radio

> *Demystifies the many ways that giant global corporations have worked to replace democratic and community values with market exchange.*
> —Elaine Bernard, Harvard University

EDWARD S. HERMAN is an economist and media analyst, Professor Emeritus of Finance at the Wharton School, University of Pennsylvania, author of *Beyond Hypocrisy: Decoding the News in an Age of Propaganda*.

286 pages ✳ Paper 1-55164-062-7 $19.99 ✳ Cloth 1-55164-063-5 $48.99

---

send for a free catalogue of all our titles
BLACK ROSE BOOKS
C.P. 1258, Succ. Place du Parc
Montréal, Québec H2X 4A7 Canada

or visit our web site at: http://www.web.net/blackrosebooks

To order books:
In Canada: (phone) 1-800-565-9523 (fax) 1-800-221-9985
email: utpbooks@utpress.utoronto.ca

In United States: (phone) 1-800-283-3572 (fax) 1-651-917-6406

In UK & Europe: (phone) London 44 (0)20 8986-4854
(fax) 44 (0)20 8533-5821 email: order@centralbooks.com

Printed by the workers of
MARC VEILLEUX IMPRIMEUR INC.
Boucherville, Québec
for Black Rose Books Ltd.